Actor–Network Theory and Technology Innovation:
Advancements and New Concepts

Arthur Tatnall
Victoria University, Australia

INFORMATION SCIENCE REFERENCE

Hershey · New York

Director of Editorial Content:	Kristin Klinger
Director of Book Publications:	Julia Mosemann
Acquisitions Editor:	Lindsay Johnston
Development Editor:	Mike Killian
Publishing Assistant:	Michael Brehm
Production Editor:	Jamie Snavely
Cover Design:	Lisa Tosheff

Published in the United States of America by
Information Science Reference (an imprint of IGI Global)
701 E. Chocolate Avenue
Hershey PA 17033
Tel: 717-533-8845
Fax: 717-533-8661
E-mail: cust@igi-global.com
Web site: http://www.igi-global.com

Library of Congress Cataloging-in-Publication Data

Actor-network theory and technology innovation : advancements and new concepts
/ Arthur Tatnall, editor.
       p. cm.
   Includes bibliographical references and index.
   Summary: "This book provides a comprehensive look at the development of
actor-network theory itself, as well as case studies of its use to assist in
the explanation of various socio-technical phenomena"--Provided by publisher.
   ISBN 978-1-60960-197-3 (hbk.) -- ISBN 978-1-60960-199-7 (ebook) 1.
Diffusion of innovations. 2. Technological innovations--Social aspects. 3.
Actor-network theory. I. Tatnall, Arthur.
   HM846.A38 2011
   303.48'3--dc22
                          2010046910

British Cataloguing in Publication Data
A Cataloguing in Publication record for this book is available from the British Library.

Table of Contents

Section 3

Section 4

Detailed Table of Contents

Section 1

Chapter 1

Dubravka Cecez-Kecmanovic, University of New South Wales, Australia
Fouad Nagm, University of New South Wales, Australia

Pre-investment evaluation of information system (IS) project proposals persists to be problematic and highly risky in practice. Numerous evaluation approaches and methodologies, offered in the literature, have not contributed to major improvements in practice. In this paper we propose a radical departure from the dominant conceptions in IS evaluation literature by adopting Actor-Network Theory (ANT) to provide a better understanding of the development and evaluation of IS proposals in practice and examine the ways in which the evaluation process shapes and ensures the selection of the best IS projects. By drawing on a field study of the IS evaluation processes in a company with a history of IS successes, we reveal the relational nature of IS project proposals and the ways they are constitutively entangled with business processes and practices. Our ANT account demonstrates: a) that the view of pre-investment IS evaluation in the literature is very narrow; b) that the practice of IS evaluation produces the 'object' it evaluates; c) that this object, that is the IS project proposal document, is a focal actor (an inscription device) produced by relations in the actor-network emerging around it; and d) that reconfiguration of these relations involving the translation of actors' expertise, experiences and interests into the IS proposal documents are critical for the evaluation of IS project proposals and their chances of success.

Chapter 2

Lorna Uden, Staffordshire University, UK
Janet Francis, Staffordshire University, UK

Our economy is becoming more and more service-oriented, with distinctions between services and non-services making less and less sense. In today's society, innovations are no longer luxury items. Instead, they are necessities and a means of economic development and competitiveness. The introduction of innovative new services is a priority for most companies. Innovation now holds the key to service performance. Currently there is a lack of understanding of the science underlying the design and operation of service systems. New conceptual understanding and theoretical underpinnings are required to systematically describe the nature and behaviour of service systems. We believe that Actor Network Theory (ANT) can be used as a theoretical lens to study the development and adoption of service innovation. ANT is a heterogeneous amalgamation of conceptual, textual and social actors. It is well suited to explain and help with the design of service systems. The development and adoption of service innovation requires the integration of multiple elements including people, technologies and networks across organisations. Technologies and interests of actors need to be aligned and coordinated for successful service innovation. In this paper we show how ANT is adopted as a theoretical framework for understanding the relationships among the actors and show how these actors have their needs shaped by the network formation during the development and adoption of service innovation for a university.

Chapter 3
The Need for Rich Theory to Realize the Vision of Healthcare Network Centric Operations:
Nimini Wickramasinghe, RMIT University, Australia
Rajeev Bali, Coventry University, UK

In a dynamic and complex global environment traditional approaches to healthcare delivery are becoming more and more inadequate. To address this von Lubitz and Wickramasinghe (2006e) proffered the need for a network-centric approach that allows free and rapid sharing of information and effective knowledge building required for the development of coherent objectives and their rapid attainment. However, to realize this vision it is essential to have rich theory and robust approaches to analyse the levels of complexity of modern healthcare delivery. This paper discusses how this might be done by drawing upon the strong rich analysis tools and techniques of Social Network Analysis combined with Actor Network Theory.

Chapter 4
Innovation Translation, Innovation Diffusion and the Technology Acceptance Model:
Arthur Tatnall, Victoria University, Australia

The process of innovation involves getting new ideas accepted and new technologies adopted and used. There are a number of different approaches to theorising technological innovation and this chapter will compare and contrast what I suggest are the most important three: Innovation Diffusion, the Technology Acceptance Model (TAM) and Innovation Translation, giving examples of how each of these approaches is used in different situations. While there are many advantages to the use of an Innovation Translation approach, it should not be said that Translation offers a better approach than the others in all circumstances and that the others have nothing at all to offer; that would be rather too simplistic a view given the widespread use of Innovation Diffusion and TAM. This chapter proposes that perhaps it should not be a case of always using either one approach or the other but rather the use of whichever is most appropriate to a particular investigation.

This paper employs the notion of translation introduced in ANT literature to study the current bio-fuel development in Indonesia. Despite the presence of some activities by scientists, businessmen, policy makers, and farmers, diffusion of bio-fuel innovation seems to remain very limited. The paper aims at understanding the bio-fuel development trajectory by seeking to disclose a variety of elements that shape the trajectory. We also make use of the notion of 'qualculation', to further diagnose the trajectory. Bio-fuel translations generated by three different scientists are described in the paper. We show that the translations follow specific patterns of qualculation, namely 'proliferation' and 'rarefaction'. We use this to make sense of the current diffusion of bio-fuel innovation in Indonesia. Beside this contextual result, the paper also seeks to contribute to ANT literature by exploring the concept of qualculation in the analysis of technological innovation.

Chapter 6

This chapter describes the development of a visual aid to depict the manner in which Internet applications are being diffused through local sporting associations. Rogers' (2003) Innovation-Decision process stages, specifically the knowledge, persuasion, adoption and confirmation stages, are used as the theoretical basis for the aid. The chapter discusses the Innovation-Decision process as an important component of Rogers' (2003) Innovation Diffusion approach. It then outlines the particular problem at hand, determining how best to represent different sporting (cricket) associations and their adoption and use of Internet applications across the innovation-decision process stages. Different data visualisation approaches to representing the data (such as line graphs and bar charts) are discussed, with the introduction of an aid (labelled I-D maps) used to represent the adoption of different Internet applications by cricket associations in New Zealand, Australia and the UK. The Internet applications considered are email, club websites, association and/or third party websites and the use of the Internet to record online statistics. The use of I-D maps provides instant interpretation of the different levels of adoption of Internet applications by different cricket associations.

Chapter 7

With a penetration rate of only about 13%, Internet usage in Thailand is lower than the world average, and is much less than the US and Australia where Internet penetration is over 70%. There are a number of approaches to modelling technology adoption, and this chapter describes a research project that modelled adoption of Internet technology by academics in Business Schools in Public Universities in Thailand. In the Internet adoption research outlined in this chapter, formulation of the research model was based mainly on TAM and its derivatives, survey methodology was used to collect primary data from academics in Thailand and analysis was performed using Structural Equation Modelling (SEM). The result was the generation of a research model: 'The Internet Acceptance Model' which demonstrates that only perceived usefulness, perceived ease of use and self-efficacy significantly influenced actual usage behaviour in this case.

Ali Alawneh, Philadelphia University, Jordan
Hasan Al-Refai, Philadelphia University, Jordan
Khaldoun Batiha, Philadelphia University, Jordan

Grounded in the technology–organization–environment (TOE) framework, we have developed an extended model to examine factors, particularly technological, organizational and environmental factors, which influence e-business adoption in Jordanian banks. For the purposes of our research some constructs were added to (TOE) framework such as IT/Business strategy alignment, adequacy of IT professionals, and availability of online revenues. Other factors were excluded such as the global scope since our research is at the national level in Jordanian banking sector. The independent variables are the (technology readiness or competence, bank size, financial resources commitment, IT/Business strategy alignment, adequacy of IT professionals, availability of online revenues, competition intensity or pressure, and regulatory support environment) while e-business adoption and usage constitutes the dependent variable. Survey data from (140) employees in seven pioneered banks in the Jordanian banking sector were collected and used to test the theoretical model. Based on simple and multiple linear regressions, our empirical analysis demonstrates several key findings: (1) technology readiness is found to be the key determinant of e-business adoption among the banks. (2) Bank size, IT/Business strategy alignment, and availability of online revenues were found to have significant influence on the e-business adoption within banks, while financial resources commitment and adequacy of IT professionals do not contribute significantly to e-business adoption. (3) Both of the competition intensity and regulatory support environment contribute significantly to e-business adoption in banks. By providing insight into these important factors, this paper can help further understanding of their role in the adoption and usage of e-business and examines the impacts of e-business usage on banks' performance in terms of sales-services-marketing, internal operations and coordination & communication. The theoretical and practical implications of these results are discussed. By extension, this could enable greater e-business usage in banks, which could improve the Jordanian overall economy.

Section 3

Chapter 9

Amany R. Elbanna, Loughborough University, UK

This chapter examines the properties of ANT in light of other approaches. It presents the theoretical and analytical inclusion of ANT in relation to other approaches. The study discusses how the properties of ANT could provide ICT researchers with a wider lens to explore the phenomena of concern. It also highlights some of the theoretical and analytical pitfalls that could be fell into at the start of the research and how a careful application of ANT could avoid it.

Chapter 10

Lars Linden, University of Central Florida, USA
Carol Saunders, University of Central Florida, USA

In June 2007, with the impending release of a revised version of the GNU General Public License (GPLv3), Linux kernel developers discussed the possibility of changing the license of the Linux kernel from being strictly the GPLv2 to a dual-licensing arrangement of both GPLv2 and GPLv3. We studied a set of Linux Kernel Mailing List (LKML) postings to better understand the relationship among the kernel developers and these licenses. Using Actor-Network Theory, we identify and describe a LKML debate about licensing. Our narrative highlights important actor-networks, their interrelationships, and a (failed) process of translation. The details suggest that the conceptualization of a copyright license as a monolithic social force maintaining the Linux community should be tempered with an appreciation of authorship and its distributed nature within Linux development.

Chapter 11

Thierry Rayna, London Metropolitan University, UK
Ludmila Striukova, University College London, UK
Samuel Landau, Gostai, France

The aim of this research is the investigate the role played by market segmentation, in general, and by the choice of initial market segment, in particular, in the ability of a product to cross the chasm. To do so, a theoretical framework, enabling to explain the ability of some firms to cross this chasm, while many others remain unsuccessful is developed. The key result of this research is that the choice of initial market segment has crucial importance as adoption in this segment can lead to a cascade of adoption in the other segments. To illustrate this proposition, three cases studies of an historical leader (Sony), a first mover (Archos) and a newcomer (Apple) in the market for digital audio players are presented.

Chapter 12

This chapter is an exploration of one particular form of non-traditional provision of higher education (HE) in England, known as higher education in further education: the provision of HE courses that are offered on a franchise basis in one or more colleges of further education (FE colleges). Focussing on assessment on one teacher-training course, this chapter offers ways of conceptualising the responses of FE colleges where the course is run to the quality assurance systems and procedures established by the university that provides the course. Assessment has been chosen as the specific focus of this paper for several reasons: it is an activity that must be performed in certain ways and must conform to particular outcomes that are standardised across colleges; it is an established focus of research; and it is a focus of specific traceable activities across both the university and the colleges. Drawing on data collected over a three-year period, the chapter suggests that the ways in which assessment processes are regulated and ordered are characterised by complexities for which actor-network theory provides an appropriate conceptual framework.

Chapter 13

In Malaysia, major information technology transfers in public sector agencies are usually due to policy implementation. This policy-led technology transfer involves central government directives to the implementation agencies. The technology transfer process usually not only involves multi-organizations that consist of many public agencies and private sector organizations but also involved many phases. Each organization plays certain roles and contributes to the achievement of the technology transfer objectives. Each phase serves a different purpose and each role during each phase has different requirements. Coordinating and encouraging the multiple organization participation in each phase is complex and a challenge that may at least result in project delays or technological decision-making that based on non-technical considerations. In such a case, understanding and managing interactions between stakeholders are important in designing activities and strategies for effective technology transfer process suitable to local environment. This is especially true for technology that requires further development to adapt with local environment. This paper explores this issue in a case study of XYZ technology transfer in a Malaysian public agency. We make use an approach based on actor-network theory and the concepts of technology transfer stages. We found that ignoring issues emerged from interactions between stakeholders will not only delay the transfer process but will also render the project's original objectives as not fully achieved.

The percentages of girls in developing countries undertaking information technology subjects in the post-compulsory years of education has remained persistently low: often under 25%. This is despite the fact that this particular phenomenon has been the subject of sustained international enquiry for at least three decades. This article investigates data collected during an Australian Research Council Linkage Grant project (2005-2007) that aimed to identify some of the contemporary reasons for this under-representation in Australian schools. The original phases of data collection proceeded from the belief that there was a clear and agreed understanding that the low numbers of girls was a problem worthy of analysis. As the project evolved, however, significant differences between the researchers' perception of the underrepresentation and the participants' views about the same issue. In this paper we make use of actor-network theory to ask key questions about the extent to which the enrolment of girls in IT is indeed 'a problem'.

Chapter 15

The S'ANT approach (Wickramasinghe and Bali, 2009) - namely the incorporation of Actor-network Theory and Social Network Analysis as proposed by Wickramasinghe and Bali 2009 in order to support a network centric healthcare solutions is proffered in the following as an appropriately rich lens of analysis in the context of the development of a chronic disease self-management model.

Chapter 16

Organisations' reliance on Information Technology (IT) is rapidly increasing. IT strategy is developed and implemented for particular purposes by different organizations. We should therefore expect that there will be network of actors within the computing environment, and that such network of actors will be the key to understanding many otherwise unexpected situations during the development and implementation of IT strategy. This network of actors has aligned interests. Many organizations are developing and implementing their IT strategy, while little is known about the network of actors and their impacts, which this paper reveals. This paper describes how Actor-Network Theory (ANT) was employed to investigate the impact of network of actors on the development and implementation of IT strategy in an organisation. ANT was used as it can provide a useful perspective on the importance of relationships between both human and non-human actors. Another example: design and implementation of a B-B web portal, is offered for comparison.

In this chapter, an attempt will be made to discuss the place of Actor Network Theory in organizational studies. To narrow the scope of the research, attention will be focused solely on companies. The concept of ANT researched within the corporate setting has been one of the author's interests for some years. Consequently, in this work the author will try to show some aspects related to Actor Network Theory in contemporary organizations. Since not every concept related to ANT within the corporate environment can be investigated in greater detail, two issues, namely ecosystem and power, have been selected to discuss the possible application of ANT in the studies on corporations.

Preface

ABSTRACT

This preface traces my own personal journey through the discovery and use of actor-network theory (ANT) for information systems research. It begins with my introduction to ANT in a small way during my research Master of Arts degree in the early 1990s and continues with the use of ANT to frame my PhD. Next it looks at how I was able to make use of ANT, and in particular Innovation Translation, with my research students and in my own research on technological innovation in business organisations. Although, in my view, Innovation Translation provides a better framework for investigation technological innovation than either Innovation Diffusion or the Technology Acceptance Model, I have been quite prepared to supervise doctoral students using either of these other approaches as well as those using my preferred approach. This preface discusses examples of these various research projects.

DISCOVERING ACTOR-NETWORK THEORY: A PERSONAL RESEARCH JOURNEY

The first developments of actor-network theory (ANT) occurred over 25 years ago, but for at least its first five or ten years ANT was regarded by many in the Information Systems (IS) community as little more than a curiosity. In the late 1990s, however, ANT began to be taken seriously by IS researchers concerned with a holistic approach to socio-technical research (Tatnall & Gilding, 1999). Today much research of this type makes use of an ANT framework. This chapter traces my personal journey of discovery with actor-network theory from my first use of ANT, through use of ANT with my research students to its current prominent place in my research.

BEGINNINGS

My first encounter with actor-network theory was in the early 1990s when I was completing a Master of Arts by research at Deakin University, Australia. I was investigating the beginnings and evolution of university-level Information Systems curriculum in Australia, and needed a way to look at the influence of both humans and technology in this development. My research supervisor was Dr Chris Bigum who has had a longstanding interest in both ANT and ICT (Information and Communications Technologies)

Research in Education. Although now partly retired, Chris is maintaining his interest in ANT as an Associate Editor of the *Journal of Actor-Network Theory and Technological Innovation*.

Beginning in the early 1960s, it might innocently be thought that university studies in Information Systems (IS) simply diverged from those in Computer Science (CS), which had been around for several years at this time. This is, however, certainly not the case. Australia made its move into electronic digital computing quite early with the CSIR Mk1 (CSIRAC) built in the late 1940s. CSIRAC was Australia's first internally stored program computer, and (depending on what machines you count) the world's fourth (McCann & Thorne, 2000). From 1948-1956 CSIRAC was located in the University of Sydney and in 1956 it moved to the University of Melbourne where it remained in service until 1964 (Pearcey, 1988), leading the way into the introduction of computing courses (Computer Science) in the Universities of Sydney and Melbourne. (CSIRAC is now on display in the Melbourne Museum – the only first generation computer intact and on display in the world (McCann & Thorne, 2000).)

In the 1960s the Australian Commonwealth Government had a need for large numbers of computer professionals to staff its rapidly developing administrative computing projects in the Department of Defence and in the Postmaster General's Department (PMG, now broken up into Telstra and Australia Post). This was a major factor in getting business computing underway in Australia. These government computing projects created a huge need for trained IT professionals in analysis, design and programming, but such people were not to be found and had to be trained. This training was initially supplied by the Commonwealth Government in the form of *Programmer in Training* (PIT) courses run by the Commonwealth Public Service Board. These PIT courses provided the impetus for university-level courses in business computing (- then know as Automatic Data Processing) as they soon moved to the Colleges of Advanced Education (later to be merged into universities) and then evolved into what we now know as Information Systems curriulum (Tatnall, 2006).

In this research project (Tatnall, 1993) I interviewed current and former academics and those who had been involved in this innovation. One of my interview subjects was Gerry Maynard who had been an inspector in the PMG and Public Service Board and been involved in the delivery of the PIT courses (Maynard, 1965, 1971). My research methodology was Curriculum History (Goodson, 1988; Goodson & Ball, 1984) which offers an ethnographic approach to the study of the evolution of curriculum. What curriculum history does *not* provide, however, is a useful approach to the consideration of the non-human entities that are an essential part of any curriculum involving technology, and this is where ANT came in. Rather than subject this data to a full actor-network analysis however, I found it more useful to draw on some aspects of ANT to help describe the socio-technical interactions which took place in the evolution of business computing. I started by looking at the non-human actors and outlining the evolution of the machines and the methods employed by the human actors in using these machines. This is where my interest in actor-network theory began.

THE ADOPTION OF VISUAL BASIC AS A UNIVERSITY CURRICULUM INNOVATION

After completing the research masters degree I commenced work on my PhD, also with Chris Bigum as research supervisor. Promotion resulted in Chris soon moving to the University of Central Queensland (CQU), and this meant that I then moved my PhD to CQU also. A suitable research topic was easy to find as in the early 1990s a colleague at RMIT University and I had recently discovered Visual Basic

(VB) and we soon each began, in a small way, teaching VB to our Information Systems students. This innovation was not, however, without some controversy in our universities. Questions were asked along the lines of: was VB an appropriate language to teach in an IS course? What about Pascal, wasn't Pascal a better language than a version of Basic to teach students about structured programming? But VB offered a much more interesting approach to programming in a graphical or Windows environment, was this not worthwhile?

These discussions suggested a suitable topic for my PhD as investigating *Innovation and Change in the Information Systems Curriculum of an Australian University* (Tatnall, 2000). My supervisor and I decided that the study would investigate the introduction of Visual Basic at RMIT University in Melbourne, and that what was needed was an approach that offered a suitable socio-technical perspective. The research approach would need to take account of the human but also the non-human (technological) actors involved. Clearly actor-network theory was seen to provide an appropriate framework.

Little of the literature on curriculum innovation at that time dealt with university curriculum, and most reported work focussed on research, development and diffusion studies of the adoption, or otherwise, of centrally developed curriculum innovations in primary and secondary schools (Nordvall, 1982). The innovation described in my thesis was of a different order, being developed initially by a single university lecturer in one of the subjects for which he had responsibility. It was important primarily because it examined something that did not appear to have been reported on before: the negotiations and alliances that allowed new material, in this case the programming language Visual Basic, to enter individual subjects of a university curriculum, and to obtain a durable place there (Tatnall, 2000).

The research investigated this single instance of innovation, and traced the associations between various human and non-human entities including Visual Basic, the university, the student laboratories, the Course Advisory Committee, and the various academic staff that made this happen. It followed the formation of alliances and complex networks of associations and how their interplay resulted in the curriculum change that allowed Visual Basic to enter the Information Systems curriculum and to fend off challenges from other programming languages in order to retain its place there. The study did this by 'interviewing' the human and non-human actors and collecting and analysing relevant documents.

As writing up progressed it became apparent that the complete study was too large to subject all parts of the thesis to an actor-network analysis. I decided instead to identify a number of *key moments*; particular events which seemed, to the actors, to be crucial in the formation of the actor-networks of interest, and to make use of an actor-network approach to describe just these moments. Although the role of the researcher in deciding which key moments to include must be acknowledged the choice was not arbitrary. In identifying these key moments I made every effort to allow the actors themselves to identify what they saw as pivotal and important. The research showed that in this curriculum innovation no pre-planned path was followed and that representations of events like this as being straightforward or well planned hides the complexity of what actually takes place. The study revealed the complex set of negotiations and compromises made by both human and non-human actors in allowing Visual Basic to enter the curriculum. The analysis mapped the progress of Visual Basic from novelty to 'obvious choice' in this university's Information Systems curriculum (Tatnall, 2007b).

The study also showed me the value of using innovation translation to describe partial adoptions, as for several of the subjects in which VB gained a place in the curriculum it was only some aspects of VB that had been of interest. For example, in the early 1990s an introductory IS subject involved use of a screen prototyping tool in one topic (Tatnall, 2010b; Tatnall & Davey, 2001). This topic had always been hard to teach because the university did not have a suitable prototyping tool that could easily be used in the MS-DOS student labs, meaning that this topic could not readily be handled practically. The academic who acted as heterogeneous engineer in the introduction of VB, we will call him Fred, wondered whether some aspects of the MS-DOS version of VB could do the job. For this subject he was not interested in the programming features of VB, just those using in its screen design and this was his *problematisation* (Callon, 1986) of VB for this subject. Fred could only use VB in this way by *translating* (Callon, 1986) it from a 'programming language and visual programming environment' into a 'screen prototyping tool'. He could do this by selecting just some features of VB while ignoring others. In further examples other IS subjects at the university required translations of VB to become: 'Visual Basic: the language for Windows operating systems programming', 'Visual Basic: the Graphical User Interface programming language', and 'Visual Basic: a language for introducing object-oriented programming'. These partial adoptions would have been difficult to explain using Innovation Diffusion (Rogers, 1995) or the Technology Acceptance Model (TAM) (Davis, 1989).

INITIAL DOCTORAL RESEARCH STUDENTS

My first two PhD students were academic staff from my own Department. The first was Jerzy, whose topic involved an investigation of the growing use of the Internet by retired people. Jerzy decided to make use of an ethnographic approach to this study and proceeded to speak with and attempt to become involved with retired people making use of computers. Although he made no direct use of ANT in his thesis we did write a joint journal article re-interpreting his data using an ANT framework (Lepa & Tatnall, 2006). In this article we noted that one reason often given by older people for adopting Internet technologies (Bosler, 2001; Gross, 1998) is, quite simply, so that the world does not pass them by and so that they won't be left out of things and seen as irrelevant by their grandchildren. The means of social interaction is increasingly moving away from posted letters to e-mail, and those not using e-mail are finding it harder to keep in touch. A growing number of older people are finding that an e-mail address has become essential (Perry, 2000). These, and related reasons for adoption of Internet technologies such as "All my friends use e-mail and I'll be left out if I don't" (Council on the Ageing, 2000) suggest that characteristics of the technology have less to do with things than do social interactions and the creation and maintenance of interpersonal networks. This makes ANT and innovation translation a useful framework for modelling this adoption and use.

The research of the other student, Tas, involved modelling the use of ICT to assist students with learning disabilities (Learning Disabilities Association of Canada, 2002; NJCLD, 1994). From the start Tas adopted an ANT approach to investigation of the networks of associations between the human and non-human actors involved. He made use of ethnographic and case study techniques to collect his data from observations at two Special Schools in Melbourne that cater for students with mild learning difficulties and also from a case study of a single student. Tas quickly identified a number of important human actors in each school including the School Principal, the teacher in charge of ICT, various other teachers, the School Council, parents and of course the students themselves. Had an actor-network approach not been used he would probably have missed the important influence of the many non-human actors involved including the school computers, the software, the laboratories and buildings they were housed in, the Internet, Education Department policy and ICT infrastructure (Adam, 2010; Adam, Rigoni, & Tatnall, 2006; Adam & Tatnall, 2007, 2008). The interactions and associations formed by these actors proved crucial to understanding how ICT can best be used to assist these students (Adam, 2010).

TECHNOLOGICAL INNOVATION AND SOCIO-TECHNICAL BUSINESS RE-SEARCH

Much of my research, and that of my doctoral students, has related to adoption of some form of new technology by a business organisation. As described in a later chapter of this book (Tatnall, 2010a), the process of technological innovation involves getting new ideas accepted or new technologies adopted and used (Tatnall, 2005a). The development of a new technology does not mean that this will automatically be adopted by its potential users, and this adoption (or failure to adopt) a new technology is what this research is about.

Models of Technological Innovation

The later chapter referred to above describes and compares three of the main approaches to theorising technological innovation: Innovation Translation (Callon, 1986; Latour, 1996; Law, 1987), Innovation Diffusion (Rogers, 1995, 2003) and the Technology Acceptance Model (TAM) (Davis, 1986, 1989; Davis, Bagozzi, & Warshaw, 1989) and also makes brief mention of several other approaches. Although I much prefer innovation translation as a research approach, I am prepared to work with either one of the other approaches if one of my students chose this. In this case I often also write a journal article with them re-interpreting their data using an innovation translation approach. In the sections that follow I will describe some of my research, and that of my students, that investigates technological innovation.

The Bizewest Portal

In June 2000 the Western Region Economic Development Organisation (WREDO), a not-for-profit organisation sponsored by the six municipalities that make up the western region of Melbourne, Australia, received a State Government grant for a project to set up a business-to-business portal. The project was to create a horizontal portal; *Bizewest*, that would enable small to medium enterprises (SMEs) in Melbourne's west to engage in an increased number of e-commerce transactions with each other (Tatnall & Burgess, 2002). The main objective of the Bizewest Portal project, in its initial stages, was to encourage SMEs in Melbourne's west to be more aggressive in their up-take of e-commerce business opportunities, and to encourage them to work with other local enterprises in the region also using the Portal. The project was to create a true business-to-business portal on which on-line trading was to occur (Tatnall, 2007a; Tatnall & Burgess, 2002).

The aim of the research project was to investigate why some SMEs in this region were keen to adopt the portal while others were not. The research methodology involved a series of case studies with SMEs and interviews with the portal's designers and the WREDO project managers, informed by actor-network theory and innovation translation. The research began by identifying some of the important actors, starting with the WREDO portal project manager. This interview revealed why the project was instigated and identified some of the other actors. One line of inquiry resulting from this interview was to approach the portal software designer and programmers. It was determined that another set of actors consisted of the proprietors of the local businesses themselves, and the project manager suggested some 'business champions' to interview first to find out why they had adopted the portal and what had influenced them in doing so. Some of these business people then pointed to the influence exerted by the computer hardware or software as a negative significant factor, so identifying some non-human actors. From this point on the key was to follow the actors, both human and non-human, searching out interactions, negotiations, alliances and networks. Negotiations between actors needed to be carefully investigated. Apart from the obvious human to human kind of negotiation, there were also human to non-human interactions such as those of the business people trying to work out how the portal operated and how to adapt this technology to their own business purposes. They 'negotiated' with the portal software to see what it could do for them, and it 'negotiated' with them to convince them to adopt its way of doing business. The process of adopting and implementing the portal could now be seen as the complex set of interactions that it was, and not just the inevitable result of the innate characteristics of this technology as innovation diffusion theory would suggest (Tatnall & Burgess, 2002). This study is further described in a later chapter of this book (Tatnall, 2010a).

A spin off from this research project was that it increased my interest in investigating other examples of portal technology and indeed of the technology of portals themselves. After producing several conference papers relating to portals (Lepa & Tatnall, 2002, 2004; Tatnall, Burgess, & Singh, 2004; Tatnall & Pliaskin, 2005), this interest resulted in the publication of the edited book: *Web Portals: the New Gateways to Internet Information and Services* (Tatnall, 2005b) and the *Encyclopedia of Portal Technology and Applications* (Tatnall, 2007c).

Rural Medical General Practitioners and the Adoption of ICT

This project was the result of a successful ARC (Australian Research Council) grant to sponsor a PhD student, Patricia, to investigate the *Adoption of Information and Communication Technologies by Rural General Practitioners*. The goal of the project was to identify and model the socio-technical factors that acted to enable or to inhibit the uptake and use of ICT and to compare two different theoretical approaches to the adoption of technological innovations: innovation diffusion and innovation translation (Deering, 2008).

The research method involved case studies of several rural medical general practices within the Central Highland Division of General Practice, to the north-west of Melbourne (Wenn, Tatnall, Sellitto, Darbyshire, & Burgess, 2002). As the study involved a comparison of two different models for theorising ICT adoption it was important from the beginning to ensure that the approach used did not privilege one of these models to the detriment of the other, and Patricia kept this in mind while collecting the data. For each of the general practices considered, Patricia identified key moments in the adoption (or non-adoption) of ICT and considered these in terms of innovation diffusion, before also applying an innovation translation analysis.

In some cases the two approaches each produced plausible explanations, but then one example showed the limitations of innovation diffusion. Initially some of the medical practices were in a position to adopt or reject the use of ICT and they chose to reject. One of the case studies points to factors that explain this (Deering & Tatnall, 2008). In this particular case the reason for non-adoption of ICT had nothing to do with the technology itself, but was because the present Practice Principal's father was not comfortable with ICT. He was not far off retirement but still practicing at the time, and no one wanted to make him feel uncomfortable by introducing technology with which he was unfamiliar as he was a strong part of the Practice. The Practice Manager said this was never articulated openly but all knew that it was so (Deering, 2008). Innovation diffusion's reliance on the characteristics of the technology is of no value as an explanation here and while it might attempt to use the characteristics of opinion leaders to explain the non-adoption this does not fully account for this type of barrier to adoption. An ANT analysis of the association between actors proved to provide a better explanation. (This study is further described in a later chapter of this book (Tatnall, 2010a)). This, and other similar examples, meant that Patricia was soon convinced of the value of innovation translation as an explanatory framework and she went on to conclude that in situations like this, translation offered more plausible explanations than did diffusion.

OTHER ANT STUDIES

Lily is undertaking a PhD to investigate: *The e-learning experience in first-year introductory accounting and its impact on learning outcomes*. She is particularly interested in determining an appropriate balance between on-line and face-to-face teaching (Wong & Tatnall, 2009, 2010). This research was started quite recently and Lily has not yet made a decision on the use of ANT, but in a recent journal article (Wong & Tatnall, 2010) we explored innovation translation as a possible approach to this research. At Victoria University the actors involved in this case include: the Bachelor of Business Course Coordinator, the Accounting Subject Coordinator, Subject Lecturers, Subject Tutors, Sessional Tutors, other lecturers, the Faculty Dean and the University Administration, the Head of the School of Accounting, University Policy, University Infrastructure, Technical Staff from Information Technology Services, students, computers, screens, computer laboratories, e-learning infrastructure (including remote access), competing technologies and the Blackboard e-learning environment itself. Each of these actors potentially has an influence on how or whether the adoption occurs and the balance between an online and a face-to-face approach.

Fernando has also just recently commenced his PhD research and is investigating *The impacts and challenges as a result of introducing and using ICT in schools for Mapuche students in Chile*. He is making use of ANT to identify the relevant human and non-human actors and intending then to use an innovation translation approach to shed light on how this adoption is taking place. One aspect of particular interest in this study is the changing role of the Mapuche elders who traditionally act as a library and vehicle for the dissemination of information and wisdom. What effect will students having access to ICT and the Internet have on this?

STUDIES USING TAM OR INNOVATION DIFFUSION

As mentioned earlier, I am quite prepared to allow my PhD students to make use of other approaches to technological innovation, as long as they have investigated the alternatives. In most cases a student wants to use Innovation Diffusion or TAM simply because they have heard of these approaches or been advised by a friend of colleague to use one of them. In these cases it is unlikely that the students have even heard of innovation translation.

One of these PhD students, Napaporn, investigated *Internet Usage by Academics within Thai Business Schools*, making use of a modified Technology Acceptance Model (Kripanont, 2007). Salim also used a modified form of TAM to study *Internet Technology Adoption in the Banking Industry* (Al-Hajri, 2005) that involved a comparison of Internet adoption in banks in Oman and Australia. In his DBA, Puripat looked into *Using the Technology Acceptance Model to investigate knowledge conversion in Thai public organisations* (Charnkit, 2010). Singha, on the other hand, made use in Innovation Diffusion in his PhD study of *The Determinants of the Adoption and Application of Business Intelligence* from an ERP perspective (Chaveesuk, 2010).

In each case, although these students were making use of different approaches to technological innovation I made sure that they were also introduced to ANT and innovation translation during their studies. In some cases we produced a joint journal article making use of the data they had collected, but using an innovation translation frame instead of TAM or innovation diffusion.

CONCLUSION

Over the last 15 or so years, actor-network theory has grown to become a fundamental part of my approach to socio-technical academic research. This chapter has outlined how I came to an appreciation of ANT and then used it in my own research and encouraged its use by my doctoral students. I have come to see considerations of human and non-human actors and of associations and interactions between actors as an important part of research analysis and have written quite a number of conference papers, book chapters and journal articles using ANT. In 2008 I was approached to become Editor-in-Chief of the new *International Journal of Actor-Network Theory and Technological Innovation* that would go into publication in 2009, hopefully bringing the value of ANT in socio-technical research projects to the attention of a wider audience.

Two of my colleagues have come to an understanding of ANT by writing joint papers with me that have used an innovation translation framework (Tatnall & Burgess, 2004; Tatnall & Davey, 2002a, 2002b, 2003). They have not studied ANT but have learned enough from writing these papers to see its value. One of the problems often mentioned by those trying to learn about actor-network theory is its jargon: they find terms like obligatory passage point, interessement and heterogeneous engineer hard to come to grips with. While it is possible to write a good socio-technical article using ANT by making good use of a large amount of ANT jargon, it is also usually possible to write just as good an article either using very little ANT jargon, or at lease explaining the jargon as the article progresses. I suggest that it is incumbent on ANT researchers to make ANT accessible to others. I suggest that it is incumbent on them to use ANT as an analytical framework and to explain its benefits to others as clearly and simply as possible.

But what of the future of what we call actor-network theory? Should we change its name to something more accurately descriptive? What of the various suggestions that ANT has run its course and needs to change fundamentally? There will always be those who make suggestions like these, but for most of us it is more important to make use of a little or a lot of ANT in our research, and to mould and shape ANT to our own needs and taste. It is important to introduce ANT to our students, but not to force it down their unwilling throats. I see no problem in letting students look at and even use other approaches to technological innovation, as long as they know that there is an alternative in innovation translation.

Arthur Tatnall
Victoria University, Australia

REFERENCES

Adam, T. (2010). *Determining an e-learning Model for Students with Learning Disabilities: An Analysis of Web-based Technologies and Curriculum.* Victoria University, Melbourne.

Adam, T., Rigoni, A., & Tatnall, A. (2006). Designing and Implementing Curriculum for Students with Special Needs: A Case Study of a Thinking Curriculum. *Journal of Business Systems, Governance and Ethics, 1*(1), 49-63.

Adam, T., & Tatnall, A. (2007). *Building a Virtual Knowledge Community of Schools for Children with Special Needs.* Paper presented at the Information Technologies for Education and Training (iTET), Charles University, Prague.

Adam, T., & Tatnall, A. (2008). Using ICT to Improve the Education of Students with Learning Disabilities. In M. Kendall & B. Samways (Eds.), *Learning to Live in the Knowledge Society* (pp. 63-70). New York: Springer.

Al-Hajri, S. (2005). *Internet Technology Adoption in the Banking Industry.* Victoria University, Melbourne.

Bosler, N. (2001). *Communication, E-Commerce and Older People.* Paper presented at the E-Commerce, Electronic Banking and Older People, Melbourne.

Callon, M. (1986). Some Elements of a Sociology of Translation: Domestication of the Scallops and the Fishermen of St Brieuc Bay. In J. Law (Ed.), *Power, Action & Belief. A New Sociology of Knowledge?* (pp. 196-229). London: Routledge & Kegan Paul.

Charnkit, P. (2010). *Using the Technology Acceptance Model to investigate knowledge conversion in Thai public organisations.* Victoria University, Melbourne.

Chaveesuk, S. (2010). *The Determinants of the Adoption and Application of Business Intelligence: An ERP Perspective.* Victoria University, Melbourne.

Council on the Ageing (2000). Older People and the Internet Focus Group: Unpublished.

Davis, F. (1986). *A Technology Acceptance Model for Empirically Testing New End-User Information Systems: Theory and Results.* MIT, Boston.

Davis, F. (1989). Perceived Usefulness, Perceived Ease of Use, and User Acceptance of Information Technology. *MIS Quarterly, 13*(3), 318-340.

Davis, F., Bagozzi, R., & Warshaw, P. (1989). User Acceptance of Computer Technology: A Comparison of Two Theoretical Models. *Management Science, 35*(8), 982-1003.

Deering, P. (2008). *The Adoption of Information and Communication Technologies in Rural General Practice: A Socio Technical Analysis.* Victoria University, Melbourne.

Deering, P., & Tatnall, A. (2008). A Comparison of Two Research Approaches to Modelling the Adoption of ICT by Rural GPs. In B. Lloyd-Walker, S. Burgess, K. Manning & A. Tatnall (Eds.), *The New 21st Century Workplace* (pp. 1-12). Melbourne: Heidelberg Press.

Goodson, I. F. (Ed.). (1988). *International Perspectives in Curriculum History.* London: Routledge.

Goodson, I. F., & Ball, S. J. (Eds.). (1984). *Defining the Curriculum: Histories and Ethnographies*. UK: The Falmer Press.

Gross, J. (1998). Wielding Mouse and Modem, Elderly Remain in the Loop. *The New York Times*.

Kripanont, N. (2007). *Examining a Technology Acceptance Model of Internet Usage by Academics within Thai Business Schools*. Victoria University, Melbourne.

Latour, B. (1996). *Aramis or the Love of Technology*. Cambridge, Ma: Harvard University Press.

Law, J. (1987). Technology and Heterogeneous Engineering: The Case of Portuguese Expansion. In W. E. Bijker, T. P. Hughes & T. J. Pinch (Eds.), *The Social Construction of Technological Systems: New Directions in the Sociology and History of Technology* (pp. 111-134). Cambridge, Ma: MIT Press.

Learning Disabilities Association of Canada (2002). Official Definition of Learning Disabilities Retrieved May 2007, from http://www.ldac-taac.ca/Defined/defined_new-e.asp

Lepa, J., & Tatnall, A. (2002). *The GreyPath Web Portal: Reaching out to Virtual Communities of Older People in Regional Areas*. Paper presented at the IT in Regional Areas (ITiRA-2002), Rockhampton, Australia.

Lepa, J., & Tatnall, A. (2004). Portals for Older People in Regional Areas: The GreyPath Virtual Community. In S. Marshall, W. Taylor & Y. Xinghuo (Eds.), *Using Community Informatics to Transform Regions* (pp. 209-222). Hershey, PA: Idea Group Publishing.

Lepa, J., & Tatnall, A. (2006). Using Actor-Network Theory to Understanding Virtual Community Networks of Older People Using the Internet. *Journal of Business Systems, Governance and Ethics, 1*(4), 1-14.

Maynard, G. B. (1965). *An Introduction to Computers and Programming; A Lecture to Melbourne Junior Chamber of Commerce*. Melbourne: Melbourne Junior Chamber of Commerce.

Maynard, G. B. (1971). *PIT Course Notes*. Melbourne: Caulfield Institute of Technology.

McCann, D., & Thorne, P. (2000). *The Last of the First - CSIRAC: Australia's First Computer*. Melbourne: The University of Melbourne.

NJCLD (1994). Learning disabilities: Issues on definition revised *Collective Perspectives on Issues Affecting Learning Disabilities* (pp. 61-66). Austin, TX: PRO-ED.

Nordvall, R. C. (1982). *The process of change in higher education institutions* (ERIC/AAHE Research Report No. 7). Washington DC: American Association for Higher Education.

Pearcey, T. (1988). *A History of Australian Computing*. Melbourne: Chisholm Institute of Technology.

Perry, J. (2000). Retirees stay wired to kids - and to one another. *U.S. News and World Report, 22*.

Rogers, E. M. (1995). *Diffusion of Innovations* (4th ed.). New York: The Free Press.

Rogers, E. M. (2003). *Diffusion of Innovations* (5th ed.). New York: The Free Press.

Tatnall, A. (1993). *A Curriculum History of Business Computing in Victorian Tertiary Institutions from 1960 - 1985*. Unpublished Major, Deakin University, Geelong.

Tatnall, A. (2000). *Innovation and Change in the Information Systems Curriculum of an Australian University: a Socio-Technical Perspective.* Central Queensland University, Rockhampton.

Tatnall, A. (2005a). Technological Change in Small Organisations: An Innovation Translation Perspective. *International Journal of Knowledge, Culture and Change Management, 4*(1), 755-761.

Tatnall, A. (2006). *Curriculum Cycles in the History of Information Systems in Australia.* Melbourne: Heidelberg Press.

Tatnall, A. (2007a). *Business Culture and the Death of a Portal.* Paper presented at the 20th Bled e-Conference - eMergence: Merging and Emerging Technologies, Processes and Institutions Bled, Slovenia.

Tatnall, A. (2007b). *Innovation Translation in a University Curriculum.* Melbourne: Heidelberg Press.

Tatnall, A. (2010a). Innovation Translation, Innovation Diffusion and the Technology Acceptance Model: Comparing Three Different Approaches to Theorising Technological Innovation. In A. Tatnall (Ed.), *Actor-Network Theory and Technology Innovation: Advancements and New Concepts.* Hershey, USA: IGI Global.

Tatnall, A. (2010b). Using Actor-Network Theory to Understand the Process of Information Systems Curriculum Innovation. *Education and Information Technologies, 15*(4).

Tatnall, A. (Ed.). (2005b). *Web Portals: the New Gateways to Internet Information and Services.* Hershey, PA: Idea Group Publishing.

Tatnall, A. (Ed.). (2007c). *Encyclopedia of Portal Technology and Applications.* Hershey, PA: Information Science Reference.

Tatnall, A., & Burgess, S. (2002). *Using Actor-Network Theory to Research the Implementation of a B-B Portal for Regional SMEs in Melbourne, Australia.* Paper presented at the 15th Bled Electronic Commerce Conference - 'eReality: Constructing the eEconomy', Bled, Slovenia.

Tatnall, A., & Burgess, S. (2004). Using Actor-Network Theory to Identify Factors Affecting the Adoption of E-Commerce in SMEs. In M. Singh & D. Waddell (Eds.), *E-Business: Innovation and Change Management* (pp. 152-169). Hershey, PA: IRM Press.

Tatnall, A., Burgess, S., & Singh, M. (2004). Community and Regional Portals in Australia: a Role to Play for Small Businesses? In N. Al Quirim (Ed.), *Electronic Commerce in Small to Medium Enterprises: Frameworks, Issues and Implications* (pp. 307-323). Hershey, PA: Idea Group Publishing.

Tatnall, A., & Davey, W. (2001). *How Visual Basic Entered the Curriculum at an Australian University: An Account Informed by Innovation Translation.* Paper presented at the Challenges to Informing Clients: A Transdisciplinary Approach (Informing Science 2001), Krakow, Poland.

Tatnall, A., & Davey, W. (2002a, 19-21 June 2002). *Curriculum Development in the Informing Sciences: Ecological Metaphor, Negotiation or Actor-Network?* Paper presented at the Informing Science and IT Education Conference, Cork, Ireland.

Tatnall, A., & Davey, W. (2002b). Understanding the Process of Information Systems and ICT Curriculum Development: Three Models. In K. Brunnstein & J. Berleur (Eds.), *Human Choice and Computers: Issues of Choice and Quality of Life in the Information Society* (pp. 275-282). Assinippi Park, Ma: Kluwer Academic Publishers / IFIP.

Tatnall, A., & Davey, W. (2003). Modelling the Adoption of Web-Based Mobile Learning - an Innovation Translation Approach. In W. Zhou, P. Nicholson, B. Corbitt & J. Fong (Eds.), *Advances in Web-Based Learning* (Vol. LNCS 2783, pp. 433-441). Berlin: Springer Verlag.

Tatnall, A., & Gilding, A. (1999). *Actor-Network Theory and Information Systems Research.* Paper presented at the 10th Australasian Conference on Information Systems (ACIS), Wellington.

Tatnall, A., & Pliaskin, A. (2005). *Technological Innovation and the Non-Adoption of a B-B Portal.* Paper presented at the Second International Conference on Innovations in Information technology, Dubai, UAE.

Wenn, A., Tatnall, A., Sellitto, C., Darbyshire, P., & Burgess, S. (2002). *A Socio-Technical Investigation of Factors Affecting IT Adoption by Rural GPs.* Paper presented at the IT in Regional Areas (ITiRA-2002), Rockhampton, Australia.

Wong, L., & Tatnall, A. (2009). The Need to Balance the Blend: Online versus Face-to-Face Teaching in an Introductory Accounting Subject. *Journal of Issues in Informing Science and Information Technology (IISIT), 6*, 309-322.

Wong, L., & Tatnall, A. (2010). Factors Determining the Balance between Online and Face-to-Face Teaching: an Analysis using Actor-Network Theory. *Interdisciplinary Journal of Information, Knowledge and Management, 5*, 167-176.

Section 1

Chapter 1

Have You Taken Your Guys on the Journey?
An ANT Account of IS Project Evaluation

Dubravka Cecez-Kecmanovic
University of New South Wales, Australia

Fouad Nagm
University of New South Wales, Australia

ABSTRACT

Pre-investment evaluation of information system (IS) project proposals persists to be problematic and highly risky in practice. Numerous evaluation approaches and methodologies, offered in the literature, have not contributed to major improvements in practice. In this paper we propose a radical departure from the dominant conceptions in IS evaluation literature by adopting Actor-Network Theory (ANT) to provide a better understanding of the development and evaluation of IS proposals in practice and examine the ways in which the evaluation process shapes and ensures the selection of the best IS projects. By drawing on a field study of the IS evaluation processes in a company with a history of IS successes, we reveal the relational nature of IS project proposals and the ways they are constitutively entangled with business processes and practices. Our ANT account demonstrates: a) that the view of pre-investment IS evaluation in the literature is very narrow; b) that the practice of IS evaluation produces the 'object' it evaluates; c) that this object, that is the IS project proposal document, is a focal actor (an inscription device) produced by relations in the actor-network emerging around it; and d) that reconfiguration of these relations involving the translation of actors' expertise, experiences and interests into the IS proposal documents are critical for the evaluation of IS project proposals and their chances of success.

INTRODUCTION

Since its infancy Information Systems (IS) research has struggled to reconcile the technological and the social nature of information systems, and to investigate them in an integrated and coherent way. Most IS research assumes a conventional separation between the technological (material) and the social (human, organizational). Such separation has been a defining feature of the discourses in the IS discipline. This is evident in both the technology focused perspective and the

DOI: 10.4018/978-1-60960-197-3.ch001

social/organisational perspective of IS studies. The technology focused research on IS development, implementation, and use typically employs a functionalist and instrumental approach producing claims about IS characteristics and their impacts on various measures of business and organisational performance. Underpinned by technologically deterministic and economic rationalist views this perspective reifies technology and largely neglects the complex and subtle ways IS are entangled with and mutually constituting human action and work practices within social, historical, cultural and political contexts. In contrast, the social and organisational perspective that adopts an interpretive, social constructivist or critical approach, focuses on how individuals make sense of, use, and engage with IS, sensitive to interpretations within and implications for particular power relations and socio-cultural and political contexts. While this perspective reveals numerous, more or less visible, ways in which IS enable transformation of work practices and organisations (e.g. increasing control and managerial domination), it privileges the social and organizational side at the expense of the technology. It considers technology as 'interpretively flexible' (Pinch and Bijker 1984) but separate and independent.

Research on IS project evaluation presents a paradigmatic case of the conceptual separation between the social/business world and the technical world. In the IS and software engineering literature IS projects (including IS specification, design and application software) are seen as autonomous entities which, once implemented, will have implications for business processes and organizational performance. The IS project evaluation literature is therefore principally concerned with the assessment of the future business implications of IS projects, including calculation of costs and benefits. Numerous IS project evaluation methodologies have been proposed and tested for this purpose (e.g. Cost-Benefit Analysis, Discounted Cash Flow Analysis, Net Present Value, Payback Period). Despite increasing sophistication of these predominantly financial evaluation methodologies, IS project evaluations and investment decisions in practice remain problematic and highly risky. The high failure rate of IS projects – as high as 50-70% according to different sources – indicates the severity of the problem (- see Standish Group International (2001), Sauer and Cuthbertson (2003), Luna-Reyes et al. (2005)).

We suggest that one of the key problems with these dominant approaches to IS evaluation in organisations is the presumption of separate existence of technology and organisation, which consequently limits research to the examination of 'the influence of the future IS on an organization's performance'. While it is assumed that IS projects are developed based on the needs of business and that once implemented and operating within a business context, the IS will influence and change this context, the IS and its business/organizational context are considered ontologically separate. This presents a conceptual difficulty when faced with the everyday ubiquity of IS in working and organising processes and the ways IS and the business, organizational and social are inextricably linked and intermeshed. Aren't we in IS research perpetuating an artificial (considered 'scientific') division between the technological and the business/social that limits our understanding of IS project evaluation and hence prevents us from doing something about such a formidable problem in the IS practice?

In this paper we propose a radical departure from the dominant conceptions in the IS evaluation literature by adopting a socio-technical approach emerging under the umbrella of Actor-network Theory (ANT) (Callon 1986; Latour 1986, 2005; Walsham and Sahay, 1999; Law 1999, 2004). This involves a key conceptual shift toward understanding the socio-technical nature of both the IS project proposals and business/organizational reality seen as entangled and mutually constituting. A similar shift has been proposed in organization studies literature. For instance, instead of "conventional framing of organizational practices as 'social practices'", Orlikowski proposed seeing organizational practices as 'sociomaterial' (2007, p. 1438; Law, 2004). Such a shift implies a change in our analytic gaze, including the sensitivity to the 'constitutive entanglement' (Barad, 2003) of the material (technological) and the social (organizational) in practice:

The notion of constitutive entanglement departs from that of mutual or reciprocal interaction common in a number of dynamic social theories. Notions of mutuality or reciprocity presume the influence of distinct interacting entities on each other, but presume some a priory independence of these entities from each other...In contrast, the notion of constitutive entanglement presumes that there are no independently existing entities with inherent characteristics (Barad, 2003, p. 816). Humans are constituted through relations of materiality – bodies, clothes, food, devices, tools, which, in turn are produced through human practice. The distinction of humans and artifacts, on this view, is analytical only; these entities relationally entail or enact each other in practice (Orlikowski, 2007, p. 1438, emphasis in the original).

This is particularly challenging in the IS project evaluation research in which the subject of study is the future IS that is constitutively entangled with business/organizational reality. To understand (and potentially improve) IS projects evaluation, therefore, we need to explore the ways in which IS projects and human actors entail and enact each other in business practice. To do this we adopt an ANT approach "to socio-technical analysis that treats entities and materialities as enacted and relational effects, and explores the configuration and reconfiguration of those relations" (Law, 2004, p. 157). The key difference in adopting ANT to study IS project evaluation in practice is the view of organizational realities and their representations and mediations via IS as relational and continuously enacted and produced.

In other words, ANT enables us to investigate the materiality and relationality of IS project development and evaluations as a recurrent envisioning and enacting of the future business realities as socio-technical realities.

We demonstrate this through an ANT account of IS projects evaluation in a case company that has extensive experience in assessing, developing and deploying IS, and a track record of successful IS projects ($3 billion worth of successfully delivered IS projects in the past few years). It also has well established processes for developing and evaluating IS proposals, including the use of a range of evaluation techniques. With its unusually high success rates of IS projects the company can be seen as an exemplary case of IS project evaluation processes. As such it provides a distinct research opportunity to examine the nature and emergence of IS project proposals and their evaluation in practice. Informed and sensitized by ANT, in this paper we seek to investigate:

- How is the socio-technical nature of IS project proposals imagined and performed through relations in business practices?
- How are socio-technical IS project/business relations configured and reconfigured in practices?
- How do these (re)configurations of IS project/business relations produce evaluations – so that some succeed and others fail?

To answer these questions we examine the practices of IS evaluation in the case company Throughout the empirical study, lasting 16 months we encountered and followed many actors, such as business managers, IS managers, project managers; a plethora of documents including an IS evaluation methodology, IS project ideas, project proposals, IS business case, etc., and their relations. We examined their relations and how IS project proposals and business realities are enacted and performed in these relations.

Before we present this analysis we first discuss the IS evaluation literature and raise some key concerns and problems. We then briefly introduce actor-network theory (ANT) and the way we adopted it as both a theoretical lens and a methodology in our study. Next we briefly introduce the case study and discuss our research design. We then seek to answer the above research questions by providing an ANT account of IS project evaluation practices in the case company, from which we draw conclusions and implications for research and practice.

IS PROJECT EVALUATION RESEARCH

The IS evaluation literature has traditionally taken quite a narrow view of IS evaluation by focussing on the development of methodologies that aid the evaluation of Information Systems. Over the years there has been a movement away from this narrow view to one which encapsulates broader social and business perspectives. Recently a new approach to IS evaluation has emerged – one that brings together both the social and technical. The literature as it has developed over the years will be briefly reviewed beginning with the narrow 'IT artefact' view of IS evaluation, then extending to the broader social and business perspective and concluding with the socio-technical view which is gaining prominence.

The IS evaluation literature is broadly divided into two distinct areas, pre and post-investment evaluation. The focus of pre-investment evaluation is on the pre-implementation evaluation of what, how and why organisations should invest in IS (Al-Yaseen, et al., 2004). It is also defined by Williams & Williams (2004) as being 'predictive evaluation', perhaps because of the speculative nature of the evaluation in predicting the impact of an IS in a certain situation in future (Remenyi & Sherwood-Smith 1999). Murphy & Simon (2001)

are of the view that the focus of pre-investment evaluation is on justification of the IS investment before it is initiated. The information needed to perform this evaluation includes future estimates which are a function of the evaluator's judgement (Remenyi & Sherwood-Smith 1999). The term evaluation used throughout this paper imply pre-investment evaluation. Post-implementation (or ex-post) evaluation is out of scope for this particular paper.

Early debates about the value of IS for business were sparked by a controversial view by Solow (1987) who argued that there was insufficient evidence to link investments in IT to gains in productivity. He said – as quoted by Brynjolfsson (1993) – that "We see computers everywhere except in the productivity statistics" (p. 67). Coined the 'productivity paradox', this has no doubt motivated an enormous amount of interest and research in the field. The result has been the introduction of a plethora of evaluation methodologies in an attempt to measure the broader value IT generates for the firm, in particular its productivity. These evaluation methodologies and the studies of their applications focussed predominately on assessing the inherent value of IT artefacts for business. They also made implicit assumptions that the IT artefact is independent from its business and organisational context.

This has been criticized by Hirschheim & Smithson (1988) who proposed an interpretive perspective to IS evaluation that is more attentive to IS practice. They criticised much of the literature for treating individuals as uniform users in a deterministic way while ignoring the role human actors play in the evaluation process. Perhaps that is because studies focused more on factors that influence evaluation rather than the evaluation process itself, which would have required a more interpretive approach – one that embraces human and social contexts.

In his review of the evaluation methodologies Powell (1992) concludes that while IS evaluation methodologies are important more work needs to focus on the way social and organisational aspects are addressed in these methodologies. As the understanding of IS in business deepened, there were more calls for studies to focus on the social and organisational aspects of evaluation. Farbey, Land & Targett (1994) state:

... if information systems are complex and pervasive socio-technical systems whose life extends over several months or even years then investment in information systems can be understood as a programme of social action, based on a complex technology and taking place over a substantial period in time. Such investments are in many ways like the programmes which are the subject to evaluation research. (p. 240)

Several other researchers have also argued for the need to incorporate social and business context of IS evaluation. Jayaruriya (1997) argues that evaluation that takes a more contextual approach provides a richer picture of information systems, its impact on the organisation and outputs. A number of studies have focussed on particular social, political and organisational dimensions of IS evaluation for example: continuous stakeholder participative evaluation (Remenyi & Sherwood-Smith 1999), involvement of stakeholder groups in evaluation (Serafeimidis & Smithson 2000), the politics of IS department involvement in evaluation (Jones & Hughes 2001), use of different criteria by different stakeholders to evaluate IS (Adelakun & Jennex 2002), and the political dimension of evaluation from multiple hetergenous stakeholder groups (Winklhofer 2002). Berghout et al. (2005) argued that eliminating politics in IS evaluation through supposedly objective evaluation methodologies is problematic because the evaluation process is not a strict rational process but rather a political process.

Heeding the call for more research in the broader context within which IS evaluations take place, a number of studies have recently emerged taking a socio-technical view. One of the first studies adopting this view was that of Wilson & Howcroft (2000) who examined political and social aspects of evaluation processes in organisations by using a social shaping approach. They found that evaluation is de facto a decision making process, and that despite being described as 'stakeholders', users did not have equal stake, if any, in the evaluation of the system. Benefits and drawbacks are also constructed through the evaluation process. As the interests of stakeholders are different the evaluation is necessarily a political process. With respect to an objectivist view of IS evaluation they state, 'no matter what claims to so-called objective methods are made, the evaluation process is skewed by those with the power to legitimize views of the system' (pp. 101-2).

Ryan et al. (2002) took a view that the operations of the organisation are made up of intertwined 'technical and social subsystems'. They state that the social subsystem consists not only of employees but of their knowledge, skills, abilities, ideas, opinions, interrelationships, and needs they bring to their tasks. The technical system on the other hand is comprised of the mechanisms, techniques and tools used within the social subsystems to carry out organisational work. They found that IT investment decisions are not only concerned with the evaluation of the technical aspects of the system but also the social subsystem which accompanies the acquisition of new information technologies.

The dominant trends in the IS evaluation literature – focusing on either IT artefacts, or on social and organisational implications or more recently attempting to incorporate both the technological and organisational aspects of IS evaluation – have a common thread; they assume the separate existence of technology and organisation even when considering both the technological and social/organisational aspects. This has been recognized by Introna & Whittaker's (2002) who argued that 'the path to better IS evaluation in organizations is to get beyond the dualisms of subject/object, mind/body, and cognition/action that limit our analysis, understanding, and practice of evaluation in the flow of organizational life' (p.155). In an attempt to overcome the issues of separate existence of the IT and the organisation Nijland (2004) adopted ANT to investigate the selection process and deployment of IT evaluation methodologies in organisations. By viewing IT evaluation methodologies as actors the deployment of these methodologies were seen as a dynamic process which is emergent and not necessarily prescriptive.

In this paper we take this challenge further. We endeavour a radical departure from the dominant trends in the IS evaluation literature by studying the IS proposals and their business and organisational context in a unified way without separating them artificially or privileging any. To do so we adopted ANT aiming to understand the sociotechnical nature of both the IS project proposals and business/organizational reality, to which we turn next.

ADOPTING ACTOR-NETWORK THEORY

ANT has been seen as having a natural affinity with the IS discipline as it is grounded in an ontology of relationality which assumes "constitutive intertwining and reciprocal inter-definition of human and material agency" (Pickering, 1995, p. 26). It enables analysis of the conditions, constraints and modification of agency within networks that intertwine the humans, culture, language, artefacts and technology (and many other things). While ANT overcomes the separation between the social and the technological it also postulates a symmetrical treatment of human and non-human actors, who are as heterogeneous actants mutually interconnected to form actor-networks (Callon 1986; Latour 1986, 2005; Law 1999, 2004).

The symmetrical treatment of human actors and technology in ANT has been questioned in the literature (Collins and Yearley, 1992; Schatzki, 2002) for attributing intentionality to technological artefacts. On the other hand studies that adopt ANT, as Orlikowski and Scott (2008) observe, often privilege one form of agency over the other, which was seen as defeating ANT's major principle. While there is no singular answer to these criticisms, we do not assume that the symmetrical treatment of human actors and technology means that they have 'equal agency' or that they 'constitute each other in *the same way*' (Suchman, 2007, p. 268) as implied by the critics. Treating humans and non-humans (technology) symmetrically should not be interpreted literally. To treat them equally means to see them as actants without precluding their roles, agency, type of actions and their importance as they get engaged in networks of relations. It means giving them a chance to act in a situation without our (researchers') intervention and pre-determination of their agency. While we see human actors and technologies entangled in emerging relations, enacting and producing each other, we do not assume that they enact and produce each other in the same way. The whole point is to abandon presumptions about how human actors enact and produce technology or how technology enacts and produces human actors (e.g. users).

Furthermore, ANT presents challenges for researchers aiming to investigate emergence of heterogeneous actor-networks. How to adopt ANT to conduct empirical studies remains open to researchers' imagination and is not prescribed by ANT's proponents and followers. For instance in their particular kinds of ethnographic studies – Latour's investigation of a "laboratory life" (1979) and later on a failed technology project called Aramis (1986), Law's aircraft stories (2002) and Mol's treatment of atherosclerosis in a hospital (2002) – they followed their objects and subjects, recorded events and collected other material evidence in many different ways. The major feature in their work is a detailed description of a story, sometimes even with fictional elements, as a basis for examining and theorizing novel and often complex concepts and questions. Latour himself describes ANT as a "very crude method to learn from actors without imposing on them an a priori definition of their world building capacity" (1999, p. 20). We learn from him and other ANTs to 'follow the actors', let them tell their own stories, use their own vocabularies and unfold their own meanings, while tracing the emergence of relations in heterogeneous actor-networks, as we explain next.

RESEARCH METHODOLOGY

In our study we aim to understand the socio-technical nature of IS project proposals and the way they are imagined and performed through relations in business practices. We also aim to follow socio-technical IS project/business relations and find out how they are configured and reconfigured in practices. Finally we aim to explain how do these (re)configurations produce evaluations – so that some succeed and others fail.

To achieve these aims we focused initially on the human actors and what they do and how they go about proposing ideas for new IS projects and how the ideas grow into official IS proposals (documents). It turned, almost intuitively, into a 'journey' of following the actors, not only humans but also objects, documents and other devices employed during projects' evaluations. By recognising mobilisation of actors and the ways they used inscription devices (such as initial PowerPoint presentations of an idea, the business case, and other documents with signatures) we began to appreciate the materiality and relationality of the emerging IS project documents and the production of their evaluation.

We conducted our study in a large multi-national financial services company in Australasia – we shall call 'ALFA Bank' – with a history spanning approximately 150 years and with an investment portfolio in excess of $1 trillion dollars. One of its divisions, ALFA Invest, was the prime focus of the study. This organisation was selected because firstly, it is known to have a well established practice of IS project proposal evaluations; secondly, it has a track record of successful IS deployment and implementation; and thirdly, the company was quite receptive to our invitation to study these practices in depth.

Our study focused on pre-investment IS project evaluation processes in ALFA Invest. However, to the degree to which these processes included actors and actions of the parent company ALFA Bank, our data collection included them as well. Data collection includes a) interviews with 36 senior executives and managers of ALFA Invest division as well as some from ALFA Bank over a 16 month period from July 2006 to October 2007 (listed in Table 1), and b) company documents in excess of 1,500 documentation related to IS project evaluation processes including examples of 25 recently approved IS project proposals.

Our investigation started with an interview with a Senior Project Analyst (see Figure 1) who explained how projects are viewed by people in the company, as well as how they are evaluated within the broader business context. From that point the inquiry emerged into several directions following the Senior Project Analyst's suggestions including the Head of the Regional Projects Board, and other Senior Business and IS Analysts. We started with semi-structured interviews guided by an interview schedule but soon departed from it and adopted unstructured interviews that proved more suitable to addressing emerging issues. The length of each interview on average was approximately one hour, but in some cases interviews spanned two hours over two separate sessions. Through these interviews we encountered non-human actors, IS project documents, evaluation methodology and strategy etc.

Table 1. Interviews conducted in ALFA invest and ALFA bank

Roles	Human actors
IS Management *(13 people)*	Head of IS Group Head of Business Demand (two people) Head of IS Architecture Head of Application Development Management Head of IS Development Head of IS Business Support IS/Business Relationship Partners (six people)
Business Management (8 people)	CEO and Chairman of ALFA Group CEO of ALFA Bank Head of Strategy Chief Operating Officer General Manager – Business Unit Head of Financial Planning Head of Central Business Operations, Head of Business Development
Projects & Project Management *(15 people)*	Senior Project Analyst (five people) Senior Project Manager (four people) Project Director (two) Head of Project Methodologies Head of Projects Head of Portfolio Management Head of Regional Projects Board

Figure 1. Interviewing actors: Following the actors' lead in ALFA Invest

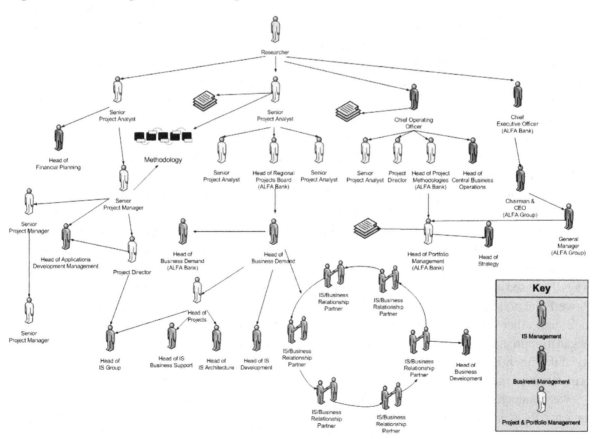

The analysis of empirical data started early on as we encountered new actors (humans and non-humans) and cannot be clearly separated from data collection. Namely, following the actors and their relations with objects and other actors prompted the chain of interviews and collection of documents. The analysis of the interviews and documents in turn led to seeking explanation of activities, events and outcomes by interviewing new actors. These interviews revealed how different business realities and interests are negotiated and inscribed in the production of IS project proposals. After data collection the analysis became more refined focusing on stages in the production of IS project proposals, the roles of specific actors or actants and the ways they enrolled and acted upon the production of the proposals while creating actor-networks. This was the basis of coding the interviews and documents using Nvivo. The coded texts were then extracted in a systematized form, assisting our writing the story of IS projects evaluation processes.

We are focusing here on the pre-investment assessment of IS projects in the ALFA Invest company that they call the 'demand' side of projects. The actual delivery of projects is referred to as being the 'supply' side. The demand side of projects in ALFA Invest is broken down into two phases - I Evaluation and II Assessment. The Phase I Evaluation consists of the emergence of the idea for an IS project, that becomes an IS Concept and is then developed into a Business Case. In the Phase II Assessment the IS Business Case is formally debated and evaluated together with other project proposals by the Regional Investment Committee. After a project is approved, funding is allocated and a Project Manager (PM) assigned. This Committee continually monitors the progress of the projects and releases further funds in stages. In our next section we provide an ANT account of this Phase I Evaluation in ALFA Invest.

PRODUCING IS PROJECTS EVALUATION WHILE PRODUCING BUSINESS REALITIES

The Nature of IS Project Proposals

In order to understand the nature of IS project proposals and the way they are imagined and performed through relations in business practices we start with the very idea for an IS project. An idea for an IS project typically includes an innovation of products or services or business improvement such as increasing productivity, better service delivery, more effective communication with customers, and the like. The IS project initiator or Project Champion presents the idea in a form of a PowerPoint presentation or a short document to communicate it to others (see Figure 2). As the Head of the Central Business Operations explains, 'you have to sell [it]…to someone else' (see Table 3). Selling the idea to other people and talking to stakeholders focuses on issues related to particular customers, business processes and their outcomes. These engagements and relations enable fermentation of the idea and garnering support from relevant people. The emergence of the idea and its maturing into an IS project proposal is illustrated by quotes from interviews in Table 2.

The idea at this moment is vague leaving enough space for other actors to read into it their view of problems, demonstrate their expertise and inscribe their interests. As it attracts other actors the idea document becomes a focal actor emerging through relations with human actors. In the words of the Head of Central Business Operations 'you garner support early and people think that guy is on to something'. An important actor, the IS/Business Relationship Partner typically engages first, as a mediating actor (see Figure 3). The Partner instigates the relations between the Champion, the idea document and business and IS stakeholders. The IS idea document thus becomes an inscription device that transforms into

Figure 2. The IS project champion proposes a short document describing the IS idea

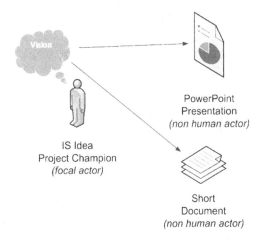

IS Idea
Project Champion
(focal actor)

PowerPoint
Presentation
(non human actor)

Short
Document
(non human actor)

different forms (versions of the document) as a consequence of the relations emerging between the document and the other actors. In such a way a core actor-network emerges through relations with and around the IS idea document. We call it a *core actor-network* to denote focal actors, relations and activities of IS proposals that are in the centre of attention at a particular time. By identifying the core network we make a distinction vis-à-vis the periphery from which other actors may act on distance or may temporarily leave the core. In Figure 3 for instance we see ALFA Group Management, a macro actor, that acts on distance and does not fully engage in mutually constituting relations.

The IS idea document is developed further by adding specific documents related to risk assessment, strategic relevance, the design of a future business, IT architecture and a crude estimation of funding. The form and content of these additional documents are determined by the methodology. We see here how the methodology acts on distance, that is, from the periphery. It can be seen as acting on behalf of the ALFA Group Management. It prescribes inscription rules and processes on behalf of Management and ensures that all relevant stakeholders get involved so that their

expertise and experience are adequately engaged in creating the vision of a new business and imagining the future IS. It also ensures that relevant, potentially conflicting, interests related to the proposed IS project, are considered and negotiated.

This initial step of proposing and strengthening an IS project idea involves enrolment and mobilization of actors – those perceived to be relevant and building initial relations around the idea as a core actor in an actor-network. In the words of the Head of Business Development, 'The influencing is the key part that...gets done in phase 1'. It is the idea document that enables people to 'come together', exchange and confront their views of business processes reality and envisage changes of this reality. By coming together and confronting their visions they also exercise their power as well as translate their interests and inscribe them in new versions of document.

We see here how the IS idea document emerges through enacted relations between the human actors and the document so that it captures the imagined future of both business and IS realities. The IS document thus arises as a relational effect that depends on configurations of the relations between the actors – in this case relevant stakeholders (Law, 2002). The IS project proposal document is not just a document. It is a relational entity that records traces of relations building among the human actors, methodology and business strategy but also and more importantly establishes links with IS and business vision and imagination of people involved. The documents describing an IS project proposal typically require signatures of responsible managers. For instance, the risk management plan for an IS project proposal should be signed by the Risk Partner and the finance case signed by the General Manager (GM) Finance. The signatures are guarantors that responsible managers' vision is engaged and that they buy-in the whole idea of the IS project proposal.

Table 2. The emergence of the IS project proposal

From an idea to the formation and evaluation of an IS project proposal	
Codes	**Extracts from interviews**
Sell an idea to someone else Relate to other people, build relations Fermentation of an idea Garner support from people, enrol and mobilize actors	*[If you have an] idea you have to sell that to someone else… [You have] to come up with the concept and then work it out, how to do it, then is anybody actually going to use it? So you have to break it down to that human thing, you have to say: does it have a need, a purpose, yeah – then its got to go. How do I sell it? I have no idea. So that's where the people have to come together. Processes are good as a framework but if people lived their life by a process then you suddenly find that things start to get hazy. … [Y]ou garner support early and people think that guy is on to something.* (Head of Central Business Operations)
Identify key people that matter in the company, that have responsibilities Influencing relevant people is the key part in phase I How to influence the business?	*I think the onus is on you as an individual to really get inside the culture, the psyche of the organisation; as part of the process you really need to identify who are the key people in that organisation, who are the people that have had that informal responsibility around? Who owns advice? Who owns investment? Who owns insurance? Who are the key strategic thinking people? You should do that as part of just coming into an organisation, in my view, because sooner or later you are going to need them. Sooner or later you are going to have to influence them and it's the influencing that's the key part and that's what gets done in phase one. How do you influence the business … is really important and gets the priority.* (Head of Business Development)
Methodology	*[T]he methodology we have built is saying what you have to do, [and] also provides the tools and templates to help project managers actually do it and to deliver [projects].* (Head of Project Methodologies)
Business and technology guys – weekly meetings IS ideas presented and discussed; hypothesis tested Idea development and testing at a more detailed level Taking people on the journey	*That's what I call the art rather than the science, but a couple of things that we are doing right now on our program from a process point of view is, we have weekly meetings – we call it the business architecture meeting – we make sure that the business engagement guys are there with the technology guys; we actually go about doing PowerPoint packs or word documents, saying here is the hypothesis at a 50,000 foot view, here are your options, then we go down to the next level, OK we have found a couple of other things here that we haven't found at this level (above), now we are testing it; now we know that we have some more decision making that we need to do, so we are sort of using a process if you like – informally making sure that we are testing it and taking people on that journey.* (Project Director)
People's suggestions and contributions to the idea encouraged Building relations around a focal actor (IS project proposal); Building an actor-network	*Its part of the culture, people are encouraged to suggest things and when they suggest something they start to buy the idea, go and talk to that person over there and see if there are implications in that area in terms of business-as-usual; go and talk to that person and get some people together and we will put some in that team and that team and become a little project committee and away it goes. Then all of a sudden it starts to grow some legs and they will say oh well lets push this up to this person, and things get filtered up.* (Head of Business Development)
Enrolling stakeholders early in the process; ownership and buying in	*… [You engage] any stakeholders that you need to be involved and onboard – we have quite a strong ethos around getting those people involved early and engaged and owning it, rather than not having them involved and handed over [something] they may not want to in the end. So I think that's definitely the culture and part of that I think is that through that collaboration is actually where a lot of the thinking happens in terms of work-shopping and working through what that actually is.* (Head of IS Business Support)
Building the actor-network – creating reality Strengthening the actor-network for the business case	*.. [building up support collectively through actual evidence as opposed to just an idea] generates interest without anybody having to put their hand in their pocket. Therefore by the time you need money you already have support so it doesn't become a big deal. Because people are engaged in what you are doing, they can see the benefits already – therefore all the formal part is putting together a paper [business case] to justify it.* (Head of Central Business Operations)
Estimates and evaluations done by the most experienced people Review of evaluations by a lot of people	*I think the approach we take in this organisation… has been more of a splatter gun approach of get the smartest people you can find, get them to put their ideas on papers and do some estimating, and then get everyone you can consider it and give you their input and try to improve and find tune it… We just try to get the most experienced people to use their best judgement to come up with evaluations and then get a lot of people to review them.* (Senior Project Manager)
Commitment to the project, electoral passion or strength of relations; sponsorship by top management	*Exactly [organisational commitment is an issue], it comes back to, if you look at it from a political context it comes down to electoral passion for it… It either goes well or not because there is no passion to make it happen. Certainly in organisations and particular on the project stuff… you need to have good passionate sponsors and passionate sponsorships comes from the top.* (Head of Projects)

Figure 3. The actor-network (the core and the periphery) is emerging around the IS idea document as a focal actor

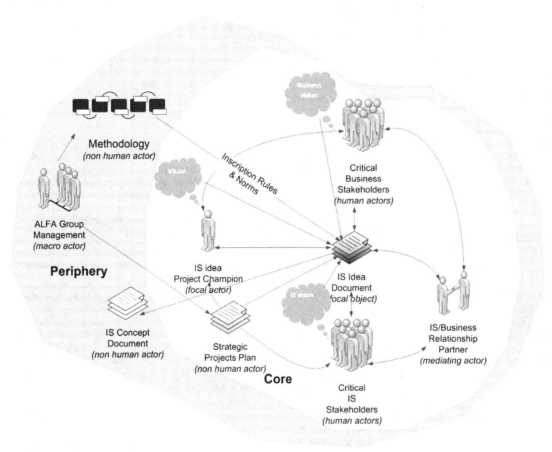

Configuring and Reconfiguring IS Project/Business Relations in Practices

A particular organizing form in ALFA Invest through which an idea for an IS project 'garners' enough support from relevant people is 'weekly meetings' also called the 'business architecture meetings'. At these meetings the 'business engagement guys' and 'technology guys' (while gendered such an expression is not seen as excluding female participants) talk together. Having different expertise and roles, often coming from different sections of ALFA Invest, they discuss, question and clarify ideas and drill down requirements to the next level of detail. In this process

their different views and visions are questioned and confronted. If their visions for the IS project proposal (IS reality) and associated changes of business processes (business reality) converge enough and if they achieve an acceptable level of agreement they produce a preliminary IS Business Case. In this process relations in the actor network around the IS Idea Document (presented in Figure 3) are reconfigured, thereby producing the IS Business Case as a new entity. Figure 4 shows a reconfigured actor-network with an IS Business Case Document at the core. This new Document emerges as a sociotechnical, relational entity constitutively entangled with Business Sponsor, Finance Partner, GM Finance and Risk Partner in the actor-network. Here again we see that the

Figure 4. The IS idea document transforms into the IS business case through reconfiguration of relations in the actor network

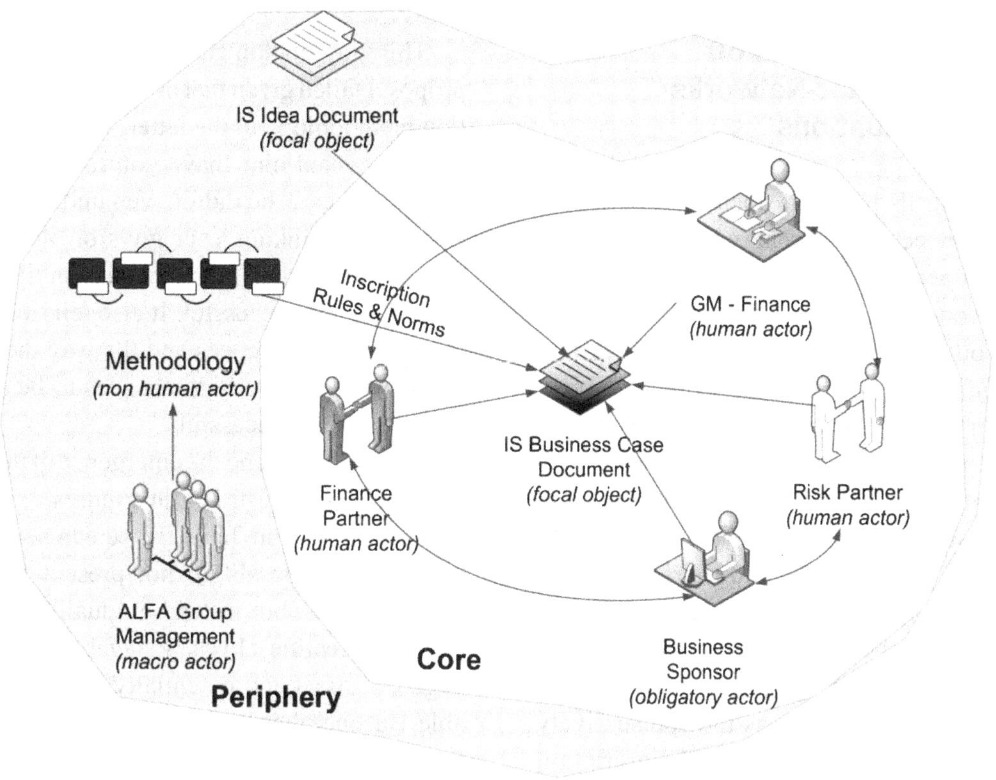

meaning of the IS Business Case Document is not residing in the documents itself, nor is it kept in the heads of people involved. The meaning of the Document is in relations through which it is entangled with other actors in the network.

As a focal actor, the IS Business Case Document (consisting of text, figures, graphs, etc.) attracts and assists enrolments of other actors into the network so that 'all of a sudden it [the proposal] starts to grow some legs' (Head of Business Development, see Table 2). As they further develop and test hypothesis about the future business and IS realities actors re-negotiate and re-create these realities. In other words they develop the IS business case further by strengthening relations and by doing so buy in and commit themselves to the constructed realities enacted by the IS proposal document. The more they commit themselves to the re-creation and (re)production of the

IS Document the more they strengthen the actor-network that brings into being the imagined business and IS realities. The document thus reflects making, negotiating and remaking of the imagined realities, hypotheses testing and arguments building. It is important to observe here that these realities do not exist outside of the actor-network. The forming of the actor-network first around an IS Idea and then emerging around the IS Business Case document (presented in Figures 2, 3 and 4) describe how IS project proposals are produced and at the same time evaluated in relations. The enrolment of key actors and strengthening of relations in the actor-network around the proposed IS Business Case Document describes how 'people are taken on the journey'. This journey is the key to our understanding the evaluation process and the emergence and transformation of the IS project document as the focal actor around which the actor-network creates and grows.

How Reconfigurations of Relations in Actor-Networks Produce Evaluations

Typically the IS proposal document, as an inscription device, first presents contested realities – different actors tend to view multiple, diffuse and non-coherent realities – but the discussions and hypothesis testing clarify differences and reduce ambiguities so that the IS proposal can transform into a sufficiently coherent reality. In other words, the negotiated business reality gets eventually inscribed in the document. It is not the result of 'objectively' and meticulously mapping the business needs into various models (diagrams), as many methodologies assume possible and prescribe, but rather the consequence of relations emerging and strengthening in the actor-network. The reality, as Law persuasively argued, is produced together with inscription devices. "Without inscription devices, and the inscriptions and statements that these produce, there are no realities" (Law 2004, p. 31).

However, network building and reconfigurations of relations, negotiation of inscriptions and realities do not necessarily converge. In ALFA Invest they talk of such cases. For example Project Director told us a story:

we had a classic case of a project, a number of years back, where the guy [who was a consultant from a leading consulting firm] followed the methodology to the letter, pissed off every stakeholder in town, and ... when the review was done, he said 'well what's the matter? I have ticked every single box! I have followed the methodology to the letter'... He used the scientific approach, he was a great left brain thinker, he had used the methodology to the letter. But he hadn't engaged his business, he hadn't engaged technology [department], he hadn't engaged a whole heap of people and he didn't get it.

This 'guy' couldn't understand why his project proposal failed given that he followed the evaluation methodology to the letter. When the Project Director asked him 'have you taken your guys on the journey?' he didn't even understand what that meant. 'Taking your guys on the journey' encapsulates what it means for an IS project proposal to be successful. It also tells a lot about the evaluation practices and the way they shape proposals that have high chances to be selected and ultimately successful.

From this case and the emergence of the evaluation process (illustrated in Figures 2, 3 and 4, and with quotes in Table 2) we can see that the IS project proposals do not present fixed and given realities, but instead gradually create and enact new realities. In early stages they tend to be vague, abstract and potentially highly questionable. But once they have become the business case the realities get more stabilized. As Mol puts it, realities are "framed as parts of events that occur and plays that are staged. If an object [in our case the IS project proposal] is real this is because it is part of a practice. It is a reality enacted." (2002, p. 44). As part of the evaluation process IS project proposals gradually become reality enacted.

During an IS project evaluation journey the same project is viewed in different ways by the risk management partners, the IS architect, the IS infrastructure expert and so on. They each see a particular side and business reality of the proposed system. While different, each side is meaningful from a particular business unit or locality vantage point. Together they often make sense, and hang together. Using Mol's concept of *fractal objects* (2002, p. 55) we can see how the enactment of an IS project proposal as it emerges through the reconfiguration of relations in the actor-network is not necessarily *singular* but *multiple* or *fractional*. Sometimes multiple enactments consolidate themselves to make coherence – Law talks of 'fractional coherence' (2002) – that typically leads to a successful IS project proposal evaluation. Alternatively they may remain a fragmented set of loosely connected realities when the proposal fails.

In this context we can see the role of the evaluation methodology as an important non-human actor. Acting on behalf of ALFA Management Group, it exerts influence on the evaluation process by providing inscription forms and rules, and common matrices, thus allowing a consistent and comparable presentation of business and IS realities and evaluations across different projects. For example, the Head of Projects explains that methodologies exist:

for consistency across the organisation. First of all methodologies exist ... to document activities. Especially with long stream projects, the likelihood of having the same people engaged at the start then at the end probably is low. The likelihood of someone hanging around to the full cycle of project is low, they need to move on, they get promoted, they work on a new project. So the whole thing about the business case and methodologies surrounding it is about communicating what are these core objectives, be it to the sponsors, be it to the project team, be it to the powers, be in the organisation, be it to the executive who sponsors it. Even though I am not on the core sponsorship team, we meet weekly, monthly, CEO is by de facto the sponsor so we need a tool to communicate to him in a simple way and in a consistent way. So when he sees Dianne's project, he compares it to Fred's project he has common metrics. So it's about the business case exists as a communications tool and as a common set of metrics in terms of being able to, if you like, bring together and be able to compare likes.

From a point of view of a single IS project proposal, as we have seen above, the methodology is not at the centre of attention but acts on distance from periphery. If we see IS project proposals as complex and fractional objects we can

understand the role of the evaluation methodology as enabling and enhancing fractional coherence. From this perspective we can see that while acting from the periphery, an evaluation methodology may be crucial for enacting sufficiently coherent business and IS realities inscribed in IS project proposals. On the other hand, at the company level at which different proposals compete for limited resources, the evaluation methodology is a more visible core actor as it regulates 'communication tools' or inscription devices, including a 'common set of matrices' that enable comparative evaluations and selection. In this sense the evaluation methodology can be seen as among the key actors in IS evaluation and selection from the company vantage point.

CONCLUSION

In this paper we proposed and empirically grounded a sociotechnical conception of IS project proposals, IS evaluation processes and methodologies. This conception departs from the dominant views of IS project proposals evaluation in the literature. The sociotechnical conception, inspired and informed by ANT, allows an investigation of IS projects evaluation in practice without pre-empting who the actors are and what they (can) do. The paper makes several key contributions.

The ANT account of the IS project evaluation processes in the ALFA Invest company enabled us to understand an eminently relational nature of IS proposals that emerge as focal actors within dynamic actor-networks. The IS project proposals are constitutively entangled with human beings and their imagined and enacted business/organizational/technological realities. Our analysis shows that the meaning of IS project proposal documents does not reside in the text of the document nor can it be subsumed by an individual understanding. Instead its meaning is in the relations emerging between the document and all other actors in the network. Such an understanding enables us to appreciate that there is no IS or future IS-enabled business or organizational reality outside the actor-network. The actor-network that emerges and reconfigures as it produces IS business case is thus key for our understanding of IS project evaluation and the role of methodologies in practices.

The traditional view of the IS pre-investment evaluation that assumes that we first develop project proposals and then evaluate them using as rigorous as possible methods, seems to be quite a mechanistic one. Our ANT account of the evaluation processes in the case company suggests that it is not possible to separate out the development of IS project proposals from their evaluation. One of our major arguments is that the IS evaluation practice (including the evaluation methodology itself) produces the object it evaluates, that is, the IS project proposal, together with evaluative statements about this object. In other words the reality of business processes and their imagined IS (inscribed in the IS project proposal documents) and the evaluative statements of these realities are produced together. If we accept that then the question of an IS project proposal success and the nature of IS evaluation processes can be seen from a different and hopefully more useful perspective.

The key to understanding the meaning of evaluation processes and methodologies in practice is to appreciate relational materiality of actor-networks forming around IS project proposals as focal actors. As actors (business managers, IS experts and managers) mobilize and enrol in an actor-network around an IS project proposal document, this document emerges and transforms (into different versions) as a consequence of the relations forming within the actor-network. The IS project proposal document – from an idea to concept to preliminary business case – is an inscription device that emerges through its relations with and among different actors. As we have demonstrated the IS project proposal document is seen as an enacted and relational entity which inscribes visions and interests of these actors. It emerges depending on configurations and reconfigurations of the

relations in the actor-network. Learning from ALFA Invest we can conclude that the enrolment of relevant actors (with required expertise and experience, from relevant parts of the business,) in the actor-network of the IS project proposal and the translation of their expertise and interests into the project document are critical for IS project proposals evaluation. In the words of actors, the success of your IS project proposal depends on knowing your key people, taking 'your people on the journey', and engaging them in the production of the document so that they become committed and feel ownership.

Another contribution of the paper is about evaluation processes and how evaluation practices cope with different perspectives of pre-existing business, social and technological realities, how new realities (a vision of business processes with embedded IS proposed to be built) and statements about these realities are created, and how (and why) these realities hang together and become sufficiently coherent. Fragmented and loosely connected realities lead to IS proposal failure. When different realities seen in an IS project proposal document converge and consolidate so as to become sufficiently coherent – while not necessarily expressing singular reality – we are dealing with 'fractional coherence'. Given that a singular meaning and perfect coherence are not likely to be achieved, fractional coherence may be sufficient to produce a successful project proposal. While it seems that actors in ALFA Invest know this and also know to recognize when sufficient coherence is achieved, their experience is not translatable into descriptions meaningful to others. Further research should address the practical meaning of fractional coherence of business and realities in the IS project proposal documents.

Finally, the practice of IS evaluation – for which various methods propose a range of rigorous and well structured processes, models and calculation techniques – is shown to be vague, sometimes messy, and seemingly unsystematic. Is the IS evaluation vagueness a sign of poor evaluation methodology? Should (could) the practice be improved by the adoption of and stringent adherence to a more precise and exact methodology as most of the literature argues? We answer this question by showing that the key part of IS evaluation process is informal and vague "because much of the world is enacted in that way" (Law, 2004, p.14). In ALFA Invest they learned the problem is not a more precise and more stringently applied methodology, but

yeah there is a methodology, and the challenge is actually in the application of the methodology. Like with a lot of methodologies it could be beautifully bound in terms of the theory and then the practice comes down to well ..., how good was I at estimating how much the costs were going to be. I said it wasn't going to cost more than x to run this, and you get to go live and you say no way we can run this without hiring 6 people so now your business case has changed from when you first started. So the challenge is in the application of the methodology not the methodology itself. (Head of Projects)

No guarantors, no golden standards or best practices. But still we learn from ALFA Invest about ways of living with ambiguity and uncertainty; we learn how the proposal and evaluation of an IS is at the same time an enactment of the new reality, that is, a vision of a business process incorporating the new IS, where IS is also a vision documented by requirements, broad design, estimated costs of development and estimated infrastructure; we learn how these visions are created and negotiated discursively through relations in heterogeneous actor-networks by the people 'taken on the journey'.

We conclude this paper with a quote from the recent book *After Method – Mess in Social Science Research* by John Law (2004) which encapsulates our experience of adopting and living ANT as a research method but also of what a method in IS research is all about:

"Method? .. It is not just a set of techniques. It is not just a philosophy of method, a methodology. ... It is also and most fundamentally, about the way of being. It is about what kind of social science we want to practice. And then, and as a part of this, it is about the kinds of people that we want to be, and about how we should live ... Method goes with work, and ways of working, and ways of being. I would like us to work as happily, creatively and generously as possible in social science. And to reflect on what it is to work well." (p.10)

REFERENCES

Adelakun, O., & Jenne, M. E. (2002) Stakeholder Process Approach to Information Systems Evaluation. *Eighth Americas Conference on Information Systems.*

Al-Yaseen, H., Eldabi, T., & Paul, R. J. (2004) A Quantitative Assessment of Operational Use Evaluation of Information Technology: Benefits and Barriers. *Proceedings of the Tenth Americas Conference on Information Systems.* New York, New York, USA.

Barad, K. (2003). Posthumanist Performativity: Toward an Understanding of How Matter Comes to Matter. *Signs: Journal of Women in Culture and Society, 28,* 801–831. doi:10.1086/345321

Berghout, E., Nijland, M., & Grant, K. (2005). Seven Ways to get Your Favoured IT Project Accepted – Politics in IT Evaluation. *Electronic Journal of Information Systems Evaluation, 8,* 31–40.

Brynjolfsson, E. (1993). The productivity paradox of information technology. *Communications of the ACM, 36,* 66–77. doi:10.1145/163298.163309

Callon, M. (1986) Some elements of a sociology of translation: domestication of the scallops and the fishermen of StBrieuc Bay. *Power, Action and Belief: A New Sociology of Knowledge, 32,* 196–233.

Collins, H. M. & Yearley, S. (1992) Journey into Space. *Science as Practice and Culture,* 369–89.

Farbey, B., Land, F., & Targett, D. (1994). Matching an IT project with an appropriate method of evaluation: a research note on 'Evaluating investments in IT'. *Journal of Information Technology, 9,* 239–243. doi:10.1057/jit.1994.23

Hirschheim, R. & Smithson, S. (1988) A critical analysis of IS evaluation. *Information Systems Assessment: Issues and Challenges,* 17-37.

Introna, L. D. & Whittaker, L. (2002) The Phenomenology of Information Systems Evaluation: Overcoming the Subject/Object Dualism. *Global and Organizational Discourse about Information Technology,* 155-175.

Jayasuriya, R. (1997). Evaluating health information systems: an assessment of frameworks. *Australian Health Review, 20,* 68–85. doi:10.1071/AH970068a

Jones, S., & Hughes, J. (2001). Understanding IS evaluation as a complex social process: a case study of a UK local authority. *European Journal of Information Systems, 10,* 189–203. doi:10.1057/palgrave.ejis.3000405

Latour, B. (1986) The powers of association. *Power, Action and Belief: A New Sociology of Knowledge, 32,* 264–80.

Latour, B. (1999) On recalling ANT. *Actor-network Theory and After,* 15–25.

Latour, B. (2005). *Reassembling the Social: An Introduction to Actor-Network-Theory.* USA: Oxford University Press.

Latour, B., & Woolgar, S. (1979). *Laboratory life.* Beverly Hills, CA: Sage.

Law, J. (1999) After ANT: complexity, naming and topology. *Actor-network Theory and After,* 1–14.

Law, J. (2002). *Aircraft Stories: Decentering the Object in Technoscience.* Duke University Press.

Law, J. (2004). *After Method: Mess in Social Science Research.* Routledge.

Lefley, F., & Sarkis, J. (2005). Applying the FAP Model to the Evaluation of Strategic Information Technology Projects. *International Journal of Enterprise Information Systems, 1,* 69–90.

Luna-Reyes, L. F., Zhang, J., Gil-García, J. R., & Cresswell, A. M. (2005). Information systems development as emergent socio-technical change: a practice approach. *European Journal of Information Systems, 14,* 93–10. doi:10.1057/palgrave.ejis.3000524

Mol, A. (2002). *The Body Multiple: Ontology in Medical Practice.* Duke University Press.

Murphy, K. E., & Simon, S. J. (2001) Using Cost Benefit Analysis for Enterprise Resource Planning Project Evaluation: A Case for Including Intangibles. *Proceedings of the 34th Annual Hawaii International Conference on System Sciences, 2001.* Hawaii

Nijland, M. H. J. (2004). *Understanding the Use of IT Evaluation Methods in Organisations.* University of London.

Orlikowski, W. J. (2007). Sociomaterial Practices: Exploring Technology at Work. *Organization Studies, 28,* 1435. doi:10.1177/0170840607081138

Orlikowski, W. J., & Scott, S. V. (2008) *The Entangling of Technology and Work in Organizations,* Working Paper Series. Department of Management, Information Systems and Innovation Group. London School of Economics and Political Science.

Pickering, A. (1995). *The Mangle of Practice: Time, Agency, and Science*. University Of Chicago Press.

Powell, P. (1992). Information Technology Evaluation: Is It Different? *The Journal of the Operational Research Society, 43*, 29–42.

Remenyi, D., & Sherwood-Smith, M. (1999). Maximise information systems value by continuous participative evaluation. *Journal of Enterprise Information Management, 12*, 14–31.

Ryan, S. D., Harrison, D. A., & Schkade, L. L. (2002). Information-Technology Investment Decisions: When Do Costs and Benefits in the Social Subsystem Matter? *Journal of Management Information Systems, 19*, 85–127.

Sauer, C., & Cuthbertson, C. (2003). *The state of IT project management in the UK. Templeton College*. Oxford University.

Schatzki, T. R. (2002). *The Site of the Social: A Philosophical Account of the Constitution of Social Life and Change*. Pennsylvania State University Press.

Serafeimidis, V. (2000). Information systems evaluation in practice: a case study of organizational change. *Journal of Information Technology, 15*, 93–105. doi:10.1080/026839600344294

Solow, R. M. (1987) We'd Better Watch Out. *New York Times Book Review, 12*, 07-87.

Suchman, L. A. (2007) Human-Machine Reconfigurations: Plans and situated actions.

The Standish Group International. (2001). *Extreme CHAOS*. The Standish Group International.

Walsham, G. (1993). *Interpreting Information Systems in Organizations*. New York, NY, USA: John Wiley & Sons, Inc.

Walsham, G., & Sahay, S. (1999). GIS for district-level administration in India: problems and opportunities. *Management Information Systems Quarterly, 23*, 39–66. doi:10.2307/249409

Williams, M. D., & Williams, J. (2004) A Framework Facilitating Ex-Ante Evaluation of Information Systems. *Proceedings of the Tenth Americas Conference on Information Systems*. New York, New York.

Wilson, M., & Howcroft, D. (2000) Power, politics and persuasion: a social shaping perspective on IS evaluation. *23rd IRIS Conference*, 725-39.

Winklhofer, H. (2002). *A Case for Soft Systems Methodology Information Analysis and Information Systems Evaluation during Organizational Change*. Gdarisk, Poland: ECIS.

This work was previously published in International Journal of Actor-Network Theory and Technological Innovation (IJANTTI) 1(1), edited by Arthur Tatnall, pp. 1-22, copyright 2009 by IGI Publishing (an imprint of IGI Global).

Chapter 2
Service Innovation Using Actor Network Theory

Lorna Uden
Staffordshire University, UK

Janet Francis
Staffordshire University, UK

ABSTRACT

Our economy is becoming more and more service-oriented, with distinctions between services and non-services making less and less sense. In today's society, innovations are no longer luxury items. Instead, they are necessities and a means of economic development and competitiveness. The introduction of innovative new services is a priority for most companies. Innovation now holds the key to service performance. Currently there is a lack of understanding of the science underlying the design and operation of service systems. New conceptual understanding and theoretical underpinnings are required to systematically describe the nature and behaviour of service systems. We believe that Actor Network Theory (ANT) can be used as a theoretical lens to study the development and adoption of service innovation. ANT is a heterogeneous amalgamation of conceptual, textual and social actors. It is well suited to explain and help with the design of service systems. The development and adoption of service innovation requires the integration of multiple elements including people, technologies and networks across organisations. Technologies and interests of actors need to be aligned and coordinated for successful service innovation. In this paper we show how ANT is adopted as a theoretical framework for understanding the relationships among the actors and show how these actors have their needs shaped by the network formation during the development and adoption of service innovation for a university.

INTRODUCTION

Over 80% of jobs in the US are now in the service sectors. This is evident in the current list of

Fortune 500 companies, in which a greater share of large companies' revenue comes from services than it did in previous decades (Möller., Rajala, & Westerlund, 2007). Many of these service jobs are highly skilled and technology-intensive, including outsourcing, consulting and process

DOI: 10.4018/978-1-60960-197-3.ch002

re-engineering. Service plays a key role in developed economies (Sheehan, 2006). Market-based services are the main drivers of productivity and economic growth in OECD countries. IT services and R&D services provide more than half of all employment growth in many developed countries. The service sectors also help improve competitive performance of firms in our modern economies.

According to Maglio, Srinivasan, Kreulea and Spohrer, J (2006), the formal representation and modelling of service systems is nascent, because of the complexity of modelling people, their knowledge, activities and intentions. Service system design cannot be achieved by traditional approaches such as product design. Firstly, customers are not typically present in R&D and product engineering processes. Secondly, the traditional product engineering approach based on a manufacturing model is not good at providing intangible, value-based services. It is therefore necessary to develop a new model for service innovation. The model should be an adaptive organisational model that enables dynamic evolution of the service system. It is important to integrate the customer perspective, learning and innovation into the development process of service systems.

A service system is defined as a dynamic configuration of resources (people, technology, organisations and shared information) that creates and delivers value between the provider and the customer through service (IfM & IBM, 2008). According to the report (IfM & IBM, 2008), a service system is a complex system having a front stage and a back stage. The front stage is about provider-customer interaction: how can customer satisfaction be ensured in the presence of multiple customer touch points and various channels of contact? The back stage is about operational efficiency: how can productivity be improved through skilled employees, streamlined processes and robust relationships with partners and suppliers (the service networks). Performance of the service depends on both the front and the back stage.

Spohrer, Golinelli, Piciocchi, and Bassano, C. (2010) argue that each service system entity is able to co-create value with other entities if its component resources can be appropriately coordinated to contribute to the purpose of the value proposition that defines the expected outcomes of the interaction. They further pointed out that in a service system network the coordination of the entities is fundamental to guarantee that the right interaction, the right agreement, the right communication takes place to realize a value co-creation outcome.

According to these authors, foundations of service systems are:

1. A dynamic configuration of resources;
2. A set of value co-creation mechanisms between suitable entities;
3. A application of competencies-skills-knowledge any person(s) in job or stakeholder roles;
4. A adaptive internal organization responding to the dynamic external environment;
5. Learning and feedback to ensure mutual benefits or value co-creation outcomes.

Service systems are also open systems capable of improving:

1. The state of another system through sharing or applying its resources;
2. Its own state by acquiring external resources" (Spohrer et al., 2010).

We concur with these authors that service systems respond to their environment (or service system ecology) to improve quality, productivity, compliance, and sustainable innovation measures. Over time, the entities, interactions, and outcomes change.

Service science, as the science of value co-creation phenomena, seeks to understand the mechanisms that account both for the structure of the entities, the patterns of their interactions, and how these structures and patterns evolve over time.

According to Sims (2007), a simple service requires numerous interactions and coordination for it to work. The relation can be between two or more individuals or organisations and machines, or between two or more machines or machine processes. Each of these interrelations can be treated as its own service relationship. This complex web of interrelated service relationships is known as a service system (Sims, 2007). According to Maglio et al (2006), service systems are value creation networks composed of people, technology and organizations. In other words, service systems are networks of relationships that afford transformations of value for those positioned as service recipients within the network. Service design exists not just between the organization and the end customer, but throughout and between organizations themselves. Each service relationship in a service system can be the object of design.

Some of the important issues that need to be addressed in service system design include:

1. How to create new service offerings based on social and cultural as well as organisational issues.
2. How can service systems be understood in terms of a small number of building blocks that get constrained to reflect the observed variety?
3. How do interactions within and between service systems lead to particular outcomes?

ANT provides a network building vocabulary for describing the process of coordinating social and technical actors as a cascading stream of translation. We believe that ANT can be used as a theoretical framework to understand, develop and adopt service innovation. This paper begins with a brief overview of service innovation. This is followed by a review of actor network theory. Subsequent sections describe a case study involving a service innovation using technology for ABC

University in order to increase productivity and meet the global economy. The paper concludes with suggestions for further research.

SERVICE INNOVATION

There are many different definitions given to services. Services are deeds, processes and performance (Zeithaml et al 2006). Vargo and Lusch (2006) define service as the application of specialised competences (knowledge and skills) through deeds, processes and performances for the benefit of another entity or the entity itself (p.4). Service plays a key role in developed economies (Sheehan, 2006). Despite the economic domination of services, there is relatively little focus from companies and government on service research and innovation compared to tangible products and technologies (Bitner & Brown, 2007).

Because of the rising significance of service in our modern society and the accelerated rate of change, service innovation is now a major challenge to businesses if they want to survive and remain competitive. Service systems are growing fast. They have become a greater part of value creation in modern economies. We are in the midst of a service-driven business revolution. Firms today are increasingly faced with sophisticated clients, market globalisation and evolving technology. For firms to survive, they must continually improve their services' delivery methods to increase client value and profitability and lower costs. Innovation is the key for survival and competitiveness in today's global economy. Global economic growth has been made possible by the rapidly evolving technology, shorter product life cycles and a higher rate of new product development. Today innovation has become increasingly complex, due to changing customer needs, extensive competitive pressure and technological change (Cavusgil., Calantone & Zhao, 2003).

The difference between invention and innovation is that invention is a new product, whereas innovation is a new value (Szmytkowski, 2005). According to Rogers (1998), innovation is concerned with the process of commercialising or extracting value from ideas. Although there are many different definitions given to innovations, we concur with du Plessis (2007) that innovation is the creation of new knowledge and ideas to facilitate new business outcomes, aiming at improving internal business processes and structures and to create market-driven products and services.

Structural Barriers to Innovation

According to Jones and Samalionis (2008), there are several well-documented structural barriers to innovation in service companies. These include:

- Service organization silos that are designed to support operational efficiency rather than rapid change; particularly true in service companies
- Many competing agendas within the organization, all vying for the same resources
- Lack of a consistent team or champion for the long time period between idea generation and bringing those ideas to market
- Measures of success (and accountability) that are ill-defined
- The large scale of some service organizations, which makes it hard for them to match the nimbleness of the marketplace
- Last but not least: the fact that change is expensive.

Service innovation is essential for firms to survive in today's global economy. Through successful innovation a firm can protect its largest revenue generators, making possible its investment in 'the next big thing' in terms of high-margin service offering (Dawson & Horenkamp, 2007). According to Dawson and Horenkamp (2007), professional services that excel at service delivery innovation have six key characteristics:

- A networked organisation.
- Flexible workflows.
- Global sourcing.
- Client and supplier collaboration.
- Continuous innovation
- Enabling technology.

Despite the importance of service sectors in our modern economy, the essence of innovation in service is to improve workforce productivity. According to IfM and IBM (2008), service innovation can impact customer-provider interactions and improve the experience of funding, obtaining, installing maintaining, upgrading and disposing of products. It can enhance the capabilities of organisations to create value with stakeholders. Another benefit of service innovation is that it can deliver better self-services, eliminating waiting and allowing 24/7 access via modern devices such as mobile phones, kiosks and web browsers. Other benefits of service innovations include:

- Improving quality of life and help with the problem of aging population.
- The creation of new service businesses such as Amazon, Google and Web 2.0.

We believe that several important factors contribute to service innovation: networks, people and technology. The new service development process cycle moves from development to analysis to design and finally to the launch of the new service product. Service systems are also networks of relationships that afford transformations of value for those positioned as service recipients within the network.

Networks

There are several reasons why network theory is useful for understanding and helping with service system design. One of the main benefits is that a service system is a complex phenomenon that involves many actors with different roles and contributions for the benefit of a shared service exchange/experience. Network Theory is both a way of thinking in relationships and interaction and a methodology to address. Network theory can also be used with different degrees of sophistication: as a basis for verbal treatise (discussion or text), graphics (from sketches of nodes and links to computer generated diagrams), or mathematical applications. (Barile, Spohrer & Polese, 2010). According to Barile et al (2010), Network Theory is both a way of thinking in relationships and inter-action and a methodology to address complexity and context. It can be used with different degrees of sophistication: as a basis for verbal treatise (discussion or text), graphics (from sketches of nodes and links to computer generated diagrams), or mathematical applications.

According to Kandampully (2002), a firm's service function concerns and interacts with every activity or component of the firm. This includes people, processes or physical evidence, internal and external customers and the various networks, alliances and partners. He also argues that external relationship networks have become an essential prerequisite if a firm is to achieve the capabilities and knowledge required to serve the holistic needs of customers. A customer's holistic requirements often extend beyond that capable of being effectively fulfilled by a single firm's product or service. It is important for firms to understand customers' holistic needs and be able to mix and match various products and services commensurate with customers' specific needs. Firms should create strategic alliances both horizontally and vertically (internal and external relationships) with individuals and firms to meet the customers' specific needs (Kandampully 2002).

Kandampully (2002) believes that the competency of the firm is derived from the various networks of stakeholders of the firm such as customers, employees, retailers, suppliers and shareholders. These five stakeholders (partners) typically constitute a service firm's basic opera-

tion. Developed as networks, the various relationships that the firm nurtures and maintains frequently constitute the life-source for many leading-edge firms (Kandampully 2002). Most firms usually involve numerous alliances and partners, especially for services.

People

The contribution of the human mind (knowledge) plays a crucial role in tomorrow's service industries (Peters, 1994).

Technology

Service innovation is rarely achieved without a strong support from technology-enabled tools. The usual communication tools like e-mail and the internet are naturally the common basis for supporting services. Service systems need tools that:

- Are available anywhere
- Cover a range of information management functions
- Cover a range of document management functions
- Allow flexible use, depending on skills of the clients
- Enable communication, collaboration and cooperation in ways that are useful for the users.

According to Abrea de Paula (2004), the perception of usefulness of technology is not statically embedded in its design, but is dynamically and constantly created and shaped by different groups. An important aim of any service design or innovation is to attempt to reconcile these often contrasting perspectives. Technology enables firms to work together in cyberspace and forge networks of relationships across the globe. Advances in technology have influenced the growth of services.

Designing of services requires that we understand the networks of relationships that afford transformations of value for service recipients within the network. We concur with Sims (2007) that each service relationship in a service system can be the object of design. It is important that we design the system as a whole, not just as atomised components.

AN OVERVIEW OF ACTOR NETWORK THEORY

Michael Callon (Callon 1986a), Bruno Latour (1986) and John Law (1987) developed the actor-network concept. The primary tenet of actor-network theory is the concept of the heterogeneous network. An actor network consists of, and links together, both technical and non-technical elements. This concept is based on the recognition that actors build networks combining technical and social elements. In ANT, actors can be defined as entities that serve as intermediaries between other actors. Actors can be humans, but also include technology, text and organizational groups. There is no difference between human and materials or the social and the natural (Murdoch, 1997).

ANT is a heterogeneous amalgamation of conceptual, social, textual and social actors. Actors in ANT, known as Actants, are any agent, collective or individuals that can associate or dissociate with other agents. Actants enter into network association that in turn defines them, names them and provides them with substance, action, intention and subjectivity (Callon, 1986a). It is via the networks that actants derive their nature and develop as networks. The main difference between actors and actants is that only actors are able to put actants in circulation in the system. In ANT, the social and technical aspects are treated as equally important. ANT denies that purely technical or purely social relations are possible. Instead it considers the world to be full of hybrid entities (Latour 1993)

containing both human and non-human components. Actors in ANT include both human beings and non-human actors (such as technology) that make up a network to be studied (Callon, 1991). In ANT innovators attempt to create a forum, a central network in which all the actors agree that the network is worth creating and maintaining. Numerous actors within an organization may be involved in a different process of translation, each with its own unique characteristics and outcomes. Each actor will have its own view of the network and its own set of objectives and goals. The process of translation seeks to align these goals with those of other candidates for the network and to create a set of shared goals.

Latour (1998) argues those actors are defined solely by their ties to other actors. Actors can be technical artefacts ranging from the smallest components to the largest. The building of an actor network is to overcome the resistance of other actors and try to weave them into network with other actors (Law, 1992). The challenge is to explore how actor networks come to generate effects like organisations, industrial structures and innovation. ANT examines the motivations and actions of human actors that align their interest with the requirements of non-human actors. It can be used to investigate the process whereby the respective interests of different human and non-human elements are aligned into a social and technological arrangement of artefacts (Gao, 2005). The core of ANT is the process of translation (Callon 1986b, Latour 1998). The important negotiation is translation, a multi-factored interaction in which actors (a) construct common definitions and meanings, (b) define representatives and (c) co-opt each other in the pursuit of individual and collective objectives. Both actors and actants share in the reconstruction of the network of interaction leading to system stabilisation.

Actors interests may vary widely. They may encourage or constrain the technology. Establishing the technology requires the aligning of the interests of actors within the network. This involves the translation of those interests into a common interest in adopting and using the technology. The translation of the network is achieved through common definitions, meaning and inscription attached to the technology.

Translation

Translation explains how artefacts become a result of negotiations between the involved subjects. ANT can be used as a theoretical lens to study the development and adoption of service innovation. Different interpretations influence the construction of an artefact. Michael Callon (1996) has defined four moments of translation.

Problematisation

This comprises the definition of the problem. During problematisation, a primary actor tries to establish itself as an obligatory passage point (OPP) between the other actors and the network, so that it becomes indispensable. The OPP is in the primary actor's direct path while others may have to overcome obstacles to pass through it (Callon, 1986b).

Intéressement

This is the moment of translation defined by Callon (1986b). Interéssement, or 'How allies are locked in place' uses a series of processes that attempt to improve the identities and roles defined in the problematisation on the other actors. According to Law (1986), it means interesting and attracting an actor by coming between it and some other actors. This is the process of recruitment of actors – creating an interest and negotiating the terms of their involvement. The primary actor works to convince the other actors that the roles it has defined them are acceptable. Where there are groups of actors with the same goal, these can be represented by a single actor.

Enrolment

This is when another actor accepts the interests defined by the primary actor. This is the third moment. It is how to define and co-ordinate the role. This leads to the establishment of a stable network of alliances. It requires more than one set of actors imposing their will on others for enrolment to be successful. In addition, it also requires others to yield (Singleton & Michael, 1993). Actors accept the roles that have been defined for them during intéressement. Enrolment means the definition of roles for actors in the newly created actor network.

Mobilisation of Allies

This fourth stage is the point where enrolled actors are given the tools of communication and are able to themselves create an interest in the network or to create sub-networks. This is the final moment. Mobilisation occurs as the proposed solution gains wider acceptance and an even larger network of absent entities is created through some actors acting as spokespersons for others (Tatnall & Burgess, 2002).

Inscription

A process of creating technical artifacts (tools) that would ensure the protection of an actor's interests. It refers to the way technical artefacts embody patterns of use. According to Akrich and Latour (1997), inscription is the act, or process, which actors perform on other actors, shaping their attitudes and properties. The properties and attributes of any actors (or networks) are a result of a complex inscription process by human and non-human actors. Human actors are able to inscribe onto non-human actors. Conversely, non-human actors are able to inscribe onto human actors. This is the translation carried out via the actor's inscriptions that enable the actor to transfer its attributes and properties to other actors in its immediate topologies. Inscription and translations are in constant flux. It is iterative in nature, therefore enabling a relative stability in the corresponding network.

Benefits of ANT for Service Innovation

We believe that ANT can provide a conceptual framework to help in the formulating and building a design methodology that can support the understanding, development and adoption of service innovation.

There are several benefits to using ANT. These include:

- ANT allows us to have an open-ended array of things that need to be aligned including work-routines, incentive structures, system modules and organisational roles.
- ANT is appropriate for preparing design strategies by aligning the interests of the actor-network, i.e. having all their influences fit together.
- ANT allows aligned interests to be inscribed into durable materials (Law 1992).
- ANT also introduces the concept of 'blackboxing' (sealed actor-networks).

USE OF ANT FOR SERVICE INNOVATION

Currently there is a lack of understanding of the science underlying the design and operation of service systems. New conceptual understanding and theoretical underpinnings are required to systematically describe the nature and behaviour of service systems. The use of technologies in service systems causes changes in an organisation. Technologies are not static entities; service systems are adapted as they are used. Ciborra (1996) called this 'drifting technology.'

It is our belief that actor-network theory can provide a theoretical lens to understand and design a service innovation. Actor-network theory

requires that we examine the process of interest alignment to form a network (Monteiro & Hanseth, 1996). Using ANT to investigate service innovation concentrates on the use of networks. It examines the use of network formation, human and non-human actors and the alliances and networks they build up (Tatnall & Burgess, 2002). ANT enables us to concentrate on the negotiations that allow the network to be configured by the enrolment of both human and non-human actors. It also enables us to consider the supposed characteristics of the technology only as network effects resulting from association (Tatnall & Burgess, 2002).

CASE STUDY

This section shows how actor network theory is used to develop ABC University service innovation and its adoption.

Background

"UK universities face "radical" and "risky" changes in the way they are funded and managed, and in the types of student they attract over the next 12 years" (Swain, 2008, p1). The rapid growth of services in the knowledge economy has vast implications for academic knowledge creation, education, business practice and government policy. Academic organisations today can no longer compete by marketing traditional educational products. Universities and other HE establishments were encouraged to respond to the need for a more diverse, highly skilled workforce and greater global competition in accordance with the Leitch agenda of 2006, to increase the number of people in the workforce with HE qualifications from 29% to 40%. This was reiterated more recently by the universities minister, David Willetts who stated "The university system is in need of "radical change to give a better deal for taxpayers and students", (BBC News, 2010).

Geoffrey Crossick, warden of Goldsmith's University of London (quoted in Swain, 2008) surmised that while the classic idea of an 18-year-old student living away from home would persist, there would be huge diversity in how and where both full and part-time courses were delivered. This is not only because of changing demographics which mean there will be fewer 18-year-olds - but also because the current model of funding for teaching and learning is unsustainable. The challenge is to find new sustainable markets and new sustainable funding streams. This will mean that universities will increasingly be funded through a mixture of public and private funding hence necessitating commitment to increase enterprise and links with industry.

It is clear that in order for a University or other HE establishment to compete in today's market it must innovate its services. As the student profile moves away from the 18-21 year old attending university on a full-time basis towards the workforce market of mature adults wishing to up-skill, the requirement for industry relevant, multi-disciplinary awards delivered in non-traditional formats and workplace settings will increase and this will inevitably lead to a requirement for resources and expertise which are neither owned nor managed by HE establishments.

HE service innovation requires not just a paradigm shift on the part of the HE institutions, but also investment. There is a risk involved in that the proposed new market is an unknown quantity and the potential return on investment is unproven. The formation of strategic partnerships provides a mechanism for risk sharing and therefore a means to move forward.

Richard Brown, chief executive of the Council for Industry and Higher Education, commenting on the government agenda to increase the number of people in the workforce with HE qualifications at the Guardian's HE summit (quoted in Swain, 2008) said "We will be looking for new products in new markets, delivered by new types of staff."

ABC is a medium size university. Like any other university, ABC must look for ways to improve the student numbers to survive. In order for ABC University to competitive, it needs to innovate. This means improving its service through the use of ICT to deliver its teaching and learning. Following lengthy discussion with the staff, ABC decided to improve and expand the facility of the university by implementing an Open Learning Network (OLN).

Open Learning Network

We have used the term open learning network to describe a learning environment that includes learners, tutors and resources separated from each other by time and space. This is in contrast to a traditional face-to-face environment constrained by the need for tutors and learners to attend sessions at a pre-defined time and place in an institution containing the required resources.

In the open learning network, we consider all the above including tutors, learners, learning materials, library texts and software to be actors in the open learning network. An important part of the case study is that while not precluding physical contact between actors, the durability of the network does not depend on it. For example, a learner may never physically open a hard copy of a book and two tutors working on an award may never physically meet.

Tutors may be employed by ABC University or by a partner and are related through contracts of employment or partnership arrangements negotiated in line with the interests of both parties. Depending on the terms of their contract, tutors will play an active role in some or all the development and management processes associated with the learning, all of which have obligatory passage points linked to the expansion and durability of the network. The learning materials, library texts, software which are available through the network may be owned and managed by different organisations but are linked in through the validation of awards. Learners join the network through their enrolment onto the awards.

In order to function effectively, the open learning environment has to be built on strong foundations and has to be able to attract and retain its actors. The case study describes how Actor-Network Theory can be utilised to establish a durable open learning network and explains the requirement of negotiation to resolve conflicts and inscription to impose standards.

Katzan (2008) defines service as the provision of assistance and expertise through a provider–client interaction to create and capture value in business, education, government, and personal endeavours. In terms of resources, services can also be understood as a series of activities in which resources of various types (employees, physical resources, goods, systems of service providers) are used in interaction with the customer to find a solution to a problem or need (Grönroos, 2006). Because of this, Barile and Polese (2010) argue that, a service system is not simply the sum of its parts; rather, the interactions form a higher-order construct. According to Polese (2010) service can thus be understood as an "… interaction between entities in a reticular system … to improve value co-creation outcomes under a win–win logic inside interrelated processes".

Service science research, highlights the centrality of a continuous interactions among actors, to the concepts of reticular relationships, to value co-creation and, finally, to the comprehension and functioning of service systems. According to service science, everything that has a name and is useful can be viewed as a resource. Service science systems are essentially dynamic configurations of resources (people, technology, organisations, and shared information) that create and deliver value between the provider and the customer through service (Spohrer, Maglio, Bailey & Gruhl, 2007). All actors are thus considered to be resources. (Barile & Polese, 2010).

The design of service innovation involves getting answers to the questions, "Who will use it, how they will use it and what service processes are involved?" The methodology for ANT requires the recording of actors' interactions, connections and effects (Latour 1987). Interactions between actors also need to be traced through documents, skills present or developed, money and control structures. The complexity of the network can then be assessed. This may influence strategies for aligning the actor-network with desired outcomes. The university service actor network involves interaction with a variety of human and non-human actors. The physical network of ICT and fibre optic infrastructure of the internet cannot be separated from the social and human networks involving administrators, professors, lecturers, students, clerks, technicians and parents. The technical and social networks must be considered together. The faculty network is a network of heterogeneous actors including the internet network, offices, professors, lecturers and students. The network also includes documents and texts that support the faculty in their teaching.

Perceptions of the usefulness of the technology as well as ease of use should also be considered. Relationships between actors in terms of current communication, level of trust, power distribution, resource control and influence should be considered. This also includes relationships between actors and local economic and natural resources. The importance of relationships or connections between actors or groups of actors needs to be examined because the strength of these connections may influence enrolment strategies.

ANT points to a need to address the social infrastructure as well as the technical infrastructure when designing service innovation. A number of questions to be asked include:

- What are the characteristics of the stakeholder groups or actors in the network?
- What are their economic and social interests?

• What meaningful inscriptions might be generated which would translate their interests into the interests of the network?

Building a service system is a social process involving both the users and developers. The system developed is a result of the social negotiations among the Director of ABC University, the staff members, business partners, students and managers. While not formally involved in the service design, customers' or users' actions have important consequences in the development process. We believe that it is important to consider all actors' points of view in order to better understand the system requirements and identity. This identity is the result of meaning given to the service system by different actors. The construction of the service system identity is a mutual and continuous process, whose complexity should be considered.

Our development of service is based on the translation process of Callon (1986a). The first moment of translation (problematisation) is where the focal actor defines identities and interests of other actors that are consistent with its own interests, and establishes itself as an obligatory passage point (OPP), thus "rendering itself indispensable" (Callon, 1986a). Problematisation is the defining of a problem and its associated 'incontestable' solution.

Problematisation

The overall problematisation for the university centres on responding to the need for a more highly skilled workforce and greater global competition by 2020 – by, in the words of Richard Brown (Swain 2008), "… looking for new products in new markets delivered by new types of staff". This in turn leads to the consideration of suitable teaching, learning and assessment modes along with the technologies to support them. For service innovation by the university, the problematisation proposed by the instigators is that to improve the university performance, there must be service innovation. Service innovation is seen by the university as an obligatory passage point to remain competitive in a global market. In the case of the students (the customers of the university), they need to be convinced that the 'improvement' is beneficial for them and will offer them a better service and return on investment. Students should be convinced that they should join the open learning network at ABC instead of going elsewhere. Having identified the problem, the next stage is to identify all stakeholders.

Identification of Stakeholders

Interviews and focus groups were used to explore the formation and development of networks and examine the alliances built as the development progresses. Interviews are a well-established means of qualitative data collection in information systems (Myers, 1999). Interviews are used because they provide opportunities for feedback and clarifying of questions. They also enable the probing for deeper and clearer responses. The following are identified as stakeholders:

• The designated manager – focal actor
• Students
• Award Staff
• Employers who are involved in award development and mentoring
• Businesses partners and their managers who may be
  ◦ University based
  ◦ Based at HE or FE colleges
  ◦ Based at Private institutions
  ◦ Independent Consultancies
• Technologies
  ◦ Email, instant messaging software
  ◦ Telephony including: Mobile, IP, texting
  ◦ Conferencing and video conferencing
  ◦ Online meeting technologies
  ◦ Social networking technologies
  ◦ VLEs

- ◦ Forums
- ◦ Databases
- ◦ Document management software
- ◦ Internet Service Providers, Browsing Software
- ◦ Groupware
- ◦ Electronic library

Intéressement

The process of Intéressement is where the focal actor has to uncover and understand the interests of each stakeholder in order to find methods of persuading the stakeholder that their key interests can be aligned to those of the network. Firstly we identified the interests of the stakeholders.

Identifying Stakeholders' Interests

This includes both organization and individuals. Organisational interests concern their political and social interests arising from their job roles in the organisation. Individual's interests concern personal interests such as status, career progress and job security.

The Designated Manager

The designated manager has been charged with meeting the challenge of looking for new products in new markets delivered by new types of staff and success in this key area will improve his/her career progress within the university and increase job security. The designated manager sets him/herself up as the focal actor and as such, sets the OPP. The focal actor enrols and mobilises the other actors by:

- Putting into place the processes for recruitment of students and staff to their respective courses and roles.
- Establishing and making available the underlying technology, standards and codes of practice to ensure ease of networking between actors.

- Defining identities and interests of other actors that are consistent with its own interests to the networks between the actors with him/herself as the OPP. Table 1 shows the relationships between actors.

Students

Non-traditional students have the opportunity to enter Higher Education and if successful, to improve their career prospects. They may also stand to benefit from increased status in society and from an extended network of contacts and new interests. Students could feel that they are not part of a community and could feel that they do not have adequate communication with staff or other students. They could find learning in a virtual environment difficult to adapt to.

Staff

Staff may benefit from flexible working arrangements in terms of time and place which may suit their lifestyle. They may find themselves working with a diverse group of colleagues based in different locations and institutions which could lead to interesting collaborations outside the scope of their day to day work. They will be exposed to a variety of virtual environments and communication technologies which will require extensive staff development and possibly open up new career opportunities. There is the potential for staff to feel isolated and for them to feel exploited since the work environment is not constrained by time or place.

Employers

The flexible nature of work-based learning means that employers can raise the educational level of their staff through the creation of awards which relate directly to the workplace and to the role of the learner. Conflicts may arise where students and mentors require time for educational and academic processes or where students leave the organisation having completed their qualification.

Table 1. Relationships Between Actors – Table continues on subsequent page

Nature	Actors*	Intéressement	Dominant Technologies	OPP
Award Development and Management (for each award)	**Award Leader** Award Development Team (including network of representatives from partners delivering the award) Course Development teams (including network of course leaders, researchers and academic supervisors from all partners) Lead Award Administrator	Award Development Award Management Award Monitoring Examination Board	Email, instant messaging software Telephony including: Mobile, IP, texting Conferencing and video conferencing Online meeting technologies Social networking technologies Document management software Internet Service Providers, Browsing Software Databases	Award Validation
Award Support (for each award)	**Lead Award Administrator** Award Leader Administration team (including network of administrators from all partners delivering the award) Students	Student Enrolment Student Records Student Communication Collation of results Monitoring of student interaction on courses.	Email, instant messaging software Telephony including: Mobile, IP, texting Social networking technologies Document management software Internet Service Providers, Browsing Software Groupware Databases	Student Enrolment on to award and associated courses (modules)
Course (module) Development and Management – for each course (modular unit)	**Course Leader** Course Development Team (including network of course leaders, researchers and academic supervisors from all partners delivering the course)	Course (Module) material development Course Monitoring Assessment setting Assessment Boards	Email, instant messaging software Conferencing and video conferencing Online meeting technologies Social networking technologies Document management software Internet Service Providers, Browsing Software VLEs Forums	Course (module) validation and approval of material
Course Support and mentoring -for each course)	**Course Leader** Academic Supervisors Mentors Students	Academic supervision Assessment marking	Email, instant messaging software Conferencing and video conferencing Online meeting technologies Social networking technologies Internet Service Providers, Browsing Software VLEs Forums E-Library	Allocation of the Academic supervisor to the student on a module.
Student Support	**Award Leader** Personal Tutors (at all institutions) Students	Personal tutoring Award guidance	Email, instant messaging software Conferencing and video conferencing Online meeting technologies Social networking technologies Internet Service Providers, Browsing Software Groupware	Allocation of the Personal Tutor to a student on an award
Partnership Management	**Partnership Manager** Business Managers at all partners	Recruitment of new partners and validation of partnership Development of existing partnerships Monitoring of processes at partner institutions	Email, instant messaging software Conferencing and video conferencing Online meeting technologies Social networking technologies Internet Service Providers, Browsing Software Document management software Groupware	Validation of a partner, award validation at partner.
Social Network	All Actors	Academic study Friendship Shared interests Activities	Social networking technologies	Instigation of the Actor-Network

Note: * Focal Actor in bold

Businesses

HE and FE establishments will be linked to the university through potentially lucrative franchise or partnership agreements which may involve them carrying out academic support and administration or may also include course development and/or academic processes such as award boards and validation and/or the handling of plagiarism and extenuating circumstances panels. In terms of finance and the security of the partnership it would be in the interest of the business partners to handle as many of these processes as possible and as many students as possible. There is the potential for competition between partners and between the university and partners which could lead to conflict of interests and the need to negotiate terms of agreement.

Technologies

The technologies used to support the virtual environment have a key role to play in its success. The environment needs to be based around technologies which are:

- Accessible to all actors in terms of price, availability, compatibility and ease of use.
- Provide levels of security and confidentiality which are acceptable to all actors and in keeping with legal, ethical and professional codes of practice.
- Capable of supporting the expected number of users and network traffic.
- Capable of providing the required functionality and interactivity.
- Reliable in terms of performance.

When setting up a network it will be necessary to introduce a set of standards and an approved list of technologies which will be supported. This will inevitably be difficult as it is likely that actors will have strong views which may not be based on the above but rather on supplier loyalty and experience.

Social Networking

An important part of the university experience for any student is the social environment. Eighteen year olds away from home for the first time will find themselves immersed in a new environment with lots of new people to meet, the opportunity to join clubs and societies and to try out new activities. As time goes on, groups will form which might be centred around

- Academic study
- Friendship
- Shared interests
- Activities

Identifying Interaction between Stakeholder

The next stage in the Intéressemment phase is to identify interactions between stakeholders. It is important to identify stakeholder interactions, the relationships between stakeholders in terms of extent of communication, power, trust, resource control and influence must be investigated. The top level interaction between the actors is shown in Figure 1.

Negotiation of Interests

Aligning stakeholder interests to those of the network is not a trivial process as there are often conflicts of interest which result in extensive negotiation until a compromise is found. For example: Consider the business stakeholder. This could for example be a local College of Further Education which wishes to offer some of the Intermediate qualifications offered at ABC University to its students as follow on courses to those already available to the college. It approaches ABC University with its proposal for service innovation. The FE College feels that offering these HE awards will improve its academic status and enable it to attract local students on to HE awards and retain

Figure 1. Build actor network

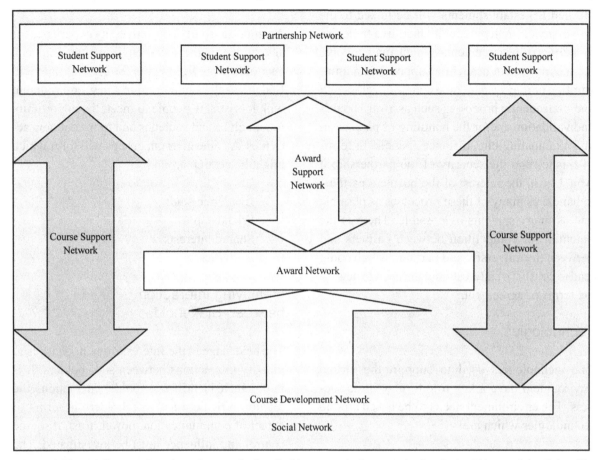

Legend. Figure 1 illustrates how the main networks described interact and relate to each other. It should be noted that these will not be the only networks in a given scenario and that each of these main networks will be made up of smaller sub-networks, which will also interact with other networks. The social network should be all-encompassing as a whole, but will usually have many discrete, unconnected parts within it.

The partnership network is linked to the university through the awards that are developed by the university, but which are validated to run at the colleges. Course development takes place through a network of university and college staff and feeds back into the award development and management process. Course support feeds into course development and into award development.

students currently on FE awards who wish to continue their education.

Unfortunately, the interests of the college conflict with those of the university. Firstly, the college wishes to attract new local students. The college is local to the university and would therefore be in direct competition with the university which is also trying to attract local (as well as distant) students into HE. Secondly, the college wishes to retain students currently on FE awards by offer-

ing follow on HE awards – the university would like those students to progress to the university.

This conflict could potentially halt the formation of a partnership. However ABC University is aware that the FE College could approach other universities which if successful could result in loss of students. There is therefore a sound business case for ABC university to find the means to align the interests of the FE college with their own. Both institutions have in common a wish to increase their student numbers and hence revenues through service innovation. This provides a starting point to negotiate a compromise.

The compromise could be that the college is allowed to offer a different type of HE award that is managed and developed by, but not available at, the university – perhaps a vocational HE diploma or a Foundation Degree. These are Intermediate level awards so ABC University could still expect the students to progress to the university for an honours year and could put into place a bridging award to facilitate this. Also, the students would still be university students and enable the university to draw down funding from external sources based on student numbers, but they would attend and pay fees to the FE College. A financial agreement would be drawn up and agreed.

Inscription

The next process is inscription. In the example, so far, ABC University has a main interest in service innovation to increase student numbers and therefore revenue. It has succeeded in aligning the key FE college interests with its own. Now there is a need to be sure that the network functions smoothly. Rules must be defined and agreed, but more importantly, obeyed.

There can be a resistance to change. Durable translations can be difficult to establish because of this. In this case study, ABC course leaders will suddenly find that they have to communicate with college course leaders, which could be time consuming. Course material needs to be available to all students including those studying at external institutions. Rules might include for example, the requirement for all staff to use a specific VLE for all shared modules. Staff at both institutions may initially contest the use of the chosen VLE for many reasons including a hesitance to release their material to external staff and students, issues relating to the functionality or performance of the VLE and time taken to learn to use the product. This is where inscription comes in.

Awards and modules go through a process of validation and this includes validation of a teaching, learning and assessment strategy. This strategy has to include the fact that modules are being delivered off-site. Award leaders will have to field questions from a panel and explain how material is shared. The use of a VLE provides this. The use of the VLE is thus inscribed into validation documentation and the subsequent use of the VLE will become an artifact of the inscription. This documentation is available for inspection by Quality Assurance agencies, accrediting bodies and students. The availability of the documentation to such an institutionally important readership and the fact that any of the readers could look easily look for confirmation through interview or by electronic means through the VLE interface makes the inscription very powerful. Because of this, the focal actor will be motivated to mobilise management processes at the highest levels of ABC University to ensure that course leaders use the VLE.

The creation of a student interface within the VLE where all courses are displayed highlights where the inscription has failed, and failure could result in complaints from students and external staff which have ramifications in viewfinder surveys and league tables. Inscription in this case study is helped by the fact that there is strong alignment in the interests of both the university and college and redundancies in the sector have focused staff on the need to generate profit and service innovation is seen as a means to do this.

The network is strengthened by other factors such as:

- FE colleges cannot currently award Foundation Degrees, so it is in their interest to link up to universities. The universities in turn need to form strategic partnerships of this kind if they are to remain competitive.
- FE college students are on an HE award which has been explicitly designed to link to a top-up award at ABC University. This would provide something of a guarantee

that students wishing to top-up their qualification would progress to the university. This in turn strengthens the inscription.

Another method of strengthening the network and the inscription is to create advantages for the college to being part of the network that is aligned to their wider interests. For example, ABC could embark on the creation and management of an alliance of many such partners. For the partners in the alliance, it means becoming part of a critical mass which can negotiate marketing arrangements and lucrative enterprise contracts and/or funding with external agencies, as well as spreading any costs to ABC University of setting up and managing the network against a greater base of potential profit.

Designing Enrolment Strategies

Enrolment strategies need to be developed. This may involve challenging the stakeholders' current assumptions, and opening existing black boxes to promote their replacement with new technology. Alignment of actors' interests with the network occurs as actors enroll others into the network. A service system may call on other actors to support the provision of the service. These may include the use of technology such as the internet. Technology, texts and documentation behave as actors because they are passively enrolled into the network. The network becomes larger and more established as the actors are enrolled. This is the stage where the FE College is validated as a partner to run the intermediate level ABC university awards. The validation documentation is prepared from the negotiations and discussions of the Intéressement stage and documents the mechanisms through which the network will function. Importantly, it also encases the inscription details.

Mobilisation of Allies

This final moment of translation is the act of building the live network and putting all the elements into place. The sub-networks at the university and college would be established and communication would begin. For enrolment it is important that there is more than one set of actors imposing their will on others. We also require those others to yield. It is not enough for the university to expose its benefits; the students must also believe that they will have their return on investment if they come to study at ABC. Evaluation of the service so far produces very positive results. However, it is too early to predict if the service innovation was a success. In order to determine if the service innovation has been successful or not, we need to consider mobilisation. That is, if students come to ABC to study.

Uniqueness of ANT for Innovation

According to Rogers (1995), an innovation can be described as an idea that is perceived to be new to a particular person or group of people. The dominant paradigm in innovation research is that of information diffusion. This consists of four elements: Characteristics of the innovation itself; the nature of the communication channels; the passage of time; and the social system. The traditional view of the success or failure of service innovation can be explained using this approach by concentrating on things such as the details of the new system itself; how the change agents helped in its adoption; why users accepted or resisted its implementation.

Actor-Network Theory views innovation differently. The core of this is translation (Law, 1992). This means one entity gives a role to others (Singleton & Michael, 1993). In translation an actor identifies other actors and arranges them in relation to each other. Chains of translation can transform a global problem into a local problem (Latour 1996). According to Latour (1986), the mere possession of power by an actor does not automatically confer the ability to cause change unless other actors can be persuaded to perform the appropriate actions for this to occur. Latour (1986) argues that it is the number of other people who enter into the business that indicates the amount of power that has been exercised. He argues that in an innovation translation model, the movement of an innovation through time and space is in the hands of people, each of whom may react to it in different ways. Latour (1986) further suggested that this is true for the spread of anything from goods and artefacts to claims and ideas. The adoption of an innovation comes as the consequence of the actions of everyone in the chains of actions who are involved with it. Each of these actors shapes the innovation to their own ends. If no-one take up the innovation then it simply stops. A process of continuous transformation takes place instead of transmission (Tatnall & Gilding, 1999).

According to McMaster and others (1997), innovations do not wait passively to be invented or discovered, but are instead created from chains of weaker to stronger associations of human and non-human alliances. Each actant translates and contributes to its own resources to the shape and ultimate form of the emerging 'black box'.

CONCLUSION

The essence of innovation in service is to improve workforce productivity. Innovation is the key for survival and competitiveness in today's global economy. We believe that more research is needed to understand the role of innovation in services. Services exist in larger networks of social, technical and sociotechnical relations, each of which is also a service. All individual relations, as well as their networked dependencies, are potential areas for design. A methodology is needed to define these types of relationships. Our case study demonstrates that ANT can be used as a tool for service innovation development and adoption. ANT as a methodology for explaining and developing service systems requires the recording of actors' interactions, corrections and efforts. Actors' interactions are traced through interviews, discussions, meetings, documents, negotiation and management. ANT allows us to have a language to describe the many small, concrete technical and non-technical mechanisms that go into development and use of service innovation. It also allows us to establish social alignments by persuasion and gentle coercion in order that individual's behaviour and practice would align with the interests of the strategy plan of ABC. We have demonstrated in this paper the power of actor network theory in explaining and implementing service innovation. It provides us the means to describe which and how actors are enabled and constrained in the service innovation. However, we do understand that there are many issues that still need to be addressed in service innovation and that these need to be researched. Further research is urgently needed to find ways of improving service innovations. Although our findings are useful, this research has limitations and there should be opportunities for further research. The findings are only our experience and should be considered tentative. Caution is required in generalising the findings beyond our particular service. Further studies could test our approach by a longitudinal experiment with a broader research sample.

REFERENCES

Abrea de Paula, R. (2004). The construction of usefulness: How uses and context create meaning with a social networking system. [http://www.ics.uci.edu/~depaula/publications/dissertation-depaula-2004.pdf]

Akrich, M., & Latour, B. (1997). A summary of a convenient vocabulary for the semiotics of human and non-human assemblies. In Bijker, W. E., & Law, J. (Eds.), *Shaping technology/building society: Studies in sociotechnical change* (pp. 259–264). Cambridge, MA: MIT Press.

Barile, S. & Polese, F. (2010). Smart service systems and viable service systems

Barile, S., Spohrer, J. & Polese, F. (2010). System thinking for service research advances Volume 2 • Number 1/2 • Spring/Summer 2010, *Service Science* 2(1/2) © 2010 SSG

Bijker, W. E., Hughes, T. P., & Pinch, T. J. (1987). *The social construction of technological systems: New directions in the sociology and history of technology.* Cambridge, Mass.: MIT Press.

Bijker, W. E., & Law, J. (1992). *Shaping technology/ building society: Studies in sociotechnical change.* Cambridge, MA: MIT Press.

Callon, M. (1986a). The sociology of an Actor-Network: the case of the electric vehicle. In M. Callon, J. Law and A. Rip, *Mapping the dynamics of science and technology.* London, Macmillan Press, pp 19-34.

Callon, M. (1986b). Some elements of a sociology of translation: domestication of the scallops and the fishermen of St Brieuc Bay. In Law, J. (Ed.), *Power, action and belief: a new sociology of knowledge?* (pp. 196–223). London: Routledge & Kegan-Paul.

Callon, M. (1991). Techno-economic networks and irreversibility. In Law, J. (Ed.), *A sociology of monsters: Essays on power, technology and domination* (pp. 132–161). London: Routledge.

Callon, M., & Latour, B. (1981). Unscrewing the big leviathan: How actors manufacture reality and how sociologists help them to do so. In Knorr-Cetina, K. D., & Cicourel, A. V. (Eds.), *Advances in social theory and methodology: Toward an integration of micro- and macro-sociologies* (pp. 277–303). Boston, MA: Routledge & Kegan-Paul.

Cavusgil, S. T., Calantone, R. J., & Zhao, Y. (2003). Tacit knowledge transfer and firm innovation capability. *Journal of Business and Industrial Marketing, 18*(1), 6–21. doi:10.1108/08858620310458615

Ciborra, C. (1996). *Groupware and teamwork.* Chichester: Wiley.

Dawson, R., & Horenkamp, M. (2007). *Service delivery innovation: creating client value and enhancing profitability.* SAP Ag.

du Plessis, M. (2007). The role of knowledge management in innovation. *Journal of Knowledge Management, 11*(4), 20–29. doi:10.1108/13673270710762684

Gao, P. (2005). Using actor-network theory to analyse strategy formulation. [Blackwell Publishing]. *Information Systems Journal, 15*(3), 255–275. .doi:10.1111/j.1365-2575.2005.00197.x

Grönroos, C. 2006. What can a service logic offer marketing theory? in R.F. Lusch and S.L. Vargo, (Eds.), *The service–dominant logic of marketing dialog, debate, and directions.* 320–333. Armonk: M.E. Sharpe

IfM & IBM. (2008). *Succeeding through service innovation: a service perspective for education, research, business and government.* Cambridge, UK: University of Cambridge Institute of Manufacturing. ISBM.

Jones, M., & Samalionis, F. (2008). From small ideas to radical service innovation, *Design Management* [http://www.ideo.com/images/uploads/thinking/publications/pdfs/08191JON20.pdf]. *RE:view, 19*(1).

Kandampully, J. (2002). Innovation as the core competency of a service organisation: the role of technology, knowledge and networks. *European Journal of Innovation Management, 5*(1), 18–26. doi:10.1108/14601060210415144

Katzan, H. (2008). Foundations of service science concepts and facilities. *Journal Of Service Science, 1*(1), 1–22.

Latour, B. (1986). The power of association. In Law, J. (Ed.), *Power, action and belief: a new sociology of knowledge?* (pp. 196–223). London: Routledge & Kegan-Paul.

Latour, B. (1987). *Science in action: How to follow scientists and engineers through society*. Milton Keynes: Open University Press.

Latour, B. (1993). *We have never been modern*. Hemel Hempstead Harvester, Wheatsheaf.

Latour, B. (1996). *Aramis or the love of technology*. Harvard University Press, Cambridge MA: Latour, B. (1998). *On actor-network theory: A few definitions*. http://ww,netime.org/lists-Archives/netime-1-9801/msg00019.html [obtained September, 2003].

Latour, B. (2005). *Reassembling the social: An introduction to actor-network-theory*. Oxford: Oxford University Press.

Law, J. (1986). The Heterogeneity of Texts. In Callon, M., Law, J., & Rip, A. (Eds.), *Mapping the dynamics of science and technology* (pp. 67–83). UK: Macmillan Press.

Law, J. (1987). Technology, closure and heterogeneous engineering: The case of the Portuguese expansion. In Bijker, W. E., Hughes, T. P., & Pinch, T. (Eds.), *The social construction of technological systems: New directions in the sociology and history of technology* (pp. 111–134). Cambridge, MA: MIT Press.

Law, J. (1992). Notes on the theory of actor-network: ordering, strategy and heterogeneity. *Systems Practice*, *5*(4), 379–393. doi:10.1007/BF01059830

Maglio, P. P., Srinivasan, S., Kreulea, J. T., & Spohrer, J. (2006, July). Service, systems, service scientists. *MMME and Innovation, CACM*, *49*(7), 81–85.

McMaster, T., Vidgen, R. T., & Wastell, D. G. (1997). Towards an understanding of technology in transition: Two conflicting theories. *Information System Research in Scandinavia,* IRIS20 Conference, University of Oslo, Hanko, Norway.

Möller, K., Rajala, R., & Westerlund, M. (2007). Service myopia? A new recipe for client-provider value creation, *The Berkeley-Tekes Service Innovation Conference in Berkeley, California* April 27-28, 2007.

Monteiro, E., & Hanseth, O. (1996). Social shaping of information structure: on being specific about technology. In Orikowski, W. J., Walsham, G., Jones, M. R., & DeGross, J. I. (Eds.), *Information technology and changes in organisational work* (pp. 325–343). London, UK: Chapman & Hall.

Murdoch, J. (1997). Towards a geography of heterogeneous associations. *Progress in Geography*, *21*, 321–337. doi:10.1191/030913297668007261

Myers, M. (1999). Qualitative techniques for data collection, Qualitative Research in Information Systems. *IS World Net*. http://www2.auckland.ac.nz/msis/isworld/#Qualitativetechniques

News, B. B. C. (2010) University system needs radical change; http://news.bbc.co.uk/1/hi/education/ [Accessed 15 June 2010]

Peters, T. (1994). *Crazy time call for crazy organisations. Tom Peters' Seminar* (p. 10). London: Macmillan.

Polese, F. (2010). The influence of networking culture and social relationships on value creation. [forthcoming].

Rogers, E. M. (1995). *Diffusion of innovations*. New York: The Free Press.

Rogers, M. (1998). The definition and measurement of Innovation Melbourne Institute Working papers No. 10/98, ISSN 1328-4991 or ISBN 07325 0973 4, [Http://www.ecom.unimelb.edu.au/iaesrwww/home.html]

ServiceScience 2 (1/2), pp. 21 – 40, © 2010 SSG

Sheehan, J. (2006). Understanding service sector innovation. *Communications of the ACM*, *49*(9), 43–47.

Sims, C. (2007). Defining services for designers: Services as systems of social and technical relations, *UCB iSchool Report* 2007-002, February 2007. http://repositories.cdlib.org/cgi/viewcontent.cgi?article=1001&context=ischool

Singleton, V., & Michael, M. (1993). Actor-Networks and ambivalence: General practitioners in the UK cervical screening programme. *Social Studies of Science, 23*, 227–264. doi:10.1177/030631293023002001

Spohrer,J, Golinelli,G, M. Piciocchi, P & Bassano, C. (2010). An integrated SS-VSA analysis of changing job roles *Service Science* 2(1/2), pp. 1- 20, © 2010 SSG.

Spohrer, J., Maglio, P., Bailey, J., & Gruhl, D. (2007). Steps towards a science of service systems. *IEE Computer, 40*(Issue 1), 71–77.

Spohrer, J., Vargo, S. L., Caswell, N. S., & Maglio, P. P. (2008) The service system is the basic abstraction of service science. *Hawaii International Conference on System Sciences*, Proceedings of the 41st Annual.

Swain, H. (2008). UK universities face 'radical' changes, Monday February 11, 2008, [Education Guardian.co.uk, http://education.guardian.co.uk/administration/story/0,,2255736,00.html]

Szmtkowski, D. (2005). Innovation definition comparative assessment (EU), DRAFT developed under GNU, free Documentation Licence, Brussels.

Tatnall, A., & Burgess, S. (2002). Using Actor-Network Theory to research the implementation of B-B portal for regional SMEs in Melbourne, Australia. *15th Bled Electronic Commerce Conference & Reality: Constructing the e-economy, Bled*, Slovenia, June 17-19, 2002.

Tatnall, A., & Gilding, A. (1999). Actor-Network Theory and information systems research. *Proceedings of 10th Australian Conference on Information Systems*, 1999

Walsham, G. (1997). Network Theory and the IS researcher: Current status and future prospect. In Lee, A. S., Liebenau, J., & DeGross, J. I. (Eds.), *Information Systems and Qualitative Research* (pp. 466–480). London, UK: Chapman & Hall.

Zeithaml, V. A., Bitner, M. J., & Gremler, D. D. (2006). *Services Marketing: Integrating Customer Focus Across the Firm*. New York: McGraw-Hill Irwin.

Chapter 3

The Need for Rich Theory to Realize the Vision of Healthcare Network Centric Operations:
The Case for Combining ANT and Social Network Analysis

Nimini Wickramasinghe
RMIT University, Australia

Rajeev Bali
Coventry University, UK

ABSTRACT

In a dynamic and complex global environment traditional approaches to healthcare delivery are becoming more and more inadequate. To address this von Lubitz and Wickramasinghe (2006e) proffered the need for a network-centric approach that allows free and rapid sharing of information and effective knowledge building required for the development of coherent objectives and their rapid attainment. However, to realize this vision it is essential to have rich theory and robust approaches to analyse the levels of complexity of modern healthcare delivery. This paper discusses how this might be done by drawing upon the strong rich analysis tools and techniques of Social Network Analysis combined with Actor Network Theory.

INTRODUCTION

Environmental complexity of healthcare operations is often magnified by the presence of multiple actors (agencies, governmental bodies, global organizations, etc.) who perform within the same space, but use a wide variety of independent and non-intercommunicating platform centric tools. As a consequence of the resulting chaos, the attainment (mission) of healthcare goals (objectives) is uncertainty- rather than information-driven (von Lubitz and Wickramasinghe, 2005; 2006e). In response to the inefficiency of the highly fragmented programs to address even the most urgent aspects of healthcare across the globe, a demand for the development of a new rule set (Barnett, 2004; Onen, 2004; Olutimayin, 2002; Banjeri, 2004)

DOI: 10.4018/978-1-60960-197-3.ch003

governing the future actions began to emerge – the quest for the "doctrine of global health."

In response to this void von Lubitz and Wick-ramasinghe (2006b-e) proffered the doctrine of network-centric healthcare. This doctrine finds its operational predecessor in the military application of information and decision support system networks based on uniform and widely distributed access, collection, processing, and dissemination standards (Cebrowski and Garstka, 1998). The doctrine calls for the development of interconnected information grids that, together, constitute a powerful and well-structured network that facilitates information sharing among all participants within the operational continuum (space, see Cebrowski and Garstka, 1998; Stein, 1998). Consequent to improved information sharing is the enhancement of its quality and integrity which, in turn, escalates the level of situational awareness that is the foundation for efficient, real-time collaboration among the involved entities, their self-synchronization, and operational sustainability. The overall operational effect of network-centricity is a dramatic increase in mission effectiveness (Cebrowski and Garstka, 1998) whose success, even at the earliest trial stages, led to its adaptation of network-centric concept by several armed forces across the globe. For the same reason, the doctrine begins to find its place in the modern, ICT-driven business world (ibid).

THE CONCEPTUAL BASIS FOR NETWORK-CENTRIC OPERATIONS

The cardinal details of the network-centric doctrine of healthcare operations have been described in detail by von Lubitz and Wickramasinghe (2006b-e). The doctrine is rooted in the pioneering work of Boyd (1987, see also von Lubitz and Wickramasinghe, 2006b-ed-e) who analyzed the process of decision making and the fundamental principles of interaction with- and control of- a fast paced and dynamic environment. Critical research-based

projects (as applicable in the area of information systems and health) have a growing tradition of qualitative inquiry. Despite its relativist ontology, actor network theory places a strong emphasis on empirical inquiry and actor network theory, is ideally suited to the generation of detailed and contextual empirical knowledge (Doolin B and Lowe A, 2002). Following its initial military applications, Boyd's OODA Loop as it is presently known, found many adherents and practical uses in a wide variety of civilian applications including medicine (von Lubitz et al., 2004 von Lubitz and Wickramasinghe, 2006a-e).

THE NATURE AND DEFINITION OF THE DOCTRINE OF NETWORK-CENTRIC HEALTHCARE

Following the essential nature of actor network theory, the intricate and mutually constitutive character of the human and technology (in the processes and relationships of illness and health) has been demonstrated (Prout, 1996). In addition to this "micro" example, successful interaction with complex sets of macro-environments (macro-environment galaxies) such as global healthcare (which comprises a vast array of independently identifiable macro-environments, *c.f.* 1) presents an insurmountable task *unless assisted by a highly sophisticated, multilayered network of ICT that incorporates a full range of telecommunication platforms, sensors, data storage elements, analytical nodes, and dispersed access points, the operation of which provides flexible command and control and rapid response capabilities.*

The doctrine of network-centric healthcare has its roots in network-centric computing (von Lubitz and Wickramasinghe, 2006b-e) whose practical development has been greatly facilitated by the rapid progress of various areas of ICTs (e.g., HTML, TCP/IP, Web, JAVA, XTML, etc – refs Hironaka, 1992, Valdes et al., 2003). The principal task of network-centricity in healthcare operations is to develop the state of *information superiority*.

The state of information superiority provides the actor(-s) with the critical *operational advantage* that allows to determine and dictate the direction and tempo of all activities in a collaborative, highly coordinated manner which, in turn, reduces the time needed to reach the preset objectives in the most effective and economical manner. Even the sketchy and largely anecdotal reports of the events surrounding Hurricane Katrina operations indicate quite clearly that the absence of the state of information superiority was one of the principal culprits in the resultant leadership failures, absence of coordination, and a number of avoidable post-hurricane fatalities (e.g., CNN News, a,b,c)

Unsurprisingly, in order to be executed efficiently, healthcare operations must be conducted within the intersecting territory of three mutually interconnected and functionally related domains (von Lubitz and Wickramasinghe, 2006b-e; Garstka, 2000):

- The *physical domain* which encompasses the structure of the entire environment healthcare operations intend to influence directly or indirectly, e.g., elimination of disease, fiscal operations, political environment, patient and personnel education, etc. Information within this domain is the easiest to collect, analyze, and disseminate
- The *information domain* contains all elements required for generation, storage, manipulation, dissemination/sharing of information, and its transformation and dissemination/sharing as knowledge in all its forms. It is here that all aspects of command and control are communicated and all sensory inputs gathered.
- The *cognitive domain* relates to all human factors that affect operations, such as education, training, experience, political inclinations, personal engagement (moti-

vation), "open-mindedness," or even intuition of individuals involved in the relevant activities. Difficulties in metrics relevant to the cognitive domain notwithstanding, a body of experimental studies begins to emerge that will, ultimately, provide close quantitative relationships to other domains that govern healthcare operations space e.g., (Bodner et al., 1986; Roberts and Clifton, 1992; Back and Oppenheim, 2001; Newby, 2001; Wetherell et al., 2002; Abel-Smith, 1989).

Hence, fundamental to the doctrine of network-centric healthcare operations (HNCO) is *"unhindered networking operations within and among all three domains that govern all activities conducted in healthcare space and are based on free, multidirectional flow and exchange of information without regard to the involved platforms or platform-systems and utilizing all available means of ICTs to facilitate such operations.*

THE PHYSICAL CONSTITUENTS OF THE HEALTHCARE NETWORK

The essential and enabling element of HNCO is the Healthcare Information Grid that allows full and hindrance-free sharing of information among individual domains, their constituents, and among constituents across the domains. In order to perform such a function, the Healthcare Information Grid must consist of an interconnected matrix of ICT systems and capabilities (including communication platforms, data collection, storage, manipulation/dissemination, and sharing), associated processes (such as information and knowledge storage and retrieval, management and their dissemination/sharing), people (e.g., healthcare providers/investigators, administrators, economists, politicians, lawyers, ICT personnel), and agencies (governmental and NGOs (Non-

Governmental Organizations) at local/national/international level.)

The required technology (von Lubitz et al., 2005) and individual components of such a grid already exist (von Lubitz and Wickramasinghe, 2006b-e), and their role and interactions in the context of network-centric operations described in a greater detail elsewhere (von Lubitz and Wickramasinghe, 2006b-e), the grid itself needs yet to be constructed based on universally accepted and shared operational and security standards and protocols that will allow free and unfettered access to all actors within the healthcare space Once developed, the Grid will facilitate information sharing and enable joint development of objectives, precise characterization of missions necessary to attain these objectives, allocation of adequate resources, and continuing monitoring of progress. The latter will, in turn, permit not only timely intra-operational interventions (e.g., modifications of the mission profile, changes in resource allocation) but, even more significantly, assist in the development of the unified command structure necessary for the synchronization of currently non-related and often disorganized and discordant efforts conducted within the same segment of healthcare space. That such controls are required in very large scale operations is demonstrated by several studies showing that, in the developing countries in particular, the currently disorganized conditions of healthcare aid often result in inefficiency and inappropriate application of the available resources (Abel-Smith, 1989; Howard, 1991; Collins and Green, 1994; Schneider and Gilson, 1999; Buse, 1999).

Access to the Healthcare Information Grid is facilitated through "smart" portals (described in detail in von Lubitz and Wickramasinghe, 2006b-e) that provide the gateway to all operationally pertinent information existing within the network. Operational (pertinent) knowledge support is derived through a semi- or fully automated search of the grid by the information processing capabilities and decision support capabilities of the smart portal, followed by the equally semi- or fully automated assembly, analysis, and pertinent knowledge derivation. Based on agent technologies, and contrary to the majority of the existing portal systems, the "smart portal" is fully active, and its operations provide relevant data, information, and knowledge based on cross-domain objective analysis of all relevant facts rather than those that may be, often erroneously and subjectively, classified as relevant by the human operator.

Many of the complexities of network-centric operations are invariable linked to the issues of security and data/information integrity and, given the total access to the Healthcare Information Grid provided by the smart portal to all actors within the operational space, it is vital that the highest level of security protocols are maintained at all times.

RICH ANALYSIS TOOLS AND TECHNIQUES

In order to design, develop and thereby successfully realize the vision of network-centric healthcare it is vital that rich analysis tools and techniques are fully utilized. In general the social theory literature is peppered with various theories that are both complex and rich. Within this body of the literature two appropriate candidates that are particularly relevant in the context of HNCO include Social Network Analysis (SNA) and Actor Network Theory (ANT).

Social Network Analysis (SNA)

SNA is a technique that facilitates the mapping and measuring of relationships and flows between people, groups, organizations, systems as well as all information/knowledge processing organizations and thereby enhances metacognition with respect to the representation of organizational knowledge in networks (Wasserman and Faust,

Figure 1. Healthcare information grid

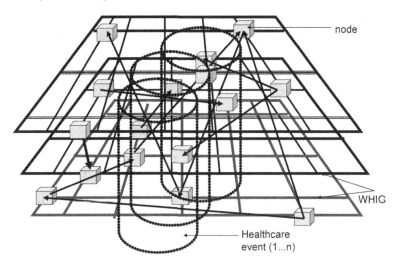

1994; Niessen 2007). People and groups are represented as nodes while the relationships or flows are represented by links. Taken together this analysis of nodes and links builds the network under consideration. The location of actors in such a network is critical to a deeper understanding of the network as a whole and the participation and position of individual actors (Wellman and Gulia, 1999). Location is measured by finding the centrality of the node.

In terms of centrality three considerations become important in any SNA; degree of centrality – in other words how many people connect with you, betweenness – or whether or not you are located between 2 key actors in the network and thus may play a "broker" role, and closeness – or ones position relative to others (especially key players) in the network. In addition, it is important to note if there exist boundary spanners -actors who bridge or overlap into different networks, or peripheral players – actors who are perceived as unimportant.

One way to improve the current state-of-the-art in SNA is to develop new ways to produce interval/ratio measures of relations between the various individuals in the organization to determine the strength of their ties (Liebowitz,

2005). Analysts of social networks are interested in how the individual is embedded within a structure and how the structure emerges from the micro-relations between individual parts (Hanneman, 2002).

To illustrate the value for SNA within HNCO let us look at Figure 1. Within the Healthcare Information Grid structure various healthcare events (denoted by cylinders labeled healthcare event 1…n) have been highlighted. In the case of an emergency and disaster scenario such as Hurricane Katrina, it is possible to think of one of these events as Hurricane Katrina. In this context the nodes (cubes on Healthcare Information Grid) represent various actors. What becomes of crucial importance in the emergency and disaster state of Hurricane Katrina is the distance or centrality of key actors since the key actors are the important decision makers and in such a context rapid prudent decision making can save lives. Clearly, in such a context the understanding of who/ where the boundary spanners are as well as the betweenness and closeness constructs are key in designing a superior network that will enable at all times appropriate and speedy decision making to ensue. It is also useful to note that SNA can be used in post facto analysis to facilitate necessary lessons learnt that can be applied to the future state. Thus the incorporation of SNA into the continuous design and development of HNCO is going to facilitate the realization of a well structured network that will indeed support all the complex and dynamic operations in healthcare.

Actor Network Theory (ANT)

As noted earlier healthcare is a complex domain. Specifically, the roles of different healthcare players including payers, providers, healthcare organizations and regulators as well as their respective interactions with Healthcare Information Grid and how Healthcare Information Grid in turn might facilitate, modify or even impede their tasks. To facilitate a superior understanding a sufficiently rich and dynamic lens of analysis can be found from the application of Actor Network Theory (ANT).

ANT embraces the idea of an organizational identity and assumes that organizations, much like humans, possess and exhibit specific traits (Brown, 1997). Although labeled a "theory", ANT is more of a framework based upon the principle of generalized symmetry, which rules that human and non-human objects/subjects are treated with the same vocabulary. Both the human and non-human counterparts are integrated into the same conceptual framework.

ANT was developed by British sociologist, John Law and two French social sciences and technology scholars Bruno Latour and Michel Callon (Latour, 1987, 2005; Law and Hassard, 1999; Law, 1992, 1987; Callon, 1986. It is an interdisciplinary approach that tries to facilitate an understanding of the role of technology in specific settings, including how technology might facilitate, mediate or even negatively impact organizational activities and tasks performed. Hence, ANT is a material-semiotic approach for describing the ordering of scientific, technological, social, and organizational processes or events.

Concepts of Actor Network Theory

Table 1 presents the key concepts of ANT and their relevance to network-centric healthcare operations.

DISCUSSION

The suggested approach is a hybrid approach that combines the respective strengths of SNA and ANT in order to facilitate the realization of HNCO. Such an approach requires the identification and tracing of specific healthcare events and networks to "follow the actors" (Latour, 1996) and investigate all the relevant leads each new actor suggests. The first step is thus to identify these actors (or actants), remembering that an actor is someone or something that can make its presence individually felt and can make a difference to the situation under investigation. Thus, in HNCO the actors would include: medical practitioners, nurses, medical instruments, healthcare organizations, regulators, patients, equipment suppliers, medical administrators, administrative computer systems, medical researchers, and so on. In a particular operation (or event) it is important to identify all relevant actors before proceeding further.

The next step is to 'interview' the actors. With human actors this is, of course, quite straightforward, but with non-humans it is necessary to find someone (or something) to speak on their behalf. For an item of medical technology this might be its designer or user, or it might just be the instruction manual. The aim of this step is to see how these actors relate to each other and the associations they create – to identify how they interact, how they negotiate, and how they form alliances and networks with each other. These 'heterogeneous networks' consists of the aligned interests held by each of the actors.

Human actors, such as medical practitioners, can 'negotiate' with non-human actors such as X-Ray or dialysis machines by seeing what these

Table 1. Key Concepts of ANT

Concept	Relevance to HNCO
Actor/Actant: Typically actors are the participants in the network which include both the human and non-human objects and/or subjects. However, in order to avoid the strong bias towards human interpretation of Actor, the neologism ACTANT is commonly used to refer to both human and non-human actors. Examples include humans, electronic instruments, technical artifacts, or graphical representations.	In HNCO this includes the web of healthcare players such as provides, healthcare organizations, regulators, payers, suppliers and the patient as well as the clinical and administrative technologies that support and facilitate healthcare delivery.
Heterogeneous Network: is a network of aligned interests formed by the actors. This is a network of materially heterogeneous actors that is achieved by a great deal of work that both shapes those various social and non-social elements, and "disciplines" them so that they work together, instead of "making off on their own" (Latour, 2005).	Healthcare Information Grid is clearly the technology network for HNCO. However it is important to conceptualise the heterogeneous network not as Healthcare Information Grid alone but as the aligning of the actors with Healthcare Information Grid so that it is possible to represent all interests and thereby provide the patient with superior healthcare delivery. Given the scope of healthcare operations and the global nature of HNCO there will be numerous power dynamics within and between groups of actors. This will be a critical barrier to enabling the well functioning of network-centric operations. The key is to carefully align goals so that healthcare delivery is truly patient centric at all times.
Tokens/Quasi Objects: are essentially the success outcomes or functioning of the Actors which are passed onto the other actors within the network. As the token is increasingly transmitted or passed through the network, it becomes increasingly punctualized and also increasingly reified. When the token is decreasingly transmitted, or when an actor fails to transmit the token (e.g., the oil pump breaks), punctualization and reification are decreased as well.	In HNCO this translates to successful healthcare delivery, such as treating a patient in a remote location by having the capability to access critical information to enable the correct decisions to be made. Conversely, and importantly, if incorrect information is passed throughout the network errors will multiply and propagate quickly hence it is a critical success factor that the integrity of the network is maintained at all times.
Punctualization: is similar to the concept of abstraction in Object Oriented Programming. A combination of actors can together be viewed as one single actor. These sub actors are hidden from the normal view. This concept is referred to as Punctualization. An incorrect or failure of passage of a token to an actor will result in the breakdown of a network. When the network breaks down, it results in breakdown of punctualization and the viewers will now be able to view the sub actors of the actor. This concept is often referred to as depunctualization.	For example, an automobile is often referred to as an unit. Only when it breaks down, is it seen as a combination of several machine parts. Or in HNCO the uploading task of one key actor, be it a provider or a regulator is in reality a consequence of the interaction and co-ordination of several sub-tasks. This only becomes visible when a breakdown at this point occurs and special attention is given to analyse why and how the problem resulted and hence all sub tasks must be examined carefully.
Obligatory Passage Point: broadly refers to a situation that has to occur in order for all the actors to satisfy the interests that have been attributed to them by the focal actor. The focal actor defines the OPP through which the other actors must pass through and by which the focal actor becomes indispensable (Callon, 1986).	In HNCO we can illustrate this by examining the occurrence of a disease or catastrophe. A recent pertinent example is SARS which caused a major epidemic crisis and required a united, co-ordinated global response to focus on finding a cure and treating affected victims. A similar co-ordianted immediate response was required in the aftermath of Hurricane Katrina or the Tsunami that struck the countries of the Indian ocean in December 2004. Such incidents form the catalyst for developing shared goals and united focus of effort so necessary to effect superior healthcare delivery.
Irreversibility: Callon (1986) states that the degree of irreversibility depends on (i) the extent to which it is subsequently impossible to go back to a point where that translation was only one amongst others and (ii) the extent to which it shapes and determines subsequent translations.	Given the very complex nature of healthcare operations (von Lubitz and Wickramasinghe, 2006b-e) irreversibility is generally not likely to occur. However it is vital that chains of events are continuously analysed in order that future events can be addressed as effectively and efficiently as possible. This is at the very essence of HNCO.

machines can do for them, how easy they are to use, what they cost to use, and how flexible they are in performing the tasks required. If negotiations are successfully completed then an association between the medical practitioner and the machine is created and the machine is used to advantage – the network has become durable. If the negotiations are unsuccessful then the machine is either not used at all, or not used to full advantage.

Once this is developed it is then important to apply the techniques of SNA to map the flows of pertinent information and germane knowledge throughout this network and thereby not only enhancing the metacognition of the system but also the ability to rapidly extract and utilize the critical knowledge to support prudent decision making and at always a state of being prepared and ready (Wickramasinghe and von Lubitz, 2007; von Lubitz and Wickramasinghe, 2006 a;f)

The main advantage of this approach to considering HNCO is in being able to identify and explore the real complexity involved. Other approaches to technological innovation, Innovation Diffusion for example, put much stress on the properties of the technology or organisation themselves, at the expense of looking at how these interact. Unfortunately in doing this they often tend to oversimplify very complex situations and so miss out on a real understanding. The ANT approach of investigating networks and associations provides a useful means to identify and explain these complexities as well as track germane knowledge and pertinent information. This is paramount if the doctrine of network-centric healthcare is to be successfully realised.

CONCLUSION

Healthcare reform is being embarked upon by most if not all OECD countries in one form or another. This is as a result of the presently disorganized state of global healthcare coupled with predicated exponentially increasing costs required to support and sustain current healthcare practices. In 2006 von Lubitz and Wickramasinghe (2006e) proffered HNCO as a solution as a remedy to the problems plaguing healthcare delivery.. This doctrine has several advantages: first, a similar concept is already implemented with significant success by the military establishment. Hence, the "lessons learned" can be readily adopted into the civilian environment. More importantly,

however, by permitting free flow of information among currently disconnected entities and fields of healthcare operations, the network-centric doctrine allows vast improvement in information management and use in all activities related to healthcare. In addition, network-centricity permits generation of the currently absent comprehensive, multifaceted, and unified body of knowledge necessary to conduct healthcare activities in a manner addressing present inequalities through a consistent knowledge-based effort rather than, as it is presently done, through the erratic application of ever increasing funds.

Sadly, still today most healthcare operations are at best platform centric and efforts to transition to a network centric approach are in general not occurring. We believe that network-centric healthcare offers the most tangible and obtainable means of such transformation, and that, in similarity to science, business, and warfare (Smarr, 1999) every effort should be made to pursue the tenets of the doctrine in changing the face of the global healthcare. However, and most importantly, if HNCO is to become the new paradigm for healthcare delivery in the 21st century it is vital that a rich set of analysis tools and techniques be employed. To this regard we have presented a hybrid analysis which draws together the strengths of two well established social theory techniques; namely social network analysis (SNA) and actor network theory (ANT). We contend that the richness of such an approach is essential if the true potential of HNCO operations are to ensue. In closing we not only call for more research in this area but also for more research into the value of using such hybrid approaches in various areas of dynamic and complex operations.

REFERENCES

Abel-Smith, B. (1989). Health economies in developing countries. *The Journal of Tropical Medicine and Hygiene, 92*, 229–241.

Alberts, D. S., Garstka, J. J., & Stein, F. P. (2000*). Network Centric Wardare: Developing and Leveraging Information Superiority, CCRP Publication Series* (Dept. of Defense), Washington, DC, pp 1-284. Retrieved from http://www.dodccrp.org/publications/pdf/Alberts_NCW.pdf

Back, J., & Oppenheim, C. (2001). *A model of cognitive load for IR: implications for user relevance feedback interaction, Information Res. 2.* Retrieved from http://InformationR.net/ir/6-2/ws2.html

Banjeri, D. (2004). The people and health service development in India: a brief overview. *International Journal of Health Services, 34,* 123–142. doi:10.2190/9N5U-4NFK-FQDH-J46W

Barnett, T. P. M. (2004). *The Pentagon's New Map* (pp. 1–435). New York: G.P. Putnam & Sons.

Bodner, G. M., & McMillen, T. L. B. (1986). Cognitive restructuring as an early stage in problem solving. *Journal of Research in Science Teaching, 23,* 727–737. doi:10.1002/tea.3660230807

Boyd, J. R. COL USAF, (1987). Patterns of Conflict. (Unpubl Briefing). Retrieved from http://www.d-n-i.net

Brailer, D. J., & Terasawa, A. B. (2003). *Use and Adoption of Computer-Based Patient Records* (pp. 1–42). California HealthCare Foundation.

Buse, K. (1999). Keeping a tight grip on the reins: donor control over aid coordination and management in Bangladesh. *Health Policy and Planning, 14,* 219–228. doi:10.1093/heapol/14.3.219

Callon, M. (1986). Some Elements of a Sociology of Translation: Domestication of the Scallops and the Fishermen of St Brieuc Bay. In Law, J. (Ed.), *Power, Action and Belief: A New Sociology of Knowledge.* London: Routledge & Kegan Paul.

Cebrowski, A. K., & Garstka, J. J. (1998). Network-centric warfare: its origin and future. *US Nav. Inst. Proc., 1,* 28–35.

Collins, C., & Green, A. (1994). Decentralization and primary health care: some negative implications in developing countries. *International Journal of Health Services, 24,* 459–475.

Doolin, B. & Lowe A (2002) "To reveal is to critique: actor–network theory and critical information systems research", Journal of Information Technology, Vol.17, No.2, June 2002, pp. 69-78(10)

Garstka, J. J. (2000). Network Centric Warfare: an overview of emerging theory. *Phalanx, 4,* 28–33.

Hanneman, R. (2002). Introduction to social network methods. Retrieved from www.faculty.ucr.edu/hanneman/

Hironaka, W. (1992, March). We must tackle population problems. *Integration (Tokyo, Japan), 31*(27).

Howard, L. M. (1991). Public and private donor financing for health in developing countires. *Infectious Disease Clinics of North America, 5,* 221–234.

Latour, B. (1987). *Science in Action: How to Follow Scientists and Engineers Through Society.* Milton Keynes, UK: Open University Press.

Latour, B. (2005). *Reassembling the Social: An Introduction to Actor-Network-Theory.* Oxford, UK: Oxford University Press.

Law, J. (1987). Technology and Heterogeneous Engineering: The Case of Portuguese Expansion. In Bijker, W. E., Hughes, T. P., & Pinch, T. J. (Eds.), *The Social Construction of Technological Systems: New Directions in the Sociology and History of Technology.* Cambridge, MA: MIT Press.

Law, J. (1992). Notes on the Theory of the Actor Network: Ordering, Strategy, and Heterogeneity.", http://www.lancs.ac.uk/fss/sociology/papers/law-notes-on-ant.pdf

Law, J., & Hassard, E. (Eds.). (1999). *Actor Network Theory and After. Oxford and Keele*. UK: Blackwell and the Sociological Review.

Liebowitz, J. (2005). Linking social network analysis with the analytic hierarchy process for knowledge mapping in organizations. *Journal of Knowledge Management, 9*(1), 76–86. doi:10.1108/13673270510582974

Markoff, J., & Schenker, J. L. (2003). Europe exceeds US in refining grid computing, *The New York Times, November 10*

Newby, G. B. (2001). Cognitive space and information space. *J. Am.Soc. Info. Sci. Technol., 12*, 1026–1048. doi:10.1002/asi.1172

Nissen, M. (2007). Keynote paper: Enhancing Organisational metacognition – flow visualization to make the knowledge network explicit. *Intl J Networking and Virtual Organisations, 4*(4), 331–350. doi:10.1504/IJNVO.2007.015728

Olutimayin, J. (2002). Communication in health care delivery in developing countries: which way out? *Pacific Health Dialog, 9*, 237–241.

Onen, C. L. (2004). Medicine in resource-poor settings: time for a paradigm shift? *Clinical Medicine (London, England), 4*, 355–360.

Prout, A. (1996). Actor-network theory, technology and medical sociology: an illustrative analysis of the metered dose inhaler. *Sociology of Health & Illness, 18*(2), 198–219. doi:10.1111/1467-9566. ep10934726

Roberts, L. W., & Clifton, R. A. (1992). Measuring the cognitive domain of the quality of student life: an instrument for faculties of education. *Canadian Journal of Education, 2*, 176–191. doi:10.2307/1495319

Schneider, H., & Gilson, L. (1999). Small fish in a big pond? External aid and the health sector in South Africa. *Health Policy and Planning, 14*, 264–272. doi:10.1093/heapol/14.3.264

Smarr, L. (1999). Grids in context. In Foster, I., & Kesselman, C. (Eds.), *The Grid: Blueprint for a New Computing Infrastructure*. San Francisco: Morgan Kaufman Publishers.

Stein, P. 1998, Observations on the emergence of network centric warfare, http://www.dodccrp.org/research/ncw/stein/_observations/steincw.htm

Sun-Tzu on the Art of War. (1910). *Project Guthenberg*. Retrieved from http://www.kimsoft.com.polwar.htm

Valdes, I., Kibbe, D., Tolleson, G., Kunik, M., & Petersen, L. A. (2003). Metcalfe's law predicts reduced power of Electronic Medical record software. *AMIA ... Annual Symposium Proceedings / AMIA Symposium. AMIA Symposium, 2003*, 1038.

Von Lubitz, D., et al. (2004). Medical Readiness in the Context of Operations Other Than War: Development of First Responder Readiness Using OODA –Loop Thinking and Advanced Distributed Interactive Simulation Technology. In *Proceedings EMISPHERE 2004 Symposium*, Istanbul, Turkey September 2004. For on-line version at the Defence and National Intelligence Network. Retrieved from http://www.d-n-i.net/fcs/pdf/von_lubitz_1rp_ooda.pdf

von Lubitz, D., & Wickramasinghe, N. (2005). Network-centric Healthcare and Bioinformatics. *Intl. J. Expert Systems with Applications., 30*, 11–23.

von Lubitz, D., & Wickramasinghe, N. (2006a). Dynamic Leadership In Unstable And Unpredictable Environments. *Intl. J. Management and Enterprise Development, 3*(4), 339–350.

von Lubitz, D., & Wickramasinghe, N. (2006b). Network-centric Healthcare: applying the tools, techniques and strategies of knowledge management to create superior healthcare operations. [IJEH]. *International Journal of Electronic Healthcare, 4*, 415–428.

von Lubitz, D., & Wickramasinghe, N. (2006c). Key Challenges and Policy Implications for Governments and Regulators in a Network-centric Healthcare Environment. *Int. J. Electronic Government*, *3*(2), 204–224.

von Lubitz, D., & Wickramasinghe, N. (2006d). Network-centric Healthcare: Outline of Entry Portal Concept. *Intl.* [IJEBM]. *J. of Electronic Business Management*, *1*, 16–28.

von Lubitz, D., & Wickramasinghe, N. (2006e). Healthcare and Technology: The Doctrine of Network-centric Healthcare. [IJEH]. *International Journal of Electronic Healthcare*, *4*, 322–344.

von Lubitz, D., & Wickramasinghe, N. (2006f). Creating Germane Knowledge In Dynamic Environments. [IJIL]. *Intl. J. Innovation and Learning*, *3*(3), 326–347. doi:10.1504/IJIL.2006.009226

von Lubitz, D., Wickramasinghe, N., & Yanovsky, G. (2006). Network-centric Healthcare Operations: The Telecommuniucations Structure. *Int. J. Networking and Virtual Organizations*, *3*(1), 60–85. doi:10.1504/IJNVO.2006.008785

Wasserman, S., & Faust, K. (1994). *Social Network Analysis*. Cambridge, UK: Cambridge University Press.

Wellman, B., & Gulia, M. (1999). Virtual communities as communities: Net surfers don't ride alone. In Smith, M. A., & Kollock, P. (Eds.), *Communities in cyberspace* (pp. 167–194). New York: Routledge.

Wetherell, J. L., Reynolds, C. A., Gatz, M., & Pedersen, N. L. (2002). Anxiety, cognitive performance, and cognitive decline in normal aging. *J. Gerontol (B). Psych. Sci. and Soc. Sci.*, *57*, 246–255.

Wickramasinghe, N., & von Lubitz, D. (2007). *Knowledge-Based Enterprise: Theories and Fundamentals*. Hershey, PA: IGI Global.

Chapter 4

Innovation Translation, Innovation Diffusion and the Technology Acceptance Model:
Comparing Three Different Approaches to Theorising Technological Innovation

Arthur Tatnall
Victoria University, Australia

ABSTRACT

The process of innovation involves getting new ideas accepted and new technologies adopted and used. There are a number of different approaches to theorising technological innovation and this chapter will compare and contrast what I suggest are the most important three: Innovation Diffusion, the Technology Acceptance Model (TAM) and Innovation Translation, giving examples of how each of these approaches is used in different situations. While there are many advantages to the use of an Innovation Translation approach, it should not be said that Translation offers a better approach than the others in all circumstances and that the others have nothing at all to offer; that would be rather too simplistic a view given the widespread use of Innovation Diffusion and TAM. This chapter proposes that perhaps it should not be a case of always using either one approach or the other but rather the use of whichever is most appropriate to a particular investigation.

TECHNOLOGICAL INNOVATION

The process of innovation involves getting new ideas accepted or new technologies adopted and used (Tatnall, 2005). After the discovery of a new idea, or the invention and development of a new technology it does not automatically follow that this will be adopted by its potential users. (The investigation of innovation processes discussed here is based on the assumption that the potential adopters *have some choice* in the adoption and I will restrict my discussion to adoptions of this type.)

It is important now to distinguish between invention and innovation. While invention involves the discovery or creation of new ideas or

DOI: 10.4018/978-1-60960-197-3.ch004

technologies, innovation is the process of putting these ideas or technologies into commercial or organisational practice (Maguire, Kazlauskas, & Weir, 1994; Tatnall, 2007b). The Oxford dictionary defines *innovation* as "the alteration of what is established; something newly introduced" (Oxford, 1973) and is concerned with individual and business decisions to *adopt* new inventions (Tatnall, 2007a). The study of innovation does not concern itself with inventors and the details of their inventions, but about individual and organisational decisions to adopt these new inventions. Invention does not necessarily invoke innovation, nor is invention necessary or sufficient for innovation to occur (Tatnall, 2005).

Making any change to the way things are done is a complex undertaking and difficult to achieve successfully. The success of any innovation is always in doubt because people who are prepared to support the innovator can be difficult to find and to convince. Although writing of *political* change almost five hundred years ago Niccolò Machiavelli summed this up as follows:

"There is nothing more difficult to handle, more doubtful of success and more dangerous to carry through than initiating changes ... The innovator makes enemies of all those who prospered under the old order, and only lukewarm support is forthcoming from those who would prosper under the new. Their support is lukewarm partly from fear of their adversaries, who have the existing laws on their side, and partly because men are generally incredulous, never really trusting new things unless they have tested them by experience." (Machiavelli, 1515:19)

One of the difficulties faced in investigating the adoption of technological innovations is that not all of these innovations are adopted in the form in which they were proposed – not all are adopted without change. This raises the question of just what was adopted in each case if it was in some way different from what was proposed by its instigator. This chapter will examine, with examples, the issue of how technological innovations are adopted or rejected, and how they might sometimes be changed during the process of adoption.

MODELS OF TECHNOLOGICAL INNOVATION

To investigate the adoption of new ideas or technologies and how innovation takes place, it is useful to follow one of the major theories of technological innovation (Al-Hajri & Tatnall, 2007; Tatnall & Dai, 2007). One important difference between some of these theories is the degree to which the adoption decision is seen as completely rational, and whether provision is made for partial adoption. A brief discussion of the main approaches to theorising innovation follows.

A number of approaches to theorising technological innovation exist, but this chapter will concentrate on just the main three: Innovation Diffusion (Rogers, 1995, 2003), the Technology Acceptance Model (TAM) (F. D. Davis, 1986, 1989; Fred D. Davis, Bagozzi, & Warshaw, 1989) and Innovation Translation (Callon, 1986; Latour, 1996), giving brief mention to the Theory of Reasoned Action (Ajzen & Fishbein, 1980; Fishbein & Ajzen, 1975) and the Theory of Planned Behaviour (Ajzen, 1991). Other approaches to theorising innovation including: Social Cognitive Theory (Bandura, 1986), the Decomposed Theory of Planned Behaviour (Taylor & Todd, 1995), the Technology Acceptance Model 2 (Venkatesh & Davis, 2000), Augmented TAM or Combined TAM and TPB (Taylor & Todd, 1995) and the Unified Theory of Acceptance and Use of Technology (Venkatesh, Morris, Davis, & Davis, 2003). These approaches are, however, not fundamentally different to Innovation Diffusion and TAM, but rather variants on these.

Figure 1. The Technology acceptance model (Fred D. Davis, et al., 1989)

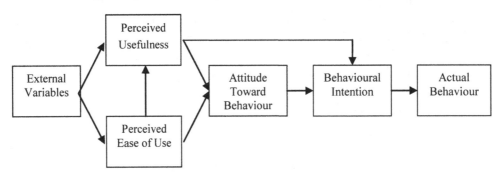

The Theory of Reasoned Action (TRA)

TRA (Ajzen & Fishbein, 1980; Fishbein & Ajzen, 1975) integrated various studies on attitude from social psychology with the aim of developing an integrated conceptual framework to predict and explain an individual's behaviour towards adoption in a general situational setting. Its designers postulated that an individual's *behavioural intention* is the immediate determinant of behaviour, their *attitude* and *subjective norm* are mediated through behavioural intention and their behavioural and normative beliefs are mediated through attitude and subjective norm.

The Theory of Planned Behaviour (TPB)

In TPB, Ajzen (1991) extended the Theory of Reasoned Action as he noted that it was designed to predict and explain behaviour, or actions, based on the assumption that the behaviour was under a person's volitional control. Ajzen argued that some behaviour that is not under a person's volitional control might be problematic due to the differences in individuals' abilities and in external forces. The modification to create TPB involved adding another construct called *perceived behavioural control*, which refers to an individual's perception of the "… presence or absence of requisite resources and opportunities"

(Ajzen & Madden, 1986:457) required to perform the specific behaviour.

The Technology Acceptance Model (TAM)

Davis (1989) developed and validated measures for predicting and explaining adoption and use of technology which focus on two theoretical constructs: *perceived usefulness* and *perceived ease of use*. These were theorised to be fundamental determinants of system use (Kripanont, 2007). TAM assumes that a computer user normally acts rationally and uses information in a systematic manner to decide whether or not to adopt this particular technology in the workplace. As shown in Figure 1 below, Davis (1986) identified major determinants of technology acceptance and, beginning with the Theory of Reasoned Action, specified a basis for causal links between the technology's perceived usefulness and perceived ease of use along with the individual's *attitude towards using technology* and *behavioural intention* to explain technology adoption (F. D. Davis, 1986, 1989; Fred D. Davis, et al., 1989).

TAM theorises that the effects of external variables (such as system characteristics, development processes or training) on intention to use the technology are mediated by perceived usefulness and perceive ease of use. Perceived usefulness is also influenced by perceived ease of use because if other things are equal, the easier the system (technology) is, the more useful it can be (Venkatesh & Davis, 2000). TAM assumes that usage of a particular technology is voluntary (F.D. Davis, 1989), and that given sufficient time and knowledge about a particular behavioural activity, an individual's stated preference to perform the activity (i.e. behavioural intention) will in fact closely resemble the way they do behave. TAM also has strong behavioural elements and assumes that when someone forms an intention to act, they will be free to act without limitation (Kripanont, 2007).

Diffusion of Innovations

Rogers describes the Diffusion of Innovations as: "… the process by which an innovation is communicated through certain channels over time among the members of social systems" (Rogers, 1995:5), and so a decision not to adopt an innovation relates to the rejection of the new idea. Rogers asserts that a technological innovation embodies information, and that this information has the potential to reduce uncertainty. He distinguishes between two kinds of information: *software information* that is embodied in the technology (or idea) itself, and *innovation-evaluation information* that relates to an innovation's expected adoption consequences (Rogers, 1995, 2003). Diffusion is thus considered to be an information exchange process amongst members of a communicating social network driven by the need to reduce uncertainty. Rogers considers the four main elements of innovation to be: *characteristics of the innovation, the communication channels, the passage of time,* and *the social system.* To explain the rate of adoption of innovations Rogers suggests consideration of the following perceived characteristics of innovations: *relative advantage, compatibility, complexity, trialability* and *observability* (Tatnall, 2005).

Innovation Translation

The view of innovation proposed by Actor-Network Theory (ANT), sometimes know as a

Sociology or Translations, considers the world to be full of hybrid entities (Latour, 1993) containing both human and non-human elements, and offers the notion of heterogeneity to help in the explanation of technology adoption (Tatnall & Davey, 2007). More specifically though, Innovation Translation (Latour, 1986, 1996; Law & Callon, 1988), informed by ANT, makes use of a model of technological innovation which uses these ideas, along with the concept that innovations are often not adopted in their entirety but only after 'translation' into a form that is more appropriate for use by the potential adopter.

Callon et al. (1983) propose that translation involves all the strategies through which an actor identifies other actors and arranges them in relation to each other, while Latour (1996) speaks of how 'chains of translation' can transform a global problem, such as the transportation needs of a city like Paris (or the design of a new information system) into a local problem like continuous transportation (or using Visual Basic to obtain data from an Oracle database).

Latour (1986) maintains that in an innovation translation model the movement of an innovation through time and space is in the hands of people, each of whom may react to it in different ways: they may modify it, deflect it, betray it, add to it, appropriate it, or let it drop. He adds that this is true for the spread of anything from goods and artefacts to claims and ideas and that the adoption of an innovation comes as a consequence of the actions of everyone in the chain of actors who has anything to do with it. He suggests that each of these actors shapes the innovation to their own ends, but if no one takes up the innovation then its movement simply stops. Here, instead of a process of transmission, we have a process of continuous transformation (Latour, 1996) where faithful acceptance involving no changes is a rarity requiring explanation. "Instead of the transmission of the same token – simply deflected or slowed down by friction – you get ... the continuous transformation of the token." (Latour, 1986:286).

McMaster et al. (1997) note that innovations do not wait passively to be invented or discovered, but that each actor translates and contributes its own resources to the final result (Tatnall & Gilding, 1999). A translation model requires the focus to be on understanding how actor-networks are created, strengthened and weakened, rather than on cause and effect (McMaster, et al., 1997).

Latour (1996) suggests that with the translation model the initial idea hardly counts and the innovation is not endowed with autonomous power or 'propelled by a brilliant inventor', but moves only if it interests one group of actors or another. Movement of the innovation is a consequence of energy given to it by everyone in the chain and when the innovation does interest a new group they transform it a little or perhaps a lot. Latour notes that, except in rare cases, there can be 'no transportation without transformation', and that "... after many recruitments, displacements and transformations, the project, having *become* real, then manifests, perhaps, the characteristics of perfection, profitability, beauty, and efficiency that the diffusion model located in the starting point." (Latour, 1996:119)

Technological Innovation and Essentialism

Grint and Woolgar (1997) contend that most views of technology attribute an "essential inner core of technical characteristics" (Grint & Woolgar, 1997:9) to the non-human elements, while portraying the human elements as secondary and transitory. They contend that contemporary ideas of technology often still rely on the idea of an essential capacity within a technological entity which accounts for its degree of acceptance or rejection, but argue that technology would be better thought of as being constructed entirely through human interpretation. A significant problem with an essentialist paradigm arises if a researcher tries to reconcile the views of all parties involved in the innovation on what *particular* essences are

significant. The difficulty is that people often see *different* 'essential attributes' in any specific technological or human entity, making it hard to identify and settle on the ones that allegedly were responsible for the adoption (Tatnall, 2002).

For example, what are the essential characteristics of a Four Wheel Drive (4WD) vehicle as seen by each of the following groups: cross country driving/camping enthusiast, travelling salesperson, young male driver, mother taking her kids to school, others ...? The problem, of course, is that each group see these characteristics quite differently. The cross country driving enthusiast will, of course, be interested primarily in the off-road aspects of the vehicle, but these will be of little interest to the mother taking her kids to school. The travelling salesperson will be concerned with the amount of space in the vehicle for goods and sales samples, while the young male driver is probably more concerned with the appearance and dominance of the vehicle. How do you then decide which characteristics led to its adoption?

EXAMPLES COMPARING EACH APPROACH

In this next section I will present and discuss several research example of the use of each approach to theorising technological innovation in the adoption of different artefacts. For each of these examples data was obtained by semi-structured interviews with the human protagonists, and from documents and discussions with other humans on behalf of the non-human actors.

Adoption of a Slide and Negative Scanner by an SME

The members of a small Australian publishing company do all their own pre-publication preparation (Tatnall, 2002). When they accept the final version of a manuscript from an author, one of them does the copy editing while another designs the cover. In the mid-1990s this small to medium enterprise (SME) decided it needed to improve the appearance of its covers and several options were considered until someone thought of using a photograph as the cover background. The problem was that most of the suitable photographs they had were not in digital format but in the form of colour slides and printed pictures (- this was before the time when everyone owned a digital camera!). The question then was how to convert these photographs into a suitable digital format to print on the cover along with the cover text. The solution decided upon was to purchase a slide and negative scanner that considerably improved the quality of the covers, also making the process of producing them much simpler. But what made them decide to adopt this particular item of technology?

Using an Innovation Diffusion approach the researcher would have considered the company to have been mainly influenced by attributes and characteristics of the technology itself. The researcher would investigate whether the directors had considered the relative advantage, compatibility, complexity, trialability and observability of this technology compared with the alternatives of using a flat-bed scanner, getting an outside printer to do the scanning, or not using a cover of this type at all. In this particular case the directors certainly did see some relative advantage in using the slide scanner, particularly as they both had large numbers of colour slides that they had taken over the years. There was, however, one major disadvantage of this technology and that was its high cost: the slide scanner was around four times as expensive as a good flat-bed scanner. The slide scanner also did not come out well on compatibility or complexity as it was quite different, and much more complex to use than the flat-bed scanner alternative. It was possible for the company to arrange trial use of the scanner, which was lucky as it had proved difficult to find anyone else using one and so its observability was

low. On this basis it is difficult to see why they would have adopted it at all.

With TAM, the researcher would need to look at whether the members of the company thought that a slide scanner would be a useful investment to meet their needs, and whether they thought it would be easy to use. It would conclude that unless these requirements were met, purchase and adoption of the slide scanner would not proceed.

When an Innovation Translation model is applied, however, the situation is seen quite differently. The socio-technical network consisting of the publishing company personnel, their computers, and their books was destabilised by the need to find a new way of producing book covers. The slide scanner (also seen as an actor seeking to enter the network) offered a new problematisation in which existing (and future) slides and negatives could easily be turned into digital images. Part of this problematisation was that *any* of the directors' old slides could easily be turned into digital images, not just those required for book covers. As well as the main application of producing book covers, the directors quickly saw advantages in a device that could also easily convert the old slides and negatives they had each taken of their children and of their holidays into digital format: this seemed to provide a good alternative to their ageing slide projectors, and produced a strong interessement in favour of this technology and against flat-bed scanners. It was thus a combination of factors, some business-related and others rather more personal, that the Translation model suggests could be seen as leading to the enrolment of this technology and hence its adoption.

Adoption of Mobile E-Training in a Factory

A large factory is keen to ensure that its workers are well trained to safely use all its new machinery and equips each employee with a Tablet PC fitted with wireless networking containing delivery software and a profiling program for the particular employee. Each factory machine has its own operating procedures, and details of safety considerations are stored in the machine. As an employee moves through the factory to use different machines this safety information is made available through wireless networking. Software on the machine recognises the Tablet PC of a new operator and automatically downloads content to this Tablet PC which configures it to what it has determined to be the learning style of the employee (Tatnall & Davey, 2003). Although factory management issues each employee with their own Tablet PC, encouraging or forcing them to use it is another matter. What factors determine the likelihood or adoption of this innovation?

With a TAM approach the researcher would look at the factory workers' behavioural intention to use the technology, based on whether the researcher thought that they perceived the technology to be easy to use and whether they perceived it to be useful to them. The researcher would need to speak with the factory workers in an to attempt to determine this. While using an Innovation Diffusion approach the researcher would begin by looking at how employees and management regarded the characteristics of the technology and whether it was useful or easy to use, in an actor-network analysis the researcher would first identify as many as possible of the (human and non-human) actors. In this case some of these actors are obvious: factory employees, management, factory machines, learning packages, Tablet PC, wireless networking, delivery software and the profiling program. But there may well also be other actors. The way to proceed now is to interview the actors. While it might seem odd to speak of 'interviewing' the non-humans, this is done by looking at instruction manuals, speaking to various humans about them, investigating how, and why, they were built and any other techniques that simulate an interview situation. One of the things that will arise in these 'interviews' is the existence of other actors not identified earlier. We then proceed to 'follow the actors' (Latour, 1996) in determining what is important and what is not.

With the ANT approach discovering networks of associations and interactions comes next. If the employer-employee relationship in this company is such that the workers are suspicious of any initiative coming from management then this is likely to be significant. At this stage we attempt not to judge the likely consequences to potential adoption, just to note this interaction. Most of the other interactions are between the factory workers and various non-human actors. In common with an approach using Innovation Diffusion we would investigate how they use the machines; is this simple and straightforward, or is it difficult and clumsy? What about the interactions with each of the computer-based technologies? How does the employee interact with the learning package? Do they like using the Tablet PC? Do they find carrying it around a nuisance? How does management view these technologies? Do they have any interactions with them? How did they decide on the learning package? Why did they decide to use mobile technologies rather than a training room? One difference between these approaches to theorising innovation is that Innovation Diffusion concentrates more of the characteristics of the technology and TAM looks at its perceived usefulness and ease of use, while Innovation Translation tries to look beyond this to investigate the human and non-human interactions involved.

Adoption of a PC-Based Accounting System by an SME

Suppose that you were researching how an Australian SME, which had previously done its accounting manually, was now considering the adoption of a PC-based accounting system. If you were using an Innovation Diffusion approach you would probably begin by considering the characteristics of PC-based accounting systems (Tatnall, 2001, 2002). For each of these you might look at its functionality, its compatibility with those used by accountants, its ease of use and so on, and then how these characteristics might help or hinder its adoption. You might then look at the channels through which the SME learned about this innovation: their accountant, the business press, training courses or friends from other companies, and how effective these were in delivering the message. Next you might consider aspects of the 'culture' of the SME; things like whether it was a family business, how much money it was prepared to spend, and the type of work it does.

With a TAM approach you would try to find out whether those people working in the SME thought that a PC-based accounting system would be easy to use and whether it would be more useful to them than a manual approach in doing their accounting work. You would then look at the likelihood that these intentions would result in action to purchase and adopt such a system.

With an Innovation Translation approach, on the other hand, you would concentrate on issues of network formation and investigate the human and non-human alliances and networks built up by the SME, their customers, the technology, and other actors involved in the implementation. Concentrating on the negotiations that allow the network to be configured by the enrolment of both human and non-human allies would be important. You would consider the accounting system's characteristics only as network effects resulting from association. ANT would suggest that it is not any innate properties of these systems that are important, but rather network associations such as the extent to which the business has been enrolled in the time-saving possibilities for use in calculating GST provisions and other things. You would look at the process of re-definition in which the SME tried to seek compromises from the accounting package, and how the accounting package sought to impose definitions of professional accounting and formal documentation on them; how it 'interested' the business and then got them to follow its interests, so becoming in-

dispensable to them. In this case what was then finally adopted for this task was probably not the accounting package originally examined as such, but a translation of this package in which it becomes a tool for their specific use (Tatnall, 2001, 2002).

Retired People Adopting the Internet and E-Commerce

One reason often given by retired people (Bosler, 2001; Gross, 1998) for adopting Internet technologies is, quite simply so that the world does not pass them by and so that they won't be left out of things. The means of social interaction is increasingly moving away from posting letters to e-mail, and those not using e-mail are finding it harder to keep in touch. Many retired people are finding that an e-mail address is becoming essential (Perry, 2000; Tatnall & Lepa, 2003) in order to converse sensibly with their overseas friends and with their grandchildren (Alexander, 2000; Lepa & Tatnall, 2006). These, and related reasons for adoption of Internet technologies such as "All my friends use e-mail and I'll be left out if I don't" (Council on the Ageing, 2000) suggest that characteristics of the technology have less to do with *things* than do social interactions and the creation and maintenance of interpersonal networks.

For retired people the issue of whether or not to adopt Internet technologies has been problematised (Callon, 1986) not as one that relates to diverse characteristics of the technology or to ease of use, but as one *largely* of communication and keeping in touch with family and friends. The Internet has been *translated* here to include a means by which these people can maintain their place in society and keep relevant to their family and friends (Bosler, 2001). What they have adopted is not the Internet as a business might know it, but a translation of the Internet resulting in technology that offers a means of maintaining contact with the world (Tatnall, 2000).

For some years now the banks have been changing the problematisation of banking from an activity carried out in-person in suburban branches to one undertaken using ATMs and the Internet. In doing this they are translating banking from a social activity to an electronic one. Many older people have resisted this change as is demonstrated by their reluctance as a group to adopt electronic banking (Tatnall & Lepa, 2001). This also is changing, and research into this topic needs to consider much more than just the 'superior' characteristics of electronic banking as might be suggested by an Innovation Diffusion approach. Perhaps TAM's constructs of perceived ease of use and usefulness in the minds of these older people might be used to explain this, but other influences such as peer group and family pressure, that would be picked up by an ANT approach, would be missed by TAM.

Adoption of the Bizewest Portal

In 2001 the Western Region Economic Development Organisation (WREDO) in Melbourne began operation of a business-to-business portal for use by small to medium enterprises. This innovative project, funded from a Government 'e-commerce early movers' grant, was to create a horizontal portal – Bizewest, which would enable SMEs in Melbourne's west to engage in e-commerce transactions with each other (Tatnall, 2007a; Tatnall & Burgess, 2002). Although quite a large number of businesses had joined with Bizewest by late 2002, a proposal at this time to introduce an annual fee to cover the costs of hosting the portal was not well received. The grant to set up the portal provided no funds for on-going maintenance and enhancement, and Bizewest was running out of money. In early 2003 the WREDO Board began considering options for the Bizewest portal, and in June 2003 reluctantly terminated its operation. The birth and death of the portal makes an interesting study.

A number of interviews were undertaken in the early stages of portal implementation to determine why different SMEs had decided to adopt the Bizewest portal. Some excerpts from a few of these follow, the first being from a medium-sized company that stores frozen food and transports it to supermarkets and other locations around the country. The general manager described benefits in adopting the portal in terms of time savings and better service. "I think it will probably just give us a chance to give the client a quicker on-line communication to know where his stock is – when it is arriving, when it's gone out, and that it is the right stuff come and gone." (Tatnall & Burgess, 2004). A major reason that this company adopted the portal, however, was in the hope that it would provide a better opportunity to deal with people in the local region (Tatnall & Burgess, 2004). He said that although he did not understand much about the portal or what it would do he thought that it was "a really good idea" and was going to provide many benefits for everybody in the region (Tatnall & Pliaskin, 2007). What this company then adopted was not the Bizewest portal in its entirety but a translation of it to become a means to deal better with people in the local region.

The next business interviewed was a small printing company where the manager remarked: "It was a great opportunity to get in at the ground floor and be one of the front runners and really I suppose that the earlier that you are in the better chance you have of reaching those new clients". He then went on to add: "The other thing was that being a small company, advertising can be quite expensive, and we thought that if we can get this free it would be fantastic." (Pliaskin & Tatnall, 2005). This business wanted to translate the portal primarily to become a means of advertising, and were not really interested in most of its other features. Another response was from the IT Manager of a small textile company: "I think the way that we will go is like many businesses; we will dip our toe in the water and do some basic ordering: stationery that's a common one." This also involved a translation of the portal, this time to become just a means for ordering supplies (Tatnall, 2007a).

A simplistic view of the portal adoption decisions would have it that the businesses involved made these decisions primarily because of the portal's characteristics or ease of use. Research, however, shows (Tatnall & Burgess, 2002) this not to be the case as interviews with the business proprietors indicated that business needs and expectations were a much more significant factor and in each case indicated that reasons for adoption were not closely related to the characteristics of the technology itself as the theory of Innovation Diffusion (Rogers, 1995) would suggest. This research also suggests that the potential users did not consider ease of use or even usefulness as TAM would require. Most of the companies that adopted the portal early knew little about the technology but were excited by the concept of getting onto the Web and just wanted to be involved. Many businesses adopting the portal did so because it seemed to them to be 'a good idea' rather than because they had any clear idea of its benefits. Few had looked objectively at the characteristics of portal technology or business-to-business e-commerce, and common reasons for adoption included: "If other businesses adopt it and we don't we will be left behind." "All the talk is about e-commerce and how it is the way of the future." and "My kids tell me that everyone will be on the Internet soon and we had better be too" (Tatnall & Pliaskin, 2005).

When put together with similar responses from other portal users it seems that the reason for the portal's initial success and later failure was that many SMEs adopted because it seemed to them to be 'a good idea' rather than because they had any clear idea of its benefits. The portal's initial success was because of the excitement generated by this new technology and because WREDO was well trusted. It had little to do with any evaluation of the technology itself and everything to do with WREDO's problematisation of the portal and its success in interesting them in the portal's possibilities, even if they did not fully understand them. It finally failed for these same reasons (Tatnall, 2007a).

Information Systems and Rural GPs

Over the last 15 years much research and development has been undertaken on the use of Medical Information Technology. In this time many Information and Communications Technology (ICT) products have been developed to support Medical General Practitioners (GP) in all aspects of their work in Australia (GPSRG, 1998), but despite this development effort many GPs are still reluctance to make full use of ICT. This is particularly true of GPs working in rural areas in Australia (Everitt & Tatnall, 2003; Tatnall, et al., 2004). If GPs are not making as much use of these systems as they could, the question then is: if these ICT products have been specially developed for GPs, then why are GPs reluctant to use them?

Increases in the complexity of health care delivery and continual increases in costs have increased the need for finding better ways of managing medical practice. While one might expect that, being highly educated professionals, most GPs would be at the forefront of the information management revolution, research shows that particularly in rural Australia this is not entirely the case (Everitt & Tatnall, 2003). When General Practices do use ICT it is often for basic record keeping only, and in many instances the GPs themselves are seen to make little of no use of ICT (Burgess & Trethowan, 2002). In the late 1990s the General Practice Strategy Review Group (GPSRG, 1998) identified a number of socio-technical reasons for the slow uptake of ICT by GPs. These included: concerns about privacy and confidentiality, concerns about a computer on the desk interfering with consultations, costs, the lack of any obvious benefit for GPs, the lack of suitable hardware and software, concerns about ICT reliability, and lack of skills and support.

This study (Deering, 2008) investigated GPs' uptake of ICT in a Division of General Practice in Central Victoria. This grouping of GPs is one of over 100 such Divisions around Australia and is primarily funded by the Commonwealth Department of Health and Aged Care to link General Practitioners with each other and to link GPs with their communities to improve health outcomes (Everitt & Tatnall, 2003). One of the main findings of the study was that it is important to note the difference between the adoption of ICT by General Practice and adoption and use by the General Practitioners themselves (Deering, 2008). The adoption process has been complex and many stakeholders have grappled with issues such as the cost of computerisation, the rapid changes in technology, the lack of agreed standards and the problems of introducing ICT solutions in to the daily work place of general practice. The study was undertaken through case studies and extended interviews, and revealed a number of interesting findings. In one case the reason for non-adoption of ICT in a particular medical practice had nothing to do with the technology itself, but was because the present Practice Principal's father was not comfortable with ICT. He was not far off retirement but still practicing at the time, and no one wanted to make him feel uncomfortable by introducing technology with which he was unfamiliar. The practice manager said this was never articulated openly but all knew it was so (Deering, 2008).

A modern medical practice is expected to have computerised, and ICT in general practice is now taken as a given. In many cases though, what the practice has adopted is not all aspects of medical ICT but a *translation* of this to fulfil the administrative needs of the practice, rather than to provide specific support for the GP through the use of electronic clinical decision-making support software. This can be well explained using innovation translation.

CONCLUSION

This chapter has illustrated some of the significant advantages of using an Innovation Translation approach to the theorising of innovation adoptions. Despite this, however, it is far too simplistic to suggest that Innovation Translation offers a better approach than Innovation Diffusion or TAM to theorising innovation in *all* situations. Many studies have shown the explanatory value of Innovation Diffusion, particularly in relation to large scale adoptions such as (to offer some samples from Rogers (1995)): bottle-feeding of babies in the third world, the diffusion of modern maths in Pittsburgh, diffusion of the News and the diffusion of a medical drug.

It might be suggested that the relationship between these two types of approach: Innovation Diffusion and TAM on the one hand and Innovation Translation on the other, has something in common to that between the macro and micro elements of Newtonian and quantum mechanics in physics. While quantum mechanics is needed to explain what goes on when fundamental particles and atoms interact, for everyday occurrences Newtonian mechanics is quite suitable. Likewise I would suggest that while Actor-Network Theory and Innovation Translation better explain the detail of how individuals and specific organisations adopt technological innovations, Innovation Diffusion does a good job in explaining large scale adoptions.

Perhaps I am being a little unfair, but personally I cannot see much value in the explanatory value of TAM, as reliance on perceived usefulness and perceived ease of use seems rather obvious and of little value in understanding what is really going on and why some innovations are adopted in one way in one place and another in a different situation. After effectively ruling out TAM, perhaps it should not be a case of using *either* Innovation Diffusion or Innovation Translation but whichever of these approaches is most appropriate to each particular investigation.

REFERENCES

Ajzen, I. (1991). The Theory of Planned Behavior. *Organizational Behavior and Human Decision Processes, 50*(2), 179–211. doi:10.1016/0749-5978(91)90020-T

Ajzen, I., & Fishbein, M. (1980). *Understanding Attitudes and Predicting Social Behavior. London*. Englewood Cliffs: Prentice-Hall.

Ajzen, I., & Madden, T. (1986). Prediction of Goal-Directed Behavior: Attitudes, Intentions, and Perceived Behavioral Control. *Journal of Experimental Social Psychology, 22*, 453–474. doi:10.1016/0022-1031(86)90045-4

Al-Hajri, S., & Tatnall, A. (2007, 4-6 June 2007). *Internet Technology in Omani Banks – a Case of Adoption at a Slower Rate*. Paper presented at the 20th Bled e-Conference - eMergence: Merging and Emerging Technologies, Processes and Institutions Bled, Slovenia.

Alexander, M. (2000, 23 April 2000). Be Online or Be Left Behind - the Older Crowd Head for Cyberspace. *Boston Globe*.

Bandura, A. (1986). *Social Foundations of Thought and Action: a Social Cognitive Theory*. Englewood Cliffs, NJ: Prentice-Hall.

Bosler, N. (2001, 22 May 2001). *Communication, E-Commerce and Older People*. Paper presented at the E-Commerce, Electronic Banking and Older People, Melbourne.

Burgess, S., & Trethowan, P. (2002, April). *GPs and their Web sites in Australia: Doctors as Small Businesses*. Paper presented at the IS OneWorld, Las Vegas.

Callon, M. (1986). Some Elements of a Sociology of Translation: Domestication of the Scallops and the Fishermen of St Brieuc Bay. In Law, J. (Ed.), *Power, Action & Belief. A New Sociology of Knowledge?* (pp. 196–229). London: Routledge & Kegan Paul.

Callon, M., Courtial, J. P., Turner, W. A., & Bauin, S. (1983). From Translations to Problematic Networks: An Introduction to Co-Word Analysis. *Social Sciences Information. Information Sur les Sciences Sociales, 22*(2), 191–235. doi:10.1177/053901883022002003

Council on the Ageing. (2000). Older People and the Internet Focus Group: Unpublished.

Davis, F. D. (1986). *A Technology Acceptance Model for Empirically Testing New End-User Information Systems: Theory and Results*. Boston: MIT.

Davis, F. D. (1989). Perceived usefulness, perceived ease of use and user acceptance of information technology. *Management Information Systems Quarterly, 13*(3), 319–340. doi:10.2307/249008

Davis, F. D. (1989). Perceived Usefulness, Perceived Ease of Use, and User Acceptance of Information Technology. *Management Information Systems Quarterly, 13*(3), 318–340. doi:10.2307/249008

Davis, F. D., Bagozzi, R., & Warshaw, P. (1989). User Acceptance of Computer Technology: A Comparison of Two Theoretical Models. *Management Science, 35*(8), 982–1003. doi:10.1287/mnsc.35.8.982

Deering, P. (2008). *The Adoption of Information and Communication Technologies in Rural General Practice: A Socio Technical Analysis*. Melbourne: Victoria University.

Everitt, P., & Tatnall, A. (2003). *Investigating the Adoption and Use of Information Technology by General Practitioners in Rural Australia and Why This is Less Than it Might Be*. Paper presented at the ACIS 2003, Perth.

Fishbein, M., & Ajzen, I. (1975). *Belief, Attitude, Intention, and Behavior: An Introduction to Theory and Research*. Reading, MA: Addison-Wesley.

GPSRG. (1998). *Changing the Future Through Partnerships.* Canberra: Commonwealth Department of Health and Family Services, General Practice Strategy Review Group.

Grint, K., & Woolgar, S. (1997). *The Machine at Work - Technology, Work and Organisation.* Cambridge: Polity Press.

Gross, J. (1998, 1998). Wielding Mouse and Modem, Elderly Remain in the Loop. *The New York Times.*

Kripanont, N. (2007). *Examining a Technology Acceptance Model of Internet Usage by Academics within Thai Business Schools.* Melbourne: Victoria University.

Latour, B. (1986). The Powers of Association. In Law, J. (Ed.), *Power, Action and Belief. A New Sociology of Knowledge? Sociological Review monograph 32* (pp. 264–280). London: Routledge & Kegan Paul.

Latour, B. (1993). *We Have Never Been Modern* (Porter, C., Trans.). Cambridge, MA: Harvester University Press.

Latour, B. (1996). *Aramis or the Love of Technology.* Cambridge, Ma: Harvard University Press.

Law, J., & Callon, M. (1988). Engineering and Sociology in a Military Aircraft Project: A Network Analysis of Technological Change. *Social Problems, 35*(3), 284–297. doi:10.1525/sp.1988.35.3.03a00060

Lepa, J., & Tatnall, A. (2006). Using Actor-Network Theory to Understanding Virtual Community Networks of Older People Using the Internet. *Journal of Business Systems. Governance and Ethics, 1*(4), 1–14.

Machiavelli, N. (1515). *The Prince* (1995th ed.). (Bull, G., Trans.). London: Penguin Classics.

Maguire, C., Kazlauskas, E. J., & Weir, A. D. (1994). *Information Services for Innovative Organizations.* Sandiego, CA: Academic Press.

McMaster, T., Vidgen, R. T., & Wastell, D. G. (1997, 9-12 August, 1997). *Towards an Understanding of Technology in Transition. Two Conflicting Theories.* Paper presented at the Information Systems Research in Scandinavia, IRIS20 Conference, Hanko, Norway.

Oxford (1973). *The Shorter Oxford English Dictionary* (3rd edition (reprinted with corrections and revisions) ed.). Oxford: Clarendon Press.

Perry, J. (2000). Retirees stay wired to kids - and to one another. *U.S. News & World Report, ¾¾¾,* 22.

Pliaskin, A., & Tatnall, A. (2005). Developing a Portal to Build a Business Community. In Tatnall, A. (Ed.), *Web Portals: The New Gateways to Internet Information and Services* (pp. 335–348). Hershey, PA: Idea Group Publishing.

Rogers, E. M. (1995). *Diffusion of Innovations* (4th ed.). New York: The Free Press.

Rogers, E. M. (2003). *Diffusion of Innovations* (5th ed.). New York: The Free Press.

Tatnall, A. (2000). *Innovation and Change in the Information Systems Curriculum of an Australian University: a Socio-Technical Perspective.* Central Queensland University, Rockhampton.

Tatnall, A. (2001, 20-23 May 2001). *Adoption of Information Technology by Small Business - Two Different Approaches to Modelling Innovation.* Paper presented at the Managing Information Technology in a Global Economy - (IRMA'2001), Toronto, Canada.

Tatnall, A. (2002). Modelling Technological Change in Small Business: Two Approaches to Theorising Innovation. In Burgess, S. (Ed.), *Managing Information Technology in Small Business: Challenges and Solutions* (pp. 83–97). Hershey, PA: Idea Group Publishing.

Tatnall, A. (2005). Technological Change in Small Organisations: An Innovation Translation Perspective. *International Journal of Knowledge. Culture and Change Management, 4*(1), 755–761.

Tatnall, A. (2007a, 4-6 June 2007). *Business Culture and the Death of a Portal.* Paper presented at the 20th Bled e-Conference - eMergence: Merging and Emerging Technologies, Processes and Institutions Bled, Slovenia.

Tatnall, A. (2007b). Innovation, Lifelong Learning and the ICT Professional. In Tatnall, A., Thompson, J. B., & Edwards, H. (Eds.), *Education, Training and Lifelong Learning* (pp. 92–101). Laxenburg, Austria: IFIP.

Tatnall, A., & Burgess, S. (2002, June 2002). *Using Actor-Network Theory to Research the Implementation of a B-B Portal for Regional SMEs in Melbourne, Australia.* Paper presented at the 15th Bled Electronic Commerce Conference - 'eReality: Constructing the eEconomy', Bled, Slovenia.

Tatnall, A., & Burgess, S. (2004). Using Actor-Network Theory to Identify Factors Affecting the Adoption of E-Commerce in SMEs. In Singh, M., & Waddell, D. (Eds.), *E-Business: Innovation and Change Management* (pp. 152–169). Hershey, PA: IRM Press.

Tatnall, A., & Dai, W. (2007, 18-20 August 2007). *Adoption of Collaborative Real-Time Information Services: a Study in Technological Innovation.* Paper presented at the 13th Cross-Strait Academic Conference on Development and Strategies of Information Management Beijing Jiaotong University, Beijing, China.

Tatnall, A., & Davey, B. (2003). Modelling the Adoption of Web-Based Mobile Learning - an Innovation Translation Approach. In W. Zhou, P. Nicholson, B. Corbitt & J. Fong (Eds.), *Advances in Web-Based Learning* (Vol. LNCS 2783, pp. 433-441). Berlin: Springer Verlag.

Tatnall, A., & Davey, B. (2007, 19-23 May 2007). *Researching the Portal.* Paper presented at the IRMA: Managing Worldwide Operations and Communications with Information Technology, Vancouver.

Tatnall, A., Everitt, P., Wenn, A., Burgess, S., Sellitto, C., & Darbyshire, P. (2004). A Study of the Adoption of Information and Communications Technologies by Rural General Practitioners in Australia. In Hunter, M. G., & Dhanda, K. K. (Eds.), *Information Systems: Exploring Applications in Business and Government* (pp. 232–253). Washington, DC: The Information Institute.

Tatnall, A., & Gilding, A. (1999). *Actor-Network Theory and Information Systems Research.* Paper presented at the 10th Australasian Conference on Information Systems (ACIS), Wellington.

Tatnall, A., & Lepa, J. (2001, December 2001). *Researching the Adoption of E-Commerce and the Internet by Older People.* Paper presented at the We-B Conference, Perth.

Tatnall, A., & Lepa, J. (2003). The Internet, E-Commerce and Older People: an Actor-Network Approach to Researching Reasons for Adoption and Use. *Logistics Information Management, 16*(1), 56–63. doi:10.1108/09576050310453741

Tatnall, A., & Pliaskin, A. (2005, September 2005). *Technological Innovation and the Non-Adoption of a B-B Portal.* Paper presented at the Second International Conference on Innovations in Information technology, Dubai, UAE.

Tatnall, A., & Pliaskin, A. (2007). The Demise of a Business-to-Business Portal. In Radaideh, M. A., & Al-Ameed, H. (Eds.), *Architecture of Reliable Web Applications Software* (pp. 147–171). Hershey, PA: Idea Group Publishing.

Taylor, S., & Todd, P. (1995). Understanding Information Technology Usage: A Test of Competing Models. *Information Systems Research, 6*(2), 144–176. doi:10.1287/isre.6.2.144

Venkatesh, V., & Davis, F. (2000). A Theoretical Extension of the Technology Acceptance Model: Four Longitudinal Field Studies. *Management Science, 46*(2), 186–204. doi:10.1287/mnsc.46.2.186.11926

Venkatesh, V., Morris, M. G., Davis, G. B., & Davis, F. D. (2003). User Acceptance of Information Technology: Toward a Unified View. *Management Information Systems Quarterly, 27*(3), 425–478.

Section 2

Chapter 5

Translating Biofuel, Discounting Farmers:
The Search for Alternative Energy in Indonesia

Yuti Ariani
Institute of Technology Bandung, Indonesia

Sonny Yuliar
Institute of Technology Bandung, Indonesia

ABSTRACT

This paper employs the notion of translation introduced in ANT literature to study the current bio-fuel development in Indonesia. Despite the presence of some activities by scientists, businessmen, policy makers, and farmers, diffusion of bio-fuel innovation seems to remain very limited. The paper aims at understanding the bio-fuel development trajectory by seeking to disclose a variety of elements that shape the trajectory. We also make use of the notion of 'qualculation', to further diagnose the trajectory. Bio-fuel translations generated by three different scientists are described in the paper. We show that the translations follow specific patterns of qualculation, namely 'proliferation' and 'rarefaction'. We use this to make sense of the current diffusion of bio-fuel innovation in Indonesia. Beside this contextual result, the paper also seeks to contribute to ANT literature by exploring the concept of qualculation in the analysis of technological innovation.

INTRODUCTION

Bio-fuel development activities in Indonesia have been intensified and wide spreading since early 2005. Scientists from major Indonesian universities have been involved in an 'invention race' by offering calculations and efficient solutions, and thousands of rural farmers have taken voluntary steps to cultivate and harvest energy plants. Top level bureaucrats and elite politicians have been in prolonged debates to defend what they see as Indonesia's energy crisis problem and its solution. However, until today, despite the variety of laboratory research involving numerous scientists, and billions of rupiah invested in the research, no technical solutions take place on the road. Despite the intensive and extensive research to supply

DOI: 10.4018/978-1-60960-197-3.ch005

technology to solve the energy crisis problem, its diffusion to the benefit of society seems to be very limited, if not totally absent.

The paper aims at understanding the bio-fuel development trajectory by seeking to disclose a variety of elements that shape the trajectory. We use some analytical concepts developed in the actor-network theory literature to achieve that aim. In particular, we deploy the notion of translation to trace the relations of heterogeneous actors that compose the bio-fuel development trajectory. To gain deeper insight into the translations, we equip the analysis by the notion of qualculation, developed by Callon and Law (2003). The field work supporting the paper began in early 2006, taking place in several laboratories in the Institute of Technology Bandung (ITB) and in the agency for technology assessment and application (BPPT), and in two villages in West Java. We also conducted interviews with informants from a variety of government institutions, political parties and mass organizations, and of course, with rural farmers and rural housewives. The 'following the actors' technique advocated by Latour (1987) is employed to trace the relations connecting heterogeneous elements.

THE TECHNICAL AND THE SOCIAL

In the ANT literature, technical and social entities are seen as 'two sides of a single coin' (Latour, 1987; Callon, 1986; Law, 2003). The social is conceived as a patterned network of relations connecting heterogeneous materials (Law, 2003). In the very similar way, scientific facts and the functioning of efficient engines draw resources from heterogeneous elements to support their durability (Latour, 1987). The heterogeneous elements include not only human actors, but also non-human actors. ANT proposes the so-called general symmetry principle that says, basically, in the analysis, human and non-human actors need to be accounted equally (Latour, 2005).

Callon (1986) and Latour (1987) propose the notion of translation to trace how an actor-network comes to existence. Thus actors are involved in a chain of translations to define the role of other actors, to set performance on trials. Network durability may result from translations, as well as network collapse. Callon (1986) goes further by analyzing translations into four moments: problematization, interessement, enrolment and mobilization. The conception of moments of translation serves as an analytical tool. Nevertheless, ANT is not a stability-seeking or equilibrium-seeking theory. As emphasized by its proponents, ANT is a descriptive theory. It seeks to describe the process of entity construction, as well as deconstruction.

The use of ANT in addressing technology assessment problems is conceptualized in the Constructive Technology Assessment (CTA) theory (Rip et al., 1995). CTA seeks to integrate social objectives and criteria by looking closely to the co-evolutionary process that connects technology and society. CTA conceptualization stems from the possibility of modulating technology in the course of its development[1], though it is not an easy task to accomplish (Schot, 1992, p. 37). In their elaboration of the notion of technology modulation and steering, Fisher et al (2006) call for the "reflexive awareness" of actors to become attentive to nested processes, structures, interactions, and interdependencies, both immediate and more removed, within which they operate. They assert that "reflexive awareness" implies equality and open process in a network.

While the notion of reflexive awareness refers to a mental entity, there is another related concept in the ANT literature that refers to a network of heterogeneous entities. That is, the concept of qualculation. This concept is employed by Callon and Law (2003) to discuss rationality and, its opponent, non-rationality. The term 'qualculation' is invented to avoid unnecessary distinction between calculation and, its qualitative counterpart, qualification or judgement. Callon and Law (2003) show that calculation, or qualification, may be conceived as an action of drawing heterogeneous resources, putting them in a single space, ordering, and totalizing. According to them, as long as we are interested in studying agency and action, "if there is a boundary at all, then it is not between the rational and the non-rational but rather between … the qualculable, and the non-qualculable" (Callon and Law, 2003, p. 13). Thus, the concept of qualculation provides us with a tool for empirical analysis, without referent to cognitive or mental entities. Callon and Law (2003) go further by identifying two different patterns of non-qualculation: proliferation and rarefaction. Proliferation refers to the pattern in which actors constantly draw resources that impede proper framing, ordering, and totalization. In the opposite sense, rarefaction is a pattern in which actors constantly withdraw qualculative resources.

INDONESIA'S OIL POLITICS

Since the early 2000s, Indonesia's status as an oil exporting country has been questioned in the energy policy discourse within the country. The climbing crude oil price in international markets has made the crude oil export-import disparity a significant matter in government revenue and expenditure calculation. Given such a situation, the 2004's election winning government had to make a complex calculation: to keep the oil subsidy at a high level and face severely limited budget, or to reduce the subsidy substantially and face the `political attacks from opposing parties that would gain momentum from the conceived social consequences of the subsidy cut-off. In March 2005, the government finalized their calculation and made the decision. It reduced the oil subsidy substantially, lifting up the national oil price 29% higher in March, and 107% in October 2005.

As an attempt to anticipate the social consequences of oil subsidy cut-off, the government devised a compensation program for the poor called direct cash aid (*Bantuan Langsung Tunai*

or BLT). The Government's affiliated economists were calculating the amount of aid based on oil related consumption (such as cooking and daily transportation) of the people living under the poverty line. It turned out to be a round number, that is 100,000 rupiah/month for each poor household. While calculating the cash is relatively simple, the distribution and targeting of the aid turned out to be a cumbersome task. Who should and who should not get the aid? In general, poor fisheries need fuel more (for transportation) than poor rural farmers living in a subsistence economy. And some poor people eat less cooked foods then others. Beside this aid distribution and targeting issues, unemployment numbers were inevitably growing since hundreds of fuel consuming small and medium scale companies could not bear the oil price-induced production cost explosion, and then collapsed. Beyond the economists' calculation, social unrest was wide spread in late 2005.

In response to the oil-induced social crisis, President Yudhoyono urged the need for a 'New Deal' program aimed at solving two problems at one strike: unemployment and oil crisis. Yudhoyono led a restricted cabinet meeting that then resulted in the introduction of a number of presidential decrees to trigger a national scale bio-fuel development program. As the decrees made applicable, it becomes mandatory to all local/district governments to foster the cultivation of fuel producing plantations by mobilizing local farmers and un-used lands. Through the decrees the government also urged Pertamina, the national oil company, to purchase bio-fuel products supplied by local farmers.

Bio-fuel research and development had taken place in Indonesia long before 2005. Since the early 1980s scientists from ITB and BPPT have introduced their bio-fuel researchers to policy makers. In 1981, the government launched the so called General Energy Policy, aimed at promoting bio-fuel development, and stimulating research by public research institutes. This policy succeeded to foster the Center of Starch Technology (*Balai Be-*

sar Teknologi Pati or B2TP) to develop bio-ethanol products. The bio-fuel research and development problem was derived from sustainable environment issues which, at that time, attracted the attention of only a few scientists and government officials. The major national technology program at that time was aircraft technology and industry; a program that drew huge financial sources from (fossil) oil export-based government revenue. For political stability purposes, the government maintained high level of (fossil) oil subsidies for end-use consumption as well as industries. Within such policy circumstances, market demand for bio-fuel products was very limited, if not totally absent. In the early 1990s Pertamina, in partnership with the Agency for Oil and Gas (Lemigas), sought to commercialize a bio-fuel product called B30[2]. But the price was significantly higher than the subsidized fossil-based fuel products in the domestic market[3].

The social crisis triggered bio-fuel development policy in 2005, and the subsequent years, differed significantly from that in the 1980s or 1990s. The 2005 bio-fuel policy derived from social problems, not from environmental problems; it gained wider political support in contrast to that of the 1980s (and 1990s). The presidential decree, named Keppres. No.5/2006, launched in early 2006, calls for "National Energy Mix" sets the target that by 2025, 5% of national energy need is supplied by bio-fuel products. A presidential instruction, named Inpres No.1/2006, defines the objective as the "Supply and Utilization of Bio-fuel as Alternative Fuel." To mobilize resources, the presidential decree, Keppres. No. 10/2006, sets on stage "The National Team for Bio-fuel Development to Accelerate Poverty and Unemployment Reduction." The national team is called the *Tim Nasional untuk pengembangan Bahan Bakar Nabati* (Timnas BBN). Two subsequent government regulations set up the rules of the game. The first is a government regulation, named PP. No. 1/2007, that devises "Income Tax Facilities for Investment Activities in Specific Industries and/ or Particular Region," and the second is PP. No. 8/2007, that defines the role of "The Government Investment" to ensure a close connection between bio-fuel development, on one hand, and job creation and poverty alleviation for farmers, on the other hand. As the decrees and the regulations took place, government affiliated experts were making calculations, pointing at as wide as 5.25 million ha of plantations to support the bio-fuel development policy implementation.

Thus, the national agenda on bio-fuel research and development has been set again, and this time it covers the supply and the demand sides simultaneously. In contrast to the bio-fuel policies in the 1980s and 1990s, in 2005 (and subsequent years) the government's determination was clearly articulated[4]: nation-wide bio-fuel production is a must, and the major goal is to solve poverty problems. Nevertheless, the situation presents new challenges to bio-fuel scientists. While framing bio-fuel research problems within environment issues have been common practices, connecting bio-fuel research to poverty, poor farmers and unused lands in remote villages turns out to be an entirely new venture to bio-fuel scientists. As the following story exemplifies, different translations were pursued by different scientists. The story traces translations enacted by three different bio-fuel scientists, all of them happen to be affiliated with one engineering department in the Institute of Technology Bandung.

BIO-FUEL ACTOR-NETWORKS

To begin our story, let us call the three bio-fuel scientists *A, B* and *C* respectively. Scientist *A* sought to proliferate connections with elite politicians, including Indonesia's President, leaders of a long established traditional organization—*Nahdathul Ulama* (NU), and leaders of the national farmer association—*Himpunan Kerukunan Tani Indonesia* (HKTI). By connecting bio-fuel research to traditional farmers' welfare, scientist *A* was able

Table 1. Graph metaphor of networks traced by scientist A, B, and C respectively

	A	B	C
Central approach	Top-down	Network; starting from existing interest	Bottom-up
Type of relation among actors	Dependent	Interdependent	Hybrid; combination between dependent and interdependent
Network graph			
Occupation	Lecture	Lecture	Entrepreneur

to attract the attention of those politicians and leaders. Scientist *B*, while also sought to established connections with top bureaucrats, moved in a different direction, reaching public research institutes, the ministry of industry, the ministry of energy and mineral resources, and several ITB-linked industry owners. Scientist *B* initiated non-formal and formal meetings, urging for the industry owners' role in bio-fuel production and supply. A bio-fuel forum called *Forum Bio-diesel Indonesia* (FBI) was then established, a major task of which is to define industrial standards for bio-diesel products. Using the stream metaphor employed by Fisher et al (2006), we may say that scientist *A* and scientist *B* trace their network via upstream engagement. The third actor, scientist *C*, set its translation strategy differently from the first two. Scientist *C* muddled through village community leaders, village housewives, cattlemen, and small business owners. Scientist *C*'s translation seems to follow 'appropriate technology' narration that 'small is beautiful' (see, for instance, IDRC/UNCTAD, 1997). Using a graph metaphor, records of network traces of those three scientists look like those shown in Table 1.

The network traced by scientist *A* displays a local/global separation, in which scientist *A* plays the role as an intermediary that draws resources from its local and global actors. In scientist *A*

network's graph above, the local actors are medium scale private companies represented by nodes on the left side of the graph, while the global actors are elite politicians and leaders. The local/global connection is represented by the dashed horizontal line. To maintain such a configuration, scientist *A* devises a specific rhetoric: a new processing technique to reduce bio-fuel production cost to benefit both the company owners and traditional farmers. And by maintaining dependencies of local and global actors to scientific facts produced inside a laboratory, allowing them only restricted, scientist *A* managed the separation of local/global networks.

In early 2005, scientist *A* achieved an agreement with NU and HKTI leaders, and a number of scientists from the Institute of Agriculture Bogor (IPB). The task delegations were made clear: IPB scientists provide agricultural technical assistance; the HKTI mobilizes lands, seeds, and farmers; and the NU mobilizes their members (which are mostly traditional farmers and small-medium scale businessmen, and religious leaders. The agreement was stabilized by a specific discourse on *jatropha curcas*. This species *Jatropha curcas* is widely known as fuel sources to traditional farmers since the Japanese colonial era back in 1940s. Its cultivation is relatively simple and low-cost. And this particular species can be cultivated on infertile soils. Framed in this way, *jatropha curcas* defines a solution to the double-edged energy crisis and poverty problem conceived by President Yudhoyono. The parties involved in the agreement were then able to convince the President that they have invented the right solution. Thus, in October 2005, scientist *A* joined a government initiated alliances to make a declaration on "National Movement to Prevent Poverty and Crisis." The declaration was signed by, to mention a few, several ministers (including the minister for national planning, the minister for internal affairs, the minister of cooperatives and small-medium enterprises), the head of regional government association, the director of state electricity enterprise (PLN), the head of Indonesia green energy society, a dean of ITB, and a representative of IPB. One point asserted in the declaration is government procurement of *jatropha curcas* kernel and oil produced by farmers.

Scientist *B* traces a different network of relations. As shown in the middle column of Table 1, the network graph does not show a grouping-separation pattern. Instead, it connects a variety of actors and maintains exchanges among them. Scientist *B* plays a role as intermediary, connecting heterogeneous actors and translating one interest to another. For instance, scientist *B* raises the issue of technical standard, and proposed the formation of a forum on bio-diesel that addresses various issues (technical, legal, environmental) related to a bio-fuel solution. Scientist *B* distributes (to a variety of actors) access to facts production in the laboratory. Compatibility with technical issues in other sectors (automotive industries, transportation and environment) was sought openly. Regular meetings were maintained, in hotels, government offices and mail lists, allowing a variety of actors to translate their rhetoric one to another. This results in a network graph in which connections are distributed evenly among nodes that compose the network. Scientist *B*'s role as circulating intermediary positions itself as the central node of the graph.

As mentioned above, scientist *C* translation follows the 'appropriate technology' rhetoric. In contrast to scientist *A* and scientist *B*, scientist *C* does not take a role in upstream bio-fuel policy engagement. While in scientist *A*'s rhetoric mass farmers involvement and land uses are central, and in scientist *B*'s rhetoric mass industrial production is a key, in scientist *C*'s rhetoric everything is local and small. Thus, no centrality or hierarchy is induced by scientist *C* translation. Negotiations between scientist *C*, the local cattlemen and housewives is mediated by bio mass, a demo plot, and technical equipment that is available and widely known locally. The cattlemen can now add value to animal waste, the local business owners allocate money for new business, and housewives get cheaper (gas) fuel. Scientist *C*, together with local leaders plays an intermediary role maintaining communication among community groups. Scientist *C* did seek to proliferate network to enroll new actors, such as provincial government officials and larger husbandry agencies. However its success seems to be limited. As shown in the right column in Table 1, the horizontal line that connects the set of nodes on the left and on the right represents local-local scientist *C*'s network proliferation.

Local actors enrolment and mobilization are key in scientist *C*'s translation. As scientist *C* described, "I try to promote local awareness so they can use the new technology for their own productivity and development. I only provide partial technical assistance.[5]" However, the situation changed when the provincial government officials and large scale husbandry agencies came to play. They distributed bio-gas reactors to the farmers for free. One of scientist *C*'s employee told us that, "This aid has promoted jealousy among cattlemen that did not get the aid." [6] This external intervention also introduced another problem. Farmers that bought the product supplied by scientist *C* did so after conceiving potential economic values. But, the farmers who received bio-gas reactors as 'free gifts,' in general, did not know how to create values from their use. Thus, the aid turned out to promote resistance among local farmers; the aid program played an anti-program against scientist *C*'s translation.

DISCOUNTED ACTORS

Are the above-described three different translations durable enough to produce beneficial effects? The answer is, apparently, no. In late 2007 Pertamina, as a party that is obligated to purchase bio-fuel products, reported a loss up to 16.9 billion rupiah, counted from May 2006 to March 2007. This loss resulted from price disparity between bio-fuel and fossil-fuel commodities. Bio-fuel price is much higher. Pertamina's director of trading and marketing described his skepticism, "Unless the government manages to provide regulatory guarantees, Pertamina will not continue the development mix-fuel".[7] The term 'mix-fuel' here refers to the Pertamina's program to develop products combining bio-fuel and fossil-fuel, e.g. mix-solar and mix-premium. Responding to the situation, the Timnas BBN proposed a financial solution to the government, specifically addressed to the department of finance, to reduce income tax from all bio-fuel transactions. But the government does not accept the proposal.

The director of Rajawali Nusantara Indonesia (RNI), a member of Timnas BBN, described that, "Bio-ethanol production is expected to start in the middle of 2009. The product is expected to be absorbed by Korea's market. ... But until now, there has been no regulatory certainty regarding trading mechanism."[8] The daily head of Indonesia Palm Entrepreneur Association (GAPKI) was also sceptical that 2008's target of 18.4 million metric ton of CPO, with 13.6 million metric ton for export could ever be met.[9]

This skepticism from the supplier's side seems to refer to the absence of a type of actor in the bio-fuel qualculation by scientists, government officials and politicians: the consumers. Consum-

ers' demand was neglected, and investors' interests were not enrolled in the bio-fuel translations. Altogether, this has resulted in inefficient bio-fuel prices. Thus, even though fossil-fuel subsidy has been cut-off, the bio-fuel products remain absent in the domestic energy market. The weak regulatory basis for bio-fuel trades has been accused as the main obstacle to investors' entrance into the sector. Scientist *A* described the situation, "The party that withdraws from the national commitment is the government itself, because of its lack of efficiency."[10] Scientist *B* described the situation by pointing at different directions, "... the regulations are not clear because it seeks to accommodate interests of all parties. In my opinion, the government has to decide its priority. ... the regulation is not consistent. Bio-fuel industry is a future industry."[11] In this statement, scientist *B* referred to the variety of parties involved in bio-fuel politicization, leading to ambiguous targets and goals. A senior researcher from the Research Division of Indonesia Natural Resources and Environment Accountant Society (MASLI) condemned that poverty alleviation and bio-fuel development are contradictory goals. Another accusation is pointed at the scientists as making incorrect calculations. For example, the Second Secretary of Bio-fuel National Team and a researcher in BPPT, suspects that the prediction is based on an immature calculation, "The information comes from a scientist that cultivates *jatropha curcas* in a small area. The calculation can be inaccurate for bigger plantations.[12]"

Farmer is another type of actor that is not enrolled in bio-fuel translations. Even though farmers are not key actors that may provide bio-fuel solutions, they are key intermediaries through which connection to soils and seeds can take place. As mentioned above, the national bio-fuel development was targeted at 5.25 million ha plantation by 2010, implying no less than 3.5 million farmers to work on farms. To mobilize such a huge number of intermediaries is not a simple matter. The situation is made worse since during the New

Order regime, many of villages have been weakly connected to urban livelihood, not to mention to the bureaucracy agencies. Rural infrastructure has been underdeveloped in most regions, since the New Order regime, and also the subsequent governments, have always prioritized urban development. Farmers have always been in a marginal position in the transaction of agricultural products. Moreover, the green revolution introduced by the government in early the 1970s has resulted in high dependency to fertilizer industries and technology donors outside villages.

According to Loekman Soetrisno, Indonesia's green revolution has raised new problems for the farmers, such as dependency on superior kernel (uniform) that stimulated farmers to leave their local kernel and the dismissal of local knowledge and wisdom (Noertjahyo, 2005). Of similar tone, Indro Tjahjono said that the central government intervention to villages had, in the past decades, led to farmer deprivation of their freedom (Tjahjono, 1996, p. 123). Now, farmers are demanded to cultivate energy plants to serve the need of urban livelihoods. From a different perspective, the executive director of *Kreatif Energi Indonesia Enterprise* worried that the farmers think *jatropha curcas* as 'green gold,' so they may set a high level of price. The head of Partnership Program in Research of Crumbs Crop and Plant for Industry Institution (BALITTRI), stated that, "Nowadays *jatropha* cultivation is like euphoria with no clear direction"[13].

Yet another discounted actor is the land itself. Fabby Tumiwa, an NGO activist, worried that increase in energy cultivation plantations would double the corn price, and called for a more integrated approach, "There should be an approach which combines different points of view, including social-structural, not only technical-economic."[14] Hardiv H. Situmeang, a member of World Energy Council sees the emerging bio-fuel discourse as lacking a balance between energy, economy, and environment values. Situmeang proposed, instead, a broader energy policy that covers low carbon energy sources, low carbon and carbon-free energy technologies, greater efficiency in energy production, distribution and use.[15] Willie Smits, the founder of Borneo Orang-Utan Survival Foundation asserted that, "When you look closely, the areas where companies are getting permission for palm-oil plantations are those of forests conservation."[16]

INSIDE THE BIO-FUEL BOX

Indonesia's present bio-fuel development seems to follow a mixed "top-down" and "bottom-up" pattern. On the one side, public participation does take place extensively. Representatives of Indonesia's farmer association and the mass organization exercised their influence in the setting of policy goals. Mass media was involved constantly in the conception of bio-fuel technology selection. On the other side, top level bureaucrats and elite politicians initiate the declarations and mobilizing of resources. Nevertheless, such a structural perspective does not reveal what goes inside the bio-fuel box: a variety of actors carrying out translations and qualculations.

Tracing the network of relations of scientists *A*, *B*, and *C* reveals the presence of competing translations and different qualculation patterns. All the three scientists sought to draw resources (scientific, political, legal, and economic) to ensure their leading role in bio-fuel innovation. Collaboration to define a common technical solution apparently is not their main concern. Thus, each of the scientists actively mobilized actors and sought to translate them be devising a variety of figures, drawings, scientific facts, and laboratories. One scientist sought connections to rural farmers, unused lands in remote areas, and political parties. Another one sought connections to automotive companies, industrial engineers, and industry related ministries. And yet another scientist muddled through the local community leaders, bio-masses, cattlemen and households.

The qualculation patterns that emerge from the translations show variations and similarities. First, in the case of scientist *A* and scientist *B* translations, the respective qualculation pattern shows a proliferation. Thus, as scientist *A* and scientist *B* constantly compete one to another. Each of them keep seeking new actors and add new qualculative resources needed to translate the new actors' interests. As Callon and Law (2003) conclude, such a proliferating translation impedes actor from performing a proper task of framing, ordering and totalizing. In the case of scientist *A* qualculation, business actors and bio-fuel consumers seem, and land missing. In the case of scientist *B*, rural farmers and households are missing. Secondly, in the case of scientist *C* translation, its qualculation seems to show a rarefaction. Scientist *C* does not compete directly with scientists *A* and *B*. Instead, scientist *C* maintained to distance itself from those two, which happened to be more senior scientists. Scientist *C* sought to disentangle any connection to scientist *A* and *B* networks. Even though scientist *C* managed to bring a technical solution to household uses and invite local investors, the solution lacks of broader legitimacy and support.

The above analysis is not meant to suggest that the global actors (top level bureaucrats, political parties, and large scale companies play only marginal roles. Surely, legislation and regulation are decided by the government, political support is in the hand of elite politicians. Nevertheless, whatever policy statements that the government officials make, and political statements that the politicians make, those statement must make referent to scientific facts corresponding to fossil fuel, oil production, lands, plantations, seeds, environments, poverty figures, machineries, automotive engines, production costs, prices, and farmers. And to make qualification and to decide priorities required calculations made by scientists to connect those heterogeneous elements into numbers and graphs—the scientific facts produced in laboratories. Thus, scientists are not the key actors, or the forceful initiators that shape the trajectory of bio-fuel development. However, the scientists modulate the roles of those key actors.

CONCLUDING REMARKS

Scientists are, of course, rational professionals according to the conventional definition of rationality, and scientific work is, as far as texts inscriptions inside laboratory is seen in isolation, politically free. However when the scientific work is seen from a broader context, a network of heterogeneous relations that shapes, and is connected to it, unfolds. Our story shows how scientists, through such a network, modulate the social, the politics, and also the trajectory of bio-fuel development in Indonesia. The way the modulation brings effect seems to be defined by the patterns of translations in which the scientists seek to establish their role. Thus, modulation of technological trajectory is not only a matter of scientists' cognitive capacities, as suggested by Fisher et al (2006). Our paper shows that the effects of such a modulation may be studied by devising the concept of qualculation.

This paper has shown specific patterns of qualculation in bio-fuel translations: proliferation and rarefaction. As noted by Callon and Law (2003), proliferating qualculation threats the mobilization stage of translation, when spokesmen are not properly able to represent those collectivities they represent, and betray them. Translations generated by scientist *A* and scientist *B*, as they have been competing one against another, seem to proliferate and improperly enrolled the interests of business actors, bio-fuel consumers, rural farmers and households, and lands. Translation generated by scientist *C* exhibits a rarefaction. Rather then trying to sum all the calculative sources, rarefaction works by letting go all the boundaries of an actor. A key in the rarefaction process is an active process of waiting to learn and appreciate (Callon and Law, 2003). Translated in this way, the technical solution brought about by scientist *C* lacks broader legitimacy and support.

To our account, the bio-fuel development and innovation could not be understood properly by devising structural perspectives such as those employed in innovation system literature (see for example Nelson, 1993). Bio-fuel related university-industry linkages have developed since 2005; scientists have been closely engaged with industries. A number of private companies have tapped the university research. But, what needs to be accounted more closely, as our story has shown, is the competition among scientists and politicians, their complex alliances, and the outcomes of such competition and alliances. In the case presented in the paper, those competitions and alliances have resulted in non-qualculabilities, leaving other business actors, farmers and lands discounted. This has blocked translations to proliferate further, and preventing the diffusion of innovation.

ACKNOWLEDGMENT

The research work supporting the paper is partially funded by the ITB's Excellent Research Scheme, and by the International Development Research Center (IDRC). The authors gratefully acknowledge the funding supports. The authors gratefully thank Erik Fisher for providing valuable comments to the earlier version of this paper.

REFERENCES

Akrich, M. (1992). The De-Scription of Technical Objects. In Bijker, W. E., & Law, J. (Eds.), *Shaping Technology, Building Society: Studies in Sociotechnical Change* (pp. 205–224). Cambridge, Massachusetts: MIT Press.

Bardini, T. (1994). A Translation Analysis of the Green Revolution in Bali,'. *Science, Technology & Human Values*, *19*(2), 152–168. doi:10.1177/016224399401900202

Boudourides, M. A. (2001). The Politics of Technological Innovations: Network Approaches,' presented in International Summer Academy on Technological Studies.

Boudourides, M. A. (2002). *Governance in Science and Technology*, contributed paper at the EASST 2002 Conference.

Callon, M. (1986). *Some elements of a sociology of translation: domestication of the scallops and the fisherman of St. Brieuc Bay,'* in J. Law, *Power, action and belief: a new sociology of knowledge?* London: Routledge.

Callon, M., & Law, J. (2003). *On Qualculation, Agency and Otherness.* published by the Centre for Science Studies, Lancaster University, Lancaster LA1 4YN, UK. Retrieved August 8, 2007 from http://www.comp.lancs.ac.uk/sociology/papers/Callon-Law-Qualculation-Agency-Otherness.pdf

de Bruijn, H., van der Voort, H., Dicke, W., de Jong, M., & Veeneman, W. (2004). *Creating System Innovation: How Large Scale Transitions Emerge*. London, UK: A. A Balkema Publishers.

Departemen ESDM. (2007). *Pokok-pokok Materi Untuk Dilaporkan pada Rakortas Energi Alternatif.* Presented in Jakarta, May 23.

Etzkowitz, H. (2000). The Triple Helix of University-Industry-Government: Dynamics of Innovation Spaces and Implications for Policy and Evaluation," *Proceedings from the 2000 US-EU Workshop on Learning from Science and Technology Policy Evaluation*, Bad Herrenalb, Germany.

Fisher, E., Mahajan, R. L., & Mitcham, C. (2006). Midstream Modulation of Technology: Governance From Within,'. *Science, Technology & Society*, *26*(6), 485–496. doi:10.1177/0270467606295402

IDRC/UNCTAD. (1997). *An Assault of Poverty: Basic Human Needs, Science and Technology.* Retrieved March, 6, 2008 from http://www.idrc.ca/en/ev-9364-201-1-DO_TOPIC.html.

Latour, B. (1987). *Science in Action.* Cambridge, MA: Harvard University Press.

Latour, B. (2001). *Technology is Society Made Durable,"* A Sociology of Monsters: Essays on Power, Technology and Domination.* London: Routledge.

Latour, B. (2005). *Reassembling the Social: An Introduction of Actor-Network Theory.* Oxford, UK: Oxford Univerity Press.

Law, J. (2003). Notes on the Theory of the Actor Network: Ordering, Strategy and Heterogeneity,' published by Centre for Science Studies, Lancaster University. Retrived March 20, 2008 from http://www.comp.lancs.ac.uk/sociology/papers/Law-Notes-On-ANT.pdf

Law, J. (2007). *Actor Network Theory and Material Semiotics,'* 25 April version. Available online at http://www.heterogeneities.net/publications/Law-ANTand MaterialSemiotics.pdf

Manurung, R. (2007). "Valorisation of *Jatropha* curcas using the Bio-refinery Concept," Presented in United Nations Expert Group Meeting on Bio fuel Meeting, New York, 29-30 March.

Nelson, R. R. (Ed.). (1993). *National Innovation Systems: A Comparative Analysis.* New York: Oxford University Press.

Noertjayo, J. A. (2005). *Dari Ladang sampai Kabinet: Menggugat Nasib Petani.* Jakarta: Kompas.

Prakoso, T. dan Tatang H. Soerawidjaja (2007). "Perkembangan Teknologi Penyediaan Energi Alternatif(Bio fuel)," Presented on Aternative Energy for Human Welfare Seminar in Aula Barat ITB, Bandung, September 5.

Prihandana, R. (2007). *Meraup Untung dari Jarak Pagar (Cet.2).* Jakarta: AgroMedia Pustaka.

Rip, A., Thomas, J., Misa, D., & Schot, J. (1995). *Managing Technology in Society: The approach of Constructive Technology Assessment.* London: Pinter Publishers.

Schot, J. W. (1992). Constructive Technology Assessment and Technology Dynamics: The Case of Clean Technologies. *Science Technology Human Values, Sage Publications, 17*(1), 36–56. doi:10.1177/016224399201700103

Sharif, N. (2006). Emergence and Development of the National Innovation System Concept. *Research Policy, 35,* 745–766. doi:10.1016/j.respol.2006.04.001

Soerawidjaja, T. H. (2007). "Bahan-bahan Bakar Hayati." Presented on Development of Industrial Estate Seminar, Jakarta, 24 February.

Tim Nasional Pengembangan, B. B. N. (2007). *Bahan Bakar Nabati: Bahan Bakar alternatif dari tumbuhan sebagai pengganti minyak bumi and gas.* Jakarta: Penebar Swadaya.

Tjahjono, S. I. (1996). Perspektif Revolusi, Pembangunan, dan Transformasi Masyarakat. In *Pembaruan dan Pemberdayaan* (pp. 106–143). Jakarta: Ikatan Alumni IA ITB.

Wie, T. K. (2004). *Pembangunan, Kebebasan, dan "Mukjizat Orde Baru.* Jakarta: Kompas.

Wiji, A. (2007). "Potensi Biogas Sebagai Sumber Energi Alternatif," Presented on Aternative Energy for Human Welfare Seminar in Aula Barat ITB, Bandung, September 5.

Winner, L. (1999). Do Artifacts Have Politics? In *Daedalus, 109*(1) Winter 1980. Reprinted in *The Social Shaping of Technology*, edited by Donald A. MacKenzie and Judy Wajcman (London: Open University Press, 1985; second edition 1999).

Yusgiantoro, P. (2007). *Kebijakan Pemerintah Dalam Penyediaan Energi Alternatif di Indonesia*. Presented on Alternative Energy for Human Welfare Seminar, Aula Barat ITB, 5 September.

ENDNOTES

[1]   Schot uses the word 'steering' in this respect.

[2]   A mix-fuel product composed by 30% biofuel and 70% fossil-fuel.

[3]   See 'BBN Bahan Bakar Alternatif dari Tumbuhan sebagai pengganti minyak bumi & gas,' Tim Nasional Pengembangan BBN, 2007.

[4]   As described by President Yudhoyono in *Losari Meeting*, 1 July 2006, "We have to launch 'New Deal' to create jobs, and to rescue the people suffering from the crisis which partially results from wrong approach, wrong prescription and wrong policies … We have to deliver hopes to our people, and to free them from fear and insecure future."

[5]   Ibid.

[6]   Interview with Isam in Lembang, 17 December 2007.

[7]   See *Kompas*, 11 May 2007.

[8]   See "PT Rajawali Nusantara Indonesia Bangun Bioetanol untuk Ekspor", *Kompas*, 8 October 2007.

[9]   See "Investasi Bio-fuel 7.67 Triliun Rupiah", *Jurnal Nasional*, 17 January 2008.

[10]   Interview with scientist A in Bandung, 12 June 2007.

[11]   Interview with scientist B in Bandung, 11 May 2007.

[12]   Interview of Unggul Prayitno with *Journal Nasional*, 6 February 2008.

[13]   Interview of Dibyo in *Info METI*, November 2006.

[14]   See *Kompas*, 17 March 2007.

[15]   Situmeang presentation in *Asia Cooperations Dialogue Co-Prime Movers on Energy Security*, Bali, 11-12 April 2007.

[16]   See *Guardian*, 4 April 2007.

Chapter 6
Using I–D Maps to Represent the Adoption of Internet Applications by Local Cricket Clubs

Scott Bingley
Victoria University, Australia

Steven Burgess
Victoria University, Australia

ABSTRACT

This chapter describes the development of a visual aid to depict the manner in which Internet applications are being diffused through local sporting associations. Rogers' (2003) Innovation-Decision process stages, specifically the knowledge, persuasion, adoption and confirmation stages, are used as the theoretical basis for the aid. The chapter discusses the Innovation-Decision process as an important component of Rogers' (2003) Innovation Diffusion approach. It then outlines the particular problem at hand, determining how best to represent different sporting (cricket) associations and their adoption and use of Internet applications across the innovation-decision process stages. Different data visualisation approaches to representing the data (such as line graphs and bar charts) are discussed, with the introduction of an aid (labelled I-D maps) used to represent the adoption of different Internet applications by cricket associations in New Zealand, Australia and the UK. The Internet applications considered are email, club websites, association and/or third party websites and the use of the Internet to record online statistics. The use of I-D maps provides instant interpretation of the different levels of adoption of Internet applications by different cricket associations.

INTRODUCTION

The Innovation-Decision Process is a key component of Rogers' (2003) theory of Innovation Diffusion and has been used to provide insights into how many different innovations have been adopted. This article focuses the use of a visual aid, I-D maps, to depict the manner in which Internet applications are diffused through sporting

DOI: 10.4018/978-1-60960-197-3.ch006

associations (specifically the game of cricket) and allows direct comparisons between different associations. After discussing the Innovation-Decision Process, data visualisation is employed as a means to represent the diffusion process of various Internet applications and I-D maps are presented with the use of data collected from cricket associations to show how the results from different associations can be compared.

BACKGROUND

There are a number of approaches that can be used to examine the adoption and use of technology. One of the most popular is known as the *diffusion of innovations*. The theory has been used to conduct research into the adoption of many different innovations and the theory itself has undergone some modifications, with the 5th edition of the book *Diffusion of Innovations* being published in 2003.

The use of Rogers (2003) Innovation Diffusion approach, and the Innovation-Decision Process, has provided an important insight into how technologies are adopted into everyday lives. The theory was introduced by Rogers in the 1960s. It has since been revised a number of times and has been used to describe change in many sectors. The approach provides a general explanation of how new ideas disseminate themselves through social systems over time (Kappelman 1995, Suraya 2005).

Rogers (2003) explains the diffusion of an innovation as "the process in which an innovation is communicated through certain channels over time among the members of a social system. It is a special type of communication, in that the messages are concerned with new ideas." (Rogers 2003: 5)

According to Rogers (2003), an innovation is "an idea, practice, or object that is perceived as new by an individual or other unit of adoption" (Rogers 2003: 12). In fact, Rogers suggests that the idea does not actually have to be new- it only

needs to *appear* to be new to the individual. The perceived attributes of an innovation explain the rate of adoption of an innovation. Research into the characteristics of innovations has described the relationship between these characteristics and the adoption of an innovation (Rogers 2003, Tornatzky and Klein 1982). In a review of 75 articles relating to innovation characteristics and their relationship to innovation adoption, Tornatzky and Klein (1982) concluded that three innovation characteristics (relative advantage, compatibility, and complexity) had the most consistent, significant relationships to the innovation process. Al-Gahtani (2003) found that relative advantage and compatibility were both positively related and complexity was negatively related to the innovation adoption process. Rogers (2003) identified five characteristics that he argued accounted for 87% of the variance in rates of adoption (Al-Gahtani 2003). These characteristics are (Rogers 2003, Al-Gahtani 2003):

- **Relative Advantage:** the degree to which an innovation is perceived to be better that the innovation it has replaced.
- **Compatibility:** the degree in which an innovation is perceived to be consistent with the present socio-cultural values and beliefs.
- **Complexity:** the degree of which an innovation is perceived to be difficult to implement, understand, or use
- **Trialability:** the degree to which an innovation may be experimented with on a limited basis by an individual.
- **Observability:** the degree to which the results of an innovation are perceptible to others.

The Innovation-Decision Process

A key component of Innovation Diffusion theory is the Innovation-Decision Process (Rogers 2003). This process is when "an individual passes from gaining initial knowledge of an innovation, to form an attitude towards the innovation, to making a decision to adopt or reject, to implementation of the new idea, and to confirmation of this decision" (Rogers 2003, 168).

The steps or stages of the Innovation-Decision Process are, in order of occurrence (Rogers 2003):

1. **Knowledge:** when a decision maker is made aware of an innovation.
2. **Persuasion:** when a decision maker forms an attitude towards an innovation. One of the aspects that can affect these attitudes are the *perceived attributes* of the innovation, which were discussed earlier, but can also be influenced by factors.
3. **Decision:** when a decision maker engages in activities that lead to either choosing the innovation or rejecting it.
4. **Implementation:** when a decision maker puts in place the new innovation.
5. **Confirmation:** when a decision maker wants reinforcement about the decision made to use the innovation. The decision to continue or discontinue use of the innovation is made.

Rogers himself commented that it might be arguable whether the particular stages can be separated from each other, but does suggest that it is probably easier to do for the first three stages (2003, 197). The next section will examine some examples of research into the Innovation-Decision Process and how it has been reported.

EXAMPLES OF RESEARCH EMPLOYING THE INNOVATION-DECISION PROCESS

This section examines some examples of research into the Innovation-Decision process and how the research has been reported.

Kendall et al (2001) used the Innovation-Decision process to scope their research into the

adoption of e-commerce by surveying 58 Singapore small and medium sized enterprises. Their results were mainly reported on the *perceived attributes* of e-commerce and were reported in *table format* using factor and regression analysis.

Fogelgren-Pedersen (2005) used the knowledge, persuasion and decision stages of the innovation-decision process as a theoretical lens for examining the adoption of 'third generation' mobile technologies in Denmark. The study was conducted with a survey of 222 participants that had prior experience of using mobile devices for data transfer. In addition to using Spearman's Rho and Kruskal Wallace tests to report on factors related to the *relative advantage* of the technology. The author also examined other stages of the Innovation-Decision process by enquiring about factors that lead to the adoption decision and reasons for continuing or discontinuing the adoption. These results were also reported in *table format*, but other stages of the Innovation-Decision Process were discussed in narrative form in the main text of the results section.

Li and Lindner (2007) used the innovation-decision process as the theoretical basis for examining the behaviour of faculty at a Chinese university in relation to the adoption of web-based distance education. The research was conducted with a survey of 273 faculty members at China Agricultural University. The authors asked questions related to different stages of the Innovation-Decision Process Each stage was initially reported as a frequency (again, in *table form*), but then also shown on *a two dimensional graph* with the stages on the horizontal axis and frequency on the y axis. Thus, the more faculty members that were situated in a particular stage the *higher* on the y axis that stage was represented.

There are examples of the use of interviews to apply the Innovation-Decision Process. For instance, Dikbas et al (2008) employed semi-structured interviews to collect data from 23 teachers in Turkey to determine what stage of the Innovation-Decision process they were at in relation to the adoption of laptop computers. They then used content analysis to determine which of the stages of the Innovation-Decision process that the teachers were at in relation to the use of laptops for practical tasks related to their employment – such as making presentations during lessons and the preparation of course materials – and presented the results as a *discussion*. This is particularly interesting as the authors did not just classify the use of laptops as a single innovation – but their use for different tasks as being multiple innovations.

ALTERNATIVES TO PRESENTING THE RESULTS OF INNOVATION-DECISION PROCESS RESEARCH

The authors were particularly interested in presenting the results of research into the adoption of Internet technologies in sporting associations in a manner that would allow easy interpretation of the results and simple comparisons to be made.

Data Visualisation is known under a number of different terms. It is described by Industry Canada (2008) as being "the art, science and technology of presenting data/information in a manner, graphically, audibly, etc., that affords the viewer the greatest appreciation and understanding of the data/information content". From a computing point of view, ZDNet refer to the Computer Desktop Encyclopedia (2008) definition of *visualisation* as "using the computer to convert data into picture form. The most basic visualization is that of turning transaction data and summary information into charts and graphs". More recent definitions of data visualisation refer to the use of 3-dimensional presentation graphics. The main goal of data visualisation is to simplify the process of understanding and interpreting data. The American University (2008) suggests that graphical presentations of data help to identify differences and relationships that might not be clearly identifiable from the numbers themselves. Forms of data visualisation (under different names) have

been occurring for centuries, going back to early map making and then later with the popularity of the use of data collection for planning and commerce in the 19th century. However, the first visual representation of statistics is thought to be the 17th century, when a line graph was used to portray different estimates of the measurement of longitude between Toledo and Rome. Of particular interest to the researchers is the use of shading (between white and black) by Baron Charles Dupin in the 1820s to represent the distribution and degree of illiteracy in France (Friendly 2006).

In relation to selecting a suitable chart format for data visualisation, the American University (2008) suggest that if the separate data items add up to 100% then a pie chart is suitable. If a set of values changes over time, then line graphs are suited. If a set of values are measured at regular intervals, a bar chart would probably be more appropriate. In statistical terms, the histogram is similar to a bar chart (Spiegel and Stephens 2008).

It is thus initially useful to set up a simple (fictional) example of the adoption of an innovation by three sporting associations (refer Table 1). The percentages relate to the proportion of clubs at each stage within each association. For instance, Table 1 shows that 95% of clubs in Association 1 had knowledge of the innovation.

Note that the Implementation stage has been left out as Rogers suggested that it might be difficult to delineate between the final two stages of the Process (Rogers 2003). Due to the difficulty, even for Rogers, to separate the latter stages of the Innovation Decision Process, the researchers have kept the first three stages and merged the 'implementation' stage with 'adoption' stage. This will show a clear difference between the decision to adopt and the decision to continue to use the innovation ('confirmation'). Also, the implementation stage is more about how the innovation is actually employed, which is important, but not to this chapter.

Using the sample data from the previous section, here are some examples of how the data

Table 1. Sample data

Association	Stages of Adoption (%)			
	Knowledge	Persuasion	Adoption	Confirmation
Association 1	95	90	90	80
Association 2	30	15	10	10
Association 3	60	50	45	40

Figure 1. Innovation decision process as a line graph

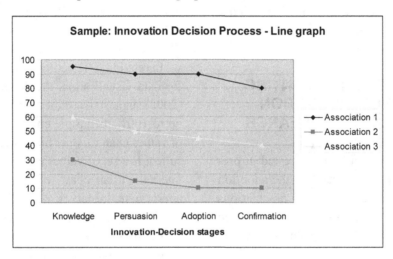

Table 2. Sample data for a fourth association

Association	Stages of Adoption (%)			
	Knowledge	Persuasion	Adoption	Confirmation
Association 4	60	55	45	40

many be presented. The first example is a line graph (Figure 1).

Now, this 'seems' to work. In this instance it is appropriate to use the line graph as each stage is 'linked' to the previous stage. However, what happens if we have another association that has similar results? Table 2 will be incorporated into the sample results.

As can be seen in Figure 2, it can be difficult to differentiate between Associations 3 and 4, especially in the adoption and confirmation stages, so the line graph will not work when val-

ues are identical. The bar chart with idetnifcal figures will now be examined (Figure 3).

This bar chart appears to work quite well with the sample data (certainly better than the line graph in relation to differentiating between Associations 3 and 4,) but it is obvious it becomes quite cramped as we start adding in more associations, as demonstrated in Figure 3.

Thus, what the researchers were after is a tool that would allow us to present the data in a different (less cramped) manner, allowing us to represent a comparison between number of associations on,

Figure 2. Innovation decision process as a line graph with a fourth association

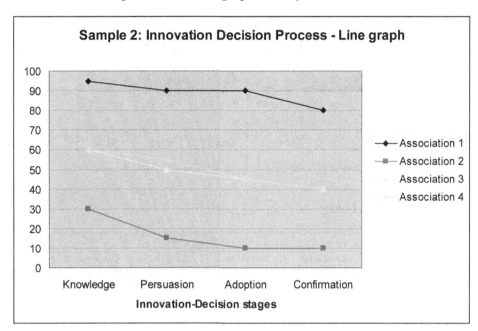

Figure 3. Innovation decision process as a bar chart

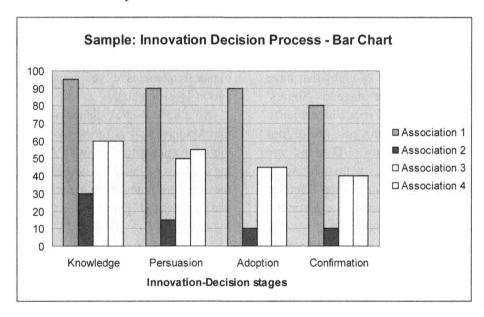

say, a single page whilst not losing (much of) the meaning of the data.

So, another approach was to try to represent the levels of 'yes' answers to each of the Innovation-Decision stages by using shading to show the different levels. This is somewhat similar to the manner in which shading has been used to represent population density in mapping.

Figure 4. MS Word's Grey Scale

Black	Gray 95	Gray 90	Gray 87.5	Gray 85	Gray 80
Gray 75	Gray 70	Gray 65	Gray 62.5	Gray 60	Gray 55
Gray 50	Gray 45	Gray 40	Gray 35	Gray 30	Gray 25
Gray 20	Gray 15	Gray 12.5	Gray 10	Gray 5	White

Figure 5. Sample Data as the I-D Map

Association	Stages of Adoption			
	Knowledge	Persuasion	Adoption	Confirmation
Association 1				
Association 2				
Association 3				
Association 4				

Introducing I-D Maps

'I-D Map' is a term coined by the researchers to represent the proportions of clubs that have passed through a particular stage of Rogers' (2003) Innovation-Decision Process in relation to a particular innovation – in this case one of four different Internet applications. "I-D Maps" are actually Microsoft Word tables, with each column representing a stage of the Innovation-Decision Process and each row representing a particular sporting association (refer Figure 5).

Microsoft Word offers a simple solution for shading table cells. Once a cell has been created, it is possible to adjust the shading in the properties of the table cell. Although only having the option round to 5% intervals in Microsoft Word 2003 (2.5% in Word 2007), it is the researchers' opinion that this offers enough depth for representation of the statistics to be meaningful at a glance. Figure 4 shows the shades (or grey scales) that Microsoft Word (2003 version) offered.

Each figure can then be mapped to its nearest percentile in the MS Word 'Gray' scale as shown in Figure 5, where the deeper shades represent higher frequencies of 'yes' responses in the Innovation-Decision stage.

Note how a quick glance at Figure 5 shows that Association 1 is further progressed through the innovation adoption, with Association 2 being the least advanced. Also, it is possible to add the details of many more associations by simply adding rows to Figure 5.

AN ACTUAL APPLICATION OF I-D MAPS

An example of how I-D Maps can be applied in an actual situation will now be presented.

Many people participate actively in sporting clubs that are based in local communities throughout Australia. These participants are supported by members (usually volunteers) that provide structure to their activities by assisting with club administration functions, such as player registration, fund raising activities and so forth. Recently, there is evidence that Internet applications are being used in various ways to support these activities.

The primary aim of this study is to examine the adoption of different Internet applications by clubs in local sporting associations. Local sporting clubs are part of the larger group known as community based organisations (CBOs). CBOs as a sector rely heavily on volunteers to support their activities. There are important differences in the manner in which CBOs adopt and use information and communications technologies, of which Internet applications are a subset, when compared with private enterprises. It is intended to examine these differences as a part of this study. In fact, there is a lag in the amount of research conducted in this sector compared to more commercial sectors, especially in relation to their use of information and communications technologies (ICTs) (Hall and Banting 2002). Very few studies investigate the role of ICT and volunteers (Boyle, et al. 1993, Madon 1999, Morgon 1995). Although there is research examining Internet adoption in general, this cannot necessarily be generalised to small CBOs and their volunteers or in this instance, local sporting clubs and their members. Therefore, more specific research is needed to investigate implications of these significant differences (MacKay, Parent and Gemino 2004).

Research into the use of ICTs in sport typically revolves around the improvement of sporting performance, not the business functions that ICTs are used for. This study fills a gap in that it not only extends research into CBOs and volunteers and their use of the Internet, it also investigates the particular applications of the Internet that are currently being adopted in local sporting clubs.

With the inherent advantages that ICTs and the Internet have to offer (Wreden 1997), it seems reasonable to assume that moving from a paper based to a computerised or Internet-based system would benefit volunteers and CBOs. However,

this move has caused some tension within CBOs. Most volunteer-based organisations are small in size (Charity Commission for England and Wales 2002). Such organisations face many ICT resource challenges not confronted by large businesses, especially in regards to the substantial risks involved in some ICT implementations, a general lack of skills and the need to rely on outside sources for technical support, inadequate hardware and software, and a lack of financial resources (MacKay, Parent and Gemino 2004).

Although the long term aim of this research project is to examine the adoption of different Internet applications across different sports, this initial phase of the study reports the results in local cricket clubs. At the highest level, cricket is predominantly played in Commonwealth countries (such as Australia, New Zealand, England, Pakistan, India and South Africa). Cricket has some similarities with baseball as the winning team scores the most runs and there are a set number of innings, each involving a team batting and a team on the field (with positions reversed at the conclusion of an innings). At the top level a game of cricket can be played over five days (a 'test match'). However, local cricket clubs predominantly play shorter versions that are played over two days or even a few hours. For instance, a local cricket match in Australia will typically take place over two Saturday afternoons, with each team usually having one innings on each day.

Thus, taking cricket clubs as an example of a local sporting club, anecdotal evidence suggests that Internet applications have become pervasive in many volunteer activities (from the researchers' experience in local sporting clubs). These activities range from the use of email to improve communications between committee members to the introduction of online systems to handle match scores and statistics related to player performance – the latter eliminating repeated data entry and saving countless hours of time. The adoption of these technologies may have been driven from the 'top' (that is, the club or even association level)

Table 3. Data Collection details

Details	New Zealand	Australia	Australia	UK
Locale	Metropolitan	Metropolitan	Rural	Rural
Date of data collection	May 2008	October 2008	November 2009	March 2009
Number of clubs (possible population)	9	25	17	86 (21/22 per division)
Number of surveys completed	7 (78% of clubs)	20 (80%)	16 (94%)	12 (14% overall or 55% of division meeting)

and imposed upon volunteers in the club – or in some instances the adoption may have been driven from the 'bottom' – via 'technology savvy' volunteers keen to apply the technology as part of their duties. However, the introduction of any new technology has an impact – and whilst improved communication and increased efficiencies might seem desirable outcomes – there can be negative impacts on those that feel marginalised from the technology or for those volunteers for whom the task of recording player statistics may have been a desirable use of their time. It is in this context that this study is being conducted.

The Innovation-Decision Process will be used as a basis for identifying how local sporting clubs have implemented the Internet applications (as an ICT). Sport is generally organised at the local level with sporting clubs being part of an association. The data collection was undertaken at the Club and Association level (an Association generally comprising 10-50 Clubs). The Sporting associations typically have regular meetings of delegates from their participating clubs..

Different sporting associations were contacted for the purpose of distributing surveys to club delegates at association meetings. This ensures a relatively captive audience and provides close to a 'full population' of clubs in each association. The surveys, which took only 5-10 minutes to fill out, asked simple questions related to the knowledge, persuasion, adoption and confirmation stages of the Rogers Innovation-Decision Process. Thus, for each Internet application, each club delegate

would answer 'yes' or 'no' as to whether they had reached a particular stage in the process.

The survey that was used was based on a flow chart diagram typically 'yes' or 'no' responses, which determined which level of the Innovation-Decision Process they were at for a particular Internet Application. In some instances the researchers were expecting that the data would be quite skewed. For example, the adoption of an association website might be a requirement of the association, so there would likely be full adoption by all clubs, and the majority of them could be in the confirmation stage.

The use of I-D maps allows for easy visual comparison of the Innovation-Decision process stages for *specific* Internet applications *across* different sporting associations – as well as *different* Internet applications *within* specific sporting associations.

Survey data was collected from four local cricket associations. The associations were selected on the basis of convenience – with the location of the researchers at the various times allowing them to investigate cricket associations in three countries. Details are as follows:

As can be seen from the results (and as was expected) the percentage response rate for the survey was quite high in relation to the *population* for three of the associations. The only exception was with the UK rural association. They had quite a large number of clubs compared to other associations and thus had separate meetings for different divisions of clubs in the association.

Table 4. Email adoption levels

Association	Stages of Adoption (%)			
	Knowledge	Persuasion	Adoption	Confirmation
NZ metropolitan	100	100	100	100
Australia metropolitan	100	100	91	91
Australia rural	94	88	70	58
UK rural	100	100	91	91

Figure 6. Email I-D map

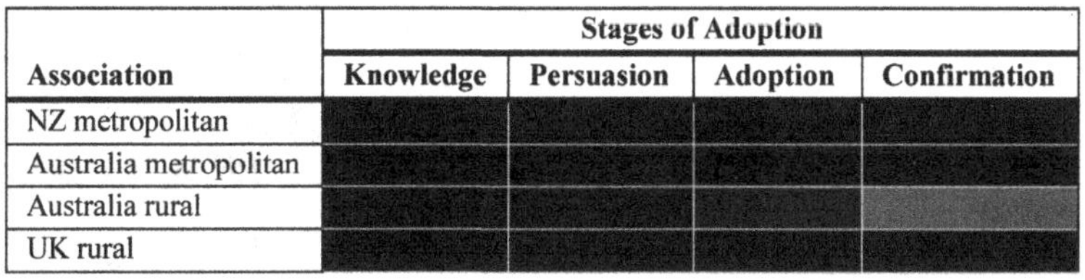

Thus, at any one meeting there would typically be 21 or 22 clubs represented at most. Thus, although the survey return is quite low (14%) for the entire association, it is quite acceptable at around 55% for the division, which the association contact suggested was representative of the association. In most cases, if a club did not complete a survey it was because it did not have a representative at the meeting. The I-D Maps are now presented for the four Internet applications that were treated as innovations:

• The use of email for club related activities;
• The adoption of a club website,
• The adoption of an association or third party website; and
• The use of the Internet for online statistics.

Email

The adoption of email was widespread through most of the associations. In all but one of the associations, at least nine out of 10 clubs were in the Confirmation stage. The only association where this was lower was the Australian rural association. Although most of the clubs in this

association (70%) had adopted email, a lesser number (58%) had confirmed that they would continue to use it. Table 4 shows the results from the surveys for email adoption.

Figure 6 shows the I-D map for email adoption in the associations. It is quite clear looking at the map that the proportion of respondents in the confirmation stage is quite high for all associations bar one. The idea behind using the I-D map is that provides the visual interpretation of the results faster than if one examines the raw figures (as in Table 4).

Club Website

This section examines the stages of adoption in relation to clubs having their own website. Both of the metropolitan associations had a high proportion of clubs in the Confirmation stage, with the UK rural association having 75% of clubs surveyed in the Confirmation stage. However, only 29% of clubs in the Australian rural association had adopted a club website (with all of these being in the Confirmation stage). Table 5 shows the results from the surveys for Club Websites.

Table 5. Club website adoption levels

Association	Stages of Adoption (%)			
	Knowledge	Persuasion	Adoption	Confirmation
NZ metropolitan	100	100	100	100
Australia metropolitan	100	100	96	95
Australia rural	94	64	29	29
UK rural	100	83	75	75

Figure 7. Club website I-D map

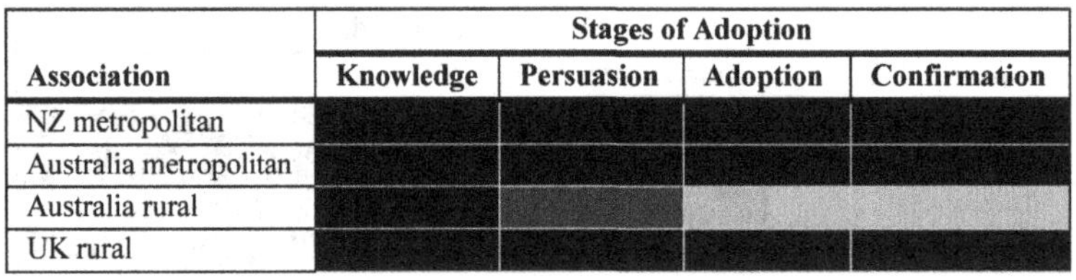

Association	Stages of Adoption			
	Knowledge	Persuasion	Adoption	Confirmation
NZ metropolitan				
Australia metropolitan				
Australia rural				
UK rural				

Table 6. Association and/or Third Party website adoption levels

Association	Stages of Adoption (%)			
	Knowledge	Persuasion	Adoption	Confirmation
NZ metropolitan	100	100	100	100
Australia metropolitan	95	95	95	95
Australia rural	64	47	17	17
UK rural	83	66	50	50

Figure 7 shows the stages of adoption of a club website for each association as an I-D map. Again, it is quite easy to spot those associations where the proportions of clubs at the various stages of adoption are lower.

Association and/or Third Party Website

In this instance, a club uses an association or third party website predominantly to access information about the association in general. Again, a higher proportion of clubs in the metropolitan associations were at the confirmation stage of adoption. In this instance, however, the Australian rural association is lagging behind the others, with only 17% of clubs being in the adoption stage and around one in three clubs not having any knowledge of the existence of an association or third party website. In this instance, the association did not actually have its own website, so the only possible awareness and adoption alternative was of a third party website. Table 6 shows these results.

Figure 8 shows the I-D map for adoption of an Association and/or third party website and highlights the low levels of awareness and adoption by clubs in the Australian cricket association.

Online Statistics

One of the reasons why cricket associations were chosen for this research project is that cricket,

Figure 8. Association and/or Third Party Website I-D map

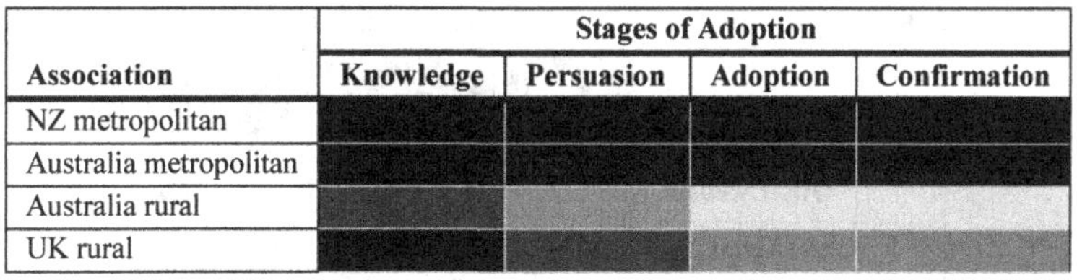

Association	Stages of Adoption			
	Knowledge	Persuasion	Adoption	Confirmation
NZ metropolitan				
Australia metropolitan				
Australia rural				
UK rural				

Table 7. Online statistics adoption levels

Association	Stages of Adoption (%)			
	Knowledge	Persuasion	Adoption	Confirmation
NZ metropolitan	100	100	71	71
Australia metropolitan	100	100	95	95
Australia rural	88	64	17	17
UK rural	100	91	75	75

Figure 9. Online Statistics I-D map

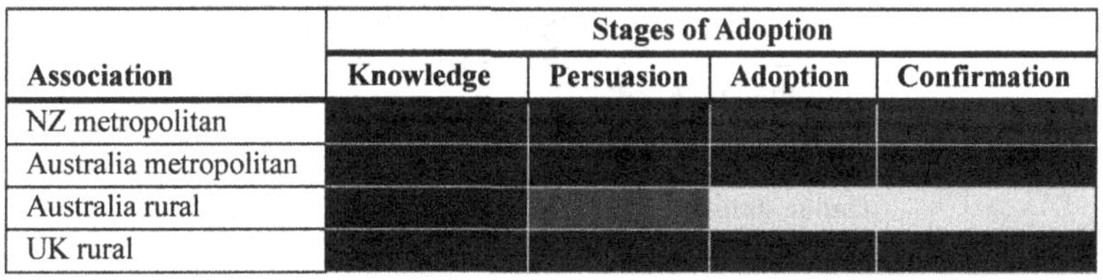

Association	Stages of Adoption			
	Knowledge	Persuasion	Adoption	Confirmation
NZ metropolitan				
Australia metropolitan				
Australia rural				
UK rural				

like baseball, is a sport that can be interpreted with a great deal of statistics. Over recent years a number of different online statistics packages have emerged for use by cricket associations and their clubs. Only one association, the Australian metropolitan association, had a similar (high) proportion of clubs at the confirmation stage as with the other Internet applications. Around three quarters of clubs in the NZ metropolitan association and the UK rural association were in the confirmation stage in relation to the use of online statistics. Again, the Australian rural association lagged well behind the other associations, with only 17% of clubs at the confirmation stage. Table 7 shows the levels of adoption of online statistics at each adoption stage.

Figure 9 shows the I-D map for adoption of online statistics. It is clear that the two Australian cricket associations are at the extreme ends of adoption.

Comparing Associations

In examining the I-D maps that have been created, it is even possible to do an association by association direct comparison for all of the Internet applications that have been developed. This has occurred in Figures 10-13. From these I-D maps it is very easy to see that the two metropolitan associations are more advanced in their use of Internet applications, followed relatively closely by the UK rural association. It is also obvious that the Australian rural association lags well behind the other associations in all areas. Whilst these observations could have been made by examining the tables of figures presented earlier, it is

Figure 10. Complete I-D map: NZ metro

Internet Application	Kdge	Pers	Adpt	Conf
Email				
Club website				
Other website				
Online statistics				

Figure 11. Complete I-D map: Aust metro

Internet Application	Kdge	Pers	Adpt	Conf
Email				
Club website				
Other website				
Online statistics				

Figure 12. Complete I-D map: Aust rural

Internet Application	Kdge	Pers	Adpt	Conf
Email				
Club website				
Other website				
Online statistics				

Figure 13. Complete I-D map: UK rural

Internet Application	Kdge	Pers	Adpt	Conf
Email				
Club website				
Other website				
Online statistics				

the instant visual clues provided by the I-D maps when examined together that show the benefits of using them to map the adoption stages.

The researchers contend that I-D maps are not limited to the adoption of Internet applications in sporting associations. They can be applied to the adoption of any innovation where there are number of parties (in this case, clubs) involved across a number of different entities (in this case, cricket associations).

CONCLUSION

When data has been captured with any project, it is important that it is presented in a way that makes the results speak for themselves. I-D maps provide, through the use of shading, instant comparison across the stages of Rogers' (2003) innovation-decision process. They do this in a more flexible manner than other graphical methods of presenting data, such as bar charts or histogram. This article has provided a practical example of how I-D maps can be used to represent the adoption of different Internet applications by sporting clubs in a range of cricket associations in New Zealand, Australia and the UK.

REFERENCES

Al-Gahtani, S. S. (2003). Computer technology adoption in saudi arabia: Correlates of perceived innovation attributes. *Information Technology for Development, 10*(1), 57–69. doi:10.1002/itdj.1590100106

American University. (2008). *Visualizing data.* Retrieved 16 Sept 2008, from http://www.j-learning.org/present_it/page/visualizing_data

Bingley, S., & Burgess, S. (2009). A framework for the adoption of the Internet in local sporting bodies: A local sporting association example. In Pope, N., Kuhn, K. L., & Forster, J. J. H. (Eds.), *Digital sport for performance enhancement and competitive evolution: Intelligent gaming technologies* (pp. 212–227). Hershey, PA: IGI Global.

Boyle, A., Macleod, M., Slevin, A., Sobecka, N., & Burton, P. (1993). The use of information technology in the voluntary sector. *International Journal of Information Management, 13*(2), 94–112. doi:10.1016/0268-4012(93)90076-G

Charity Commission for England and Wales. (2002). *Giving confidence in charities: Annual Report 2001–2002.* London.

Computer Desktop Encyclopedia. (2008). *ZDNet definition for: Visualization.* Retrieved 17 Sept 2008, from http://dictionary.zdnet.com/definition/Visualization.html

Dikbas, T. E., Kocak, U. Y., & Ilgaz, H. (2008). Teachers' adoption of laptops in the stages of innovation decision process. *Proceedings of World Conference on Educational Multimedia, Hypermedia and Telecommunications 2008,* Vienna, Austria. 3147-3152.

Fogelgren-Pedersen, A. (2005). The mobile internet: The pioneering users' adoption decisions. *Proceedings of the 38Th Hawaii International Conference on Systems Sciences,* Hawaii.

Friendly, M. (2006). A brief history of data visualization. In C. Chen, W. Hardie & A. Unwin (Eds.), *Handbook of Data visualization,* Springer-Verlag, 15-54

Hall, M., & Banting, K. (2002). *The nonprofit sector in Canada: An introduction.* Working Paper, School of Policy Studies, Queen's University.

Industry Canada. (2008). *Technology roadmaps: Geomatics technology roadmap — appendix D: Glossary.* Retrieved 17 Sept 2008, from http://www.ic.gc.ca/epic/site/trm-crt.nsf/en/rm00196e.html

Kappelman, L. A. (1995). Measuring user involvement: A diffusion of innovation perspective. *ACM SIGMIS Database, 26*(2-3), 65–86. doi:10.1145/217278.217286

Kendall, J., Tung, L., Chua, K. H., Ng, C. H. D., & Tan, S. M. (2001). Receptivity of Singapore's SMEs to electronic commerce adoption. *The Journal of Strategic Information Systems, 10*(3), 223–242. doi:10.1016/S0963-8687(01)00048-8

Li, Y., & Lindner, J. R. (2007). Faculty adoption behaviour about web-based distance education: A case study from china agricultural university. *British Journal of Educational Technology, 38*(1), 83–94. doi:10.1111/j.1467-8535.2006.00594.x

MacKay, N., Parent, M., & Gemino, A. (2004). A model of electronic commerce adoption by small voluntary organizations. *European Journal of Information Systems, 13*(2), 147–159. doi:10.1057/palgrave.ejis.3000491

Madon, S. (1999). International NGOs: Networking, information flows and learning. *The Journal of Strategic Information Systems, 8*(3), 251–261. doi:10.1016/S0963-8687(99)00029-3

Morgon, G. (1995). ITEM: A strategic approach to information systems in voluntary organisations. *The Journal of Strategic Information Systems, 4*(3), 225–237. doi:10.1016/0963-8687(95)96803-G

Rogers, E. (2003). *Diffusion of innovations* (5th ed.). New York: Free Press.

Spiegel, M. R., & Stephens, L. J. (2008). *Statistics* (4th ed.). USA: McGraw Hill.

Suraya, R. (2005). Internet diffusion and e-business opportunities amongst Malaysian travel agencies. In *Proceedings of the Hawaii International Conference on Business*, Honolulu.

Tornatzky, L. G., & Klein, K. J. (1982). Innovation characteristics and innovation adoption-implementation: A meta-analysis of findings. *IEEE Transactions on Engineering Management, 29*(1), 28–45.

Wreden, N. (1997). Business boosting technologies. *Beyond Computing, 6*(9), 26-32.

Chapter 7
Modelling the Adoption and Use of Internet Technologies in Higher Education in Thailand

Napaporn Kripanont
Kasetsart University, Thailand

Arthur Tatnall
Victoria University, Australia

ABSTRACT

With a penetration rate of only about 13%, Internet usage in Thailand is lower than the world average, and is much less than the US and Australia where Internet penetration is over 70%. There are a number of approaches to modelling technology adoption, and this chapter describes a research project that modelled adoption of Internet technology by academics in Business Schools in Public Universities in Thailand. In the Internet adoption research outlined in this chapter, formulation of the research model was based mainly on TAM and its derivatives, survey methodology was used to collect primary data from academics in Thailand and analysis was performed using Structural Equation Modelling (SEM). The result was the generation of a research model: 'The Internet Acceptance Model' which demonstrates that only perceived usefulness, perceived ease of use and self-efficacy significantly influenced actual usage behaviour in this case.

SOME MODELS FOR TECHNOLOGY ACCEPTANCE

An important area of research in information systems is that of technology acceptance – the adoption and use of specific technologies. The research described in this article (Kripanont, 2007) involved coming up with a modified model to best describe the adoption of Internet technologies by academics in Business Schools in Thai Public Universities. Several models could have been used to investigate and explain technology acceptance, and the first step was to consider the theoretical perspectives of these in order to formulate the theoretical framework for this study. These technology acceptance theories are as follows.

1. **Innovation-Diffusion** comprises five functions or stages (Rogers, 1983, 1995): knowledge, persuasion, decision, implementation

DOI: 10.4018/978-1-60960-197-3.ch007

and confirmation. In the persuasion stage, five attributes that persuade an individual to adopt the innovation are: relative advantage, compatibility, complexity, trialability, and observability.

2. **Social Cognitive Theory**, by Bandura (1986), views: (a) personal factors in the form of cognition, affect, and biological events, (b) behaviour, and (c) environmental influences that create interactions that result in a triadic reciprocality.

3. The **Theory of Reasoned Action** (TRA) (Ajzen and Fishbein, 1980) postulates that beliefs influence attitude and social norms which in turn shape a behavioural intention guiding or even dictating an individual's behaviour. Intention is the cognitive representation of a person's readiness to perform a given behaviour, and is considered to be the immediate antecedent of behaviour.

4. The **Theory of Planned Behaviour** (TPB) was evolved by Ajzen (1985) from the Theory of Reasoned Action, with a third independent determinant of intention: perceived behaviour control (PBC).

5. The **Decomposed Theory of Planned Behaviour** (DTPB) (Taylor and Todd, 1995b) suggests that behavioural intention is the primary direct determinant of behaviour. Nevertheless the original three core constructs still exist and include attitude toward behaviour (ATB), subjective norm (SN), and perceived behaviour control (PBC) as first introduced in TPB.

6. The **Technology Acceptance Model** (TAM) was developed from TRA by Davis (1989). This model used TRA as a theoretical basis for specifying the causal linkages between two key concepts: perceived usefulness and perceived ease of use, to users' attitudes, intentions and actual computer usage behaviour. Behavioural intention is jointly determined by attitude and perceived usefulness, while attitude is determined by perceived

usefulness (PU) and perceived ease of use (PEOU), replacing those from TRA. The goal of TAM is to provide an explanation of the determinants of computer acceptance that is in general capable of explaining user behaviour across a broad range of end-user computing technologies and user populations, while at the same time being both parsimonious and theoretically justified. But because it incorporates findings accumulated from almost two decades of IS research, it may be especially well-suited to modelling computer acceptance (Davis, Bagozzi, and Warshaw, 1989).

7. In 1995 Taylor and Todd developed the model called **Augmented TAM** or **Combined TAM and TPB** by adding two factors: subjective norm and perceived behavioural control to TAM to provide a more complete test of the important determinants of IT usage, because of their predictive utility in IT usage research and their wide use in social psychology (Taylor and Todd, 1995b).

8. Venkatesh and Davis (2000) later developed **TAM2**. Their goal was a theoretical extension of TAM to: (1) include additional key determinants that explain perceived usefulness and usage intensions in terms of social influence and cognitive instrumental processes and (2) to understand how the effects of these determinants change with increasing user experience over time with the target system.

9. The **Unified Theory of Acceptance and Use of Technology** (UTAUT) (Venkatesh, Morris, Davis, and Davis, 2003) introduced four core determinants (performance expectance, effort expectancy, social influence and facilitating conditions) of intention and usage, and up to four moderators (age, gender, experience and voluntariness of use) of key relationships.

A great deal of previous research has been based on these theories/models, and especially on TAM and its extensions. Despite the popularity and usefulness of TAM, many researchers still want to investigate whether it should be revised, extended or modified to account for rapid change in both technologies and their environments. More importantly, much of the research has been conducted in the U.S. and it is questioned whether technology acceptance models that have been developed in U.S. can be used in other regions like South East Asia and especially in Thailand.

The main objective of the research described in this article was to generate a modified model of technology acceptance that best describes usage adoption behaviour by academics with Internet experience within Business Schools in the Thai Public University Sector. The generated model was expected to be both substantively meaningful and statistically well-fitting (Jöreskog, 1993) and Structural Equation Modelling (SEM) was used in conjunction with the computer package AMOS. The study comprised two stages:

1. Formulation of a technology acceptance model based on TAM and other models.
2. Generation of a technology acceptance research model that best describes usage behaviour of academics using the Internet in their work. This was to make use of SEM through AMOS.

THE INTERNET AND UNIVERSITIES IN THAILAND

The Thai public university sector is supported by the government and Thai higher education institutions are under the supervision of the Office of the Higher Education Commission, Ministry of Education (Commission of Higher Education, 2007). These universities can be classified into four types with specific patterns of coordination

and institutional governance (SEAMEO RIHED, 2007):

1. public universities and institutes,
2. private universities and colleges,
3. other institutes and colleges,
4. specialised training institutions.

Even though worldwide use of the Internet began to grow less than two decade ago (Hyperdictionary, 2006) it is now very popular in many countries. Despite this popularity world Internet penetration (percentage of the population that use the Internet) is still quite low. Only 15.7% of all people in the world use the Internet, accounting for 1,023 million people from a total population of 6,500 million ("Internet Usage Statistics - The Big Picture" 2006). The low Internet penetration rates in some countries raises questions on what determinants influence use of the Internet and how to motivate people to make full use of this technology in their work.

With a penetration rate of 12.7%, Internet usage in Thailand is lower than the world average and cannot be compared with that of the U.S. (68.6%) ("Internet Usage Statistics for the Americas," 2006) and Australia (68.4%) ("Internet Usage and population in Oceania," 2006). The total population of Thailand is 66.6 million, and Internet users make up only 8.4 million people ("Internet Usage for Asia," 2006). Despite the low overall penetration rate, the Internet is most widely used in the central part of Thailand especially in Bangkok – the capital, and the cities around Bangkok. Other than this, the Internet is also widely used in the big cities (or provinces) in other part of the country (Students of the World, 2006). The usage growth in Thailand from 2000-2006 was 266.1% (Internet World Stats, 2006). Noticeably, each Thai public university is located where the Internet is widely used. The Thai government has a policy of supporting IT to facilitate teaching and learning processes (Government of Thailand, 2001) and so there are networks that link to all state universities around the country. All Thai Public Universities have computer facilities and networking including intranet, extranet and the Internet to facilitate the teaching and learning environment.

Thai National Plans (NECTEC, 2001; Office of the Education Council, 2004) have consistent targets and aim to use Internet technologies to support continuous learning. The critical issues of how to increase usage and make full use of ICT are important national concerns. It is seen as essential for all academics in higher education to use ICT, and especially the Internet as most students already do so (Office of the Education Council, 2004).

An understanding of the determinants of usage behaviour will enable higher education institutions to better plan policies and design organisational interventions to increase user acceptance and usage of Internet technologies.

RESEARCH MODEL AND HYPOTHESES

Previous Cross-Sectional Studies

In previous TAM research using cross-sectional studies, if a technology had not been introduced before or had been introduced recently and individuals had no experience of it, or were in the early stage of experience with very few users of the technology at that time, usually only behavioural intention was measured. An example is the study by Chau and Hu (2002). By contrast, if the technology had been in use for quite a period of time, actual usage behaviour was usually measured.

Previous Longitudinal Studies

For longitudinal studies of a new technology, behavioural intention to use was captured before actual usage behaviour was measured. For example, Venkatesh et al. (2003) first investigated behavioural intention and then investigated usage

behaviour from the time of the initial introduction of the technology to stages of greater experience. Thus, in a longitudinal study the role of intention as a predictor of usage behaviour is critical and has been well-established in IS and the reference disciplines (Ajzen, 1991; Sheppard, Hartwick, and Warshaw, 1988; Taylor and Todd, 1995b).

Since the Internet has been used in Thailand for over fifteen years (NECTEC, 2007), in this study *actual usage* was measured in order to explain usage behaviour. In addition, because this is a cross-sectional study it was necessary to use *behavioural intention* as a predictor of future behaviour (Venkatesh et al., 2003) as experience in using the technology will impact on intention to use the technology in the future. For this study both actual usage and intention to use the technology were thus measured concurrently.

The proposed research model for this study was formulated according to the basic concept shown in Figure 1 which is adapted from Venkatesh et al. (2003). This suggests that individual reactions to use of information technology may influence actual usage and actual usage may influence intentions to use the technology. A research model, based on this concept after some tests and modifications (if necessary), could have power in explaining usage behaviour and could predict future usage based on user' intention to use the technology.

The research model was based mainly on TAM (Davis, 1989), TAM2 (Venkatesh and Davis, 2000), C-TAM-TPB (Taylor and Todd, 1995b) and UTAUT (Venkatesh et al., 2003) and specified the causal linkages between five key concepts (perceived usefulness, perceived ease of use, social influence, facilitating conditions and self-efficacy), actual Internet usage, and intention to use the Internet (see Figure 2, later). Usage behaviour is jointly determined by five core constructs including perceived usefulness, perceived ease of use, social influence, facilitating conditions and self-efficacy. Behavioural intention is determined by usage behaviour. In other words, the

Figure 1. Basic concept of the research model (Adapted from Venkatesh et al., 2003)

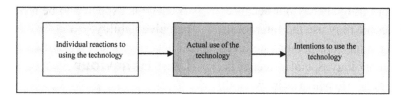

proposed research model was formulated by theorising these five constructs to play important roles as direct determinants of usage behaviour and user acceptance. Several hypotheses were tested regarding whether determinants affect user behaviour, and behavioural intention.

Perceived Usefulness (PU)

This is used as the core construct of interest and as a direct determinant of usage behaviour in this study. It is expected that a person will use a particular technology if they believe that that technology would enhance their job performance, so this determinant will directly influence technology use. Significantly, many models also theorised that perceived usefulness is a direct determinant of behavioural intention and usage behaviour in TAM (Davis, 1989), TAM2 (Venkatesh and Davis, 2000), and Augmented TAM or C-TAM-TPB (Taylor and Todd, 1995b). In addition, perceived usefulness is analogous to the relative advantage of perceived characteristics of an innovation according to Innovations Diffusion by Rogers (1995).

In this study therefore, perceived usefulness is defined and used as the degree to which a person believes that using a particular system would enhance their job performance according to the definition from Davis (1989) and Davis et al. (1989).

Perceived Ease of Use (PEOU)

PEOU is also theorised as a direct determinant of behavioural intention in a number of theories including TAM, TAM2, and C-TAM-TPB. In ad-

dition, strong evidence supports perceived ease of use as a direct determinant of usage behaviour (Davis, 1989; Gefen and Straub, 1997; Igbaria, Zinatelli, Cragg, and Cavaye, 1997; Szajna, 1994; Thompson, Higgins, and Howell, 1991). It is analogous to the complexity of perceived characteristics of an innovation by Rogers (1983), although in the opposite direction. Perceived ease of use is similar to effort expectancy in the concept, construct definitions and measurement scales (Venkatesh et al., 2003). Effort expectancy is defined by Venkatesh, et, al. (2003, p. 450) as: "The degree of ease associated with the use of the system."

For this study, perceived ease of use is considered to be a direct determinant of usage behaviour because it is expected that an academic would use the Internet if he or she believes that the technology is easy to use. Thus in this research, perceived ease of use is defined and used here as the degree to which a person believes that using a system would be free of effort in accordance with Davis (1989) and Davis et al. (1989).

Social Influence

According to Venkatesh et al. (2003), social influence is a direct determinant of behavioural intention and is represented as a subjective norm in the Theory of Reasoned Action (Ajzen and Fishbein, 1980; Fishbein and Ajzen, 1975), TAM2 (Venkatesh and Davis, 2000), Theory of Planned Behaviour (Ajzen, 1991), Decomposed Theory of Planned Behaviour (Taylor and Todd, 1995b), and Augmented TAM or C-TAM-TPB (Taylor and Todd, 1995b), etc.

In this study, social influence is also used as a direct determinant of usage behaviour because it is expected that people may use the Internet if they think that other important persons believe they should use the technology. Social influence is defined here as "The degree to which an individual perceives that other important persons believe he or she should use the technology/system" (Venkatesh et al., 2003, p. 451).

Facilitating Conditions

This is defined as "The degree to which an individual believes that an organisational and technical infrastructure exists to support use of the system" (Venkatesh et al., 2003, p. 453). The empirical results also indicated that facilitating conditions did have a direct influence on usage beyond that explained by behavioural intention alone. Consistent with TPB/DTPB, facilitating conditions was also modelled as a direct antecedent of usage (Ajzen, 2006; Taylor and Todd, 1995b). The researchers expected that facilitating conditions would not have any influence toward behavioural intention but only on usage behaviour as the more the facilitating conditions exist to support use of the technology, the more the technology is used.

Self-Efficacy

Self-efficacy is defined in this study as the internal notion of the individual and is related to perceived ability (Bandura, 1986). With respect to Information Technology usage it was anticipated that higher levels of self-efficacy lead to higher levels of behavioural intention and IT usage (Compeau and Higgins, 1991). Taylor and Todd (1995b) suggested that in DTPB, self-efficacy was a significant determinant of perceived behavioural control, and also a significant determinant of behaviour intention and actual behaviour. However, for this study it was expected that self-efficacy would be a significant direct determinant of usage behaviour because the perceived ability of a person will influence them to use the technology. The level of usage is expected to be related to the level of perceived ability.

User Behaviour

Normally in Thai Public Universities, Internet usage by academics depends on their volitional control, in the other words on their own choice. This research was conducted in the context of voluntary use (similar to most previous research). Since an individual's stated preference to perform the activity (i.e. behavioural intention) will be closely related to the way they do behave, this assumption only applies when the behaviour is under a person's volitional control (Ajzen and Fishbein, 1980). Therefore, academics' intention to use the Internet will be closely related to their usage behaviour if the use of the technology is their own choice. This suggests that actual usage may influence behavioural intention in this cross-sectional study, and that usage behaviour will have a significant positive influence on behavioural intention to use the technology in the future.

Behavioural Intention (BI)

Behavioural intention plays an important role in predicting behaviour but it is important to note that BI is more predictive of behaviour when individuals have had prior experience (Taylor and Todd, 1995a). Since this study is a cross-sectional study, and because individual academics already have experienced using the Internet, at the time of the survey academics' behavioural intention was influenced by actual usage (usage at the time of survey). Behavioural intention thus plays an important role in predicting usage behaviour of individual academics using the Internet in the future.

Figure 2. The proposed research model

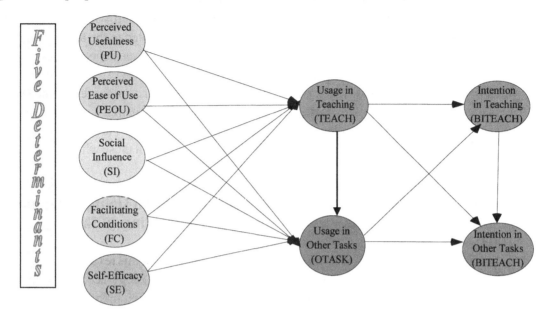

Direct Path Hypotheses

The direct path hypotheses are divided into three groups, the first group containing hypotheses for testing the significant influence of determinants on usage behaviour of the Internet in teaching and teaching related tasks (TEACH). The second group is for testing the significant influence of determinants on usage behaviour of the Internet in other tasks (OTASK). The third group is for testing the influence of usage behaviour toward behaviour intention.

1. Determinants and Usage Behaviour in Teaching and Teaching Related Tasks (TEACH)

    H₁1a: Perceived usefulness has a significant influence on usage behaviour (TEACH).

    H₁2a: Perceived ease of use has a significant influence on usage behaviour (TEACH).

    H₁3a: Social influence has a significant influence on usage behaviour (TEACH).

    H₁4a: Facilitating conditions has a significant influence on usage behaviour (TEACH).

    H₁5a: Self-efficacy has a significant influence on usage behaviour (TEACH).

2. Determinants and Usage Behaviour in Other Tasks (OTASK)

    H₁1b: Perceived usefulness has a significant influence on usage behaviour (OTASK).

    H₁2b: Perceived ease of use has a significant influence on usage behaviour (OTASK).

    H₁3b: Social influence has a significant influence on usage behaviour (OTASK).

    H₁4b: Facilitating conditions has a significant influence on usage behaviour (OTASK).

    H₁5b: Self-efficacy has a significant influence on usage behaviour (OTASK).

3. Usage Behaviour and Behavioural Intention

    H₁6: Usage behaviour in teaching (TEACH) has a significant influence on usage behaviour in other tasks (OTASK).

$H_1$7: Usage behaviour in teaching (TEACH) has a significant influence on behaviour intention in teaching (BITEACH).

$H_1$8: Usage behaviour in teaching (TEACH) has a significant influence on behaviour intention in other tasks (BIOTASK).

$H_1$9: Usage behaviour in other tasks (OTASK) has a significant influence on behaviour intention in teaching (BITEACH).

$H_1$10: Usage behaviour in other tasks (OTASK) has a significant influence on behaviour intention in other tasks (BIOTASK).

$H_1$11: Behaviour intention in teaching (BITEACH) has a significant influence on behaviour intention in other tasks (BIOTASK).

RESEARCH METHODOLOGY

This research employed survey methodology using semi-structured interviews to gather preliminary data during the exploratory stage. The results from the interviews helped in designing the questionnaire used in the next stage to collect primary data. The questionnaire design was pre-tested twice, and then the pilot survey was conducted. From the results of reliability, content validity, convergent validity tests and data analysis of the pilot survey, a minor change was also made to the questionnaire design before distribution.

Questionnaires were distributed to all academics within 22 Business Schools in 24 Universities in the Thai Public University sector around the country. From an estimated 1,045 academics, 109 academics were on educational leave, and 9 academics had no Internet experience, so the target population was 927 academics. Subjects for this study were individual full-time academics within Business Schools (or equivalent) who have had some Internet experience. Because the size of the population was relatively small (927 academics) it was important to use all subjects in the popula-

tion as targets of this survey (Sekaran, 2003). A questionnaire was created with items validated in prior research adapted to the technologies and organisations studied (see items on questionnaire in Table 2 in Appendix A).

After three months, the survey yielded a total of 455 usable questionnaires, so the response rate of this survey was 49%. Participation was on a voluntary basis, and all those who responded had Internet experience.

Model Generation Using Structural Equation Modelling (SEM)

The main objective of this research was to generate a model of technology acceptance that best described usage behaviour of academics, with some Internet experience, within Thai Business Schools. The generated model needed to be one that was both substantively meaningful and statistically well-fitting (Byrne, 2001, 2006).

In order to achieve this objective, structural equation modelling (SEM) was used. SEM is a multivariate technique combining aspects of multiple regression (examining dependence relationships) and factor analysis (representing unmeasured concepts-factors with multiple variables) to estimate a series of interrelated dependence relationships simultaneously (Hair, Black, Babin, Anderson, and Tatham, 2006; Schumacker and Lomax, 1996). A structural equation model, or path model, depicts the structural relationships among constructs (Sharma, 1996). In other words, SEM is a model of relationships among variables (Hayduk, 1987).

There are three important general strategic frameworks for testing structural equation models (Jöreskog, 1993): strictly confirmatory, alternative model and model generating.

1. For a strictly confirmatory approach (SC) the researcher postulates a single model based on theory, collects the appropriate data, and then tests the fit of the hypothesised model to the

sample data. The researcher either rejects or accepts the model based on the results of the test; no further modifications to the model are made. This is not commonly found in practice because with the many costs associated with the collection of data, it would be a rare researcher indeed who could afford to terminate his or her research on the basis of a rejected hypothesised model.

2. An alternative model (AM) approach has been relatively uncommon in practice, since, after proposing several alternative (i.e., competing) models, all of which are grounded in theory following analysis of a single set of empirical data, the researcher selects one model as most appropriate in representing the sample data.

3. This research was based on the third strategic framework – a model generating (MG) strategy. MG is the most common of the three scenarios because the researcher could postulate and reject a theoretically derived model on the basis of its poor fit to the sample data, and proceed in an exploratory (rather than confirmatory) fashion to modify and re-estimate the model. The primary focus is to locate the source of misfit in the model and to determine a model that better describes the sample data. In this strategy further modification to the model could be made.

By using SEM with AMOS (the SEM software package) the hypothesised model can be tested statistically in a simultaneous analysis of the entire system of variables to determine the extent to which it is consistent with the data. If the goodness of fit is adequate, the model argues for the plausibility of the postulated relations among variables; if it is inadequate, the tenability of such relations is rejected. However, despite the fact that a model is tested in each round, the whole approach is model generation rather than model testing (Byrne, 2001, 2006).

TECHNOLOGY ACCEPTANCE MODELLING

Core Constructs

The proposed research model comprised nine latent constructs. A latent construct cannot be measured directly but can be represented or measured by one or more variables (indicators). An observed (measured) variable is a specific item or question, obtained either from respondents in response to questions in a questionnaire or from some type of observation. Measured variables are used as the indicators of latent constructs. In other words, indicators associated with each latent construct are specified by the researcher (Hair et al., 2006).

Nine latent constructs include five exogenous constructs (independent variables) including perceived usefulness, perceived ease of use, social influence, facilitating conditions and self-efficacy, and four endogenous constructs (dependent variables) including actual Internet usage behaviour (TEACH, OTASK) and intention to use the Internet (BITEACH and BIOTASK). An exogenous construct is a latent, multi-item equivalent of an independent variable. It is a construct that is not affected by any other constructs in the model. Endogenous constructs are latent, multi-item equivalents to dependent variables. They are constructs that are affected by other constructs in the model (Hair et al., 2006; Sharma, 1996).

In this study, consideration of which items belong to a specific latent construct was based on the literature. Each construct comprised at least four, and no more than five, items. For example, a perceived usefulness latent construct (PU) consists of 4 items (indicators/observed variables) including pu1, pu2, pu3, and pu4 according to the literature. In addition, a teaching in class latent construct (TEACH) consists of 5 items and using the Internet in other tasks latent construct (OTASK) also consists of 5 items, etc. (see Table 1 in Appendix A). All indicators of core constructs and their measurement scales were adapted from Venkatesh et al. (2003), Venkatesh and Davis (2000) and Taylor and Todd (1995b), and are presented in Table 2 in Appendix A.

This study was conducted using the two-step approach to SEM recommended by Anderson and Gerbing (1988) where firstly the measurement models are evaluated to ensure that the items used to measure each of the constructs is adequate. The second step is carried out only after the measurement models are shown to be proper measures of the constructs. This involves assessment of the structural model showing the relationships between the constructs. By using this two-step approach, the typical problem of not being able to localise the source of poor model fit associated with the single-step approach (which assesses measurement and structural models simultaneously (Singh and Smith, 2001)) is overcome (Kline, 1998).

Construct Reliability and Discriminant Validity

The Squared Multiple Correlation (SMC) was used to measure construct reliability. This is referred to an item reliability coefficient and is the correlation between a single indicator variable and the construct it measures. The SMC for an observed variable is the square of the indicator's standardised loading. For example, if the standardised loading for an observed variable is 0.80, the corresponding squared multiple correlation is 0.64 and the error variance is 0.36 accordingly. The SMC of a good observed variable should exceed 0.50 although an SMC of 0.30 indicates an acceptable indicator variable. An SMC of 0.50 is roughly equivalent to a standardised load of 0.70 (Holmes-Smith, Cunningham, and Coote, 2006). It was found that most SMCs of the 21 observed variables belong to the five exogenous latent constructs (PU, PEOU, SI, FC, and SE) exceeded 0.50 and that most SMCs of the 20 observed variables of the four endogenous latent constructs (TEACH, OTASK, BITEACH,

and BIOTASK) exceeded 0.50. These indicated construct reliability.

In discriminant validity analysis, it was found that these five latent constructs in the research model were different because correlations between latent constructs were not larger than 0.8 or 0.9. The maximum correlation (between PEOU and SE) was 0.71. In addition, four other constructs in the research model, after deleting some indicators, were different because correlations between latent constructs were not larger than 0.8 or 0.9, and the maximum correlation (between TEACH and BITEACH) was 0.73. These indicated discriminant validity of the five exogenous latent constructs, and four endogenous constructs in the model.

It can thus be concluded that the constructs in a model reflect construct reliability and discriminant validity.

Results of Hypotheses Testing

In generating the research model three groups of hypotheses were tested. The results, with modifications, formed the modified model of technology acceptance, in this study called the 'Internet Acceptance Model'.

For Group-1 hypotheses (determinants and usage behaviour), only five null hypotheses were accepted out of ten ($H_1$1a-$H_1$5a, and $H_1$1b-$H_1$5b). This indicates that perceived usefulness (PU) ($H_1$1a), perceived ease of use (PEOU) ($H_1$2a) and self-efficacy (SE) ($H_1$5a) significantly influenced actual usage behaviour of academics in using the Internet in teaching (TEACH).

For Group-2 hypotheses, perceived usefulness (PU) ($H_1$1b), and self-efficacy (SE) ($H_1$5b) significantly influenced actual usage behaviour of academics in using the Internet in other tasks (OTASK).

For Group-3 hypotheses (usage behaviour and behaviour intention), all hypotheses were accepted ($H_1$6-$H_1$11), indicating that actual us-

Figure 3. Internet acceptance model (In experience and voluntary settings)

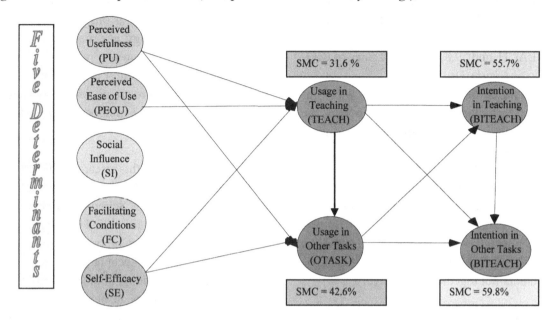

age behaviour of academics in using the Internet significantly influenced their intention to use the Internet in the future.

The Internet Acceptance Model

The Internet Acceptance Model posits three significant determinants of usage in teaching (TEACH): perceived usefulness (PU), perceived ease of use (PEOU) and self-efficacy (SE), and two significant determinants of usage in other tasks: perceived usefulness (PU) and self-efficacy (SE). Social influence and facilitating conditions did not play an important role in influencing usage behaviour. All six direct paths between usage behaviour and behavioural intention are statistically significant (see Figure 3).

From this finding, it can be suggested that academics used the Internet in teaching and in other tasks because of perceived usefulness (PU) and self-efficacy (SE) and noticeably in teaching. One more motivation to used the Internet was perceived ease of use (PEOU). This indicates that sometimes academics may not have used the

Internet in teaching and teaching related tasks because they thought that the Internet was not easy to use or there were obstacles related to using it. In other words, academics still use the Internet in teaching less than in other tasks, but those who use the Internet in teaching did so because they perceived that the Internet was easy to use.

Perceived usefulness was an important determinant and the findings suggest that academics used the Internet because they believed that it was useful. This perception motivated them to utilise the technology for their work. Self-efficacy was another important determinant and the findings suggest that whenever academics used the Internet either in teaching or in other tasks the rationale behind usage was their perception that they were able to use the technology. They thus used the technology because of self-confidence associated with their abilities in using the technology.

The generated model is well capable of explaining the variances in four latent constructs by examining the Square Multiple Correlation (SMC). SMC is analogous to the R^2 statistic

(Sharma, 1996). The model has the power to explain 31.6% of the variance of TEACH, 42.6% of the variance of OTASK, 55.7% of the variance of BITEACH, and 59.8% of the variance of BIO-TASK (see Figure 3).

It should be noted that the study was conducted in a voluntary setting (academics used the Internet by their own free will). The capabilities in explaining the variances of usage behaviour and behaviour intention of the model, presented an improvement over almost all of the original nine theories and their extensions. According to a study of Venkatesh et al. (2003) R^2 of ID was 39%, SCT 36%, TRA 19%, TPB 21%, TAM 37%, TAM2 37%, C-TAM-TPB 39%, and UTAUT 36% (pooled data not together) respectively.

Methodological and Practical Implications

This study illustrates how Structural Equation Modelling can provide a very useful statistical technique for generating models, especially together with AMOS, as there are significant benefits of using SEM over other multivariate techniques (Byrne, 2001, 2006):

- SEM presents itself well to analysis of data for purposes of inferential statistics. On the other hand, most other multivariate techniques are essentially descriptive by nature (e.g. exploratory factor analysis) so that although hypothesis testing is possible, it is rather difficult to do.
- SEM can provide explicit estimates of error variance parameters, whereas traditional multivariate techniques are not capable of either assessing or correcting for measurement error.
- Data analysis using SEM procedures can incorporate both unobserved (latent variables) and observed variables, but the for-

mer data analysis methods are based on observed measurements only.

- SEM methodology has many features for modelling multivariate relations and for estimating point and/or interval indirect effects, whilst there are no widely and easily applied alternative methods for these kinds of features.

The key findings of this research could provide significant benefits not only for individual academics within Business Schools, but also to the Universities in the Thai Public University sector as well as the country. An important implication is that using the Internet Acceptance Model, which provides an understanding about relationships of key determinants and usage behaviour and usage behaviour with behaviour intention, will help promote Internet usage within Thai Business Schools and may also be applied to other universities.

The Internet Acceptance Model has been carefully considered in terms of both parsimony and its contribution to understanding. For predictive, practical applications of the model, parsimony may be more heavily weighted. On the other hand, if trying to obtain the most complete understanding of a phenomenon, a degree of parsimony may be sacrificed (Taylor and Todd, 1995b). With this rationale, in this study the Internet Acceptance Model comprised three important determinants: perceived usefulness, perceived ease of use and self-efficacy. This has provided useful information about how to promote usage of the Internet. The more academics perceive usefulness and ease of use of the Internet the greater these determinants encourage them to use the Internet. The more academics perceive their ability (self-efficacy) the more they increase their Internet usage. As previously mentioned, the way to promote self-efficacy is by continuous training, and especially training that reinforces these perceptions. Training was found to be very significant in encouraging individuals to have more self-confidence in their use of the technology, and they will use the technology more because of their self-confidence associated with their abilities in using the technology. In conclusion, if Internet usage in all types of work increase, it will enable positive changes in teaching and learning processes (Leidner and Jarvenpaa, 1995).

CONCLUSION

From a theoretical perspective, the Internet Acceptance Model provides an understanding of the relationships of determinants and usage behaviour and refines the view of how usage behaviour relates to behavioural intention in a cross-sectional study. Behavioural intention was significantly influenced by actual usage: the more experience of the technology, the more significantly this affects their intention to use the technology in the future. More specifically, in order to increase the power of explaining behaviour by the model, usage behaviour was separated into two categories: teaching (TEACH), other tasks (OTASK), behavioural intention was separated into two categories: intention to use in teaching (BITEACH) and intention to use in other tasks (BIOTASK). Five determinants in the research model were theorised according to the theories of technology acceptance but the findings did not perfectly fit as theorised when testing the model using SEM.

- Firstly, regarding perceived usefulness and perceived ease of use, not only have these received considerable attention in the technology acceptance research literature (rather than self-efficacy) but both also have significant influence on usage behaviour particularly in teaching. Only perceived usefulness has a significant influence on usage behaviour in other tasks.
- Secondly, self-efficacy was found to be another important determinant in this re-

search, which is consistent with previous studies such as Lopez and Manson (1997) and Ramayah and Aafaqi (2004). It has a very strong influence on usage behaviour both in teaching and in other tasks, although it has received less attention in the technology acceptance research literature compared to the two determinants previously mentioned.

- Thirdly, it has been found that social influence has no significant influence on usage behaviour, although some researchers have argued to integrate social influence in models of adoption and use (for example, Taylor and Todd (1995b), and Thompson, Higgins and Howell (1991)). Others, however including Davis, Bagozzi and Warshaw (1989) have not integrated this into their models. For this study, social influence had no significant influence on usage behaviour, possibly because academics already had Internet experience of 6 to 10 years. According to empirical evidence from a study by Karahanna, Straub and Chervany (1999) which suggested that experience moderated the relationship between subjective norm (social influence) and behaviour, social influence becomes less important with increasing levels of experience.
- Fourthly, it has also been found that facilitating conditions have no significant effect on usage behaviour. This finding was not consistent with those of Venkatesh et al. (2003), who suggested that facilitating conditions have a significant effect on usage behaviour. Noticeably, the path between facilitating conditions and usage in other tasks was deleted from the Internet Acceptance Model because it was never significant.

REFERENCES

Ajzen, I. (1985). From intentions to actions: a theory of planned behaviour [Electronic Version]. *Action Control: From Cognition to Behavior*, 11-39. Retrieved February 2, 2004, from http://search. epnet.com/login.aspx?direct=true&db=aph&au thdb=epref&an=ACFCB.AJZEN.SPRINGER. AIHE.AA

Ajzen, I. (1991). The Theory of Planned Behaviour [Electronic Version] [from http://search. epnet.com/login.aspx?direct=true&db=aph&aut hdb=epref&an=OBHDP.EJ.AGI.AJZEN.TPB]. *Organizational Behavior and Human Decision Processes*, *50*, 179–211. Retrieved September 2, 2004. doi:10.1016/0749-5978(91)90020-T

Ajzen, I. (2006). Theory of planned behaviour (Publication. Retrieved November 4, 2006, from http://people.umass.edu/aizen/tpb.diag.html

Ajzen, I., & Fishbein, M. (1980). *Understanding attitudes and predicting social behaviour.* Retrieved August 4, 2004, from http://search. epnet.com/login.aspx?direct=true&db=aph&au thdb=epref&an=UAPSB.AJZEN.PRENTICE-HALL.AIHJ

Anderson, J. C., & Gerbing, D. W. (1988). Structural Equation Modelling in practice: a review and recommended two-step approach. *Psychological Bulletin*, *103*(3), 411–423. doi:10.1037/0033-2909.103.3.411

Bandura, A. (1986). *Social foundations of thought and action: a social cognitive theory.* Englewood Cliffs, NJ: Prentice-Hall.

Byrne, B. M. (2001). *Structural Equation Modelling with AMOS: Basic Concepts, Applications, and Programming.* Mahwah, NJ: Lawrence Erlbaum Associates, Inc.

Byrne, B. M. (2006). *Structural Equation Modelling with EQS: Basic concepts, applications, and programming* (2 ed.). Mahwah, NJ: Lawrence Erlbaum Associates, Inc.

Chau, P. Y. K., & Hu, P. J. (2002). Examining a model of information technology acceptance by individual professionals: An exploratory study. *Journal of Management Information Systems*, *18*(4), 191–229.

Commission of Higher Education. (2007). Commission of Higher Education. Retrieved January 15, 2007, from http://www.mua.go.th/default1. php

Compeau, D. R., & Higgins, C. A. (1991). *A Social Cognitive Theory Perspective on Individual Reactions to Computing Technology.* Paper presented at the Proceedings of the 12th International Conference on Information Systems, New York.

Davis, F. D. (1989). Perceived usefulness, perceived ease of use and user acceptance of information technology [Electronic Version]. *MIS Quarterly, 13*, 319-340. Retrieved 5 June 2004 from http://search.epnet.com/login.aspx?direct= true&db=aph&authdb=epref&an=MQ.AC.CAI. DAVIS.PUPEUU

Davis, F. D., Bagozzi, R. P., & Warshaw, P. R. (1989). User acceptance of computer technology: a comparison of two theoretical models [Electronic Version] [from http://search.epnet.com/login. aspx?direct=true&db=aph&authdb=epref&an= MS.CE.IHB.DAVIS.UACTCT]. *Management Science, 35*, 982–1003. Retrieved June 7, 2004. doi:10.1287/mnsc.35.8.982

Fishbein, M., & Ajzen, I. (1975). *Belief, Attitude, Intention and Behavior: An Introduction to Theory and Research B2 - Belief, Attitude, Intention and Behavior: An Introduction to Theory and Research.* Reading, MA: Addison-Wesley.

Gefen, D., & Straub, D. W. (1997). Gender differences in the perception and use of e-mail: An extension to the Technology Acceptance [Electronic Version]. *MIS Quarterly*, 21, 389. Retrieved 7 September 2004 from http://search.epnet.com/login.aspx?direct=true&db=aph&an=36297

Hair, J., Black, W., Babin, B., Anderson, R., & Tatham, R. (2006). *Multivariate data analysis* (6th ed.). Upper Saddle River, NJ: Pearson Education, Inc.

Hayduk, L. A. (1987). *Structural equation modelling with LISREL: Essentials and advances*. Baltimore, MD: The Johns Hopkins University Press.

Hyperdictionary. (2006). *Internet: Definition*. Retrieved July 5, 2006, from http://www.hyperdictionary.com/dictionary/Internet

Igbaria, M., Zinatelli, N., Cragg, P., & Cavaye, A. L. M. (1997). Personal computing acceptance factors in small firms: A structural equation model. *Management Information Systems Quarterly*, 21(3), 279–305. doi:10.2307/249498

Internet Usage and population in Oceania. (2006). *Internet Usage and population in Oceania*. Retrieved July 7, 2006, from http://www.internetworldstats.com/stats6.htm

Internet Usage for Asia. (2006). *Internet Usage for Asia*. Retrieved July 7, 2006, from http://www.internetworldstats.com/stats3.htm#asia

Internet Usage Statistics for the Americas. (2006). *Internet Usage Statistics for the Americas*. Retrieved 7 July 7, 2006, from http://www.internetworldstats.com/stats2.htm#north

Internet Usage Statistics-The Big Picture. (2006). Retrieved July 7, 2006, from http://www.internetworldstats.com/stats.htm

Internet World Stats. (2006). *Internet Usage in Asia*. Retrieved 9 January, 2007, from http://www.internetworldstats.com/stats3.htm#asia

Jöreskog, K. G. (1993). Testing structural equation models. In *B. M. Byrne (2006), Structural Equation Modelling with EQS: basic concepts, applications, and programming* (2nd ed.). Mahwah, NJ: Lawrence Erlbaum Associates, Inc.

Karahanna, E., Straub, D. W., & Chervany, N. L. (1999). Information technology adoption across time: a cross-sectional comparison of pre-adoption and post-adoption beliefs [Electronic Version]. *MIS Quarterly*, 23, 183-213. Retrieved August 31, 2004 from http://search.epnet.com/login.aspx?direct=true&db=aph&authdb=epref&an=MQ.BC.AHC.KARAHANNA.ITAATC

Kline, R. B. (1998). *Principles and practice of Structural Equation Modelling*. New York: Guilford Press.

Kripanont, N. (2007). *Examining a Technology Acceptance Model of Internet Usage by Academics within Thai Business Schools*. Melbourne, Australia: Victoria University.

Leidner, D. E., & Jarvenpaa, S. L. (1995). The use of information technology to enhance management school education: a theoretical view. *Management Information Systems Quarterly*, 19(3), 265–292. doi:10.2307/249596

Lopez, D. A., & Manson, D. P. (1997). *A study of individual computer self-efficacy and perceived usefulness of the empowered desktop information system* [Electronic Version], 83-92. Retrieved December 5, 2005 from www.csupomona.edu/~jis/1997/Lopez.pdf.

NECTEC. (2007). *Internet Users in Thailand*. Retrieved January 12, 2007, from http://iir.ngi.nectec.or.th/internet/user-growth.html

Office of the Education Council. (2004). *Education in Thailand*. Retrieved January 29, 2005, from http://www.edthai.com/pulication/edu2004/content.

Ramayah, T., & Aafaqi, B. (2004). Role of self-efficacy in e-library usage among students of a public university in Malaysia [Electronic Version]. *Malaysian Journal of Library and Information Science*, 19, 39-57. Retrieved December 8, 2006 from http://majlis.fsktm.um.edu.my/document.aspx?FileName=276.pdf.

Rogers, E. M. (1983). *Diffusion of innovations* (3 rd ed.). New York: The Free Press.

Rogers, E. M. (1995). *Diffusion of Innovations* (4 th ed.). New York, NY: The Free Press.

Schumacker, R. E., & Lomax, R. G. (1996). *A beginner's guide to Structural Equation Modelling*. Mahwah, NJ: Lawerence Erbaum.

SEAMEO RIHED. (2007). Higher Education System of Thailand. Retrieved January 15, 2007, from http://www.rihed.seameo.org/hesystem/thailandHEIs.htm

Sekaran, U. (2003). *Research methods for business: a skill-building approach* (4 th ed.). New York: John Wiley and Sons, Inc.

Sharma, S. (1996). *Applied Multivariate Techniques*. New York: John Wiley and Sons, Inc.

Sheppard, B. H., Hartwick, J., & Warshaw, P. R. (1988). The Theory of Reasoned Action: a meta-analysis of past research with recommendations for modifications and future research [Electronic Version] [from http://search.epnet.com/login.aspx?direct=true&db=aph&authdb=epref&an=JCR.AE.CBE.SHEPPARD.TRAMAP]. *The Journal of Consumer Research*, 15, 325–343. Retrieved March 4, 2004. doi:10.1086/209170

Singh, P. J., & Smith, A. J. R. (2001). *TQM and Innovation: An empirical examination of their relationship*. Paper presented at the 5th International and 8th National Research Conference on Quality and Innovation Management. from http://www.eacc.unimelb.edu.au/pubs/proceedings6.pdf#search=%22TQM%20and%20Innovation%3A%20An%20Empirical%20Examination%22.

Students of the World. (2006). *Thailand*. Retrieved January 13, 2007, from http://www.studentsoftheworld.info/country_information.php?Pays=THA

Szajna, B. (1994). Software evaluation and choice: predictive validation of the technology acceptance instrument [Electronic Version]. *MIS Quarterly, 17*, 319-324 from http://search.epnet.com/login.aspx?direct=true&db=aph&authdb=epref&an=MS.DB.HE.SZAJNA.EERTAM

Taylor, S., & Todd, P. A. (1995a). Assessing it usage: the role of prior experience [Electronic Version]. *MIS Quarterly*, 19, 561-570. Retrieved August 30, 2004 from http://search.epnet.com/login.aspx?direct=true&db=aph&authdb=epref&an=MQ.AI.EFA.TAYLOR.AIURPE

Taylor, S., & Todd, P. A. (1995b). Understanding information technology usage: a test of competing models [Electronic Version] [from http://search.epnet.com/login.aspx?direct=true&db=aph&authdb=epref&an=ISR.F.ADD.TAYLOR.UITUTC]. *Information Systems Research*, 6, 144–176. Retrieved August 30, 2004. doi:10.1287/isre.6.2.144

Thompson, R. L., Higgins, C. A., & Howell, J. M. (1991). Personal computing: toward a conceptual model of utilization [Electronic Version] [from http://search.epnet.com/login.aspx?direct=true&db=aph&authdb=epref&an=MQ.AE.ABD.THOMPSON.PCTCMU]. *Management Information Systems Quarterly*, 15, 124–143. Retrieved September 1, 2004. doi:10.2307/249443

Venkatesh, V., & Davis, F. D. (2000). A theoretical extension of the Technology Acceptance Model: four longitudinal field studies [Electronic Version]. *Management Science, 46*, 186-204. Retrieved August 4, 2004, from http://search.epnet.com/login.aspx?direct=true&db=bth&an=2958359

Venkatesh, V., Morris, M. G., Davis, G. B., & Davis, F. D. (2003). User acceptance of Information Technology: toward a unified view [Electronic Version]. *MIS Quarterly, 27*, 425-478. Retrieved July 31, 2004, from http://search.epnet.com/login.aspx?direct=true&db=aph&an=10758835

APPENDIX A

Table 1. Nine constructs in the proposed research model

Construct	Number of Items	Items/Indicators/ Observed Variables	Codes/Name of Constructs	Definitions of the Constructs
1*	4	pu1-pu4	PU	Perceived usefulness
2*	4	peou1-peou4	PEOU	Perceived ease of use
3*	5	si1-si5	SI	Social Influence
4*	4	fc1-fc4	FC	Facilitating Conditions
5*	4	se1-se4	SE	Self-Efficacy
6**	5	tclass, tweb, tmateria, tknowled, temail	TEACH	Usage behaviour (actual usage of the Internet in teaching and teaching related tasks)
7**	5	oresearc, oadmin, person, operknow, oemail	OTASK	Usage behaviour (actual usage of the Internet in other tasks)
8**	5	bitclass, bitweb, bitmater, bitknow, bitemail	BITEACH	Behaviour intention (Intention to use the Internet in the future in teaching and teaching related tasks)
9**	5	Bioresea, bioadmin, bioperso, bioperkn, bioemail	BIOTASK	Behaviour intention (Intention to use the Internet in the future in other tasks)

* = Exogenous Latent Construct, ** = Endogenous Latent Construct

Table 2. Indicators/items, questions on the questionnaire and measurement scale

Indicator (Code)	Core Construct	Description (Question on the Questionnaire)	*Scale
pu1	PU	1. Using the Internet enables me to accomplish tasks more quickly.	7-point
pu2	PU	2. Using the Internet enhances the quality of my work.	7-point
pu3	PU	3. Using the Internet makes it easier to do my work.	7-point
pu4	PU	4. I find the Internet useful in my work.	7-point
peou1	PEOU	1. Learning to use the Internet is easy for me.	7-point
peou2	PEOU	2. I find it easy to use the Internet to do what I want to do.	7-point
peou3	PEOU	3. I find it easy to become skilful in using the Internet.	7-point
peou4	PEOU	4. I find the Internet easy to use.	7-point
si1	SI	1. Peers think that I should use the Internet.	7-point
si2	SI	2. Family and friends think that I should use the Internet.	7-point
si3	SI	3. Students think that I should use the Internet.	7-point
si4	SI	4. Management of my university thinks that I should use the Internet.	7-point
si5	SI	5. In general, my university has supported the use of the Internet.	7-point
fc1	FC	1. The resources necessary (e.g. new computer hardware/software, network etc.) are available for me to use the Internet effectively.	7-point
fc2	FC	2. I can access the Internet very quickly within my University.	7-point
fc3	FC	3. Guidance is available to me to use the Internet effectively.	7-point
fc4	FC	4. A specific person (or group) is available for assistance with Internet difficulties.	7-point

continued on following page

Table 2. continued

Indicator (Code)	Core Construct	Description (Question on the Questionnaire)	*Scale
se1	SE	1. I feel comfortable when I use the Internet on my own.	7-point
se2	SE	2. I am able to use the Internet even if there is no one around to show me how to use it.	7-point
se3	SE	3. I can complete my task by using the Internet if I can call someone for help if I get stuck.	7-point
se4	SE	4. I can complete my task by using the Internet if I have a lot of time.	7-point
tclass	TEACH	1. I use the Internet when teaching in classes.	7-point
tweb	TEACH	2. I use the Internet in providing a Personal Web-Base for facilitating teaching *(e.g. on-line syllabus, lectures, noted, tutorials, tests, quizzes, and providing grade etc.)*	7-point
tmateria	TEACH	3. I use the Internet for preparing teaching materials.	7-point
tknowled	TEACH	4. I use the Internet for enhancing my teaching knowledge.	7-point
temail	TEACH	5. I use Email for student contact and giving my advice	7-point
oresearc	OTASK	1. I use the Internet for searching information for my research.	7-point
oadmin	OTASK	2. I use the Internet to assist administrative tasks (e.g. searching information to assist administrative tasks, email to help accomplishing administrative tasks.)	7-point
operson	OTASK	3. I use the Internet for personal tasks.	7-point
operknow	OTASK	4. I use the Internet for enhancing personal knowledge.	7-point
oemail	OTASK	5. I use Email for personal contact.	7-point
bitclass	BITEACH	1. I intend to use the Internet more when teaching in classes.	7-point
bitweb	BITEACH	2. I intend to use the Internet more in providing a Personal Web-Base for facilitating teaching (e.g. on-line syllabus, lectures, noted, tutorials, tests, quizzes, and providing grade etc.)	7-point
bitmater	BITEACH	3. I intend to use the Internet more for preparing teaching materials.	7-point
bitknow	BITEACH	4. I intend to use the Internet more for enhancing teaching knowledge.	7-point
bitemail	BITEACH	5. I intend to use Email more for student contact and giving my advice.	7-point
bioresea	BIOTASK	1. I intend to use the Internet more for searching information for my research.	7-point
bioadmin	BIOTASK	2. I intend to use the Internet more to assist administrative tasks.	7-point
bioperso	BIOTASK	3. I intend to use the Internet more for personal tasks.	7-point
bioperkn	BIOTASK	4. I intend to use the Internet more for enhancing personal knowledge.	7-point
bioemail	BIOTASK	5. I intend to use Email more for personal contact.	7-point

*7- Point Scale: 1= Strongly Disagree 2= Quite Disagree 3= Slightly Disagree, 4= Neutral 5=Slightly Agree 6= Quite Agree 7= Strongly Agree

Chapter 8
E–Business Adoption by Jordanian Banks:
An Exploratory Study of the Key Factors and Performance Indicators

Ali Alawneh
Philadelphia University, Jordan

Hasan Al-Refai
Philadelphia University, Jordan

Khaldoun Batiha
Philadelphia University, Jordan

ABSTRACT

Grounded in the technology–organization–environment (TOE) framework, we have developed an extended model to examine factors, particularly technological, organizational and environmental factors, which influence e-business adoption in Jordanian banks. For the purposes of our research some constructs were added to (TOE) framework such as IT/Business strategy alignment, adequacy of IT professionals, and availability of online revenues. Other factors were excluded such as the global scope since our research is at the national level in Jordanian banking sector. The independent variables are the (technology readiness or competence, bank size, financial resources commitment, IT/Business strategy alignment, adequacy of IT professionals, availability of online revenues, competition intensity or pressure, and regulatory support environment) while e-business adoption and usage constitutes the dependent variable. Survey data from (140) employees in seven pioneered banks in the Jordanian banking sector were collected and used to test the theoretical model. Based on simple and multiple linear regressions, our empirical analysis demonstrates several key findings: (1) technology readiness is found to be the key determinant of e-business adoption among the banks. (2) Bank size, IT/Business strategy alignment, and availability of online revenues were found to have significant influence on the e-business adoption within banks, while financial resources commitment and adequacy of IT professionals do not contribute significantly to e-business adoption. (3) Both of the competition intensity and regulatory support environment contribute significantly to e-business adoption in banks. By providing insight into these important factors, this paper can help further understanding of their role in the adoption and usage of e-business and

DOI: 10.4018/978-1-60960-197-3.ch008

examines the impacts of e-business usage on banks' performance in terms of sales-services-marketing, internal operations and coordination & communication. The theoretical and practical implications of these results are discussed. By extension, this could enable greater e-business usage in banks, which could improve the Jordanian overall economy.

1. INTRODUCTION

The banking and other financial services sector is one of the most advanced in the usage and diffusion of technologies. Being essentially information business, they do not produce physical products and have been trading electronically for decades. For these reasons hardly any other sector is better suited for e-business which, in fact, is progressing very quickly. ICT impacts on all aspects of the activity and is undoubtedly one of the main driving forces in the sector.

Electronic business (e-business) is a major force in the global economy. Businesses and consumers alike increasingly engage in e-business. Despite the burst of the dot-com bubble, many firms continue to deploy e-business extensively in their enterprise value chains. Indeed, firms face a series of obstacles in adopting and carrying out e-business, particularly their ability to transcend significant technical, managerial, and cultural issues (Sato et al., 2001).

The adoption and usage of electronic business (e-business) have emerged into an active research area in the information systems (IS) discipline (Straub et al., 2002). Drawing on the literature of (Barua et al., 2001), we define e-business as using the Internet to conduct or support business activities along the value chain. We focus on sales/services/ marketing, internal operations, and coordination & communication because we are studying banking services industry (Alawneh and Hattab, 2008).

The financial services industry differs in important ways from industries such as manufacturing or retailing, and its use of IT and e-business technologies reflect those differences (Olazabal, 2002). Financial institutions are linked to custom-

ers and each other in an extensive network of interrelationships that is more complex, reciprocal, and less linear than traditional manufacturing and retailing industries (Mulligan and Gordon, 2002). There is a primary market in which customers interact with financial institutions such as retail banks, insurance agencies, real estate agencies and stock brokers. There is also a larger secondary market in which those institutions interact with each other and with others such as mortgage brokers, commercial banks, insurance companies, and investment bankers (Hess and Kemerer, 1994). Financial services, which are both immaterial and relatively standardized, and have hence already been widely affected by information technology innovations (Buzzacchi, and Mariotti, 1995), would therefore be one of the first arenas where that "new information economy" would arise (Dewan, Freimer and Seidmann, 2000).

The nature of IT in this industry is complex and heterogeneous. On the front end, IT is used to execute and record customer transactions, whether they are handled in person, by phone, by electronic funds transfer, or on the Internet. On the back end, funds are transferred among institutions via electronic transfer systems, such as Fedwire, CHIPS, and Swift, which handle hundreds of trillions of dollars in transactions yearly. Financial EDI systems are used to support information flows among institutions. Internal IT systems include a mix of packaged and custom applications that maintain account records and support internal financial and managerial functions.

E-business technologies have the potential to add significant value in all of these areas. Most striking is the potential for Web-based applications to improve customer service. Loan applications and insurance forms can be filled out, stock trades initiated, bills paid, and funds transferred online with no human interaction required. Research tools such as mortgage calculators or retirement planning applications can be made available, and account information can be accessed online. On the back end, applications based on common Internet standards can enable data sharing across firms in an industry marked by limited standardization of IT systems. Internally, e-business applications can likewise improve integration of various proprietary systems to move toward "straight-through processing," improving the links between decision (swap, credit extension, trade) and execution (funds transfer, account updates, settlement finality).

There is substantial evidence to suggest that e-business is being embraced by financial institutions in developed and emerging markets to the extent that explosive growth is almost at hand. There are two different strategies for usage of e-business in banking sector: First, an existing bank with physical offices can establish a web site and offer Internet banking to its customer as an additional delivery channel. A second alternative is to establish an Internet-only bank or virtual bank, almost without physical offices. Recent years have seen the industry rapidly moving towards a "click and bricks" strategy that emphasizes an online supplement to the conventional banking services. Banking institutions are using their web sites not only to provide classical operations such as fund transfer or accounts information, but also to provide stock trading, bill payments, credit card request and investment advice.

Banks are endeavoring from conducting e-business to the provision of retail and small value banking products and services through electronic channels. It would run the gamut from direct deposits, ATMs, credit and debit cards, telephone banking, to electronic bill payment and web-based banking (Basel Committee Report on Banking Supervision, 1998).

Electronic banking (e-banking) covers various operations that can be conducted from home, busi-ness or on the road instead of at a physical bank location (Turban et al., 2003). These operations include: retrieving account balances and history of accounts, fund transfers, check-book request, opposition to check and credit card payments... some banks also offer other services such as security trading, bill payments, etc.

As technology evolves, different kinds of electronic business systems emerge, among these the Automated Teller Machine (ATM), phone banking, Internet banking and Mobile banking (Claessens et al., 2002).

The term Internet banking refers to the use of the Internet as a remote delivery channel for banking services. Some banking institutions limit their Internet Banking services to an informational website. Others are using their web sites not only to provide the basic operations such as fund transfer or account details, but also to provide new services such as securities trading, bill payments, check book requests, credit card requests and investment advice. These organizations rushed to provide Internet based services in order to gain competitive advantage:

These services permit to banks and other financial institutions to lower their overhead costs on one side and to add extra fees on the online services on the other side, increasing therefore their margins and profit base. Internet also permits to tap a larger client base with its positive impact on the banks turnover.

Internet E-business technology represents a variety of different services, ranging from common automatic teller machine (ATM) services and direct deposit to automatic bill payment (ABP), electronic transfer of funds (EFT), and computer banking (PC banking) (Kolodinsky et al., 2004).

The common motivation for banks to implement e-business is to provide a faster, easier, and more reliable service to clients, to improve the bank's competitive position and image, and to meet clients' demands. E-business may also provide other benefits. For instance, creating new markets, and reducing operational costs, administrative costs, and workforce are increasingly important aspects for the banks' competitiveness, and e-business may improve these aspects as well.

Banks are highly focusing on e-business for the last ten years that is expected to continue in order to achieve varieties of outcomes such as: creating consumer-centric culture and organization, securing customer relationships, maximizing customer profitability, and aligning effort and resource behind most valuable customer groups (Alawneh and Hattab, 2009).

The value of e-business has become widely recognized, accepted and offered many benefits to banks as well as to customers. Organizations invest in information systems for many reasons, for example cutting costs, producing more without increasing costs, improving the quality of services or products (Lederer et al., 1998).

Jordanian banks have invested heavily to leverage the Internet and transform their traditional businesses into e-businesses in the last ten years. Jordanian banks like their international counterparts have increasingly resorted to e-business to capitalize on the opportunities of business efficiencies. These banks adopted the B2C e-business model to increase market share, offer better customer service and to reach out to customers at greater geographic distances.

An enhanced extended model based on assumptions of (TOE) framework has been developed, and explored the role and function of each factor in the framework. It is expected that the extended model will provide a deeper insight into banks e-business adoption and usage. Then, we will test that model using survey data from banks in the banking sector in Jordan that had already adopted e-business, i.e., Clicks-and-mortars banks which have supplemented their existing business using the Internet in their operations. We chose the above mentioned industry because it was one of the first movers to adopt the Internet technologies and to innovate with e-business applications. Data analysis will be performed to determine the role

and influence of factors on e-business deployment and on bank performance.

Our empirical survey was carried out in an interesting and homogenous market, the Jordanian Banking sector. Jordan is one of the regionally leading countries regarding the national IT infrastructure available for online services. Also, the population's motivation and ability to conduct online transactions are one of the highest regionally.

2. AIMS AND MOTIVATION OF THE RESEARCH

In essence, technological innovation diffusion and adoption rests on the three main contexts that surrounded any firm, the technological context, organizational context and environmental context, they are recognized the source of adoption of any technological innovation. Consideration of each of these various contexts and the relationships between them is necessary for a comprehensive understanding of e-business deployment in banks.

Why some banks adopted and conducted e-business in doing their financial transactions whereas others didn't is the problem that motivated this study, and because the lack of empirical examination of e-business adoption in Jordanian banking sector is another motivation of this study. In that context, the aim of this study is to contribute to a better understanding of the e-business usage and its application to the sector of financial services to commercial banks in Jordan.

From both research and applied perspectives there are few studies published on this topic. There is a need to combine and concentrate the efforts of academic researchers in a holistic approach to e-business technology deployment. There is a limited understanding of what are the key factors that affect e-business adoption in banks and there is currently no tested framework that unifies all relevant factors in an easy to understand and practical way. As such, one of the principal goals of this study is to develop an enhanced framework, which can explain e-business technology adoption in banks. Such a framework would benefit research in e-business-e-banking and also help to eliminate confusion as to where a bank should focus its efforts, strategies and investments for optimum organizational performance.

There is a lack of substantial empirical studies in e-business adoption and deployment, as the majority of studies reported in the literature still rely heavily on case studies and anecdotes, with few empirical data to measure Internet-based initiatives or gauge the scale of their impact on bank performance, partly because of the difficulty of developing measures and collecting data. A more fundamental issue is the lack of theory to guide the empirical work. So far, the literature has been weak in making the linkage between theory and measures. Hence, there is a need for theoretical development.

3. E-BUSINESS IN JORDANIAN BANKING SECTOR

Traditional branch-based retail banking remains the most widespread method for conducting banking transactions in Jordan as well as any other country. However, Internet technology is rapidly changing the way personal financial services are being designed and delivered. For several years, commercial banks in Jordan have tried to introduce electronic business (e-business) systems to improve their operations and to reduce costs. Despite all their efforts aimed at developing better and easier e-business systems, these systems remained largely unnoticed by the customers, and certainly were seriously underused in spite of their availability.

In this Internet age, when the customer is having access to a variety of products and services it is becoming very difficult for banks to survive. In this situation, when customer inquires are not met easily or transactions are complicated, the customer will asks for new levels services, and only chose those institutions who are making a real effort to provide a high level of quality, fast and efficient service through all the bank's touch points, call centers, ATMs, voice response systems, Internet and branches.

The financial sector in Jordan has witnessed media blitzes announcing electronic banking. Banks that have implemented e-business are showing up of being modernized; some of those that have not are drastically trying to catch up.

The financial sector in Jordan is composed of the Central Bank of Jordan (CBJ), 37 commercial and/or investment banks, 39 insurance companies, 16 special credit institutions, the Social Security Corporation, a number of provident funds, and foreign exchange bureaus. It is considered as one of the better financial sectors in the region and generates in total close to 8% of the GDP (Gross Domestic Product). One of the weakest points in the financial sector is, with the exception of mortgage lending, the lack of long-term lending and the absence of secured loans (www.abj.org. jo, www.cbj.gov.jo accessed on 12/8/2009).

It is worth mentioning that the percentage of Jordanian households who own personal computer 15.9%, Internet access 6%, 1,000,000 regular telephone lines, around a 1.6 million mobile telephony subscribers, 21 licensed Internet service providers, more than 500,000 Internet users and close to 250 Internet cafes in the year 2004. However, Jordan is in the Guinness Book of World Records as the highest per capita in Internet cafes, and the number of Internet cafes located in the city of Irbid, is ranked number one in the world, with regard to so many Internet cafes located in a small region. It is worth mentioning that the number of Internet users in the world will reach three billion in year 2010 (www.moict.gov.jo, accessed on 1/9/2009).

The banking sector is very dynamic and liberal in Jordan. Moreover, some of the commercial banks in Jordan are offering electronic services. Samples of these services are:

1. **Internet banking:** Arab Bank is the first bank to launch Internet banking service. This service has been started in Jordan in May 2000.

2. **Internet Shopping Card (ISC):** it provides convenient and easy access to on-line shopping transactions with small limits and it can be used at any website that displays the Visa logo.

3. **WAP banking:** customers can use WAP mobile phone and access their accounts.

4. **SMS banking:** customers can use a mobile and access their accounts.

5. **Phone bank service:** This provides access to customers' accounts.

6. **On-line stock trading:** Jordan Kuwait Bank (JKB) offers this service in collaboration with its affiliate United Financial Investment Co. (UFICO). The service allows JKB customers to trade in Amman Bourse through UFICO's website and settle the value of shares traded through JKB's Internet banking service (Net banker) directly from their accounts with the bank.

7. **Net banker:** for performing banking transactions.

8. **Mobile Banking:** this service allows the customers to perform banking transactions by using a mobile.

9. **Automated Teller Machines (ATM):** The banks are providing ATM services through their branches.

10. **Cyber branch:** Jordan Kuwait Bank (JKB) opened its first Cyber branch on the first of May 2001 in Sweifiyyah area. It is a comprehensive electronic bank providing banking services directly to the clients on a 24 hours basis.

11. **Money transfer:** money transfer service allows customers to transfer and receive money.

12. **Pre-paid mobile cards:** customers can buy the mobile prepaid cards electronically.

13. **Banking via SMS:** it enables the customers to receive information on their transactions through their mobile telephones.

14. **E-com card:** the E-com card is a pre-paid electronic card, which allows you to buy any product of the World Wide Web, the phone or mail order. This new product at Jordan National Bank (JNB) can help you minimize the risk of using your credit card on the Internet since the card has a fixed limit 25 JD. After you have used your card's limit you can re-charge it within the card's validity without the need for re-issuing a new card.

15. **The call free hotline:** the customer can call the bank free of charge. The bank staff will answer all inquiries.

16. **WAP phone services:** current account and savings account customers are eligible for using this service to facilitate balance inquiry, obtaining a simplified account statement, demanding a balance statement, demanding a checkbook.

4. THE TECHNOLOGY-ORGANIZATION- ENVIRONMENT (TOE) FRAMEWORK

To gain a comprehensive view on what factors may affect the deployment of e-business, we adopt the TOE framework developed by Tornatzky and Fleischer (1990). The TOE framework identifies three aspects of a firm's context that influence the process by which it adopts and implements a technological innovation: technological context, organizational context, and environmental context. Technological context describes both the internal and external technologies relevant to the firm. These include existing technologies inside the firm, as well as the pool of available technologies in the market. Organizational context is defined in terms of several descriptive measures: firm size

118

and scope; the centralization, formalization, and complexity of its managerial structure; the quality of its human resources; and the amount of slack resources available internally. Environmental context is the arena in which a firm conducts its business—its industry, competitors, access to resources supplied by others, and dealings with government (Tornatzky and Fleischer, 1990). These three groups of contextual factors influence a firm's intent to adopt an innovation, and affect the assimilation process and eventually the impacts of the innovation on organizational performance.

A theoretical model for e-business use needs to take into account factors that affect the propensity to use e-business, which is rooted in the specific technological, organizational, and environmental circumstances of an organization. Reviewing the literature suggests that the TOE framework (Tornatzky and Fleischer 1990) may provide a useful starting point for looking at e-business use. The TOE framework identifies three aspects of a firm's context that influence the process by which it adopts, implements, and uses technological innovations: (a) Technological context describes both the existing technologies in use and new technologies relevant to the firm. (b) Organizational context refers to descriptive measures about the organization such as scope, size, and the amount of slack resources available internally. (c) Environmental context is the arena in which a firm conducts its business—its industry, competitors, and dealings with government (Tornatzky and Fleischer 1990, pp. 152–154).

This framework is consistent with the innovation diffusion theory of Rogers (1983, pp. 376–383), in which he emphasized technological characteristics, and both the internal and external characteristics of the organization, as drivers for technology diffusion.

Based on our literature review of (Zhu et al. 2003, 2004), we found that the TOE framework has consistent empirical support in various IS domains, such as electronic data interchange (EDI), open systems, and material requirement planning (e.g., Iacovou et al. 1995, Chau and Tam 1997, Thong 1999). As a generic theory of technology diffusion, the TOE framework can be used for studying different types of innovations. According to the typology proposed by Swanson (1994), there are three types of innovations: Type I innovations are technical innovations restricted to the IS functional tasks (such as relational databases, CASE); Type II innovations apply IS to support administrative tasks of the business (such as financial, accounting, and payroll systems); and Type III innovations integrate IS with the core business where the whole business is potentially affected and the innovation may have strategic relevance to the firm. We consider e-business a Type III innovation, in the sense that e-business is often embedded in a firm's core business processes (e.g., making use of the open standard of the Internet protocol to streamline information sharing among various functional departments); e-business can extend basic business products and services (e.g., leveraging Internet-enabled two way connectivity to offer real-time customer service); and e-business can streamline the integration with suppliers and customers (e.g., using XML-based communication to increase the capability of exchanging data on product demand and inventory availability throughout the supply chain).

Prior IS research has sought to study Type I and Type II innovations, but relatively limited attention had been devoted to Type III innovations (Swanson 1994) until the recent studies of EDI and enterprise resource planning (ERP) systems (Iacouvou et al. 1995, Hart and Saunders 1998). E-business is a new Type III innovation and warrants investigation along with these innovations (Straub et al. 2002, Zhu 2004b). In particular, the migration toward the Internet and the transformation of traditional processes require firms and their subunits to orchestrate the coevolutionary changes to their technologies in use, business processes, and value chain structures to successfully assimilate the Internet technologies into their e-business initiatives (Chatterjee et al. 2002).

The TOE framework has been examined by a number of empirical studies in various information systems (IS) domains. In particular, electronic data interchange (EDI), an antecedent of Internet-based e-business, has been studied extensively in the past decade. Iacovou et al. (1995) developed a model formulating three aspects of EDI adoption— technological factors, organizational factors, and environmental factors—as the main drivers for EDI adoption, and examined the model using seven case studies. Their model was further tested by other researchers using larger samples. For example, Kuan and Chau (2001) confirmed the usefulness of the TOE framework for studying adoption of complex IS innovations.

Drawing on the empirical evidence combined with literature review and theoretical perspectives discussed above, we believe that the TOE framework is appropriate for studying e-business usage. Based on the TOE framework, the use of e-business in organizations will be influenced by three types of antecedents: technological factors, organizational factors, and environmental factors (Zhu et al., 2004). One might ask why we need to develop a theoretical model for e-business, given that there are already several studies on EDI adoption. To answer this question, we need to articulate how e-business differs from EDI (or other previous Type III innovations) and explain the theoretical necessity of extending TOE to e-business.

Although specific factors identified within the three contexts may vary across different studies, the TOE framework has consistent empirical support. Drawing upon the empirical evidence combined with the literature review, we believe that the TOE framework is an appropriate theoretical foundation for studying e-business adoption.

5. THE RESEARCH MODEL AND HYPOTHESES

The proposed outline for the extended framework that will be developed and tested in this research is seen in Figure 1. It depicts the main statement of the problem. An important aspect of the problem is whether e-business technology is deployed if the bank uses adequately the factors of e-business technology adoption.

To examine the points previously discussed and address the issues raised, we have formulated the following eight hypotheses based on the Figure 1.

H1: The technology readiness or competence positively affects e-business adoption in the bank.

H2: The bank size negatively affects e-business adoption in the bank.

H3: The financial resources commitment positively affects e-business adoption in the bank.

H4: The alignment of IT/Business strategy positively affects e-business adoption in the bank.

H5: The availability of online revenues positively affects e-business adoption in the bank.

H6: The adequacy of IT professionals positively affects e-business adoption in the bank.

H7: The competition intensity or pressure negatively affects e-business adoption in the bank.

H8: The regulatory support environment positively affects e-business adoption in the bank.

Figure 1. An Extended Framework of e-business diffusion (By Researchers)

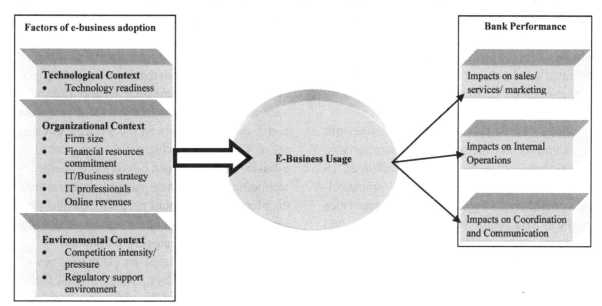

6. PREVIOUS WORK

A summary of some of the literature related to technological innovation adoption is given below.

Zhu and Kraemer (2005) developed theoretically and evaluated empirically an integrative research model incorporating technological, organizational, and environmental factors, for assessing e-business use and value at the firm level, based on which a series of hypotheses are developed. The theoretical model is tested by using structural equation modeling (SEM) on a dataset of 624 firms across 10 countries in the retail industry. For e-business use, their study has examined six factors, within the TOE framework, as drivers of e-business use. For e-business value, their study has demonstrated that the extent of e-business use and e-business capabilities, both front-end functionalities and back-end integration, contribute to value creation of e-business. The study found that technology competence, firm size, financial commitment, competitive pressure, and regulatory support are important antecedents of e-business use. In addition, the study found that, while both front-end and back-end capabilities contribute to

e-business value, back-end integration has a much stronger impact [16].

Zhu et al., (2003) Based on (TOE) framework they examined the factors: Technology competence, Organizational factors (firm scope, size) and Environmental context (consumer readiness, trading partner readiness, competitive pressure) for studying E-business adoption by European firms using a survey on a sample size of (3100) firms

Kuan and Chau (2001) confirmed the usefulness of the TOE framework for studying adoption of complex IS innovations. Based on (TOE) framework they examined the factors: Technological context (perceived direct benefits), Organizational context (perceived financial cost, technical competence) and Environmental context (perceived industry pressure/government pressure) for studying EDI innovation using a survey on a sample size of (575) firms [18].

Ramamurthy et al. (1999) posited the impact of EDI on firm performance as the consequence of technological, organizational, and environmental factors. Based on (TOE) framework they examined the factors: Organizational factor (management support, expected benefits, resource intensity, compatibility, costs) and Interorganizational factor (competitive pressure, customer support) for studying EDI innovation using a survey on a sample size of (181) firms. Their empirical results indicated that the impact of EDI on operational and market-oriented performance was significantly affected by these factors [19].

Thong (1999) Based on (TOE) framework he examined the factors: CEO characteristics (CEO's innovativeness and IS knowledge), IS characteristics (relative advantage/compatibility, complexity), Organizational characteristics (business size, employees IS knowledge) and Environmental characteristics, for studying and developing an integrated model of information systems adoption in small business using a survey on a sample size of (168) firms [20].

Chau and Tam (1997) Based on (TOE) framework they examined the factors: Characteristics of the innovation (perceived barriers, importance of compliance) Organizational technology (satisfaction with existing systems) and External environment, for studying adoption of open systems using a survey on a sample size of (89) firms.

Damanpour (1996) Based on (TOE) framework he examined the factors: Organizational complexity (organization size, horizontal complexity) and Contingency factors (environment uncertainty), for studying Organizational complexity and innovation using meta-analysis methodology on various innovations.

Iacovou et al. (1995) developed a model formulating three aspects of Electronic Data Interchange (EDI) adoption—technological factors (perceived benefits), organizational factors (organizational readiness), and environmental factors (Interorganizational context and external pressure)—as the main drivers for EDI adoption, and examined the model using seven case studies. Iacovou et al., using the technology-organization-environment (TOE) framework, found that the impact of EDI on performance was directly affected by its level of integration with other IS and processes. Their

model was further tested by other researchers using larger samples [23].

Swanson (1994) examined the three contexts of the TOE framework and contended that adoption of complex IT innovations requires a facilitating technology portfolio, certain organizational attributes such as diversity and sufficient slack resources, and a strong emphasis on the strategic environment. We extend this theoretical argument to the e-business environment: e-business is enabled by technology development, requires organizational enablers and may entail necessary business and organization reconfiguration, and may shape (and be shaped by) the strategic environment.

Grover (1993) Based on (TOE) framework he examined the factors: Organizational factors (IS-related factors, firm size) Environmental factors (market assessment, competitive need) Interorganizational (IOS) factors (compatibility, complexity) and Support factors (top management support) for studying EDI innovation using a survey on a sample size of (226) firms.

7. RESEARCH FINDINGS: TESTING THE THEORETICAL HYPOTHESES

7.1 Hypothesis H1 Technological Context vs. E-Business Usage

Table 1 and Table 2 summarize the results of simple linear regression for hypothesis 1. The table shows the standardized regression coefficient of each predicator, R, R^2 and F, for all the predictors in linear regression analysis.

The entire model has a significant effect on e-business usage ($p<0.01$). R^2 In the entire model of the technological context explains 13.8% of the variance related to e-business usage. As shown in Table 1, the standardized coefficient (beta) value for the technological context is positive and significant ($p<.01$), and thus supports hypothesis H1.

Table 1. Results of simple regression analysis of e-business usage vs. technological context

Model~	Standardised Coefficient	t
Technology readiness (H1)	.372	4.703**
Equation		
R	.372	
R^2	.138	
F	22.116**	

**p<.01 *p<.05 ~ dependent variable: e-business usage

Table 2 shows the dependent variable as three impacts of e-business usage are: sales-services-marketing, internal operations and coordination & communication. The technological context explains 7.4% of the variance of sales-services-marketing as an impact of e-business usage, 6.4% of the variance of internal operations as an impact of e-business usage, and 18.7% of the variance of coordination and communication as a impact of e-business usage. Furthermore, the technology readiness contributes more significantly to e-business usage on coordination and communication (0.432) more than to e-business usage on internal operations and sales-services-marketing (0.254, 0.272) respectively.

7.2 Hypotheses H2-H6 Organizational Context vs. E-Business Usage

The entire model has a significant effect on e-business usage (p<0.01). R^2 In the entire model of the organisational context explains 54.6% of the variance related to e-business usage. As shown in Table 3, the standardized coefficient (beta) value for the bank size is positive and significant (p<. 01), and thus does not support hypothesis H2. The standardised coefficient (beta) value for the financial resources commitment is positive but is not significant and thus, the result does not support hypothesis H3. The standardised coefficient (beta) value for the IT/Business strategy

alignment is positive and significant (p<. 01), and thus supports hypothesis H4. The standardised coefficient (beta) value for the IT professionals is positive but is not significant and thus, the result does not support hypothesis H5. The standardised coefficient (beta) value for the online revenues is positive and significant (p<. 05), and thus supports hypothesis H6. Further, IT/Business strategy alignment contributes more to e-business usage than the other factors.

Table 4 shows the dependent variable as three impacts of e-business usage are: sales-services-marketing, internal operations and coordination & communication. All of the organisational context variables explain 44.4% of the variance of sales-services-marketing as an impact of e-business usage, 33.6% of the variance of internal operations as an impact of e-business usage, and 50.9% of the variance of coordination and communication as an impact of e-business usage.

On the other hand, the bank size contributes significantly to e-business usage on sales-services-marketing and coordination & communication (0.271, 0.199) respectively, but the financial resources commitment don't contribute significantly to e-business usage in any impact, while IT/Business strategy alignment contributes significantly to e-business usage on sales-services-marketing, internal operations and coordination & communication (0.543, 0.476, 0.475) respectively , but the online revenues contributes significantly to e-business usage on coordination & communication (0.174) respectively. Finally, the IT professionals don't contribute significantly to e-business usage in any impact.

7.3 Hypotheses H7-H8 Environmental Context vs. E-Business Usage

The entire model has a significant effect on e-business usage (p<0.01). R^2 In the entire model of the environmental context explains 29.7% of the variance related to e-business usage. As shown

Table 2. Results of multiple regression analysis for impacts of e-business usage vs. technological context

Independent	e-business Usage Impacts(Dependent)		
Technological Context	Sales/services/marketing R^2=.074 F=11.038**	Internal operations R^2=.064 F=9.514**	Coordination and communication R^2=.187 F=31.718**
Technology readiness (H1)	β=.272 t=3.322**	β=.254 t=3.084**	β=.432 t=5.632**

**p<.01, *p<.05

Table 3. Results of multiple regression analysis of e-business usage vs. organizational context

Model~	Standardised Coefficient	t
Bank Size (H2)	0.215	3.643**
Financial Resources Commitment (H3)	0.090	1.236
IT/Business Strategy (H4)	0.573	7.110**
IT Professionals (H5)	0.013	0.178
Online Revenues (H6)	0.132	1.923*
Equation		
R	0.739	
R^2	0.546	
F	32.262**	

**p<.01 *p<.05 ~ dependent variable: e-business Usage

Table 4. Results of multiple regression analysis of impacts of e-business usage vs. organizational context

Independent	e-business Usage Impacts(Dependent)		
Organizational Context	Sales/services/marketing R^2 =.444 F=21.417**	Internal operations R^2=.336 F=13.566**	Coordination and communication R^2=.509 F=27.778**
Bank size (H2)	β=.271 t=4.159**	β=.084 t=1.185	β=.199 t=3.240**
Financial Resources Commitment (H3)	β=.027 t=.338	β=.124 t=1.401	β=.086 t=1.127
IT/Business Strategy (H4)	β=.543 t=6.087**	β=.476 t=4.880**	β=.475 t=5.665**
IT Professionals (H5)	β=-.014 t=-.175	β=-.144 t=-1.663	β=.105 t=1.469
Online Revenues (H6)	β=.104 t=1.371	β=.136 t=1.644	β=.174 t=2.335*

**p<.01, *p<.05

Table 5. Results of multiple regression analysis of e-business usage vs. environmental context

Model~	Standardised Coefficient	t
Competition Intensity (H7)	0.363	4.801**
Regulatory Support Environment (H8)	0.306	4.041**
Equation		
R	0.545	
R^2	0.297	
F	28.902**	

**p<.01 *p<.05 ~ dependent variable: e-business usage

Table 6. Results of multiple regression analysis for impacts of e-business usage vs. environmental context

Independent	e-business Usage impacts(Dependent)		
Environmental Context	Sales/services/marketing R^2=.329 F=33.540**	Internal operations R^2=.124 F=9.717**	Coordination and communication R^2=.238 F=21.430**
Competition Intensity (H7)	β=.392 t=5.305**	β=.219 t=2.596*	β=.330 t=4.192**
Regulatory Support Environment (H8)	β=.311 t=4.205**	β=.214 t=2.540*	β=.269 t=3.415**

**p<.01, *p<.05

in Table 5, the standardized coefficient (beta) value for the competition intensity is positive and significant (p<. 01), and thus does not supports hypothesis H7. The standardised coefficient (beta) value for the regulatory support environment is positive and significant (p<. 01), and thus supports hypothesis H8.

Table 6 shows the dependent variable as three impacts of e-business usage are: sales-services-marketing, internal operations and coordination & communication. All of the environmental context variables explain 32.9% of the variance of sales-services-marketing as an impact of e-business usage, 12.4% of the variance of internal operations as an impact of e-business usage, and 23.8% of the variance of coordination and communication as an impact of e-business usage.

On the other hand, the competition intensity contributes significantly to e-business usage on sales-services-marketing, internal operations and coordination & communication (0.392, 0.219, 0.330) respectively, but the regulatory support environment contributes significantly to e-banking usage on sales-services-marketing, internal operations and coordination & communication (0.311, 0.214, 0.269) respectively.

8. CONCLUSION

The main purpose of this research is to provide a context for better understanding of e-business adoption and how the factors of the technological, organizational, and environmental contexts that surrounding the banks are necessary for diffusion and deployment of e-business usage and its impacts on banks performance.

This paper provides empirical evidence on factors that influence e-business deployment among commercial banks in Jordan. It contributes to the few pieces of literature on e-business experiences among banks operating in the Middle East region particularly Jordan. The study contributes several insights into banks e-business usage. First of all, this study sheds light on the e-business adoption in Jordanian banks and examines the impacts of e-business usage on the banks' performance in terms of sales-services-marketing, internal operations and coordination & communication.

Many managers and investors are facing strong pressure to answer the question of what are the most important factors that influence on adoption of any technological innovation they might deploy in their firms, and how their investments on that technological innovation will betterment the performance of firms in terms of sales-services-marketing, internal operations and coordination & communication, because it is not clear to them what are the most important and significant factors that determine adoption or non adoption of that innovation. This study will help managers of banks to make critical decisions toward deployment of e-business technology in their banks. This study endeavors to find a conceptual model that joins and classifies these factors, unifying them with e-business usage and bank performance.

The current research is limited to one industry type, the banking services as belong to the financial services industry. Nonetheless, other domains in the financial services industry (e.g., securities, brokerage, credit institutions, trading, loan, mortgage, credit cards and real estate) can be studied.

The current study was conducted only in Jordan, and so future cross-cultural research would be valuable. It is assumed that there will be, to some degree, a difference in the factors affecting the adoption of e-business technology across different cultures.

REFERENCES

Alawneh, A., & Hattab, E. (2008). E-Business Value Creation in Jordanian Banking Services Industry: An Empirical Analysis of Key Factors. In *Proceedings of the International Arab Conference on e-Technology* (IACeT'2008). Arab Open University, Amman-Jordan. October 15-16, 2008.

Alawneh, A., & Hattab, E. (2009). An Empirical Study of the Sources Affecting E-Business Value Creation in Jordanian Banking Services Sector. *The International Arab Journal of e-Technology (IAJeT)., 1*(2).

Alawneh, A., & Hattab, E. (2009). E-Banking Diffusion in the Jordanian Banking Services Sector: An Empirical Analysis of Key Factors. *International Journal of Actor-Network Theory and Technological Innovation, 1*(2), 50–65.

Barua, A. (2001). P., Konana, A. B., & Whinston, F. (2001). Driving e-business excellence. *MIT Sloan Management Rev., 34*(1), 36–44.

Basel Committee Report on Banking Supervision. (1998). Bank of International Settlements. In *Molina and Ben-Jadeed 2004*. Basel: Risk Management for Electronic Banking and Electronic Money Activities.

Buzzacchi, L. M., Colombo, G., & Mariotti, S. (1995). Technological regimes and innovation in services: the case of the Italian banking industry. *Research Policy, 24*, 151–168. doi:10.1016/0048-7333(93)00756-J

Chatterjee, D., Grewal, R., & Sambamurthy, V. (2002). Shaping up for e-commerce: Institutional enablers of the organizational assimilation of Web technologies. *Management Information Systems Quarterly, 26*(2), 65–89. doi:10.2307/4132321

Chau, P. Y. K., & Tam, K. Y. (1997). Factors affecting the adoption of open systems: An exploratory study. *Management Information Systems Quarterly*, *21*(1), 1–21. doi:10.2307/249740

Claessens, J., Dem, V., Decock, D., Preneel, B., & Vandewalle, J. (2002). On the security of today's online electronic banking systems. *Computers & Security*, *21*(3), 257–269. doi:10.1016/S0167-4048(02)00312-7

Cooper, R. B., & Zmud, R. W. (1990). Information technology implementation research: A technological diffusion approach. *Management Science*, *36*(2), 123–139. doi:10.1287/mnsc.36.2.123

Damanpour, F. (1996). Organizational complexity and innovation: Developing and testing multiple contingency models. *Management Science*, *42*(5), 693–716. doi:10.1287/mnsc.42.5.693

Dewan, R., Freimer, M., & Seidmann, A. (2000). Organizing Distribution Channels for Information Goods on the Internet. *Management Science*, *46*(4), 483–496. doi:10.1287/mnsc.46.4.483.12053

Fichman, R. G. (2000). *The diffusion and assimilation of information technology innovations. R. Zmud, ed. framing the Domains of IT Management: projecting the future through the past*. Cincinnati, OH: Pinnaflex publishing.

Grover, V. (1993). An empirically derived model for the adoption of customer-based inter organizational systems. *Decision Sciences*, *24*(3), 603–640. doi:10.1111/j.1540-5915.1993.tb01295.x

Hart, P. J., & Saunders, C. S. (1998). Emerging electronic partnerships: Antecedents and dimensions of EDI use from the supplier's perspective. *Journal of Management Information Systems*, *14*(4), 87–111.

Hess, C. M., & Kemerer, C. F. (1994). Computerized loan origination systems: An industry case study of electronic markets hypothesis. *Management Information Systems Quarterly*, *18*(3), 251–275. doi:10.2307/249618

Kolodinsky, J. M., & Hilgert, M. A. (2004). the adoption of electronic banking technologies by US consumers. *International Journal of Bank Marketing*, *22*(4), 238–259. doi:10.1108/02652320410542536

Kuan, K. K. Y., & Chau, P. Y. K. (2001). A perception-based model for EDI adoption in small business using a technology-organization-environment framework. *Information & Management*, *38*(8), 507–512. doi:10.1016/S0378-7206(01)00073-8

Lacovou, C. L., Benbasat, I., & Dexter, A. S. (1995). Electronic data interchange and small organizations: Adoption and impact of technology. *Management Information Systems Quarterly*, *19*(4), 465–485. doi:10.2307/249629

Lederer, A. L., Maupin, D. J., Sena, M. P., & Zhuang, Y. (1998). The role of ease of use, usefulness and attitude in the prediction of world wide web usage. In *Proceedings of the 1998 Association for computing machinery special interest group on computer personnel research conference*, 195-204.

Mulligan, P., & Gordon, S. R. (2002). The impact of information technology on customer and supplier relationships in the financial services. *International Journal of Service Industry Management*, *13*(1), 29–46. doi:10.1108/09564230210421146

Olazabal, N. G. (2002). Banking: The IT paradox. *The McKinsey Quarterly*, *1*, 47–51.

Ramamurthy, K., Premkumar, G., & Crum, M. R. (1999). Organizational and inter organizational determinants of EDI diffusion and organizational performance: A causal model. *Journal of Organizational Computing and Electronic Commerce*, *9*(4), 253–285. doi:10.1207/S153277440904_2

Rogers, E. M. (1983). *Diffusion of Innovations* (3rd ed.). New York: Free Press.

Sato, S., Hawkins, J., & Berentsen, A. (2001). *E-finance: Recent developments and policy implications. In Tracking a Transformation: E-Commerce and the Terms of Competition in Industries*. Washington, DC: Brookings Institution Press, pp.64-91.

Straub, D., Hoffman, D., Weber, B., & Steinfield, C. (2002). Toward new metrics for Net-enhanced organizations. *Information Systems Research, 13*(3), 227–238. doi:10.1287/isre.13.3.227.80

Swanson, E. B. (1994). Information systems innovation among organizations. *Management Science, 40*(9), 1069–1092. doi:10.1287/mnsc.40.9.1069

Thong, J. Y. L. (1999). An integrated model of information systems adoption in small business. *Journal of Management Information Systems, 15*(4), 187–214.

Tornatzky, L. G., & Fleischer, M. (1990). *The Processes of Technological Innovation.* Lexington, MA: Lexington Books.

Turban, E., King, D., Warkentin, M., & Chung, H. M. (2003). *Electronic Commerce 2003: A managerial perspective*. Prentice Hall. In Achour and Bensedrine, 2005.

Zhu, K., Kraemer, K., Xu, S., & Dedrick, J. (2004). Information Technology Payoff in E-Business Environments: An International perspective on Value Creation of E-Business in the Financial Services Industry. *Journal of Management Information Systems, 21*(1), 17–54.

Zhu, K., & Kraemer, K. L. (2002). E-commerce metrics for Net-enhanced organizations: Assessing the value of e-commerce to firm performance in the manufacturing sector. *Information Systems Research, 13*(3), 275–295. doi:10.1287/isre.13.3.275.82

Zhu, K., & Kraemer, K. L. (2005). Post-Adoption variations in usage and value of E-Business by organizations: cross-country evidence from the retail industry. *Information Systems Research, 16*(1), 61–84. doi:10.1287/isre.1050.0045

Zhu, K., Kraemer, K. L., & Xu, S. (2003). E-business adoption by European firms: A cross-country assessment of the facilitators and inhibitors. *European Journal of Information Systems, 12*(4), 251–268. doi:10.1057/palgrave.ejis.3000475

Section 3

Chapter 9

The Theoretical and Analytical Inclusion of Actor Network Theory and its Implication on ICT Research

Amany R. Elbanna
Loughborough University, UK

ABSTRACT

This chapter examines the properties of ANT in light of other approaches. It presents the theoretical and analytical inclusion of ANT in relation to other approaches. The study discusses how the properties of ANT could provide ICT researchers with a wider lens to explore the phenomena of concern. It also highlights some of the theoretical and analytical pitfalls that could be fell into at the start of the research and how a careful application of ANT could avoid it.

OVERVIEW

Actor Network Theory was developed more than two decades ago in the sociology of science. The theory was initially an attempt to investigate the emergence of scientific knowledge and was later extended to study a range of topics. It draws on a variety of fields, such as linguistics (especially semiotics), anthropology, and the ethnomethodology tradition in sociology.

ANT consistently argues that scientific knowledge is a product of a network of heterogeneous materials that are partly social, partly technical, and partly natural. Its field of study has been

extended from investigating the creation of scientific knowledge to studying technology and the construction of technological artefacts. Its focus has been also broadened from the production of knowledge towards agents, social institutions, machines, economic markets, and organisations to form a comprehensive theory.

This chapter suggests that ANT could provide an opportunity for information and communication technology researchers to widen their focus of enquiry and include actors that would traditionally been excluded when applying other approaches. It discusses the inclusion properties of ANT in two fronts: theoretical and analytical. The chapter has five sections. Following the introduction, the second section critically reviews different theoreti-

DOI: 10.4018/978-1-60960-197-3.ch009

cal approaches and argues that ANT provides a balanced view of the society and technology. The third, discusses the analytical inclusion properties. The fourth section examines the implication of the inclusion property of the theory on ICT research. The fifth section provides a summary and conclusion.

THEORETICAL INCLUSION

The relationship between technology and society has been for long debated in the history and sociology field and recently in the information systems field. Two main perspectives have dominated the view of the relationship between society and technology: technology determinism and social constructivism. However the discussion of these approaches is not new to the information systems field, yet it is here presented only to show how ANT could theoretically resolve the tension between the two polars of determinisms and include some of the approaches that could go under the label 'social constructivism' as follows.

Technology Determinism Perspective

Technology determinism refers to the line of thinking that supports the argument that technology determines the nature of society and drives it along a predetermined path. According to this approach, a given technology imposes certain social and political characteristics upon the society in which it is applied, resulting in a determinate pattern of social relations in that society (Heilbroner, 1994a).

The approach could vary between 'hard' and 'soft' determinism. The hard version views technology as a natural, independent force that has the power to shape society and social relations. Sturken and Thomas (2004) critically discuss this view as follows: "the transformative power awarded to new technologies is directly related to the idea that technologies arise not of the world

in which we live but as a force that comes magically from elsewhere, a force seemingly outside of social and political influences" (Sturken & Thomas, 2004, p.4).

In contrast, soft determinism finds difficulty in eliminating completely the role of society in the relationship between technology and society. For example, Heilbroner (Heilbroner, 1967, 1994a) embraced in his classic article *"Do Machines Make History?"* the technology determinism stand, but ended with a "note of caution" that states: "... even where technology seems unquestionably to play the critical role, an independent 'social' element unavoidably enters the scene in the design of technology (Heilbroner, 1994a, p.61). He then states: "the machine will reflect, as much as mould, the social relationships of work" and urges historians to practice a 'soft determinism' with regard to the influence of the machine on social relations. His version of soft determinism views technology as a strong "mediating factor" rather than the determining influence on history. In a later article, he revisited the concept and suggests that history cannot embrace either a fully determined or a wholly undetermined narrative of events (Heilbroner, 1994b). He calls for an even softer version of determinism that considers social factors such as political decisions, social attitudes, and cultural fads and fashions.

Most researchers who adopt the technology determinism perspective recognise that technology is rarely autonomous and independent of the forces of society, yet they struggle to fit the role played by different societal forces within their framework without losing the technological focus of their analysis. Soft determinism, for example, locates technology in a far more complex social, economic, political, and cultural context that renders it power. At the same time, however, it tries to maintain that once the technology is developed and has gained societal power, its deterministic efficacy may then become sufficient to direct the course of events (Marx & Smith, 1994).

Such debates led some authors to seek a middle ground by trying to include the social as an undeniable force that could affect technology. For instance, Misa suggests that the level of analysis adopted by a researcher emphasises one side of the phenomena of technological change over the other (Misa, 1994). Hence, those who conduct 'macro-level' studies are prone to technology determinism, while those who conduct 'micro-level' studies tend to find more contingent and multiple societal forces at work. He concludes by "proposing a methodological advance toward synthesizing the social-shaping of technology thesis with the technological shaping of society antithesis" (ibid).

Scranton (1994) also calls for a contextual view of technology development (Scranton, 1994). He dismisses 'universal' approaches to thinking about technology and calls for an emphasis on locality as there may be sites, sectors, and periods in which a technology-oriented logic governs. Such a concept of local determination calls for specification and differentiation.

Along similar line, Perdue (1994) proposes a contextual account that integrates environmental, technological, social, and cultural elements. He adds, "it is the interrelationship of all the elements, not any single one, that determine the whole" (Perdue, 1994).

Hughes (1994) seeks a middle ground by proposing the concept of 'technological momentum' to be "somewhere between the poles of technological determinism and social constructivism" (Hughes, 1994). He shows that technological systems in their earlier stages of development tend to be more open to socio-cultural influences than older, more mature systems as the latter is found to be more independent of outside influences and therefore more deterministic in nature. He views technological momentum as an alternative to technology determinism and contends that it is a more valuable interpretative concept than either technology determinism or social constructivism

because it is time dependent, yet sensitive to the 'messy' complexities of society and culture (ibid). Technological momentum, in that sense, could be seen as an integrative concept that gives equal weight to social and technical forces.

Social Constructivism Perspective

Social constructivism suggests, with different degrees of strength, the importance of the social in shaping the technology, either in use or in production. The specific approach of the social construction of technology (SCOT) (Pinch & Bijker, 1987) and the early version of the social shaping of technology approach (Mackenzie & Wajcman, 1985) focus on revealing the role played by the social in directing the development of technology along certain directions and not others. Studies adopting this approach tend to have a narrow perspective that sees only the role played by the social as the main determinant of the technological development. They generally try to reveal empirically that technology is a product of only its social construction.

There are several approaches that could be classified under the label 'social constructivism'. These include the Social Construction of Technology (SCOT), the social shaping of technology, the political approach, the systems approach, and the Actor Network Theory approach.

The Social Construction of Technology (SCOT)

The social construction of technology (SCOT) was developed to confront and challenge the technology determinism perspective.[1] Thus, it focuses on revealing the role played by the social in directing the development of technology along certain directions and not others. Studies adopting this approach tend to have a narrow perspective that sees only the role played by the social as the main determinant of the technological development. They generally try to reveal empirically that technology is a product of only the social construction.

SCOT investigations typically examine the different interests of social groups and institutions in an attempt to explain why a certain design of technology eventually prevails. The model followed by this approach is based on three principles (Pinch & Bijker, 1987): "relevant social groups", "interpretive flexibility", and "closure and stabilisation". The first principle seeks to identify the institutions, organisations, and groups of individuals that share an attachment to the same set of meanings relating to a certain artefact. The second principle deals with revealing the different interpretations that each social group develop for the technology under study and the flexibility in the ways in which artefacts are designed. The third addresses how certain interpretations of the technology gain more power over others and prevail at the end. It maps the mechanisms relating to the closure of debate and the stabilisation of an artefact.

Although SCOT opposes technology determinism, "it nevertheless shares with it one fundamental concern. In differing ways, both firmly root their focus on the first sphere of a technology - its conception, invention, development and design" (Mackay, 1995). For instance, SCOT has no mechanism to follow the technology in its use and appropriation by its users (Mackay & Gillespie, 1992).

SCOT is also criticised for its social determinism on the ground that it ignores the technology itself and considers its development as a mere social matter. SCOT tends to assume that: "once one has done the detective work necessary to reveal the social origins - power holders behind a particular instance of technological change - one will have explained everything of importance" (Winner, 1986, p.27). In doing so, "it denies the obduracy of objects and assumes that only people can have the status of actors" (Akrich, 1992).

This approach also received criticism for its exclusive focus on the micro context of technology and avoidance of the wider social context that might inform its social construction (Rosen, 1993).

The principle of closure and stabilisation was also criticised on the ground that: "to suggest that once a technology is produced, or even sold, it reaches the end of its social shaping, however, is to ignore both its marketing and how the technology comes to be used or implemented; is it 'finished' once it is made? For example, who does 'produce' software? Software is malleable through its entire life, through the process of customisation, modification and maintenance; is the producer the original developer, or the purchaser who customises it, or the software house, which maintains it? The reality is that most technologies never stabilise in the way which so many sociology of technology accounts suggest" (Mackay, 1995).

Bijker later recognises the weak areas of the SCOT approach and offers suggestions for repairing it (Bijker, 1993). These suggestions moved SCOT to become very close to ANT. For example, Bijker proposes that SCOT should adopt a sociotechnical ensemble as a unit of analysis and endorse the principle of generalised symmetry, in a similar way to ANT. He also adopts the ANT stance in suggesting that the SCOT model should not compel researchers to make any *a priori* choices as to the social, technical, or scientific character of the pattern that would let itself visible to the researcher.

Bijker also extends the SCOT's social concept of a "frame of meaning" that was once adopted from SSK to develop the concept of "technological frame" (Bijker, 1993, 1995). This extension aims to capture the heterogeneous nature of technological development and its interactive character (Bijker, 1993, 1995). This extension brought it very close to both the 'system' concept (Hughes, 1983) and the 'translation' concept in actor network theory (Law, 1992a). Furthermore, Bijker agrees with ANT in accepting that the analyst must transcend the dichotomy between the social and the technical and recognise that "all relations are both social and technical" and that "the technical is socially constructed, and the social is technically constructed" (Bijker, 1993). He then takes a further step towards accepting the ANT stance by admitting: "society is not determined by technology, nor is technology determined by society. Both emerge as two sides of the sociotechnical coin, during the construction process of artefacts, facts, and relevant social groups". He accepts that neither technical reductionism nor social reductionism should be the basis for an analysis of technology and society. More significantly, he argues that human and non-human actors should be treated symmetrically in case studies descriptions. He contends that this significant move would overcome the shortcomings of SCOT.

The Social Shaping of Technology

A book edited by Mackenzie and Wajcman (1985) called *The Social Shaping of Technology* is a primary source for the approach of the same name (Mackenzie & Wajcman, 1985). Although it is of much value, this book adopted a "social determinist" view since it identified the social shaping of technology in terms of the influence of social relations upon artefacts. In the book's second edition, the editors admitted the shortcomings of the first editions and the previous approach in neglecting the influence of technology upon social relations. The solution they propose in the second edition is to bring it closer to ANT, as they say: "to put it in other, more accurate, words, it is mistaken to think of technology and society as separate spheres influencing each other: technology and society are *mutually constitutive* [emphasis added]" (Mackenzie & Wajcman, 1999). This is similar to the ANT stance. To emphasise their shifted stance, the editors include in the second edition of the book an additional article by Strum and Latour (1999) that explains the mutual constitution of technology and society (Strum & Latour, 1999).

The Political Approach

The political approach is developed by Winner to complement the social constructivism perspective (Winner, 1986). It emphasises the characteristics of technical objects and the meaning of those characteristics, as well as recognising the political power of technology. It distinguishes between two political views of technology. The first is that technology is developed with a certain notion of power in mind. The second is that technology is "inherently political" in a way that requires, or is strongly compatible with, particular kinds of political relationship.

This approach could be positioned under the social constructivism perspective on the ground that it deals with politics, which is subsumed in the social phenomena (Edge, 1995; Mackay, 1995). On the other hand, it could be seen as giving technology a kind of political determinism, in the sense that once a particular technology has been designed with a certain political notion in mind it will continue to impose and stabilise this specific political notion in the social life affected. A technology that requires, or is compatible with, certain social relations could also be seen as determining the direction of the social.

Therefore, the political approach is contested on the basis that it undermines the role played by the social in appropriating the political content of an artefact. The political property of an artefact is argued to be inherently susceptible to multiple interpretations (Pfaffenberger, 1992). The interpretation that prevails is not necessarily the one the designer sought to embed into the technology. The political property of the technology could also, in principle, be negotiated by the social subjects, resulting in counter activity that refutes the political contents of the technology. For Pfaffenberger (1992), both the political intentions and the technological effects are constructed in a reciprocal and discursive process. The politics of technology therefore needs to be actively created and sustained.

This discussion indicates that the political approach stands short of explaining the construction of the political content and its negotiation with the social subjects, which are dimensions that ANT could provide.

The Systems Approach

Thomas Hughes' (1986) "systems" or networks approach refutes the contextual view of technology and society and proposes a more interactive relationship between technology and society, rather than a context-content conception. He recognises that "system builders were no respecters of knowledge categories or professional boundaries (Hughes, 1986), and points to Thomas Edison as an example of someone who mixed matters commonly labelled "economic", "technical", and "scientific" so thoroughly that his thoughts composed a "seamless web" (Hughes, 1999).

Hughes says system builders drop practically all dichotomies, such as between the internal and the external or the technical and the social, and instead incorporate them in a seamless web that contributes to the system-building goal. It is for this reason that this approach suggests that technological systems "seamlessly" interconnect components as diverse as physical artefacts, mines, manufacturing firms, utility companies, academic research and development laboratories, and investment banks. These components make up a system because they come under central control and interact functionally to fulfil a system's goal, or to contribute to a system's output. For example, a power utility system could break down if all generators were removed or equally if an investment bank providing funds withdrew from the system (ibid).

The systems approach is inspired by ANT. For instance, the notions of a seamless web and system builders are the same as those of "network" and "network builder" in ANT. Hughes not only cites but openly discusses and agrees with both Law and Callon's ANT ideas of "network", "heterogeneous

engineers", and "actor-network" (Callon, 1987; Callon & Law, 1982; Hughes, 1986). Hughes has studied primarily large technological systems that affect the whole of society and involve many institutions, organisations, and social groups, such as the electrification of America (Hughes, 1987). The level of detail and analysis of these studies is therefore significantly different from most early ANT studies, as discussed next.

The Actor Network Theory Approach

Actor Network Theory maintains that the social and the technical are in constant dialogue and negotiation, and regards the settlement of each negotiation as an empirical matter.

ANT could also be seen as a mean of reconciling the technology determinism and social constructivism schools by providing an alternative way of looking at the social and the technical. It views the social and the technical as being enmeshed in a network built to achieve the network builder's goals. This makes ANT capable of offering a better conceptualisation than other approaches of the actual processes of interaction between the technology and society.

ANT incorporates most of the previous thinking in social constructivism and could provide a balanced view of technology. It does this by finding a way of speaking about the 'capacities of technology' that other social approaches struggle to achieve (Rappert, 2001). For instance, SCOT and the social shaping approaches focus merely on the social and its influence on technology, but neglect the technology and its capacity to influence the social. The influence of the social and the implications of the technical are issues for negotiation in ANT, not a starting point of the research, since this approach moves beyond the typical dichotomy of essentialist-relativist to provide a contingent performative perception of the relationship between technology and society. ANT also resolves the highly criticised issue of "closure" that SCOT proposes. It sees stability as being negotiated as a continuous process of aligning interests. Hence, there is no closure for once and forever and, in principle, the network could break down at any point (Cadili & Whitley, 2005; Hanseth & Braa, 1998).

Authors who have attempted to address the shortcomings of the first two approaches have widely acknowledged that their modifications bring their approach closer to ANT (Bijker, 1993). At the same time, ANT does not dismiss the technology determinism approach entirely. Its view of the social as a network of humans and non-humans, with the outcome of their interactions as a result of a process of negotiation between the social and the technical, opens the door to both technology determinism and social constructivism arguments. This leaves it to the actors in the field to negotiate their existence, rather than expecting the researcher to decide *a priori* which is the correct viewpoint. In this sense, ANT provides an open-minded approach for enquiry. For example, ANT does not deny the possible political power of technology but leaves it to the social to negotiate this power. The approach itself is open to accept any stance that 'people in the field' accept and *vice versa.*

ANT maintains a balanced view of the technical and the social, as it recognises that sociotechnical networks could be inscribed in machines, technical devices, texts, documents, and training materials (Akrich, 1992; Bloomfield & Vurdubakis, 1997). ANT also acknowledges the social de-scription that takes place once the technology network is opened, negotiated, and reconstructed. Moreover, its notion of punctualisation - that is reducing the infinitely complex world to a set of entities that are well defined, instead of dealing with the whole networks of the world[2]- allows the technology to be sometimes nodded in a wider sociotechnical network. At the same time, it does not deny that this node is not always well perceived and taken for granted. Thus, it considers that the node could be opened in case of controversy to reveal its once invisible network. This maintains its stance that

there is no essentiality either on the technology or society side.

ANALYTICAL INCLUSION

The analytical inclusion of ANT is manifested in its inclusion of non-human actors and actors with different scale and level of analysis as follow.

Including Non-Humans

ANT fundamentally reviews the notion of society by arguing that "society is constructed, but not just *socially* constructed" (Latour, 1994, p.793; 1999, p. 198). It suggests that society is constructed through intertwining networks of heterogeneous materials: some of these are human and others are non-human, and their intertwining constitutes 'the social'. This contends that all artefacts incorporate social relations and it is not possible to define a social structure without the integration of non-humans into it, as every human interaction is sociotechnical (Latour, 1994).

The theory arguably (for criticism see: Collins & Yearley, 1992) renders agency to non-human entities (artefacts) and claims that these non-human actors or "actants" offer the possibility of "holding society together" (Latour, 1991). ANT distinctively views artefacts as the 'glue' or 'cement' that lends social relations relative durability. A common example here is of a baboon community that is purely social, so baboons constantly need to re-construct their social relations through physical, direct, and personal interactions (Strum & Latour, 1987). This is because they have few resources for time-space distanciation and hence nothing stays in place for long. On the other hand, human society is different because of the existence of an intertwined relationship of the social and the technical. According to Law (1997), people are "heterogeneous engineers" who deal with social and technical relations simultaneously to create a network of associated heterogeneous entities (Law, 1987).

Law suggests that such networks are composed of people, machines, animals, texts, money, architectures, and "any material that …[researchers] care to mention" (Law, 1992a). Thus, ANT invites more sensitivity and detailed account of the observed and investigated phenomena as it allows the researcher to include many actors that might otherwise be forgotten or excluded. In general, ANT recognises "texts of all sorts, machines or other physical objects, and people, sometimes separately but more frequently in combination, … to be the obvious raw materials for the actor who seeks to control others …" (Law, 1986).

Including Actors with Different Scale and Level Of Analysis

ANT adopts a symmetrical view of traditional sociological dichotomies, such as those between global and local, and macro and micro phenomena. It regards the sociotechnical world as not having a fixed, unchanging scale, and maintains that "it is not the observer's job to remedy this state of affairs" (Latour, 1991). The theory does not see any difference in kind between the macro-structure and the micro-structure, so treats both with the same analytical tool. Latour emphasises that "respecting such changes of scale, induced by the actors themselves, is just as important as respecting the displacement of translations" (ibid). In that sense, ANT is largely empirical. It does not impose *a priori* structure on actors. On the contrary, it follows actors in their construction, modification, and negotiation of their macro - and micro - structures.

ANT also treats the distinction of 'inside' and 'outside' as open to question and negotiation. It therefore leaves it to actors to define what is inside and what is outside, and the boundary between them. This may be a physical, organisational, or legal boundary (Law, 1992b). The agreed boundary determines the 'intermediaries' or what is

involved in the exchange between the global and local network.

The actors define one another in their interaction and in the intermediaries that they put into circulation (Callon, 1991). By defining what is local and inside, actors try to create a "negotiation space", a notion developed in (Law, 1987; Law & Callon, 1988) as having two essential characteristics: first, it is a private area, physical and/or metaphorical, that is relatively inaccessible to those outside; second, it is an area in which plans, ideas, designs, and/or possibilities with implications for control of the outside world may be generated, explored, and tested in a way that is largely invisible to those on the outside (Law, 1992b).

The negotiation space thus represents an area of relative autonomy approved by actors in the global network in order to build a local network. The establishment of a negotiation space is one of the strategies that actors adopt in order to build stable networks of sociotechnical objects. Law and Callon (1988) explain that a negotiation space makes it possible for mistakes to occur in private. Within a negotiation space it is also possible to experiment and, if all goes well, it is possible to create relatively durable sociotechnical combinations (Law & Callon, 1988).

Continuous work and many negotiations take place on the boundary between the global and local or the outside and inside in order to secure the existence of the inside. For example, in his book *Science in Action*, Latour (1987) identified the inside as the laboratory itself, with all its heterogeneous combinations of scientists, machines, and natural phenomena. On the other hand, the outside of the laboratory is the combination of financial institutions, governments and others. The internal/external division becomes the provisional outcome of a relationship between the outside recruitment of interests and the inside recruitment of new allies with "each step along the path the constitution of what is 'inside' and what is 'outside' alters" (Latour, 1987, p. 158).

IMPLICATIONS FOR ICT RESEARCH

ICT could be seen as a cause of societal change. This view is problematic as it maintains a deterministic view of technology that is dismissed and opposed by the social constructivism argument. The social constructivism argument while holds some truth, has been accused of being socially deterministic in its focus of society and ignoring the technology itself. In this regard, ANT could help researchers investigating the ICT related phenomena to better conceptualise the relationship between technology and society away from the traditional dichotomy. This is because ANT can account for both the social and the technical without loosing any thread in favour of the other providing a more balanced view of both.

ANT presents a theoretical framework and analytical vehicle that provides an alternative way of analysing the role of technology in society, which supports the social constructivism view but without undermining the role played by the technology. This could provide a solution to one of the main difficulties of ICT research, namely accounting for the capacity of technology without losing the social focus.

Moreover, ANT provides a wider lens for investigation, as the material heterogeneity of networks suggests a discourse of "liberal democracy", as it "grants the right of representation to anything - anything at all" (Lee & Brown, 1994). With ANT, there is "nothing which cannot be brought into the fold" (ibid). This commitment to the heterogeneity of the materials of the networks provides a flexible and powerful analytical and conceptual tool. This could be particularly of benefit to ICT research as it allows for investigating a wide range of actors regardless of their nature.

There is a wide range of actors that affect any ICT phenomenon under study. This wide range of heterogeneous actors are usually interrelated and hence require a more comprehensive and holistic approach to research. ANT treats all actors symmetrically despite their scale. Therefore it provides a wider lens for inquiry that could account for these different actors and their relationship and allows analytic flexibility in moving from the global to the local and from the micro to the macro and back. This is particularly useful for ICT studies where the level of analysis vary broadly between global, national, international, individual, institutional, and demographic level.

CONCLUSION

The ANT approach provides a process and interactionist view of the relationship between technology and society. It is largely empirical and avoids any *a priori* assumption about either the social or the technical. The role played by the social and the technical, and their effect on each other, is left as a local empirical matter that needs to be explored, rather than being a theoretical starting point for research. Hence, it provides a way out of the controversial dichotomy of technology determinism and social construction of technology (SCOT), since it recognises no social or technological necessity on either side.

The reconciliation and the fresh view ANT brings to the technical/social debate could be valuable to research on ICT as it takes the research beyond the determinism view that technology would impact society or the social view that society shapes technology. The relationship itself between technology and society and what each can and cannot is open for research rather than being a starting point for research.

On the analytical level, ANT could provide researchers with a wider binocular for investigations. It has the capacity to include and account for non-humans as an integral part of its distinctive view of society. It also provides a capacity to include a wider range of actors that are traditionally divided into Macro/ micro, outside/ inside, global/local into a holistic analysis which is needed for analysing the ICT based social inclusion and exclusion.

This study argues that ANT with its analytical and conceptual properties could open up research questions, include different stream of actors, and maintain a balanced view of the social and the technical. This argument does not mean that ANT is a theory that could explain it all. Any theory provides a way of seeing and not seeing but in different degrees. The argument of this chapter shows that ANT could provide just a high degree of seeing through phenomenon. It should also be noted that the application of ANT could bring some difficulties and challenges to researchers. These research challenges have to be considered and accounted for.

REFERENCES

Aanestad, M., & Hanseth, O. (2000, 10-12 June). *Implementing Open Network Technologies in Complex Work Practices: A case from telemedicine.* Paper presented at the IFIP 8.2, Aalborg, Denmark.

Akrich, M. (1992). The De-Scription of Technical Objects. In Bijker, W. E., & Law, J. (Eds.), *Shaping Technology/Building Society: studies in sociotechnical change* (pp. 205–224). Cambridge, MA: MIT Press.

Atkinson, C. J. (2000). The 'Soft Information Systems and Technologies Methodology' (SISTeM): An actor network contingency approach to integrated development. *European Journal of Information Systems*, *9*, 104–123.

Bijker, W. E. (1993). Do Not Despair: There is life after constructivism. *Science, Technology & Human Values*, *18*(1), 113–138. doi:10.1177/016224399301800107

Bijker, W. E. (1995). *Of Bicycle, Bakelite and Bulbs: Towards a theory of sociotechnical change.* Cambridge, MA: MIT Press.

Bloomfield, B. P., Coombs, R., Knights, D., & Littler, D. (Eds.). (1997). *Information Technology and Organizations: Strategies, Networks, and Integration.* Oxford, UK: Oxford University Press.

Bloomfield, B. P., & Vurdubakis, T. (1997). Paper Traces: inscribing organizations and information technology. In Bloomfield, B. P., Coombs, R., Knights, D., & Littler, D. (Eds.), *Information Technology and Organizations: Strategies, Networks, and Integration* (pp. 85–111). Oxford, UK: Oxford University Press.

Cadili, S., & Whitley, E. A. (2005). *On the Interpretive Flexibility of Hosted ERP Systems* (Working Paper Series No. 131). London: Department of Information Systems, The London School of Economics and Political Science.

Callon, M. (1987). Society in the Making: the study of technology as a tool for sociological analysis. In Bijker, W. E., Hughes, T. P., & Pinch, T. (Eds.), *The Social Construction of Technological Systems* (pp. 83–103). Cambridge, MA: MIT Press.

Callon, M. (1991). Techno-Economic Networks and Irreversibility. In Law, J. (Ed.), *A Sociology of Monsters: essays on power, technology and domination* (pp. 132–161). London: Routledge.

Callon, M., & Law, J. (1982). On Interests and their Transformation: Enrolment and Counter-Enrolment. *Social Studies of Science*, *12*, 615–625. doi:10.1177/030631282012004006

Cetina, K. K. (1993). Strong Construtivism- From a sociologist's Point of View. *Social Studies of Science*, *23*(3), 555–563. doi:10.1177/030631279302300305

Collins, H. M., & Yearley, S. (1992). Epistemological Chicken. In Pickering, A. (Ed.), *Science as Practice and Culture* (pp. 301–326). Chicago: The Universty of Chicago Press.

Edge, D. (1995). The Social Shaping of Technology. In Heap, N., Thomas, R., Einon, G., Mason, R., & Mackay, H. (Eds.), *Information Technology and Society: A reader*. The Open University.

Hanseth, O., & Braa, K. (1998, 13-16 December). *Technology as Traitor: emergent SAP infrastructure in a global organization*. Paper presented at the Nineteenth International Conference on Information Systems (ICIS), Helsinki, Finland.

Hanseth, O., & Monteiro, E. (1997). Inscribing Behaviour in Information Infrastructure Standards. *Accounting. Management and Information Technology*, *7*(4), 183–211. doi:10.1016/S0959-8022(97)00008-8

Heilbroner, R. L. (1967). Do Machines Make History? *Technology and Culture*, (July): 335–345. doi:10.2307/3101719

Heilbroner, R. L. (1994a). Do Machines Make History? In Smith, M. R., & Marx, L. (Eds.), *Does Technology Drive History? The dilemma of technological determinism*. Cambridge, MA: MIT Press.

Heilbroner, R. L. (1994b). Technological Determinism Revisited. In Smith, M. R., & Marx, L. (Eds.), *Does Technology Drive History? The dilemma of technological determinism*. Cambridge, MA: MIT Press.

Hughes, T. P. (1983). *Networks of Power: Electrification in Western Society, 1880-1930*. Baltimore: Johns Hopkins University Press.

Hughes, T. P. (1986). The Seamless Web: Technology, Science, Etcetera, Etcetera. *Social Studies of Science*, *16*(2), 281–292. doi:10.1177/030631278601600200

Hughes, T. P. (1987). The Evolution of Large Technological Systems. In Bijker, W. E., Hughes, T. P., & Pinch, T. J. (Eds.), *The Social Construction of Technological Systems: New direction in the sociology and history of technology*. Cambridge, MA: MIT Press.

Hughes, T. P. (1994). Technological Momentum. In Smith, M. R., & Marx, L. (Eds.), *Does Technology Drive History? The dilemma of technological determinism*. Cambridge, MA: MIT Press.

Hughes, T. P. (1999). Edison and electric light. In Mackenzie, D., & Wajcman, J. (Eds.), *The Social Shaping of Technology* - (2nd ed.). Buckingham, Philadelphia: Open University Press.

Klischewski, R. (2000). *Systems Development as Networking*. Paper presented at the Americas Conference on Information Systems (AMCIS), Long Beach, CA.

Latour, B. (1987). *Science in Action: How to follow scientists and engineers through society*. Cambridge, MA: Harvard University Press.

Latour, B. (1991). Technology is Society Made Durable. In Law, J. (Ed.), *Sociology of Monsters: essays on power, technology and domination* (pp. 103–131). London: Routledge.

Latour, B. (1994). Pragmatogonies. *The American Behavioral Scientist*, *37*(6), 791–808. doi:10.1177/0002764294037006006

Latour, B. (1999). *Pandora's Hope: Essays on the reality of science studies*. Cambridge, MA: Harvard University Press.

Law, J. (1986). On the Methods of Long-Distance Control: vessels, navigation and the Portuguese route to india. In J. Law (Ed.), *Power, Action and Belief: a new sociology of knowledge* (pp. 234-263): Routledge & Kegan Paul plc.

Law, J. (1987). Technology and Heterogeneous Engineering: The case of the Portuguese Expansion. In Bijker, W. E., Hughes, T. P., & Pinch, T. (Eds.), *The Social Construction of Technological Systems: New directions in the sociology and history of technology* (pp. 111–134). Cambridge, MA: MIT Press.

Law, J. (1992a). Notes on the Theory of the Actor-Network: Ordering, Strategy, and Heterogeneity. *Systems Practice*, 5(4), 379–393. doi:10.1007/BF01059830

Law, J. (1992b). The Olympus 320 Engine: A case Study in Design, Development, and Organizational Control. *Technology and Culture*, 33(3), 409–440. doi:10.2307/3106632

Law, J., & Callon, M. (1988). Engineering and Sociology in a Military Aircraft Project: A network analysis of technological change. *Social Problems*, 35(3), 284–297. doi:10.1525/sp.1988.35.3.03a00060

Lee, N., & Brown, S. (1994). Otherness and the Actor Network. *The American Behavioral Scientist*, 37(6), 772–790. doi:10.1177/0002764294037006005

Lilley, S. (1998). Regarding Screens for Surveillance of The System. *Accounting. Management and Information Technology*, 8, 63–105. doi:10.1016/S0959-8022(97)00012-X

Mackay, H. (1995). Theorising the IT/ Society Relationship. In Heap, N., Thomas, R., Einon, G., Mason, R., & Mackay, H. (Eds.), *Information Technology and Society: A reader*. The Open University.

Mackay, H., & Gillespie, G. (1992). Extending the Social Shaping of Technology Approach: Ideology and Appropriation. *Social Studies of Science*, 22(4), 685–716. doi:10.1177/030631292022004006

Mackenzie, D., & Wajcman, J. (Eds.). (1985). *The Social Shaping of Technology - first edition* (the first edition ed.). Buckingham and Philadelphia: Open University Press.

Mackenzie, D., & Wajcman, J. (Eds.). (1999). *The Social Shaping of Technology - second edition* (The second edition ed.). Bukingham and Philadelphia: Open University Press.

Marx, L., & Smith, M. R. (1994). Introduction. In Marx, L., & Smith, M. R. (Eds.), *Does Technology Drive History? The dilemma of technological determinism*. Cambridge, MA: MIT Press.

McGrath, K. (2001, June 27-29). *The Golden Circle: A case study of organizational change at the London Ambulance Service (Case Study)*. Paper presented at the The 9 th European Conference on Information Systems, Bled, Slovenia.

Misa, T. J. (1994). Retrieving Sociotechnical Change from Technological Determinism. In Smith, M. R., & Marx, L. (Eds.), *Does Technology Drive History? The dilemma of technological determinism*. Cambridge: The MIT Press.

Perdue, P. C. (1994). Technological Determinism in Agrarian Societies. In Smith, M. R., & Marx, L. (Eds.), *Does Technology Drive History? The dilemma of technological determinism*. Cambridge, MA: MIT Press.

Pfaffenberger, B. (1992). Technological Dramas. *Science, Technology & Human Values*, 17(3), 282–312. doi:10.1177/016224399201700302

Pinch, T. J., & Bijker, W. E. (1987). The Social Construction of Facts and Artifacts: Or How the Sociology of Science and the Sociology of Technology Might Benefit Each Other. In Bijker, W. E., Hughes, T. P., & Pinch, T. J. (Eds.), *The Social Construction of Technological Systems: New Directions in the Sociology and History of Technology*. The MIT Press.

Rappert, B. (2001). The Distribution and Resolution of the Ambiguities of Technology, or Why Bobby Can't Spray. *Social Studies of Science*, 31(4), 557–591. doi:10.1177/030631201031004004

Rosen, P. (1993). The Social Construction of Mountain Bikes: Technology and Postmodernity in the Cycle Industry. *Social Studies of Science*, 23(3), 479–513. doi:10.1177/030631279302300303

Scranton, P. (1994). Determinism and Indeterminacy in the History of Technology. In Smith, M. R., & Marx, L. (Eds.), *Does Technology Drive History? The dilemma of Technological determinism*. Cambridge, MA: The MIT Press.

Strum, S., & Latour, B. (1987). The Meaning of the Social: From Baboons to Humans. *Information Sur Les Science Socials. Social Sciences Information. Information Sur les Sciences Sociales, 26*, 783–802. doi:10.1177/053901887026004004

Strum, S., & Latour, B. (1999). Redefining the Social Link: From baboons to humans. In Mackenzie, D., & Wajcman, J. (Eds.), *The Social Shaping of Technology*. Buckingham, Philadelphia: Open University Press.

Sturken, M., & Thomas, D. (2004). Introduction: Technological visions and the rhetoric of the new. In Sturken, M., & Thomas, D. (Eds.), *Technological Visions: The hopes and fears that shape new technologies*. Philadelphia: Temple University Press.

Vidgen, R., & McMaster, T. (1996). Black Boxes, Non-Human Stakeholders and the Translation of IT Through Mediation. In Orlikowski, W. J., Walsham, G., Jones, M. R., & De Gross, J. I. (Eds.), *Information Technology and Change in Organizational Work* (pp. 250–271). London: Chapman and Hall.

Winner, L. (1986). *The Whale and The Reactor*. Chicago, London: The University of Chicago Press.

ENDNOTES

[1] Some authors call it the social constructivist approach (Cetina, 1993).

[2] A punctualised actor is itself a network that was successfully translated and aligned.

Chapter 10
Linux Kernel Developers Embracing Authors Embracing Licenses

Lars Linden
University of Central Florida, USA

Carol Saunders
University of Central Florida, USA

ABSTRACT

In June 2007, with the impending release of a revised version of the GNU General Public License (GPLv3), Linux kernel developers discussed the possibility of changing the license of the Linux kernel from being strictly the GPLv2 to a dual-licensing arrangement of both GPLv2 and GPLv3. We studied a set of Linux Kernel Mailing List (LKML) postings to better understand the relationship among the kernel developers and these licenses. Using Actor-Network Theory, we identify and describe a LKML debate about licensing. Our narrative highlights important actor-networks, their interrelationships, and a (failed) process of translation. The details suggest that the conceptualization of a copyright license as a monolithic social force maintaining the Linux community should be tempered with an appreciation of authorship and its distributed nature within Linux development.

INTRODUCTION

The first sentence of *Anna Karenina* is one of the best-known openings of any novel: "All happy families are alike: each unhappy family is unhappy in its own way." We studied the electronic mailing list discussions of the Linux kernel developers and found many posts that expressed the developers' dislike for revised version of the GNU General Public License (GPLv3) — all for

DOI: 10.4018/978-1-60960-197-3.ch010

different reasons. On the Linux Kernel Mailing List (LKML) the posters explored the possibility of a dual-licensing arrangement under which the Linux Kernel would be licensed by both the GPLv2, the current license, and the GPLv3, the revision version of the license. We analyzed these opinions about the GPLv2 and GPLv3 to better understand the relationships between the Linux kernel developers and copyright licenses. Using the analysis perspective of Actor-Network Theory (ANT), these opinions provide details of differences between "open sources" software and "free software." While the consensus of arguments on the LKML favored the GPLv2 over the GPLv3, the arguments were numerous and varied. The support for the GPLv2 was comprised of many individual arguments. Linux kernel developers have an author-centric view of licensing (i.e., that benefits the contributors of code), and reject a commanding, user-centric view (i.e., that emphasizes the free use of the software) they attributed to free software advocates.

The communities surrounding open source software and free software have a fuzzy and overlapping boundary. It is easiest to consider them as one, with the term Free/Open Source Software (FOSS) referring to an overall category of software that is contrasted with proprietary software. FOSS allows others to inspect the source code, provided they follow the terms of the code's license. FOSS can be contrasted with proprietary software which releases programs only in machine-readable form so as to guard the secrecy of the program's executed instructions. The term FOSS, even while referencing the overall category that is different from proprietary software, still maintains the distinction between free software and open source software, a distinction that began in the late 90s (Dempsey, Weiss, Jones, & Greenberg, 2002; Weiss, 2001), and still exist as is evident in the posts of the Linux kernel developers that we studied. The revision of the GPL has widened the gap between the two communities.

The difference between free software and open source software has been described in terms of the goals and the organizations founded to achieve these goals. Free software is championed by the Free Software Foundation whose mission is to achieve freedoms for users of software (Free Software Foundation, 2008). The definition of open source is stewarded by the Open Source Initiative, an organization which has its roots in the same programmer community as the free software advocates but which devotes attention to the areas of business and government (Open Source Initiative, 2005). The term "open source"

(Open Source Development Network, 2006) was strategically adopted into use to help create a more business-friendly approach and to overcome the perceived poor reputation that "free software" had as connoting a "moralizing" attitude; programmers wanted to better market the burgeoning open development environment to business contexts (Fitzgerald, 2006; Tiemann, 2008). The difference between free software and open source software has also been described in terms of values, with open source advocates assuming that technical values are the basis of quality software and free software advocates assuming that freedom is the basis of cooperation (AlMarzouq, Zheng, Rong, & Grover, 2005). Ideology has consequences for FOSS communities. Stewart and Gosain (2006) find freedom beliefs negatively impact effectiveness, explaining that people with strong freedom beliefs distribute their efforts across many projects throughout the greater FOSS community as they strive to accomplish their social goals. Also, the reduced attention to individual projects hinders trust and communication.

The free software/open source software differences are of interest to licensing of the Linux kernel because there is a paradox: the license applied to the Linux kernel is the GPLv2, a license regarded by GPL's author as a free software license, while the Linux kernel is regarded by the Linux project leader as open source software. Prior to the release of the revised license, a licensing debate on the LKML included many statements relating to the paradox. The opinions expressed during the debate present an opportunity to increase our understanding of the relationships among the Linux kernel developers and the licenses.

The GPL is the quintessential free software license. Created by Richard Stallman to support the freedoms of software users, the GPL describes the terms by which people can execute the copyrighted code, study the code, redistribute the code, modify the code, and release any modifications (Stallman, 2002). Those who use, modify, and distribute the software contractually agree to make the source code available and to refrain from imposing any licensing restrictions that would deny software freedoms (Rosen, 2005).

The revision of the GPL is itself a response to innovation in the marketplace. Richard Stallman, the creator of the GPL, the Free Software Foundation (FSF), the organization that manages many of the affairs related to the GPL, and the Software Freedom Law Center, an organization active in the legal aspects of FOSS, managed a process of revising the GPL license (Free Software Foundation & Software Freedom Law Center, 2006). The GPLv3 revision process began in 2006 with the release of a process document and an initial discussion draft. Inputs were garnered from both public comments and discussion committees. The purpose of the GPLv3 revision was to respond to perceived threats to user's software freedom, including, (1) "tivoization," which uses asymmetric modification privileges to restrict users from changing the free software contained inside a device, (2) anti-circumvention legislation, which prohibits people from writing software that breaks Digital Restrictions Management tools asserting control over their data, and (3) discriminatory patent deals, which aim to extract payment from free software users (Smith, 2008; Stallman, 2007). The GPL allows use of the software for making private profits on the public good, but only after first contributing any modifications of the code to the public under an equivalent license (Franck & Jungwirth, 2003). A majority of FOSS software projects use the GPL or compatible licenses (de Laat, 2005). For example, as of December 2008, the GPL accounted for over 59% of projects listed on Freshmeat (freshmeat.net, 2008), a repository of FOSS projects.

The revision process of the GPL is comparable to the standardization process of information infrastructure standards (i.e. Internet Protocol standards) that are described by Hanseth, Monteiro, and Hatling (1996). The license revision process is similar in that the process was open for anyone to participate and a single organiza-

tion (i.e. FSF) supervised the process. However, the revision process for the GPL must produce a document that is not only technically meaningful, but also the basis for a legally binding contract. The additional constraint of having to function within the legal domain dictates that the output of the revision process is arguably even less flexible to change than what is produced, for example, by the process of creating an Internet standard.

The creation of the GPLv3 is an indication that licenses are susceptible to innovation in the commercial environment. The consequences of such change are potentially significant. If Torvalds and other copyright holders of the Linux kernel were to respond to GPLv3 license changes by changing the license of the Linux kernel, their decision might reverberate not only through the Linux kernel developer community but also through the user and business communities. Information technology trade press (Babcock, 2007; Martens, 2007; Shankland, 2007) reported on the Linux community's reaction to license, an indicator of the prominence of the Linux kernel and the existence of interest within the business community.

The current license of the Linux kernel, the GPLv2, has not always been the kernel's license. The Linux kernel was created by Linux Torvalds in 1991 after he grew dissatisfied with the cost and design of the Unix-clone operating system he was using during his university studies (Linux Online, 1994-2008; Torvalds & Diamond, 2001). Torvalds made Linux available on the Internet to other kernel developers for no charge. Torvalds added features himself and incorporated the code that programmers sent. Each file that comprises the Linux kernel is individually licensed by one or more authors. Torvalds releases the collected arrangements of these files, called a compilation (in the copyright sense of the word), and so not only are the individual files copyrighted but the aggregate is licensed with the GPLv2. When Torvalds initially released Linux, a self-written license was applied to the code.

The first license stated that Linux could not be distributed for money. Early in Linux's history, two factors motivated Torvalds to switch from the self-written license to the GPLv2. First, people requested permission to sell copies to recoup the cost of the disks, and, second, the free software tools (e.g. GNU gcc compiler) were used to develop the kernel (Torvalds & Diamond, 2001). In 1992, on the mailing list, Torvalds proposed the adoption of the GPLv2 as the Linux kernel's license, allowing anyone with grievances to contact him (Torvalds, 1992).

The relationship between Linux and the GPL is a paradox. Linux Torvalds, the leader of the Linux kernel project, states that the last time he referred to Linux as "free software" was more than 10 years ago and that he prefers to call the Linux kernel "open source" (Torvalds, 2007). So, despite the code being licensed by the preeminent free software license, the GPLv2, the project leader considers the project to be an open source project. The opinions expressed by other Linux kernel developers in the LKML suggest that Torvalds views are shared. In consideration of this paradox we seek to analyze these discussions about the GPLv2 and GPLv3 to further understand the relationships among the copyright license, the people, and other entities of a project.

We begin by describing the literature that models how a FOSS license relates to a FOSS project. We then describe several concepts drawn from Actor-Network Theory (ANT) that we use during our analysis to aid us in identifying and describing relationships. After we describe our methodology, we narrate our analysis of the LKML postings from our adopted ANT perspective. We relate both the actor-networks found and the moments of translation which describes an effort (that failed) to alter the licensing scheme of the Linux kernel. Before concluding, we elaborate on a pattern comprised of many arguments provided by the developers, a pattern we call an *argument mosaic*.

LITERATURE ON FOSS LICENSING

The literature on FOSS provides several conceptualizations of licenses. Licenses are a governance mechanism, a means by which control is achieved. Licenses are metaphorical fences, encircling the commons of code to protect it from those who would appropriate the code. Licenses are textual artifacts that reflect the natural practices of the early programmer community. The section below describes the many aspects of the FOSS licensing phenomenon.

License as Governance Mechanism

Several authors describe FOSS licenses as governance mechanisms. Bonaccorsi and Rossi (2003) rank licenses as "the most important institution in the governance structure of Open Source projects" (p. 1248). The GPL as a governance mechanism insures that the code remains visible and is not hidden. This is important because the code is a common language by which programmers express their skills and ideas, and wide circulation of the code increases intellectual and other intrinsic motivations.

Franck and Jungwirth (2003) also describe the license as a governance mechanism. The crux of the design is that a party is able to extract private profits, but only after contributing their modifications to the public good. The GPL prevents fraud of the public good yet allows private profits.

In a review of open source software governance literature, Markus (2007) lists several categories of structures and rules that make up the multidimensional phenomenon of open source software governance. A license falls within the "ownership of assets" category of open source software governance. The ownership rules of a license hypothetically solve the problems of who owns the output of the community's work, how to prevent free riders, and how to create an organizational climate that is positive in that it motivates contributors.

License as Fence Protecting the Commons

The literature also describes FOSS licenses in terms of a metaphor: the fence around the commons. The fence metaphor pictures the license as a safeguard, one backed by legal sanctions and community norms, preventing people from taking code and placing it in proprietary systems. The license, in this view, is inconsequential to most developers and users. The important feature of licenses like the GPL is that they restrict people from taking the code for proprietary use (O'Mahony, 2003).

AlMarzouq, Zheng, Rong, and Grover (2005) provide a model that employs the fence metaphor. The model depicts a FOSS project as an Input-Process-Output (IPO) system comprised of four components: license, community, development process, and software. The license is described as a governance mechanism that provides the boundaries of the system. The license compels the observation of community norms and establishes that the code base represents a commons, thus helping to motivate programmers to participate. In an illustration of the model the license is depicted as a barbed-wired fence on the perimeter of a FOSS project.

License as Just Another Actor

Researchers adopting the methodological perspective of ANT identify additional relationships related to licenses. Lanzara and Morner (2005) argue that the copyleft license is merely the legal institutionalization of natural practices that programmers perform using the Internet. The license is a legal inscription of their particular "way of creating and distributing knowledge" (p. 88). Lanzara and Morner (2005) describe that

licenses aid innovation by making it easy for new programmers to engage a project (which increases variety), and by restricting modified code from being placed into a non-GPL program (a selection process that thwarts forking the code base and encourages upstream contributions).

Another way of relating licenses to FOSS communities is contributed by Tuomi (2001), who writes that licenses serve to guarantee that actants (i.e. software) in the development network are available for use by the Linux kernel developers. For example, the GPL-licensed GNU gcc compiler is an important software program that enables Linux development.

Also adopting an ANT-guided perspective, Cornford, Ciborra, and Shaikh's (2005) produce a narrative about their research in which open source software is described as grand social experiment. Drawing inspiration from Science and Technology Studies, all of FOSS is likened to a laboratory. The focus of their study, a controversy within the Linux collective over which version control software to use, appeared to the researchers as "a big episode in Laboratory Life" (p. 520). The focus of the study was upon Linux's version control system used and licensing controversy surrounding it (Shaikh & Cornford, 2003). The version control system being used at that time (BitKeeper) was unacceptable to some developers because the system had a license that was not compatible with the GPL.

Understanding More about Relationships with Licenses

The literature on FOSS licenses increases our understanding of FOSS by providing three different views of the FOSS license: as a governance mechanism, fence and just another actor. These conceptualizations are helpful but do not readily explain the paradox of an open source software project with a free software license and the controversy that this situation generates. We consider a given license to be just another actor, as is the case with the third conceptualization discerned from the literature. But, we seek to contribute additional understanding of FOSS licensing in relationships. We aim to do this by analyzing a discussion that reflects the FOSS controversy within the licensing relationship. The free software/open source software divergence is a consideration that the literature does not readily accommodate. We search for an analytical description that complements the current literature and adds to it a tentative explanation of the relationships between developers and licenses in light of the open source software/free software controversy.

ANALYSIS WITH ACTOR-NETWORK THEORY

This study uses ANT as a theoretical lens to trace and describe relationships among Linux kernel developers and the entities related to both the current license (GPLv2) and the revised license (GPLv3) as they are discussed on the LKML. The aim is to use ANT to reveal relationships and to produce a description of how Linux kernel developers, copyright licenses, and other actors impact each other. Rather than starting with an assumption that a copyright license has an essence that exhibits a social force upon the kernel developers, the license is viewed as just another entity and its influence is observed in the relationships discussed by the posters.

ANT is a relevant theory for the analysis, because the FOSS environment contains a variety of technology, from programming tools to Internet-based communication systems, and the GPLv3 represents a response to innovative maneuvers in the information technology marketplace. ANT has been advocated as a useful point of view when studying the innovations of information system implementations (Tatnall & Gilding, 1999). The following is a description of the particular ANT concepts used during the analysis.

Adopting the Three Principles of ANT

Analysis with ANT is guided by three principles: generalized agnosticism, generalized symmetry, and free association (Callon, 1986). These methodological imperatives aid in the relinquishing of the idea that the license has a pre-established influence upon the social. The imperatives aid in the tracing of associations among heterogeneous entities.

The first principle is *generalized agnosticism*. During ANT analysis, the observer reports on the doubts that actors have about the social and the natural. The goal of this principle is to not only strive to be objective about the license with respect to its legal or technical language but also to strive to be objective with how the Linux kernel developers discuss their social relationships. The knowledge pertaining to the Linux kernel developers and the licenses is regarded to be equally uncertain. The objective is to not assess the license and developers too soon, but to allow their social identities to fluctuate (Callon, 1986).

The second principle is *generalized symmetry*. During ANT analysis, the observer adopts an impartial attitude toward human and non-human actors. The list of agents that actively interpret the network of relationships surrounding the Linux kernel includes not just developers, users, and lawyers, but also code, computers, devices, electronic mailing lists, venture capital funding, and the mascot penguin Tux. Both humans and non-humans shape the relationships that constitute the social. In this analysis, a vocabulary of actor-networks and a vocabulary of translation are maintained and applied equally to actors of differing types.

The third principle is *free association*. This imperative requires that the analysis begins by having no assumptions of existing socio-technical structures or macro-social systems (Law, 1992). This means, for example, that the copyright license has no essence that allows it to have social influence; the social influence of a license, if any, is found in the license's associations as events transpire.

Identifying Actor-Networks

Actors are the people and things that interact, make associations, and define one another through the intermediaries which pass between them (Callon 1991). Actors engage in relationships and form alliances with other actors, using artifacts to strengthen the alliances. Actors both inscribe and are inscribed. In so doing, actors assemble heterogeneous networks each of which can then be treated as an independent actor (Sarker, Sarker, & Sidorova, 2006). Once assembled, a heterogeneous network is referred to as an actor-network, notable because the interests of the actors are aligned and "working toward achievement of a common goal" (Abrahall, Cecez-Kecmanovic, & Kautz, 2007, p. 25). *Punctualization* is said to occur when a complex actor-network is treated as singular whole. The simplification of an entire complex actor-network occurs when the details of the network are taken for granted and become effectively hidden, such as with a bug-free, smoothly-executing computer program. However, this simplification is precarious in that a failure in the network may suddenly reveal the complexities of the network (Law, 1992). *Depunctualization* refers to the collapse of the unified view and the unclustering of the network that exposes the details of the network.

There are four types of actors making (or attempting to make) associations. First, human beings are actors. A Linux kernel developer is a flesh and blood actor who can also be viewed as an actor-network by considering "the skills, the knowledge, and the know-how" that the person brings together and posses (Callon, 1991, p. 135). Being a kernel developer implies the network that makes kernel hacking possible. For example, the skills of compiling a kernel imply associations

with compiler software and computer hardware, manuals of some form, a source of electricity, etc.

Second, texts are actors, for example, "reports, books, articles, patents, notes," and copyright licenses (Callon, 1991, p. 135). The ANT view of a text as a network encourages the observer to understand more than the semantic meanings of the words on the page. The observer should also consider the network of social and technical entities which contribute to the definitions (Callon, 1991). A license, such as the GPLv3, is a network of association with outward links (e.g. copyright terminology links to legal definitions) and inward links (e.g. public speeches containing commentary about the GPLv3). These texts "rework and extend the network" (Callon, 1991, p. 136).

Third, technical objects are a type of actor. This set includes "scientific instruments, machines, robots, and consumer goods" (Callon, 1991, p. 135). Any electronic device that executes a compiled Linux kernel is a technical object.

Fourth, money or, more generally, any instrument of exchange, is a type of actor. Money actors influencing licenses range from the profits (or losses) of business models commercializing products and services around software products that are provided *gratis* to credit cards that are swiped through Linux-based cash registers.

Vocabulary of ANT's Moments of Translation

ANT is referred to as the sociology of translation. Actors enact strategies to influence other actors and assemble actor-networks (Callon, 1986). Actors strive to align interests and form cohesive entities, which can be treated as a unified whole. Callon (1986) describes four moments found during the process of translation:

- **Problematization** occurs when focal actors frame a problem and portray to others a solution as being irresistibly beneficial.

- **Interessement** is a process by which focal actors attempt to convince other actors that their interests are aligned with the innovative *social ordering* that is being attempted. During this stage actors are enticed to accept their new roles and to abandon resistance.
- **Enrollment** occurs when actors accept a role in the newly-created actor-network. An alliance is created when actors accept a particular issue as being beneficial to them and when they align their interests with that particular issue.
- **Mobilization** is performed to position particular actor-networks such that they successfully represent collectives and do not betray these collectives.

These four moments describe a process that may achieve an alignment of interests that is social stable. However, the social entity of aligned interests is not necessarily permanent. Translation is a temporary, precarious process of social ordering (Law, 1992). The process may collapse (Fox, 2000). Although the opposite can happen, once established, a newly assembled social actor-network may exhibit *irreversibility,* a measure of convergence representing stability (Callon, 1991). The *obligatory passage point* (OPP) represents what must be achieved by all actors in order for a new social stability to be established.

RESEARCH METHODOLOGY

The data for our study was downloaded from the LKML (www.tux.org/lkml/), an electronic mailing list that is used primarily to discuss technical issues of kernel development. The LKML is the main mode of communication of the developers of the Linux kernel and has been used in the past to study the Linux community (Shaikh & Cornford, 2005).

To select the postings, subject lines of the LKML posts were downloaded and searched for keywords. If a subject line contained the terms "GPL" or "gpl," the entire text of the post was downloaded. Using this technique, we identified and examined a set of LKML posts just prior to the official release of the GPLv3 on June 29, 2007. This set consisted of 1,133 posts that span from June 9, 2007 to June 30, 2007. The debate addresses whether or not it is advisable—or even possible—to change the terms of the Linux kernel's license. We analyzed postings using the analytical lens of Actor-Network Theory using a prepared list of ANT concepts. We followed the three principles of ANT.

The posts were written by 101 participants, including the project leader (Linus Torvalds), core members, active developers, and peripheral developers. A histogram showing the frequency distribution illustrates that most posters only contributed a few posts and a few posters contributed a large number of posts (Figure 1).

ANALYSIS OF LKML LICENSING DISCUSSION

The discussion began when a LKML poster asked if it was possible to dual license the kernel. Here is an excerpt of the post that started a multi-week flamewar:

But; if the Linux Kernel should Dual-Licensed (GPL V2 and GPL V3), it will allow us the both worlds' fruits like code exchanging from other Open Source Projects (OpenSolaris etc.) that is compatible with GPL V3 and not with GPL V2 and of course the opposite is applicable, too. (Tarkan Erimer, 2007/6/9/11)[1]

The poster was unsure if dual-licensing is possible. The question posed is a moment of problematization. This poster used the prospects of code gained from other projects to interest

Figure 1. LKML participants' frequency by number of posts

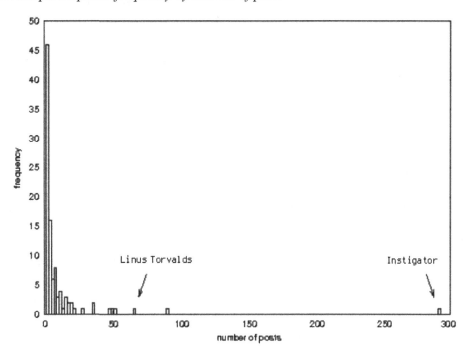

others and enlist their support of the GPLv3. A debate ensued.

Persistent Poster of Arguments was an Instigator

One poster supported the GPLv3 and provided reasons as to why the Linux community would benefit from adopting the license. The poster's primary argument is that the spirit of the GPL's Preamble has not changed with the new version.

However, it seems to me that GPLv3 would do an even better job at serving these goals than GPLv2, even if the holes v3 plugs that enabled players to disrespect others' freedoms might steer away the participants who are not willing to contribute, to really be part of your community. (Alexandre Oliva, 2007/6/13/246)

This person posted 291 messages, more than three times the number of posts made by the person with the second-most posts. This person argued in

support of GPLv3. Only one other person provided significant support supportive arguments. Hence only 2 of 101 participants posted comments in favor of adopting GPLv3.

The most persistent poster instigated many responses. Other posters expressed annoyance with the instigator's inordinate number of posts. The instigator is associated with the FSF, based on the similarity of the tactic of relentlessly insisting of one particular interpreting of the license.

I see the smiley, but I hate it how the FSF thinks others are morons and cannot read or think for themselves. Any time you disagree with the FSF, you "misunderstand" (insert condescending voice) the issue. _Please_ don't continue that idiocy. (Linus Torvalds, 2007/6/13/221)

The instigator's arguments are not accepted. However, there is enrollment to the extent that the actors in the network consider the issue to be worthy of exploration as to the extent to which the adoption of GPLv3 may possibly align with their interests.

Linux Torvalds Uploading and Posting his Way to Kernel Spokesperson

When the pro-GPLv3 instigator persists in arguments, Torvalds states that it is his choice he because he originated the project:

It was my right to use the license of my choice for a project that I started. (Linus Torvalds, 2007/6/14/276)

Torvalds' interpretation of the license has strength because he created the project and is the person who releases new aggregated versions of Linux. Typical of many FOSS projects, there are no formal organizational structures in the Linux kernel development community (Fontana, 2008), although Torvalds is informally called the "benevolent dictator" (Kerner, 2008; Zemlin, 2008). The existence of Torvalds' leadership position is found in statements that other developers post. For example, more than once kernel developers deferred to Torvalds' view of the license:

On top of that, Linus clarified his position back in 2000? (Rob Landley, 2007/6/13/244)

Kernel developers are aligned with the license in as much as they are aligned with the project leaders' view of the license. The license is not viewed in isolation; rather, it is viewed with respect to the relationship between the project leader and the license.

Kernel Developers Revisit their Convergence

In addition to expressing deference to Torvalds' opinions, kernel developers also expressed their own opinions:

From the very _beginning_ of the v3 process the kernel developers have showed their objection to that section of the license ["anti-tivo" clause], and we were told, to our face, with no uncertain terms, that it was going to stay, in one form or another, no matter what we thought or said about it. (Greg KH, 2007/6/18/221)

As this post reveals, this controversy has a history. Several times references are made to the kernel developer's consensus. For example, one actor that is mentioned is an open letter entitled "The Dangers and Problems with GPLv3" (Bottomley et al., 2006), signed by ten prominent Linux kernel developers. This letter is a text intermediary; the mere mention of the letter signifies the Linux kernel developers' denouncement of the GPLv3. Another reference to previously documented kernel developer's positions is an informal poll in which 28 voters expressed their opinion about the GPLv3.

In case you haven't followed previous discussions, here's a pointer: ... http://lkml.org/lkml/2006/9/22/176 The major kernel developers (and probably most of the total number of developers) are perfectly aware of the kernel license and chose GPL v2. (Paulo Marques, 2007/6/15/222)

Open letters and polls are textual actor-networks used to defend against the GPLv3. Meanwhile, the advocates of the GPLv3 mention actor-networks to support their position. One text that is repeatedly mentioned by the instigator and advocates for the GPLv2 is the Preamble. The instigator uses it as an interessement device, with the argument being that because the Preamble exists in both licenses, a person should embrace both licenses equally. The Preamble argument fails because a Preamble is not a substantial part of the license.

Figure 2 illustrates the actor-networks described up to this point in the analysis and shows

Figure 2. Linux and two versions of the GPL

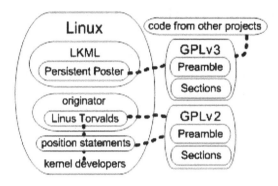

how code from other projects would be available upon acceptance of a relationship with the GPLv3.

Richard Stallman and Linux: Interests Not Aligned

The creator of the General Public License, Richard Stallman, never makes a post, but he is mentioned several times in during the discussion. Stallman is strongly associated with the GPLv3 and the process by which it was created.

The GPLv3 process was pretended to be "open", but regardless of what the "GPL committees" said, in the end it was one person: the president of the FSF (Richard Stallman) who singlehandedly decided what went into the GPLv3 draft and what not. (Ingo Molnar, 2007/6/14/401)

The concept of betrayal can be drawn from the ANT lexicon to describe the dynamics of this poster's frustration. The poster portrays Stallman failing to abide by the open process of the GPLv3 drafting and unfairly dominating the views of the stakeholders of the GPLv2. Evidence from the posts suggests that the Linux kernel developers seek to distance themselves from Stallman.

But your argument fatally falls down on the fact that rms has had *nothing* to do with the Linux Kernel. (Linus Torvalds, 2007/6/15/336)

Stallman and the Linux community are no longer aligned, despite the fact that the Linux kernel is licensed by the Stallman-authored GPLv2.

Free Software Foundation Encapsulates Only One Definition of Freedom

No poster was identified as an official representative of the FSF. However, posters interpret the intent of FSF.

Neither is the fact that I've never agreed with the FSF's agenda about "freedom" (as defined by _them_ - I have a notion of "freedom" myself, and the FSF doesn't get to define it for me). I don't call Linux "Free Software". I haven't called it that for close to ten years! Because I think the term "Open Source" is a lot better. (Linus Torvalds, 2007/6/14/306)

In addition to the declarations that the Linux kernel is not associated with Stallman, the posters declare that the FSF agenda is also not associated. The term "free software" is not permanently inscribed on the GPLv2 license.

And I don't like the FSF's radical world-view, but I am able to separate the license (the GPLv2) from the author and source of the license (rms and the FSF). (Linus Torvalds, 2007/6/14/253)

Figure 3 illustrates the how the GPLv3 is associated with Stallman, the FSF, and their definition of freedom.

Authors as Copyright Owners

Several posters agreed that it is possible to change from GPLv2 to another license, or a dual-license arrangement. However, the change would be difficult to bring about.

Figure 3. Stallman inscribes a definition of freedom

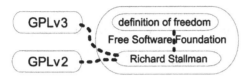

But one thing is pretty clear and nonspeculative: *nobody* has the right to upgrade the kernel to GPLv3. Not me, not you, not anybody. Not without clearing it with every single person whose copyright is involved and who didn't already give that permission. (Linus Torvalds, 2007/6/15/374)

The appearance of this argument weakens the nascent proposed translation of a dual-licensed Linux kernel as beneficial. The number of actors that need to be convinced are too numerous. Direct engagement to promote the dual-licensing scheme diminishes, and the obligatory passage point of dual-licensing fails as ideas of a union of licenses are outnumbered by messages creating a division between the licenses.

The attempt to entice the kernel developers with the code of outside projects upon the adoption of the GPLv3 fails in part because kernel developers refuse to betray the role of authorship. In stating that no person is allowed to unilaterally upgrade the kernel, Torvalds is strengthening a conviction about the license that was apparent in several posts. The community responds positively to the rights of authorship, the foundation of the copyright. In essence there is a type of mobilization in that the members of the LKML appear to agree that the best action to adopt is not to take any action on GPLv3. This action (or rather lack of action) appears to represent the collectives in the LKML community, even though the reasons for doing so are varied.

GPLv2 and GPLv3: Cut and Pasted, Reworked and Extended

Posters inserted short clips of text when discussing the licenses, splicing them into discussion, primarily using them as evidence. Actors depunctualize the licenses to associate parts of the licenses' text with entities in the environment, as in the following example:

Section 6 is inherently broken. It tries to gerrymander the "bad" cases and ends up with a huge mess. (Al Viro, 2007/6/15/13)

The discussion of the GPLv2 and GPLv3 reworked and extended the text of these licenses. Not only are there many associations with the license text, but there is not one common understanding of the license text. In more than a dozen instances posters accused others of not having read the license. Posters also asked others to re-read a text.

Linux Kernels, Hacked in More Than One Way

Several posters depunctualize the Linux kernel by discussing the various parts. One example of this is the mentioning of the COPYING file. This file contains the text that associates the Linux kernel to the GPLv2. During the discussion, the COPYING file is described, strengthening the relationship between the licensing and the aggregate of kernel files.

... though there is a consensus that the COPYING file was indeed a license for the whole kernel (Krzysztof Halasa, 2007/6/13/109)

The parts of the Linux kernel are mentioned in other ways. Adding value to the discussing, a poster apparently wrote a small program to analyze the copyright declarations in the kernel files.

Because almost half (Around %60 of the code licensed under "GPLv2 Only" and the rest is "GPLv2 or above", "GPL-Version not specified, others that have not stated which and what version of License has been used) of the code is "GPLv2 or above" licensed. (Tarkan Erimer, 2007/6/10/27 discussing Linux 2.6.20)

Another relationship between the Linux kernel developers and the license is based upon the technical skills of a kernel developer. One argument against adopting the GPLv3 is that the GPLv3 is not aligned with these technical values associated with the Linux's goals.

*In the GPLv3 world, we have already discussed in this thread how you can follow the GPLv3 by making the TECHNICALLY INFERIOR choice of using a ROM instead of using a flash device. Quite frankly, I don't *want* to attract developers that are not technically "up to snuff". (Linus Torvalds, 2007/6/18/403)*

These threads suggest that the relationship between the kernel developers and the programming realm impacts the inscription of the licenses.

Hardware Manufacturers Playing by the Software Rules While Inventing the Hardware Rules

During the discussion, several pieces of hardware are mentioned. The discussion about a digital video recorder (DVR) designed and sold to consumers by TiVo Inc. is central to the license controversy.

Obviously Linus feels that the spirit of the GPLv2 is exactly what he wanted and that it allows TiVo to lock down their hardware. You obviously disagree. Stop telling everyone else they are wrong and you are right when they disagree with your intepretation. (Chris Adams, 2007/6/15/533)

TiVo Inc. sells a device that contains a Linux kernel. The GPLv3 was written to prevent the use of GPLv3-licensed software being used in a device with such a design. However, Torvalds has a different opinion. During the discussion, Torvalds relates that the relationship between TiVo and the Linux kernel object code is not in jeopardy because the device manufacturer diligently followed the conditions of GPLv2. Torvalds' strong relationship with TiVo contrasts greatly with those attributed to GPLv3 advocates. As a result, the relationship between the Linux kernel and the GPLv3 is weakened.

Another quote clearly differentiates the GPLv2 and GPLv3 actor-networks because it defines a Linux guideline pointing to the dichotomy of software and hardware.

I agree with Linus that software licenses should have their influence only on the software part and leave the freedom of the hardware on which the software runs to the hardware manufacturers. (debian developer, 2007/6/10/183)

The argument is that the GPLv3, in its attempt to thwart asymmetric modification privileges, limits the hardware designer's range of possibilities. The TiVo DVR hardware/software issue highlights Linux kernel developers as having focused on how best to design software and being of the opinion that hardware design beyond the scope of their mission. The kernel confines the project. The developers are interested in the kernel and the kernel is software. Kernel developers are interested in writing device drivers, not designing devices.

Figure 4 illustrates all of the previous actor-networks as well as the ones just discussed. The kernel developers recognize authors as being directly associated with the files that comprise the Linux kernel. The COPYING file serves to strongly associate the GPLv2 with the Linux kernel. And, a manufacturer of hardware is associated to Linux, first, via the product it produces which contains the object code of a compiled kernel and,

Figure 4. Actor-networks associated with licenses in differing patterns

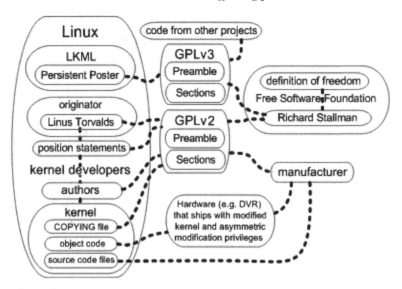

second, via the GPLv2 which is adhered to when releasing the modified source code files used in the hardware product.

Subscribers to the Linux Kernel Mailing List: Paying Attention is the Cost of Admission

Lanzara and Morner (2005) observed two "everyday mundane practices" performed by Linux developers: writing programs and conversing with e-mails (p. 69). The act of writing and reading messages is a fundamental task performed by kernel developers. Reflexively, the LKML, the system enabling discussion, is an actor that has a relationship among other actors.

But I agree with you - the thread was fun. And then I realized that the discussion was going nowhere at all. So I'm going to answer the last few messages in my inbox and then start filtering messages with this topic off without reading them. (Daniel Hazelton, 6/15/115)

The electronic mailing list system enables the debate and, because it embodies a design,

helps determine the pattern of the discussion. An example of the design impacting the discussion is its openness. The instigator elicited responses even after others had expressed their annoyance. A large amount of the collective mailing list attention span—"bandwidth" in terms of community—was used up with the discussion of the issue continued during the three-week period. One reason explaining why the kernel developers discussed the licensing issue to such an extent is to test ideas.

The most important purpose of the discussion is to TEST if someone could force this "upgrade" in the future when leadership is less clear. So, I think it's good that some people are willing to take the side of version 3 and try to go all the way to prove that it's better and/or possible to "upgrade" etc - as if they REALLY want that. (Carlo Wood, 2007/6/15/174)

By practicing these arguments in-house, they sharpen their arguments. The community discusses as a way to test themselves. Having an open discussion allows the actors to submit answers to problems, hear from other supporting actors, and enlist the support of as many as possible for when they will be needed in the future. The relationships between a license and software exist in a changing environment. Voicing arguments is one tactic that exposes arguments to the current environment to determine their strengths and weaknesses.

ARGUMENT MOSAIC

In response to the possibility of a dual-licensing arrange, it is discussed that to change the license arrangement of the Linux kernel it would be necessary to obtain agreement from all copyright owners. The difficulties of this task are discussed, but no movement is made to attempt to set up a dual-licensing arrangement. The discussion of dual-licensing is just a discussion. Support for dual-licensing is weak.

Although the idea of dual-licensing the Linux kernel fades, the support for the GPLv2 continues. The discussion is not short. A variety of arguments are offered to support the GPLv2 and reject the GPLv3: The process for creating the new license was not open even though it was said to be open. The project leader is interested in a license that encourages technically correct decisions. A group of kernel developers have gotten together and agreed that there are some real problems with the revised license. The license applied to the Linux kernel should only cover the software and should not dictate how the hardware should be designed. The revised license is the result of the FSF pushing their agenda. The revised license is a messy document.

The 3-week, asynchronous, virtual conversation is a mosaic of arguments. It resists being summarized with one primary reason. If one was to attempt to provide one major argument as to why there is little chance in the licensing status quo, it would neglect many important arguments. Dual-licensing is not likely because it is not feasible to obtain agreement from all copyright owners. Dual-licensing is not likely because the Linux project leader favors the GPLv2. Dual-licensing is not likely because the revision process was not considered by some Linux kernel developers to be open. Each of these reasons has a quality of being correct and being strong enough to extinguish any effort to dual-license the Linux kernel. The combination of these arguments is argued to be significant not because the combination changes the results but because the combination accounts for the sources of the arguments. These arguments are expressed by many posters. The arguments are distributed.

Lanzara and Morner (2005) describe open source software projects as interactive systems, and a structuring on mailing lists when the members of the group focus upon a particular topic. The 3-week LKML discussion about licensing represents a "cluster of activity" that Lanzara and Morner (2005, p. 71). The focus point of licensing has captured the attention of the LKML and many people were posted. To this concept of the common theme around which members of community virtually congregate, we draw attention to the characteristic of this cluster of activity: there is a variety of opinions submitted to support the status quo creating ht impression of overwhelming the opposition.

An argument mosaic is a set of arguments supporting a particular position with a wide variety of reasons and with a much larger number of reasons than may be necessary to win the argument. The GPLv2 is favored over the GPLv3 for no single reason; yet one reason may have been enough. The distributed quality of these arguments may be attributable to the distributed nature of the electronic mailing list system, the persistent postings of the instigator, and the fact that each Linux kernel developer posting may have an individual favorite reason, or a combination of these. Regardless of what provokes the variety of arguments, the variety of arguments expressed by the developers relates the license of the code to several actors. This characterizes the license of the Linux kernel as an intricate and diversified across relationships, rather than a community-wide, monolithic force.

CONCLUSION

We set out to describe the relationships between the license and the kernel developers and other entities related to kernel development. Our analysis of the LKML discussion associates several actor-networks with respect to the Linux kernel developers and the licenses. The copyright license is more than a legal text applied to computer code.

The GPLv2, as the license of the Linux kernel, exhibits an irreversible quality, at least for this current time period. The set of relationships that have converged in agreement with this relationship is numerous and strong. Based upon the support found in the discussion, a change in this licensing arrangement would require a multitude of a variety of reasons. In the discussion, the primary benefit of dual-licensing was the offer of code from other projects, but this now appears far from what would be necessary to bring about a change in the licensing of the Linux kernel. Especially when considering the technical-author-centric values to the Linux kernel developers, which suggest that the Linux kernel community can just write whatever code they need for themselves by themselves.

While a change in licensing arrangement appears remote, the idea was debated. A change is not out of the question. No sustainable alliance is created around the idea of a dual license for Linux. There is no convergence upon the OPP urged by proponents of GPLv3. Yet, there is an acceptance to discuss the idea. It is conceivable that an OPP regarding a license change could embark upon a process of translation whereby actors are aligned in favor of change. If a focal actor were to emphasize the benefits to the authors of the code, address sections of the license in detail, align with the project leaders and major kernel developers, and be mindful of the mailing list conventions,

the Linux kernel developers would likely give attention to the potential arrangement. However, that was not the case for GPLv3.

REFERENCES

Abrahall, R., Cecez-Kecmanovic, D., & Kautz, K. (2007). Understanding Strategic ISD Project in Practice – An ANT Account of Success and Failure. In G. Magyar, G. Knapp, W. Wojtkowski, W. G. Wojtkowski & J. Zupančič (Eds.), *Advances in Information Systems Development, 1*, 23-33. Springer US.

AlMarzouq, M., Zheng, L., Rong, G., & Grover, V. (2005). Open Source: Concepts, Benefits, and Challenges. *Communications of the AIS, 16*, 756–784.

Babcock, C. (2007). What Will Drive Open Source? *InformationWeek, Mar 19, 2007*, 36-44.

Bonaccorsi, A., & Rossi, C. (2003). Why Open Source software can succeed. *Research Policy, 32*(7), 1243–1258. doi:10.1016/S0048-7333(03)00051-9

Bottomley, J. E. J., Chehab, M. C., Gleixner, T., Hellwig, C., Jones, D., Kroah-Hartman, G., et al. (2006). *The Dangers and Problems with GPLv3*. Retrieved January 9, 2008, from http://lwn.net/Articles/200422/

Callon, M. (1986). Some Elements of a Sociology of Translation: Domestication of the Scallops and the Fishermen of the St Brieuc Bay. In L. J. (Ed.), *Power, Action and Belief: A New Sociology of Knowledge* (pp. 196-229). London: Routledge & Kegan Paul.

Callon, M. (1991). Techno-economic networks and irreversibility. In Law, J. (Ed.), *A Sociology of Monsters: Essays on Power, Technology and Domination* (pp. 196–223). London: Routledge.

Cornford, T., Ciborra, C., & Shaikh, M. (2005). Do penguins eat scallops? *European Journal of Information Systems, 14*(5), 518–521. doi:10.1057/palgrave.ejis.3000583

de Laat, P. B. (2005). Copyright or copyleft? An analysis of property regimes for software development. *Research Policy, 34*(10), 1511–1532. doi:10.1016/j.respol.2005.07.003

Dempsey, B. J., Weiss, D., Jones, P., & Greenberg, J. (2002). Who is an Open Source Software Developer? *Communications of the ACM, 45*(2), 67. doi:10.1145/503124.503125

Fitzgerald, B. (2006). The Transformation of Open Source Software. *Management Information Systems Quarterly, 30*(3), 587–598.

Fontana, J. (2008). *Torvalds Breaks Down Linux.* Retrieved January 11, 2008, from http://www.networkworld.com/news/2008/011008-torvalds-linux.html

Fosfuri, A., Giarratana, M. S., & Luzzi, A. (2008). The Penguin Has Entered the Building: The Commercialization of Open Source Software Products. *Organization Science, 19*(2), 292–305. doi:10.1287/orsc.1070.0321

Fox, S. (2000). Communities of Practice, Foucault and Actor-Network Theory. *Journal of Management Studies, 37*(6), 853–867. doi:10.1111/1467-6486.00207

Franck, E., & Jungwirth, C. (2003). Reconciling Rent-Seekers and Donators–The Governance Structure of Open Source. *Journal of Management and Governance, 7*(4), 401–421. doi:10.1023/A:1026261005092

Free Software Foundation. (2008). *Free Software and the GNU Operating System.* Retrieved December 17, 2008, from http://www.fsf.org/about

Free Software Foundation, & Software Freedom Law Center. (2006). *GPLv3 Process Definition.* freshmeat.net. (2008). *Statistics and Top 20: License breakdown.* Retrieved December 11, 2008, from http://freshmeat.net/stats/#license

Hanseth, O., Monteiro, E., & Hatling, M. (1996). Developing Information Infrastructure: The Tension between Standardization and Flexibility. *Science, Technology & Human Values, 21*(4), 407–426. doi:10.1177/016224399602100402

Kerner, S. M. (2008). *Torvalds Still Keen On GPLv2: The Linux creator explains why he's sticking with the older version of the General Public License.* Retrieved January 11, 2008, from http://www.internetnews.com/dev-news/article.php/3720371

Lanzara, G. F., & Morner, M. (2005). Artifacts Rule! How Organizing Happens in Open Source Software Projects. In Czarniawska, B., & Hernes, T. (Eds.), *Actor-Network Theory and Organizing* (pp. 197–206). Malmo, Sweden: Liber & Copenhagen Business School Press.

Law, J. (1992). *Notes on the Theory of Actor Network: Ordering, Strategy and Heterogeneity.* Center for Sciences Studies.

Linux Online, I. (1994-2008). *The Linux Home Page at Linux Online,* 2008, from http://www.linux.org/

Markus, M. L. (2007). The governance of free/open source software projects: monolithic, multidimensional, or configurational? *Journal of Management and Governance, 11*(2), 151–163. doi:10.1007/s10997-007-9021-x

Martens, C. (2007). *GPLv3 third draft: Linus likes it, ACT hates it.* Retrieved January 11, 2008, from http://www.computerworld.com/action/article.do?command=viewArticleBasic&articleId=9014878

O'Mahony, S. (2003). Guarding the commons: how community managed software projects protect their work. *Research Policy*, *32*(7), 1179–1198. doi:10.1016/S0048-7333(03)00048-9

Open Source Development Network. (2006). *Software Map*. Retrieved December 17, 2008, from http://www.dwheeler.com/frozen/sourceforge-stats-20031110.html

Open Source Initiative. (2005). *The Open Source Definition*. Retrieved December 10, 2008, from http://www.opensource.org/docs/osd

Rosen, L. (2005). *Open source licensing: software freedom and intellectual property law*. Upper Saddle River, NJ: Prentice Hall PTR.

Sarker, S., Sarker, S., & Sidorova, A. (2006). Understanding Business Process Change Failure: An Actor-Network Perspective. *Journal of Management Information Systems*, *21*(1), 51–86. doi:10.2753/MIS0742-1222230102

Shaikh, M., & Cornford, T. (2003). *Version Management Tools: CVS to BK in the Linux Kernel*. Paper presented at the Taking Stock of the Bazaar, 3rd Workshop on Open Source Software Engineering, Portland, OR.

Shaikh, M., & Cornford, T. (2005). *Learning/organizing in Linux: a study of the 'spaces in between'*. Paper presented at the Open Source Application Spaces: Fifth Workshop on Open Source Software Engineering, St. Louis, MO.

Shankland, S. (2007). *Open-source Solaris makes GPL 3 more attractive: Linus Torvalds*. Retrieved January 11, 2008, from http://www.zdnet.com.au/news/software/soa/Open-source-Solaris-makes-GPL-3-more-attractive-Linus-Torvalds/0,130061733,339278528,00.htm

Smith, B. (2008). A Quick Guide to GPLv3.

Stallman, R. (2002). *Free Software, Free Society: Selected Essays of Richard M. Stallman*. Boston, MA: Gnu Press.

Stallman, R. (2007). *Why Upgrade to GPL Version 3*. Retrieved December 11, 2008, from http://gplv3.fsf.org/rms-why.html

Stewart, K. J., & Gosain, S. (2006). The Impact of Ideology on Effectiveness in Open Source Software Development Teams. *Management Information Systems Quarterly*, *30*(2), 291–314.

Tatnall, A., & Gilding, A. (1999). Actor-Network Theory and Information Systems Research. *Proc. 10th Australian Conference on Information Systems*.

Tiemann, M. (2008). *History of the OSI (Open Source Initiative)*. Retrieved December 10, 2008, from http://www.opensource.org/history

Torvalds, L. (1992). *RELEASE NOTES FOR LINUX v0.12*. Retrieved January 9, 2008, from http://www.kernel.org/pub/linux/kernel/Historic/old-versions/RELNOTES-0.12

Torvalds, L. (2007). *LKML.ORG - the Linux Kernel Mailing List Archive*, from http://lkml.org/2007/6/14/306

Torvalds, L., & Diamond, D. (2001). *Just for fun: the story of an accidental revolutionary*. New York, NY: HarperBusiness.

Tuomi, I. (2001). Internet, Innovation, and Open Source: Actors in the Network. *First Monday*, *6*(1).

von Hippel, E., & von Krogh, G. (2003). Open source software and the 'private-collective' innovation model: issues for organization science. *Organization Science*, *14*(2), 209–223. doi:10.1287/orsc.14.2.209.14992

Weiss, A. (2001). The politics of free (software). *netWorker*, *5*(3), 26–31. doi:10.1145/383719.383727

Zemlin, J. (2008). *Linus Torvalds - Part I: Open Voices: The Linux Foundation Podcast*. Retrieved January 11, 2008, from http://linux-foundation.org/weblogs/openvoices/linus-torvalds-part-i/

·ENDNOTE

[1] Quotes were obtained from the Linux Kernel
Mailing List Archive (htttp://lkml.org/).

This work was previously published in International Journal of Actor-Network Theory and Technological Innovation (IJANTTI) 1(3), edited by Arthur Tatnall, pp. 15-35, copyright 2009 by IGI Publishing (an imprint of IGI Global).

Chapter 11
The Critical Role of Market Segmentation:
Evidence from the Audio Player Market

Thierry Rayna
London Metropolitan University, UK

Ludmila Striukova
University College London, UK

Samuel Landau
Gostai, France

ABSTRACT

The aim of this research is the investigate the role played by market segmentation, in general, and by the choice of initial market segment, in particular, in the ability of a product to cross the chasm. To do so, a theoretical framework, enabling to explain the ability of some firms to cross this chasm, while many others remain unsuccessful is developed. The key result of this research is that the choice of initial market segment has crucial importance as adoption in this segment can lead to a cascade of adoption in the other segments. To illustrate this proposition, three cases studies of an historical leader (Sony), a first mover (Archos) and a newcomer (Apple) in the market for digital audio players are presented.

INTRODUCTION

In many industry sectors, the key rule that enables companies to remain on the market is continuous innovation. Nonetheless, innovating, while necessary, is seldom sufficient to succeed and although some innovations are adopted by the consumers, many fail to do so. In most cases, successfully innovating requires innovative products or services to be adopted by a majority of consumers. While many new products encounter initial success and are successfully adopted by early adopters, only a few are able to 'cross the chasm' that separates early adopters from the rest of consumers.

Although such a chasm exists in the diffusion of many products, high-tech products are particularly known to experience such discontinuities. The large investments required to successfully develop and initially market new products with high technological content make it even more

DOI: 10.4018/978-1-60960-197-3.ch011

crucial to understand how this chasm is created and how to cross it.

The aim of this article is to shed a light on the complex question of crossing the chasm by considering the impact of the initial choice of market segment that is targeted by innovative firms. The key argument is that a fine balance has to be found in order for the initial market segment to 'naturally' spread its adoption to adjacent segments and, eventually, to the whole market.

To assess the relevance of this approach, three case studies of firms producing Digital Audio Players – Sony, Archos and Apple – are presented in the article. The reason for such a choice is that the number of innovations is particularly high in consumer electronics sector, in general, and in portable players, in particular. Thousands of new models have been released since the introduction of the Walkman, the first cassette based portable audio player. The changes introduced in this sector were both radical and incremental and while some of them were successful, the adoption of many new products never went beyond a small number of early adopters.

For many years, the innovation in this sector was led by the market leader, Sony, whose subsequent generations of portable audio players were successfully adopted by the majority of consumers. However, after several cycles of successful introduction of new products in this sector, Sony missed the digital audio player revolution and this led to a shift in market power towards a newcomer in consumer electronics – Apple. The fact that the long-time leader, Sony, failed to cross the chasm while a new entrant succeeded emphasises the importance of this issue.

After briefly presenting the determinants of diffusion of innovation, its non-linear and discontinuous nature, the article proceeds with an analysis of the role of market segmentation in the ability of a firm to cross the chasm. Then, case studies of Sony, Archos and Apple are presented as an illustration of the developed theories.

THE DETERMINANTS OF DIFFUSION OF INNOVATION

Transforming an invention into an innovation (which requires successful commercialisation) is often a difficult task. The introduction of a new product is only the first step in a long process that will or will not lead to a sustainable demand for this new product. Diffusion of innovation is a major determinant of sustainability of new products. However, the diffusion paths of innovations may differ strongly. It is, therefore, crucial to understand the particular characteristics of each individual innovation to influence the process of diffusion (Rogers, 2003). Rogers (2002) identifies five characteristics that affect the adoption of a particular innovation. First of all, the relative advantage of the new product or, in other words, the degree to which users see the innovation as being better than previously existing products. The second characteristic, compatibility, refers to how the innovation is consistent with the existing habits and values of consumers. A third characteristic, complexity, assesses the ease of use of the innovation. The last two characteristics, trialibility and observability, refer to the ability consumers have to, respectively, try and observe the innovation. All these characteristics, which are intrinsic to each innovation, play an important part in the diffusion path of new products and, ultimately, are a determinant of the successful adoption of the innovation (or, to be more precise, of whether the diffusion of innovation will reach a sufficient scale for the new product to be viable and sustainable).

Nonetheless, the diffusion of innovation does not solely depend on characteristics intrinsic to the innovation. There are other characteristics such as costs, communicability, divisibility, profitability and social approval that affect the distribution of innovation (Tornatzky and Klein, 1982). The distribution of innovation also depends on the distribution of the competing and complementary products (Metcalfe, 2005). For example, when the broadband internet diffusion started to grow in Korea, the demand for related applications started to increase as well (Park and Yoon, 2005). In contrast, if there are already similar products on the market, it may be more difficult to diffuse new technologies and services (Katz and Shapiro, 1994). This may be the case even if the existing products are inferior (Shy, 1996) in terms of quality and/or features.

Furthermore, even when favourable conditions exist (e.g. the product has good intrinsic characteristics, is not too expensive, does not cause social disapproval and has complements and few competitors), the adoption may be delayed if potential adopters do not have enough information or knowledge about innovation and, therefore, have problems evaluating it (Oliver, 1991). Similarly, consumers may not be aware of the product, in general, or of its new features, in particular.

The existence (or entry) of competitors makes the diffusion of innovation even more complex. The novelty of the product and the lack of available information about it affect not only the adopters but also competitors as well. When innovation is radical, competitors will wait longer before they start imitating, as they do not have sufficient knowledge about the new product (MacMillan et al., 1985). On the other hand, when innovation diffuses quickly, this may make competitors innovate faster (D'Aveni, 1994). More information means, at the same time, a larger initial adoption, but also a quicker entry of competitors which may, in turn, curb the diffusion of the new product. In contrast, less information both hinders diffusion and entry of competitors.

Competition, in fact, greatly affects the overall pattern of innovation. For instance, Cohen et al. (1996) explored the effects of competition on the launch dates and the performance of new products and found that a firm facing more intense competition should aim either at greater product performance or at earlier product launch. It is not guaranteed, however, that the first-mover will be successful in achieving a long-term competitive advantage over the followers (Rayna and Striukova, 2008).

As to the diffusion of the next generation of a particular technology, it is adopted depending on the diffusion effects (how the technology is adopted over time) and substitution effects (how the old technology is replaced by the new one (Norton and Bass, 1992)). However, usually, when there is already an installed base of a new technology, it is easier to diffuse the next generation of this technology (Islam and Meade, 1997).

FROM INNOVATORS TO LAGGARDS: THE NON-LINEARITY OF DIFFUSION OF INNOVATION

Although the probability of adoption of an innovation increases once a critical mass has been achieved (Rogers, 2003), the path to long-term adoption is complex and the acceptance of new products by the general public is known to be non-linear.

A reason for the non-linearity of the diffusion of innovations is given by Rogers in 1962 (Rogers, 2003). According to Rogers, the adoption of innovation is closely linked to different types of adopters. Rogers' classification scheme distinguishes five categories of adopters (innovators, early adopters, early majority, late majority, laggards), whose distribution follows a normal, bell-shaped curve[1]. All five categories have distinctive characteristics. Innovators are nearly obsessed with innovation and have an ability to understand and apply complex knowledge. Early adopters evaluate the innovation and pass this information to their peers. Early majority are used as opinion leaders and point of reference by other potential adopters. Late majority often adopt new products either because of the economic necessity or under the peer pressure. Finally, laggards' adoption is deferred because they need to be certain that the innovation will not fail before adopting it, thereby deferring their use of the new technology. Rogers' classification has been subsequently used to analyse diffusion of innovation in many sectors and for numerous products.

Moore (1995) provides a similar classification scheme of adopters: technological enthusiasts, visionaries, pragmatists, conservatives and sceptics. Chun (2003) matched these two schemes and proposed that technological enthusiasts could be seen as innovators, visionaries as early adopters, pragmatists as early majority, conservatives as late majority and sceptics as laggards.

According to Rogers, innovators and early adopters are different from the users who follow them, in the sense that, at the time when they adopt the new product, the new technology may not be fully developed as yet and there are few users with previous experience they can gain hindsight from. The difference between innovators and early adopters is that the former bring the innovation inside the social system and the latter diffuse it in the system. As the technology matures and the number of users who have experienced the product grows, early adopters are then followed by early and late majority. Laggards are the latest to adopt the innovations, sometimes years after the product was initially introduced.

However, it is important to note that laggards are not necessarily consumers resistant to innovation, but instead might not be aware of the innovation (Rogers, 2003; Valente, 1996) or have the information but are not able to afford the new product. Laggards typically have low income and low levels of education (Mahajan et al., 1990) and low social status (Rogers, 2003). The two extremes of the spectrum of technology adoption, adopters and laggards, therefore, are different both in regard to skills, knowledge, income, risk aversion and future expectations.

Furthermore, since laggards represent a small proportion of the population and are the last to adopt the product, their adoption is not required for an innovation to be successful. This tends to reinforce their late adoption, because firms have often no reason to actively target this consumer segment (at least not until the adoption of the product is well advanced).

THE DIFFUSION CHASM: DISCONTINUITY IN THE DIFFUSION OF INNOVATION

While countless number of firms have been able to achieve a relative success when releasing new products, very few are, in fact, able to transform this initial success into a long-term competitive advantage. The diffusion of innovation is not only problematic because of its non-linearity, but also because it is sometimes discontinuous.

Moore (1991) added to Rogers' work by showing that during the diffusion of some innovations (disruptive or discontinuous), there is a chasm between early adopters and early majority. The reality of such a chasm, in other words, an initial peak in sales soon followed by an abrupt decline in sales, was verified empirically (Golder and Tellis, 2004; Stremersch and Tellis, 2004).

The existence of a chasm may seem, at first, surprising. Indeed, the traditional view of diffusion of innovation is that early adopters ('visionaries') influence the decisions of the early majority ('pragmatists') regarding the adoption of innovation. However, Moore (1991) suggests that when it comes to the diffusion of high-tech products, visionaries do not necessarily affect the opinions of pragmatists. One of the reasons, according to Moore, is that visionaries have different expectations than pragmatists. For example, in spite of possible issues of reliability and compatibility, visionaries tend to prefer new technology to functional and effective solutions, which are, in contrast, appreciated by pragmatists. Thus, the opinions of visionaries are only important for other visionaries and only pragmatists can influence pragmatists.

According to Goldenberg et al. (2002), who studied consumer electronic products in the U.S., the chasm in product adoption occurs 52% of the time and is caused by the lack of communication between visionaries and pragmatists. Because of the differences that exist between visionaries and pragmatists, communication may not be possible, as these two types of consumers may, in fact, never have the opportunity to communicate with each other. Furthermore, even when they get a chance to do so, visionaries and pragmatists may be 'speaking different languages' and simply misunderstand each other. Finally, visionaries and pragmatists are likely to have very different tastes and the excitement of a visionary related to the complexity of a product (which triggers the adoption of the product by the visionary) may be seen as a product disadvantage by a pragmatist (thereby hindering the pragmatist's adoption).

Ram and Sheth (1989) argue that two types of barriers, functional and psychological, can cause a chasm and prevent the adoption of the innovation. Functional barriers are related to usage (incompatibility with consumer's existing habits and practices), value (high performance/price ration is needed to overcome resistance to change) and risk (uncertainty related to any innovation). In contrast, psychological barriers are linked to tradition, i.e. the necessary changes in one's routines caused by the adoption of a new technology or product, and image barriers, e.g. the consumer perception of the innovation in terms of class, brand, etc. Other reasons for a chasm to take place are external factors, such as technological inertia, economic recessions and slow repurchases by early adopters (Chandrasekaran and Tellis, 2008).

The above-mentioned reasons help explain both the rapid initial growth of sales of some products and their subsequent rapid decline. The sales go up as technological enthusiasts (innovators) influence other visionaries (early adopters) and decline, as the adoption of the product by visionaries does not trigger the adoption of the product by pragmatists. Indeed, once all visionaries have adopted the product, sales drop.

Yet, while such a chasm exists in the diffusion of most high-tech products, some firms have been able to successfully cross it and conquer the mass market of pragmatic consumers. Although the quality of the product introduced certainly plays an important role, recent history has shown many examples of good products that never crossed the chasm, while some inferior ones did. Beyond the simple question of product quality, it is thus important to understand the factors that determine the ability for an innovation to cross the chasm.

CASCADING MARKET SEGMENTS: THE CRITICAL CHOICE OF THE INITIAL TARGET

As mentioned in the previous section, the chasm in the diffusion of innovation is related to a lack of diffusion of information and/or a lack of linkage between visionaries and pragmatists. Although there are ways to overcome such a divide among adopters, this is likely to be quite costly for the company.

Advertisement, for example, can be used to propagate information about the product when information does not diffuse naturally among consumers. However, not only is advertising very costly, especially for a company that, most likely, has already spent large amounts of money on research and development, it is also not necessarily sufficient to trigger adoption. Indeed, many consumers, in particular pragmatic ones, are risk averse and will not adopt the new product, even if there is a lot of information available, until the product is adopted by a significant number of their peers.

Furthermore, when the divide between groups of consumers is large, crossing the chasm is likely to require, because different groups have different skills, abilities and tastes, the development and commercialisation of several versions of the new product, which creates an additional burden for the firm, both financially and in terms of risk.

In contrast, successful diffusion of innovation sometimes occurs without requiring a significant push from the innovating company. Indeed, market segments are sometimes arranged in such a way that the innovation fills in the first segment and then 'cascades' into adjacent segments and progressively, in a domino effect, conquers the whole market.

It is, therefore, crucial for firms introducing innovative products to choose the right market segment. If the chosen segment happens to be isolated, the enthusiasm of the innovators in this segment will not be 'naturally' communicated to other segments and the firm will have to resort to other strategic means, such as marketing or versioning, to foster diffusion and adoption. The difficulty to choose the right initial market segment and to change marketing strategies, from those aimed at early adopters to those designed to gain market majority has been emphasised by Moore (1991).

The difficulty to choose the initial market segment is due to the multi-dimensional nature of market segmentation. Indeed, depending on the dimension considered (sociological, geographical, economic, demographical), consumers can belong, simultaneously, to many different segments. Likewise, as mentioned in the previous sections, the difference between visionaries and pragmatists has also multiple dimensions and the frontier between the two is often fuzzy because most consumers are, depending on the context, at the same time visionaries and pragmatists. Even the greatest technophiles have domains (usually related to low-tech products), where they are pragmatists and not innovators.

In order to foster adoption and diffusion efficiently, firms have to consider a market segmentation that is such that the degree of linkage between all the segments is relatively high. Yet, the chosen segmentation strategy should also be such that a large number of visionaries are present in the segments that are targeted initially. Indeed, adopting a new product can be risky and only few people accept to take such a risk, while the others wait for someone else to test the product first. Social networks are, therefore, an important factor when individuals take adoption decisions, even when individuals have the same propensity to adopt. If there are many members in a particular social network who adopt innovation, others will follow, though some networks fill in with initial adopters quicker than others (Valente, 1996).

Another key element of diffusion of innovation is observability (Rogers, 2002). Observability provides the missing link between social networks, as consumers who do not personally know adopters, but observe that others have adopted the innovation, are more likely to opt for the new product, thereby triggering diffusion in their own network. For this reason, market segmentation should be done in such a way that adoption in one segment can be observed in other segments. Observability also explains why market ought to be segmented and why market segments should not be too large. Indeed, segments should be small enough for adoption to be observable by both the consumers of the segment and consumers of adjacent segments. If an appropriate segmentation (i.e. interconnected small segments) cannot be devised, firms can rely on changes in product designs to create an 'artificial' proximity between distant segments. Thereby, the product can be made more appealing for visionaries and early adopters (for example, by integrating more technology) and, once initial adoption has occurred, the product can be adapted to the needs and tastes of others (e.g. simplified, made more colourful, etc.). However, it is important to note that, although such remodelling is sometimes necessary, it is unlikely to compensate for a poor choice of market segmentation. Indeed, the fewer links exist between the segments, the more the product has to be changed in order to cross the chasm. Consequently, there is the risk that the changes made to the product weaken the adoption in the original segment without being sufficient to target adoption in other segments.

Proposition 1 (Cascading adoption of innovation)*An effective diffusion of innovation can be achieved by choosing an initial market segment that:*

1. *has a large proportion of visionaries;*
2. *is small enough for adoption to be visible from within and outside the segment;*
3. *consumers in this segment have a close proximity (in terms of social networks, geographically, socially, etc.) to consumers in other segments;*

If such market segmentation can be achieved, the early adoption in the initial segment will result, at a minimal cost, in the diffusion of the innovation in the adjacent segments and, further on, progressively, to all other segments, thereby avoiding the creation of a chasm.

Ultimately, being able to target a segment that is a representative subset of the mass market with a higher proportion of early adopters is the key to a successful diffusion process.

In the next sections, an empirical analysis is conducted to confirm the above proposition. In particular, the analysis focuses on the diffusion of digital audio players by Sony, Archos and Apple. The information for these case studies was collected from companies' websites, financial documents and related consumer forums.

SONY, THE HISTORICAL LEADER

Sony Corporation was established in 1945 and, from the 1950s until early 1980s, released a significant number of radically innovative products. These included the world's first compact transistor in 1963, the first portable cassette player (Walkman) in 1979, the Compact Disc in 1982, followed by the CD-based Walkman released in 1984. Sony also continued to produce incrementally innova-

tive products in the 1980s, such as Vaio notebook computers and PlayStation video game consoles.

In regard to Sony's previous innovations, the first Sony digital audio player, released in 1999, was an incremental, rather than a radical, innovation. While Sony had been, in the past, successful with both radical and incremental innovations, its digital audio player never matched the success of products such as the Walkman (radical) or PlayStation (incremental) that dominated the market for many years. In this context it is important to consider whether it was the nature of the product or the marketing strategies of Sony that led to the failure of digital Walkman.

One of the reasons to explain this lack of success could be that none of Sony digital audio players was a radical innovation. However, the lack of radical innovation did not prevent Sony from dominating the market of game consoles, for example. Neither did it prevent Apple's iPod from conquering the majority of the digital audio player market. In fact, being a second or a third mover may even be advantageous for a company, since it can enable to save on the costs of product and market development as well as on customer education (Schnaars, 1994). According to Schnaars (1994) the advantage of a late entrant is especially significant if it aims at the majority of adopters rather than at early adopters who often have different tastes and expectations. A well-defined target market is, therefore, very important for a late entrant.

The release of the Sony's first digital player was not the first time when Sony was not the original inventor of the concept. Its most successful product – Walkman – was based on the first portable personal stereo audio cassette player invented by Andreas Pavel in 1972 and patented in 1978[23]. One of the reasons behind Walkman's success was that the existing players were marketed to professional journalists whereas Walkman was aimed at general consumers.

Later, Sony continued to incrementally improve the Walkman and to tailor these improvements in relation to the different niches they were targeting. For example, according to Sanderson and Uzumeri (1995), Sony produced different types of Walkman for Japanese and the U.S. markets. It also released new versions of the Walkman to meet different customer demands (e.g. waterproof, etc.), which resulted in Sony's product line having the greatest number of models in both U.S. and Japan markets. There were, for example, around 20 new models released each year in the U.S. (almost 250 models altogether in the 1980s). Incremental innovation was, therefore, as important as the release of new products. Interestingly, however, 85% of Sony's models were rearranged versions of existing features with slight changes in the external case. Such minor changes were quite inexpensive and Sony only needed to sell 30,000 players of a particular version to break even (Sanderson and Uzumeri, 1995).

The first version of Walkman, besides being targeted at general consumers, was not aimed at any particular market segment. Nonetheless, since Sony was the absolute first mover (there was, at the time, no other substitute means to listen to recorded music on the go), the lack of competition and the interest in such product made the Walkman being progressively adopted by consumers from different market segments. Similarly, Sony's digital Walkman was initially not aimed at a particular market segment. However, the situation, at the release of the first digital Walkman was quite different. Not only Sony was not the first mover and other competitors were already in the market (The first mass produced digital audio payer was released by SaeHan Information Systems in 1997), but also many other substitute portable devices existed at the time (portable tape players, portable CD players, portable Mini-Disc players, etc.).

By not targeting any particular market segment, Sony's digital Walkman did not attract a number of visionaries sufficient to trigger a large adoption. The original (tape) Walkman did not need to target a particular market segment, since being the absolute first mover meant that the

initially small size of the market guaranteed that enough visionaries would adopt the product (each subsequent growth of the market being, in fact, a market segment). Walkman's digital successor failed to achieve a large market adoption because not targeting a particular segment meant that not enough visionaries could be reached in a market that was already mature.

The second important factor that impeded the adoption of Sony digital players was their lack of observability, which is an important determinant of diffusion of innovation (Rogers, 2002). Not targeting a particular market segment meant that even a significant number of adopters looked small in comparison to the rest of the market. Furthermore, Sony did not attempt to improve the observability of the adoption of their DAPs. In contrast, during the initial diffusion stage of the Walkman Sony hired, as a part of their advertising campaign, young people to walk around and offer people to listen to Walkman players.[4]. Furthermore, Sony employees were given Walkman with the instruction to use them in Tokyo's underground while commuting to work. More traditionally, Sony also asked Japanese celebrities to try the new product and published the photos of them listening to Walkman[5]. The mouth-to-mouth communication helped Sony sell 30,000 units of Walkman one month after its launch, and more than 150 million players in two years.

Similar strategy could not be applied to the new digital model, because it did not look significantly different from other Sony models. Similarly, using young people with headphones, which was so successful during the original Walkman campaign would have little effect in an environment where most other young people already used cassette and CD versions of Walkman or other audio players. Another reason for Sony's digital Walkman to never cross the chasm is the fact that it was not, originally, compatible with the MP3 format. Similarly to observability, compatibility plays a significant role in diffusion of innovations (Ram and Sheth, 1989; Rogers, 2002). At the time of its release in 1999, there were already a significant number of MP3 files available for download on the internet. Yet, in contrast to its competitors, Sony decided to use exclusively a proprietary format, ATRAC, for its digital audio players. The reason for this was twofold. Firstly, Sony's aimed to protect itself (as content distributor as well as a manufacturer) from piracy (most pirated content was, at the time, available in MP3 format). Furthermore, MiniDisk, another innovation of Sony, introduced in 1992, and its successors (MiniDisk Long Play, introduced in 2000 and Hi-MD introduced in 2004) were already based on the ATRAC format. For Sony, this new technology was meant to be the successor of CDs and, therefore, had a chance of creating a standard. Basing the digital players on ATRAC format was, therefore, expected to strengthen the standard.

While most companies producing consumer electronics acknowledged MP3 format as a *de facto* standard by making their players compatible with this format, ATRAC remained the only format supported by Sony digital Walkman until 2003. This had heavy consequences in terms of usage, since consumers who purchased Sony digital player were either forced to buy (even, in some cases, item they already owned in another format) all their music from Sony's online music store (which was a costly option) or use Sony's SonicStage software (only compatible with Microsoft Windows) to convert all the CDs they owned (which was very time consuming). Later on, Ken Kutaragi from Sony admitted that only supporting the ATRAC3 format was a mistake.[6]

In 2003, Sony finally released its first MP3 player, which was the smallest MP3 player of the market at the time. However, by that time, Sony's competitors, Apple and Archos (among others) had already released several generations of MP3 players (Apple's iPod was already a third generation player). Releasing the smallest player was not, therefore, sufficient for Sony to win the market over. The later versions were not very successful either. Unlike the radical innovations

released by Sony in the beginning of the firm's existence, the MP3 Video Walkman released by Sony in 2007 was an attempt to catch up with the existing products rather than being a truly innovative product. Its advertised new features such as 'clear audio technology', 'time machine', shuffle function and 'initial search' already existed in models released by competitors. The company was already very much behind its competitors and far from being able to catch up with them.

Finally, the failure of Sony to cross the chasm can be related to the issue of complementarities, whose distribution might often affect the distribution of the innovation itself (Metcalfe, 2005). In order to lock its customers in and keep up with the competition (Apple opened its online store in 2003), Sony opened its music online store 'Connect' in 2004. Despite joining in rather late, Sony had the advantage of being part of the content industry, since its purchase of CBS Records in 1987, and having numerous famous artists already signed in. The incompatibility of its content with any other formats but ATRAC, however, balanced this advantage off. Due to the lack of success of both players and store, the store was finally closed down in 2007 (giving a possibility to its clients to use the songs they had purchased until the end of 2008). The customers who purchased content in ATRAC format were advised by Sony to rip it to CD and then re-rip it to MP3 in order to play it on the new Walkman digital players. Such complicated manipulations, as well as the loss of quality they entailed, did not play to Sony's advantage either.

ARCHOS, THE TECHNOLOGICAL FIRST-MOVER

Archos, a French consumer electronics company, was established in 1988. Until 1999, when the company started to operate solely under its brand name, only 10% of the company's products were sold under Archos brand. Archos is well known in the world of digital audio players for its Jukebox 6000, released in 2000, which was the first hard disk-based digital audio player. This player opened the way to high-capacity DAPs, which led to the large adoption of digital players[7]. In the following years, Archos pursued a similar strategy of technological leadership and introduced several generation of products, each more technologically advanced than the previous ones and more technologically advanced, at the time of their release, than those of their competitors.

After an initial relative success, Archos started to experience some difficulties. In 2007 Archos revenues were €102 million, down from €124 million earned in 2006 and not reaching the break-even point of €115 million. The reason given by the company to explain this decline was the (alleged) global decrease in demand for media players. Therefore, in June 2008 Archos decided to pull out of the portable media players market and concentrate on broadband-capable Internet tablets [8].

When compared to Apple, Archos provides a clear example that being the first on the market and being more technologically advanced is not necessary the key to success. After releasing its DAP one year before Apple, Archos released the first ever portable media player (or PMP, an advanced version of DAP that can display pictures and films) in July 2002. In comparison, the first photo-enabled iPod was released in October 2004, while the first iPod Video appeared in the market in October 2005. Despite this significant head start, Archos only managed to capture a small market niche and despite its late arrival, the iPod Video was far more successful and quickly became the best selling PMP. Similarly, Archos introduced its first range of large screen PMP in 2004 and upgraded it in 2006 and September 2007. Yet, the iPod Touch, which is the first iPod with a large screen, released in September 2007, has far exceeded the sales of Archos large-screen PMP, despite having fewer features.

While Archos has always been able to raise an interest in its product and achieved a moderate amount of sales, it has never, for any of its products, been able to actually cross the chasm and has been contained to a niche market of a small number of faithful users. In contrast to Apple[9] or Sony users, Archos' users are, for most of them, technophiles and highly skilled consumers who are quite different from the mass market consumers that Archos has hopped to conquer.

The fact that the faithful followers of Archos are mostly technophiles has affected both the strategy used by Archos and its difficulties to cross the chasm. In regard to the market segment initially targeted, Archos has followed a 'logical' strategy that has been used, with mixed result, by many other companies. Since the diffusion of innovation requires visionaries/early adopters and, since technophiles are very likely to be visionaries, Archos has designed products aimed at this type of consumers.

As mentioned in the previous sections, the problem of such strategy, even though it is very likely to trigger, at least, a beginning of diffusion, is that technophiles are unlikely to affect adoption decisions of the majority and that, moreover, differences in tastes and skills are such that a product designed for technophiles is, most probably, unsuitable for the mass market. Furthermore, according to Mick and Fournier (1998) the emotions that consumers experience may be positive (when consumers are excited or confident) and negative (when they are scared or annoyed). Archos' products created positive emotions for technological enthusiasts and negative emotions for pragmatists.

Targeting technophiles is easier in the short term and provides 'instant gratification', because of the almost certain and steady demand for high-tech products by this type of consumers. However, such strategy is a double-edged sword, since it makes crossing the chasm much more difficult. In this case, reaching the mass market often requires remodelling the original product, a strategy used by Archos. In order to cut down the price of the products to more suitable for the mass market, Archos, for some of its product, made advanced features, that were previously available for free, optional and started to charge a fee for them.

This illustrates the difficulty to remodel product in order to cross the chasm. Indeed, ultimately, the changes in the product may alienate early adopters without giving access to the early majority (which was the case for Archos). Removing advanced functions has reduced the value of the products for technophiles. At the same time, this has not changed the 'philosophy' of a product that was designed for advanced users and may still be perceived as too complex for the average user (simply for the sole reason that, regardless of the number of features embedded, traditional Archos products have many more buttons than iPod). Overall, on the way to crossing the chasm, firms may lose early adopters to such extent that it can undermine their ability to conquer the mass market and even their viability.

The problem faced by companies which, like Archos, choose to target technophiles is that such consumers are, in fact, quite independent and much less likely to be attracted, or retained, by a particular brand, because their prime interest is purely technology. Any more technologically advanced competitor is then likely to attract the majority of technophiles. This puts a particular strain on the firm, as it has to innovate constantly to retain technological leadership. This might explain why Archos has always been in advance and has introduced a new generation of products every year (in contrast to Apple who has introduced new products at a slower rate and with fewer incremental changes). The main inconvenience of this strategy is that, when products are released, the technology and/or the market may not be mature enough. Customers may be confused by a variety of options and frustrated if their products become obsolete very quickly (Lambert and Slater, 1999). Furthermore, when new generations are released too frequently, it tends to decrease the demand, as consumers delay their purchase until the next generation arrives.

In contrast, firms such as Apple, who target as initial market segment less expert customers, are more likely to retain their customers, since these customers are less independent and more sensible to branding and other switching costs. Furthermore, the level of expertise of such consumers is likely to be such that they incur significant learning costs, which makes it unlikely (as opposed to technophile who can use any product) that they will switch to another brand.

In regard to the other determinants of diffusion of innovation, Archos has tried to maximise complementarities. To do so, it made its products compatible with most computers (Windows, Mac, Linux). Also, Archos' DAPs support a large number of audio and video formats. In addition to its own DRM system, Archos has also licensed in other DRM systems (including Microsoft's PlayForSure). However, the large number of complementarities created through compatibility have not helped Archos much. To this respect, it is important to note that most small competitors of Archos are also compatible with most computers and most file formats and, thus, also display *a priori* a high level of complementarity. In contrast, the market leaders have opted for restricted compatibility and, thus, *a priori* less complementarity. A reason for this apparent contradiction can be found in the fact that a high degree of compatibility, while increasing the number of potential complementarities, make these rather weak (since substitutes exist), whereas a lack of compatibility create a very strong link with the few existing complements.

In 2007, Archos has introduced the Archos Content Portal, which is a complementary service to its DAPs. However, this online store offers significantly less content than the stores of the competitors. Furthermore, Archos players are also compatible with the content available form other, larger stores, and as such, the complementarity with their own store is also rather loose.

Also, while observability of Archos products was fairly high in the small circles of technophiles, the lack of connection between this market segment and the rest of the market made the overall visibility of Archos products rather poor. Furthermore, the design of Archos products has always been very generic (technophiles are often more focused on technology than design), which made them unnoticeable (as opposed to Apple's white iPod and headphones). Over the years, Archos has spent significant amounts on advertising and has signed many promotion deals with distributors (consumer electronic chains). Nonetheless, despite having been the first mover for almost a decade, Archos product and brand awareness in the general public has remained fairly low.

APPLE, THE WELL INSPIRED NEWCOMER

Apple Computer, Inc.[10] was founded in 1976 and was first known for being one of the first movers in the personal computer market. Over the years, Apple has introduced many innovations (the first successfully commercialised: PC graphical interface, mouse, laptop, Personal Digital Assistant, digital camera, among others) and democratised the usage of many others (laser printers, desktop publishing, etc.). Until 2001, the core market of Apple was personal computers (although devices had been released by Apple, they were merely complement to the main computer business rather than a business *per se*) and Apple was only mildly successful (Apple's market share had rapidly slumped to just below 5% and Apple went nearly bankrupt in 1997).

In 2001, there was a shift in Apple's strategy with the entry of Apple into a market of digital audio players, a market Apple had no prior experience of. In contrast to what happened before, when Apple had introduced devices and peripherals, this new activity soon became part of Apple's core business (hence the name change from Apple Computer, Inc. to Apple Inc.).

When Apple released its first Digital Audio Player, iPod, in October 2001, such players had been present in the market for quite a while (at least since 1997; Sony entered in 1999 and Archos in 2000). While iPod rapidly became a success (with a market share greater than 70%[11]), it did not bring any radical innovation and had, in fact, features similar to many other DAP present in the market at the time (it even had fewer features that some of the competing products, such as Archos's Jukebox). Despite not being a radical innovation, iPod was perceived as such by many consumers, which was sufficient (Rogers, 2003) to make iPod an innovation. While the fact that Apple was, at the time, a known brand, could help explain iPod's rapid success, it is important to note that the popularity of Apple was, when iPod was introduced, at one of its lowest point and that Apple was not identified at all as a brand for consumer electronics.

The key differences between iPod and its competitor were its design (at the time of its release, iPod looked more solid, being made half of metal and half of hard Plexiglas-like material, and more appealing than any other DAP) and its operating mode. iPod was not better because it had many features, but because the few features included were better than those of other DAPs. While, at the time, most DAPs were quite complex to operate, the iPod interface was very easy to use. For instance, iPod was operated through one click-wheel and four buttons, whereas competing products had many buttons (which resulted in rather steep learning curve).

In terms of features, Apple applied an opposite strategy to its competitors. While most DAPs embedded a myriad of features that could be fully used only by very few consumers, Apple included a minimal number of features that could be fully used by most of the population. This simplicity of the iPod is quite representative of the strategy chosen by Apple to diffuse its innovations. As discussed in the previous section, Archos made the 'logical' choice to target technophiles as innovators, but then found it impossible to cross the chasm. Apple, in contrast, designed a product that could be used by (almost) anyone. The strategy chosen by Sony, was similar to Apple's, however, the absence of initial segment target (combined with a pursued strategy of incompatibility) caused Sony's products to remain unnoticed by the mass market.

While Apple ensured that its DAP was such that it could easily trigger a cascade adoption between market segments, it also targeted an adequate initial market segment: the Mac users [12]. Apple has been able to develop a segment of faithful consumers that remained behind Apple (and bought Apple products) even in the most critical moments. The devotion of these consumers (which is the reason for which Mac Users are sometimes qualified as a cult (Belk and Tumbat, 2005) ensured that a quick adoption occurred in the initial market segment. Although they were a small minority (less than 5% of personal computers at a time) of the consumer population, Mac Users were, at the time, well distributed (geographically, socially, economically, age-wise, etc.) among consumers. In fact, with the difference that Apple computers are, on average, more expensive than entry level PCs, which implies incomes slightly higher than average, the subgroup of Mac Users could almost be a representative subset of the mass market. Thus the initial segment chosen by Apple had a higher proportion of early adopters, was small enough for adoption to be noticed from inside and integrated enough in the society for adoption to be observable in other segments.

To ensure its new product would cross the chasm, Apple took additional precautions and designed a product that would fit the needs of the average Mac Users, instead of targeting the technophiles among Mac Users (who complained, as expected, about 'missing features' in iPod). While technophiles were not entirely satisfied with the new product, their taste for novelty was sufficient to make them purchase the product. At the same time, since the product had been designed with the average Mac Users in mind, this triggered the adoption of traditionally reluctant and risk averse users.

Apple already had used such a conquest strategy a few years before, when it released the iMac, a redesigned easy-to-use version of the Macintosh. However, although the iMac was an instant success among Mac Users and even converted some Windows Users and newcomers, Apple failed to convert the majority and after a brief surge in sales, the market share of Apple returned to its usual less than 5% level.

The proposition presented in Section 4 helps understand the failure of iMac to cross the chasm. While adoption was successful in the initial market segment, the observability of the diffusion was very weak within the segment and, most importantly, from the other segments, thereby impeding the crossing of the chasm and the adoption of the product by the mass market.

With the iPod, Apple introduced a change that was almost trivial, but which played an essential role in iPod's ability to cross the chasm: while almost all media players and headphones at the time were black, iPod and, more importantly, the headphones supplied with it were white. With this simple change of colour and due to the portable nature of the DAPs (as opposed to iMac, that stayed indoors), Apple ensured that the progression of adoption of iPod was fully observable not only from within the segment, but also from all other segments. By making its product white, Apple achieved a similar effect as when Sony hired young people to walk around with Walkman, but without havinging to pay for it. Furthermore, as the popularity of iPod grew and other manufacturers started to change the colour of their products to white to benefit from the 'iPod effect', this naturally increased even more the perceived adoption of the iPod, since consumers identified white headphones with iPod.

With regard to compatibility, iPod was, initially, only compatible with Macintosh computers. However, the demand from early adopters outside the initial segment (e.g. Windows users), grew quickly and, barely three months after the initial release of iPod, several third-party software applications had already been developed to enable the use of iPod with Windows. The second version of iPod, released nine months after the first one, was made compatible with Windows. Subsequently, third-party software was developed to make iPod compatible with Linux/Unix systems, which made the iPod, *de facto* compatible with any computer.

As to the content, Apple, in contrast to Sony, decided from the very start to support the already *de facto* standard MP3 format as well as its 'successor', the MP4/AAC format. As a complement, Apple developed its own DRM system, FairPlay, which, to this day remains the only DRM system compatible with iPod.

In terms of complement, Apple opened the iTunes Music Store as a retail music outlet for iPod products in 2003. In 2005, videos and films were introduced in the store, which was renamed iTunes Store. Since Apple has refused to licence out its DRM technology, the iTunes Store has the monopoly of protected content for the iPod. This has forced competing stores to offer unprotected MP3, as it was the only means for them to access the iPod's 70% market share. Although iTunes Store was launched at a time when iPod had already reached a significant popularity, the complementarity between the two has, undoubtedly, been instrumental in consolidating and expending further iPod's market dominance.

CONCLUSION

The aim of this article was to study the phenomenon of chasm that often exists in the diffusion of innovation and to devise a theoretical framework enabling to explain the ability of some firms to cross this chasm, while many others remain unsuc-

cessful. The proposition developed in this article is that the choice of initial market segment has crucial importance. This initial market segment has, at the same time, to contain a large proportion of visionaries, be small enough for adoption to be observed from within the segment and from other segment and be sufficiently connected with other segments. If this is the case, the adoption in the first segment will progressively cascade into the adjacent segments, thereby triggering the adoption by the mass-market.

Three cases studies were then presented to assess the validity of this proposition. The analysis of the diffusion of portable digital players released by Archos, Apple and Sony confirmed the 'golden rule' of adoption of innovation introduced in this article. The successful diffusion of iPod was due to a well-defined initial segment (Mac users), which did not exist in case of Archos and Sony. The consumers in this segment form a very close community which enabled a rapid exchange of information between the community members. The new design (white colour) made iPod extremely visible to the users outside the Mac community, the fact intensified by some of the competitors trying to use 'the iPod' effect and releasing white headphones as well.

Finally, this article has emphasised several strategic mistakes made by Apple's competitors (and also by Apple itself). In particular, these mistakes include the decision of Sony to exclusively used a proprietary format and Archos' attempt to capture the mass market resulting in alienating early adopters without gaining access to the early majority. Such mistakes have led to the creation of a greater chasm and have undermined the competitiveness of these firms.

Overall, thus article demonstrates that, in high-tech industries, being the first mover or the historical leader have, often, little importance. Being well placed, in term of market segment, may reveal itself as far more important than having a stronger brand or being technologically more advanced.

REFERENCES

Belk, R. W., & Tumbat, G. (2005). The cult of Macintosh. *Consumption Markets and Culture, 8*(3), 205–217. doi:10.1080/10253860500160403

Chandrasekaran, D., & Tellis, G. J. (2008). The global takeoff of new products: culture, wealth, or vanishing differences. *Marketing Science, 27*(5), 844–860. doi:10.1287/mksc.1070.0329

Chun, I. C. J. (2003). Tasks and theories in the marketing strategy of innovative new product. *Korean Journal of Marketing, 5*(1), 1–16.

Cohen, M. A., Eliashberg, J., & Ho, T. (1996). New product development: The performance and time-to-market trade-offs. *Management Science, 42*(2), 173–186. doi:10.1287/mnsc.42.2.173

D'Aveni, R. A. (1994). *Hypercompetition: Managing the dynamics of strategic maneuvering*. New York: Free Press.

Goldenberg, J., Libai, B., & Muller, E. (2002). Riding the saddle: How cross-market communications can create a major slump in sales. *Journal of Marketing, 66*, 1–16. doi:10.1509/jmkg.66.2.1.18472

Golder, P., & Tellis, G. (2004). Growing, growing, gone: cascades, diffusion, and turning points in the product life cycle. *Marketing Science, 23*, 207–218. doi:10.1287/mksc.1040.0057

Islam, T., & Meade, N. (1997). The diffusion of successive generations of a technology: A more general model. *Technological Forecasting and Social Change, 56*(1), 49–60. doi:10.1016/S0040-1625(97)00030-9

Katz, M., & Shapiro, C. (1994). Systems competition and network effects. *The Journal of Economic Perspectives, 8*(2), 93–115.

Lambert, D., & Slater, S. F. (1999). Perspective: first, fast, and on time: the path to success. or is it? *Journal of Product Innovation Management, 16*(5), 427–438. doi:10.1016/S0737-6782(99)00017-X

MacMillan, I., McCaffrey, M. L., & Van Wijk, G. (1985). Competitor's responses to easily imitated new products: Exploring commercial banking product introductions. *Strategic Management Journal, 6*, 75–86. doi:10.1002/smj.4250060106

Mahajan, V., Muller, E., & Srivastava, R. (1990). Determination of adopter categories by using innovation diffusion models. *JMR, Journal of Marketing Research, 27*(2), 37–50. doi:10.2307/3172549

Metcalfe, J. (2005). Ed Mansfield and the diffusion of innovation: an evolutionary connection. *The Journal of Technology Transfer, 30*(1/2), 171–181.

Mick, D., & Fournier, S. (1998). Paradoxes of technology: consumer cognizance, emotions, and coping strategies. *The Journal of Consumer Research, 25*, 123–143. doi:10.1086/209531

Moore, G. A. (1991). *Crossing the Chasm*. New York: Harper Business.

Moore, G. A. (1995). *Inside the Tornado: Marketing Strategy from Sillicon Valley's Cutting Edge*. New York: Harper Collins.

Norton, J., & Bass, F. (1992). Evolution of technological generations: The law of capture. *Sloan Management Review, 33*(2), 66–77.

Oliver, C. (1991). Strategic responses to institutional processes. *Academy of Management Review, 16*, 145–179. doi:10.2307/258610

Park, S., & Yoon, S.-H. (2005). Separating early-adopters from the majority: the case of broadband internet access in korea. *Technological Forecasting and Social Change, 72*, 301–325. doi:10.1016/j.techfore.2004.08.013

Ram, S., & Sheth, J. (1989). Consumer resistance to innovations: The marketing problem and its solutions. *Journal of Consumer Marketing, 6*(2), 5–14. doi:10.1108/EUM0000000002542

Rayna, T., & Striukova, L. (2008). (forthcoming). The curse of the first-mover: When incremental innovation leads to radical change. *International Journal of Collaborative Enterprise.*

Rogers, E. (2003). *Diffusion of innovations.* New York: Free Press.

Rogers, E. M. (2002). Diffusion of preventive innovations. *Addictive Behaviors, 27*(6), 989–993. doi:10.1016/S0306-4603(02)00300-3

Sanderson, S., & Uzumeri, M. (1995). Managing product families: The case of the sony walkman. *Research Policy, 24*(5), 761–782. doi:10.1016/0048-7333(94)00797-B

Schnaars, S. P. (1994). *Managing Imitation Strategies: How Late Entrants Seize Marketing from Pioneers.* New York: The Free Press.

Shy, O. (1996). Technology revolutions in the presence of network externalities. *International Journal of Industrial Organization, 14*(6), 785–800. doi:10.1016/0167-7187(96)01011-9

Stremersch, S., & Tellis, G. (2004). Understanding and managing international growth of new products. *International Journal of Research in Marketing, 21*(4), 421–438. doi:10.1016/j.ijresmar.2004.07.001

Tornatzky, L., & Klein, K. (1982). Innovation characteristics and innovation adoption-implementation: a meta-analysis of findings. *IEEE Transactions on Engineering Management, 29*(1), 28–45.

Valente, T. (1996). Social network thresholds in the diffusion of innovations. *Social Networks, 18*, 69–89. doi:10.1016/0378-8733(95)00256-1

ENDNOTES

[1] The cumulative distribution of which gives the famous "S-Curve" of technology adoption.

[2] It is only in 2003 that Sony fully recognised him as an original inventor the Walkman. http://www.iht.com/articles/2005/12/16/news/profile.php?page=2

[3] http://lowendmac.com/orchard/06/sony-walkman-origin.html

[4] http://www.technoreadymarketing.com/case_studies5.html

[5] http://www.neoseeker.com/news/4244-sony-admits-mp3-error/

[6] Until then, DAP players could barely store more than one or two albums and were, thus, not significantly better than portable CD players or MiniDisc players.

[7] http://www.shephard.co.uk/Inflight/default.aspx?Action=-1000945703&ID=89a4c4a0-50df-447a-9718-63b6d2f9c40d

[8] see Section 7.

[9] Nowadays, Apple Inc.

[10] http://www.bloomberg.com/apps/news?pid=conewsstory&refer=conews&tkr=AAPL:US&sid=ap0bqJw2VpwI

[11] Since 1987, Apple only produces and sells Macintosh computers. Thus Apple users are commonly referred to as 'Mac Users'.

Chapter 12
Actors, Networks and Assessment:
An Actor–Network Critique of Quality Assurance in Higher Education in England

Jonathan Tummons
University of Teesside, UK

ABSTRACT

This chapter is an exploration of one particular form of non-traditional provision of higher education (HE) in England, known as higher education in further education: the provision of HE courses that are offered on a franchise basis in one or more colleges of further education (FE colleges). Focussing on assessment on one teacher-training course, this chapter offers ways of conceptualising the responses of FE colleges where the course is run to the quality assurance systems and procedures established by the university that provides the course. Assessment has been chosen as the specific focus of this paper for several reasons: it is an activity that must be performed in certain ways and must conform to particular outcomes that are standardised across colleges; it is an established focus of research; and it is a focus of specific traceable activities across both the university and the colleges. Drawing on data collected over a three-year period, the chapter suggests that the ways in which assessment processes are regulated and ordered are characterised by complexities for which actor-network theory provides an appropriate conceptual framework.

WIDENING PARTICIPATION THROUGH HIGHER EDUCATION IN FURTHER EDUCATION

Holgate University is a university in the north of England with a history of training teachers for the further education (FE) sector in England, that

DOI: 10.4018/978-1-60960-197-3.ch012

stretches back forty years. For much of this time, the university has delivered its teacher-training courses on a collaborative basis with a large number of further education (FE) colleges. FE colleges predominantly cater for students aged 16-19 who are following technical or vocational programmes of study. On completion of their courses, most students will enter employment although some will progress to university. FE colleges offer a range of programmes for adults, some of whom may be returning to learning after a protracted period away from formal education and training and some of whom may be returning to college to update or refresh existing skills. FE colleges also provide basic skills courses in literacy and numeracy to adults.

The vast majority of teachers in the FE sector enter the profession on the basis of their vocational or technical qualifications, rather than whether or not they have a teaching qualification. For example, a new lecturer in electrical installation would be expected to have appropriate and up-to-date trade qualifications or endorsements. After being appointed, s/he would then study for a teaching qualification on a part-time, in-service basis, and the course would therefore take two years to complete. Over four-fifths of teacher training for practitioners in the FE sector is carried out in this way; the remainder rests on a model that is more akin to schools-based training (that is, a full-time course with a teaching placement, completed within one year). The course is available as a postgraduate certificate in education (PGCE) to graduates, or as a certificate in education (Cert Ed) to non-graduates, who are teaching either part-time or full-time in post-compulsory education. These teaching contexts include FE colleges (the majority of students on the course), accredited adult education, and higher education. The course is endorsed by both Lifelong Learning UK (the body responsible for professional standards in teaching in the further education sector in England and Wales) and the Higher Education Academy (the body that holds equivalent responsibility for the higher education sector). It takes two years to complete on a part-time in-service basis. Throughout this chapter, the course will be referred to as the PGCE/CertEd.

A little over half of all of the students on the course take the Cert Ed route: for these students, this teacher-training course represents a first experience of higher education (HE). Consequently, this aspect of the provision can be seen as being one of a number of methods through which wider participation in HE more generally can be offered (Parry et. al., 2003; Parry and Thompson, 2002; Thomas, 2001). Such provision of higher education courses within further education institutions is generally referred to as *Higher Education in Further Education* (HE in FE) provision, and has expanded considerably over recent years (Bird and Crawley, 1994; Connolly et al., 2007; Hilborne, 1996; West, 2006).

Holgate University delivers the course across a network of nearly thirty colleges, involving over one hundred tutors working with nearly two thousand students. Although the scale of provision varies between colleges, a broadly similar set of structures exists at each. At each college there is a course manager who is responsible for the academic and managerial leadership of the programme. The course manager oversees the applications process at a college level (which are then, on a sample basis, checked by the university), and is responsible for the return of final marks to the university at the end of the academic year. As well as this, they teach on the programme, usually with a small number of other tutors as well. In some colleges, PGCE/CertEd tutors maintain a teaching load within other curricular areas; in other cases, tutors are seen as 'education specialists' and work solely within the teacher-training curriculum. The course is modular, and course content is mapped onto the relevant professional standards (Tummons, 2010). The course is rolled out across the college network through an infrastructure that consists of handbooks, course meetings, visits to colleges by Holgate staff, websites and emails: in this way, the university maintains contact with all of the colleges, and colleges are in turn enabled to maintain useful working relationships with each other, for example through the regional organisation of assessment moderation. Put simply, there is a considerable amount of communication between and amongst the university and the colleges that serves to ensure the quality of the PGCE/CertEd provision.

QUALITY ASSURANCE FOR HE IN FE

The ubiquitous demands of quality assurance, as they might relate to any HE programme, raise particular concerns when considering the systems involved in HE in FE provision. Quality assurance (QA) is understood here as consisting of those processes that can be seen as ensuring the quality and fitness for purpose of the HE programme under discussion. Benchmarking, external verification, audit and evaluation: these are the ways in which the work of an HE in FE network tends to be evaluated, for the purposes of quality assurance, within a managerialist culture (Avis, 2005; Barnett, 2003; Gleeson et. al., 2005). Quality assurance and audit processes need to satisfy relevant interested parties that HE provision, as it is delivered in an FE context, has a sufficient level of equivalence to what might be found within a university, to be considered of appropriate rigour and quality. This might be in terms of resources, of learning and teaching processes (which will include assessment, the focus of this paper), even of the quality of accommodation (Hilborne, 1996). The tools by which the demands of audit are satisfied include people, including tutors and managerial professionals; processes, such as inspections and audit; and outputs, such as inspection reports, all of which are commonly found within audit cultures (Shore and Wright, 1999; Shore and Wright, 2000).

The Holgate teacher-training network draws on many such QA processes and tools in order to satisfy relevant stakeholders (funding agencies, professional bodies and government inspectorates) as to the quality of the provision across the different colleges. This is not to say that there is an expectation that each college would deliver the PGCE/CertEd in exactly the same way. But there is an expectation that, variances in delivery notwithstanding (although such variances are, as we shall see, constrained), the different components of the PGCE/CertEd are understood, managed and experienced in ways that, although

mindful of local factors (for example, class size or student catchment area), are nonetheless not paradigmatically conflicting. Put another way, there is an expectation, a sense or an understanding relating to the work of the PGCE/CertEd that is shared by all of the people involved in delivery, assessment and management.

All aspects of the PGCE/CertEd are therefore enmeshed in quality assurance processes. One example is the admissions system. An admissions handbook, written by the course quality manager at Holgate, is sent out to each college. It contains details as to those prior qualifications and other pre-requisites that an applicant to the course has to have if her/his application is to proceed. Once completed by the applicant, the admissions form (again, designed by Holgate and mailed out to colleges in time for the start of the academic year) is returned to the college where s/he wishes to study. Once all of the forms have been returned, each college then sends all of its forms back to the university, which samples them to ensure that they have been completed correctly. A second example is in the appointment of staff to teach the PGCE/CertEd within the colleges. Staff are interviewed and employed by colleges, but in order to teach on the PGCE/CertEd, have to be approved by the university. This process involves the submission of a curriculum vitae (using a standard format designed by the university) and attendance at a mandatory training day for new tutors. Attendance at further development events such as moderation meetings (to which I shall return shortly) is also a condition of approval.

However, amongst the many quality assurance practices that are carried out within this teacher-training network, those that surround assessment provide particularly useful and insightful opportunities for research. There are two reasons for this. Firstly, assessment is such a central aspect of the work of this HE in FE network, that it provides a wealth of material for the researcher: all participants do it, both students and tutors, and there is a considerable amount of documentation of various kinds relating to it, such as course handbooks and external examiners' reports. Secondly, assessment practice is in and of itself, a focus of research and scholarship, not least relating to both the role of assessment as preparing people for a professional role (Atkins, 1995; Katz, 2000; Taylor, 1997), but also in terms of the assessment methodology used on teacher training courses (Klenowski, 2002; Tigelaar, 2005; Young, 1999). Consequently, assessment can be conceptualised as a *nexus of practice* (Scollon, 2001): that is to say, it is a place where a number of strands – pedagogy, policy, audit – conflate.

Assessment processes within this teacher training course are subject to considerable managerialist scrutiny: internally, through assessment moderation and course committees; and externally through external examination, inspection by the Office for Standards in Education, Children's Services and Skills (Ofsted), and accreditation by Standards Verification UK (SVUK, the body that endorses all teacher training qualifications for the learning and skills sector). These and other activities and procedures are all geared towards making sure that the assessment process is carried out correctly, from a quality assurance perspective.

Such QA systems are complex, involving the coordination of work that has been done across institutional, geographic and temporal boundaries. Internal moderation provides a good example. Over the course of a single academic year, internal moderation, within this teacher-training network, consists of two day-long meetings in twelve different locations, with all of the tutors on the programme poring over a total of 200 different student portfolios. Tutors talk with each other, discuss the work that they are reading, occasionally argue over the interpretation of learning outcomes, or whether a student's work is of an acceptable standard. However, by the time of the writing of the internal moderation report, as required by the QA systems of the franchising university, all of these processes are distilled within a report that summarises, and thereby necessarily simplifies,

the process. Audit culture values unambiguity and simplicity. All the complexity and ambiguity of the internal moderation process is absent (Law, 2004).

So, how to restore this complexity and detail to an investigation of not just moderation, but assessment systems as a whole? How is assessment done? How does a geographically distant university manage to make things to do with assessment happen in different places, at different times, and with different people involved? Somehow, the University manages to get lots of different people to do different things relating to the course at different times: how can these relationships be explored and theorised, without over-simplification? How can the complexity, the ambiguity, the mess, be brought back? Or, to turn the question around, how might the ordering of the social project of assessment across the network of colleges be explored in such a way that its complexities can be maintained, rather than lost? A suggested framework through which to approach these questions is provided by actor-network theory (ANT) (Barton and Hamilton, 2005; Clarke, 2002; Edwards 2003; Fox, 2000, 2005; Latour, 2005; Law, 1994, 2004).

FROM QA TO ANT

Perhaps appropriately, bearing in mind its antecedents in post-structuralism, ANT defies a simple definition. It comes in several varieties. Having said this, extant literature allows a few themes to be teased out. Firstly, ANT is a *sociology of association* (Latour, 2005), or of *ramifying relations* (Law, 2004): it is a way of thinking about how social projects are joined together (in ways which can be traced) using networks of associations or links. Secondly, ANT provides ways of thinking about how associations influence each other, and the ways in which people are made to do things across networks of geography or time or institutional boundaries: "how to make someone do something" is a central concern (Latour, 2005:

59). Thirdly, ANT goes on to explore the ways in which people are made to do things through analysing the technologies which are used to achieve this: both people and objects can make people do something; that is to say, both people and objects are granted *agency* within ANT. Objects can travel across networks, and can carry meaning and intention. Many such objects are text-based (Barton and Hamilton, 2005; Law 1994). They are referred to as immutable mobiles: they are stable in form, but are transportable (Latour, 2005). Finally, ANT moves attention away from the role of amorphous social forces such as 'culture' or 'society', employing an anti-reductionist commitment to complexity, whilst foregrounding the practical means by which social ties are kept in place (Clarke, 2002; Law, 2004). So how might ANT contribute to an exploration of the *ordering work* (Law, 1994) that goes into the assessment process across this network of colleges?

ANT provides a way to investigate the strategies, activities and resources that are used by the university to reify, distribute, monitor and standardise (that is to say, to *order*) the assessment process across the network. The assessment process has both a pedagogic aspect and a managerial aspect, and these are linked. In terms of pedagogy, it is the process of the actual act of assessment, and hence the validity, reliability and sufficiency of the process, that is of importance. In terms of management, it is the processes of moderation and standardisation of assessment procedure that are of importance. The artefacts that accompany these processes are all either text-based (course handbooks and module packs, feedback pro-formas and internal moderation schedules created by the university and delivered to the colleges) or involve talk around text (moderation meetings involve talk around a range of texts: assignments; report forms; internal moderation feedback forms). But people are necessarily involved as well: there are monthly meetings for tutors; twice-yearly internal moderation events; twice-yearly meetings that see a member of the university's staff going out

to one of the colleges within the network. And, of course, it is important to remember that all of the text-based artefacts, or immutable mobiles already referred to, are written by people.

What ANT provides, in sum, is a framework that allows a detailed account of the actual ways by which the social project of assessment is ordered, through exploring the movement of both people and artefacts, how successful their movement is, how they are read or acted on or responded to when they arrive at their destination, and how, why and when what they say might be unwittingly misinterpreted or wilfully deviated from. With ANT, we can follow a chain of activities, actors and artefacts in order to explore the ways by which the university gets assessment done in the colleges.

EXPERIENCING ASSESSMENT PROCEDURES: ACTORS' ACCOUNTS

Assessment practices within this PGCE/CertEd are captured, or *reified* (Wenger, 1998), within several text-based artefacts: the course handbook, and the module guides (the course consists of seven different modules, and each has a different genre or mode of assessment). The course handbook is a 96 page A4 document. As well as containing module specifications for the whole course, it also includes a wealth of other information, such as guidance on Harvard referencing; an introduction to reflective practice; and more general information such as deadlines, plagiarism warnings, and the like. Module packs are much smaller: only a dozen pages or so. There is a pack for each module, containing: the module specifications and assignment brief; a module cover sheet for use when students submit their work; and a blank feedback pro-forma for use by tutors. The module specifications include: learning outcomes; indicative reading; outline syllabuses; and assessment details. They constitute written instructions for assessment, to be delivered to the colleges. In sum, the course handbook and module packs constitute text-based immutable mobiles that are used to synchronise or order the work of (amongst other things to do with the course) the assessment process. Reading lists and syllabuses privilege some texts, authors and perspectives over others, and assessments privilege some forms of academic writing or genre, such as essayist literacy or reflective writing, over others (Lillis, 2001; Swales, 1990; Tummons, 2008). A calendar dictates the timing of particular activities such as the submission of assessed work or the internal moderation process, to synchronise the work done in the network of colleges, in order to coincide with university deadlines (Crook et. al., 2006). In short, the university owns the assessment process, and the other partners in the network conform to these processes.

Before the module arrives at a college the writing of the module specifications constitute a significant *moment* where power can be seen at work. Richard is the teacher-training course leader at the university and co-leader of the module in question:

Jonathan: *...imagining either the course handbook or the module pack in front of us with the, what I think I'm right in saying is not the full module specification but a significant chunk of it that the students actually see, is that correct?*

Richard: *yeah, the way it is at the moment is probably 75% of the [board of studies] version of the module spec [...] We do miss out a few more important things like, for example, there's a specification of the expected hours and I think it's pretty obvious why we don't put that in what we give to the students.*

Jonathan: *Do you think that at [board of studies] everyone knows it doesn't quite happen, I don't know, it's almost like a game or...*

Richard: *No, no, let me clarify that a little bit. The tutor led hours here we do stay quite scrupulously to*

Jonathan: *independent study and assessment for example*

Richard: *yeah that will obviously vary from student to student. I mean we would take a dim view if [colleges] departed significantly from 48 hours for a 20 credit module but one of the reasons we don't put in the module spec is if for some reason you're only able to deliver 46 hours, or you might decide you want an extra couple of hours, and you don't want the students saying "it says in this module specification forty-eight".*

It is perhaps superfluous to note that the handbooks or packs that will be read by students on the course will have been written or designed or shaped *for* them, not *with* them. But these are also the versions of the module specifications that will be read by tutors at the colleges. Some knowledge, in this one example relating to guided learning hours and independent study hours, is kept at the university, which has the power to do so because it creates both the procedures and the artefacts which reify them. That is to say, it has the power to shape conversations within the colleges, about the construction of the course. In this small example, the number of guided learning hours and private study hours (or, rather, the lack of a specific number) constitutes an example of the uneven distribution of power between university and colleges.

The course handbook and all the module packs are distributed electronically. Each college receives electronic versions either via email or by downloading them from the university's virtual learning environment. It is up to each college to reproduce and distribute them for the students. How people in the colleges respond to them is another matter. Emma is a college-based tutor with a background in literacy teaching, now in her second year of teaching the PCET course:

Emma: *the graphology isn't good [...] well, erm, we're looking at the visual aspect of it now. Font size, font style, no white space. This is all things that do not support literacy. And I think that supporting literacy isn't just about teaching somebody how to put full stops in. It's actually about supporting the whole reading, and if you make reading accessible, then that is what is necessary.*

Jonathan: *[...] do you think this is something that is noticed by your own students?*

Emma: *they don't, they've all said they look at these and they don't like them, they don't like reading them. And I also think that they are rather confusing because they have the assessment there on one page, then they have the assessment on another page. Which bit is the student supposed to refer to, which bit is the tutor supposed to refer to? It's cluttered. And clutter does not make for good reading, and it doesn't invite anybody to read. And one of the principles that I, that we look at on the literacy courses [...] is reorganising information. It's critical.*

Emma's critique of the material form of the module pack rests on her own professional knowledge, experience and identity as a literacy tutor. So can anything be done to ameliorate this problem? After all, since colleges are responsible for the reproduction of these module packs as well as the course handbooks that are delivered in electronic form, it would be a straightforward task to, for example, enlarge the font size as an aid to legibility. I spoke to the course leaders at six of the colleges within the network about the reproduction of course documents: of these, four reproduced the documents exactly as they received them; the other two introduced a small innovation by using coloured paper. According to the course leader at the university, colleges are free to adapt

or add to the module packs because they are not auditable documents. Few of the college-based tutors are aware of this adaptability, however.

Once in circulation, the packs and handbooks settle down, as do the students and tutors, to the task at hand: that is, the business of the course: of reading, of the module outcomes, of the assessment strategies for the module. And both tutors and students should know what to do: it's in the paperwork, after all. Working out exactly what is required sometimes needs some effort, however, as demonstrated by the tutors and students quoted above. They might not necessarily like them, but they have to use them. To that end, tutors engage in a range of exercises designed to introduce students to what needs to be done. They prepare powerpoint presentations, additional handouts, close-reading exercises and writing frames. These are done at a local level: different tutors do different things in different colleges. But the effort is uniform insofar as these different actions are all aimed at the successful interpretation and negotiation of the assignment brief.

It may not be a surprise to learn that a majority of students do not always read large documents such as the course handbook from cover to cover: they rely on their tutor to tell them what sections to read, what they need to know. Nor may it come as a surprise to learn that a majority of tutors do not read large documents such as the course handbook from cover to cover, either: as well as dipping in and out of it, they can and do rely on other resources: people, conversations, meetings, internal moderation events, university web sites, perhaps their own memories of being students on the very same course. In different ways, such activities as these help to fix, to render less slippery, the key messages that the university wants to send out regarding how assessment should be done. The text-based artefacts that Holgate has created are being used, but not in isolation. They need to be sponsored and responded to by people (Brandt and Clinton, 2002).

If social action is, in part, done by things as well as by people, then the action in question can be transported further than might otherwise be the case (Latour, 2005). Packs and handbooks are a practical, and relatively cheap, way for the university to get the assessment process 'out there'. But ANT "is not the empty claim that objects do things 'instead' of human actors"; rather, things might "authorise, allow, afford, encourage, permit, suggest, influence, block, render possible, forbid, and so on" (ibid: 72). Assignment briefs do indeed make students and tutors go about the process of assessment in certain ways. And they work that way, in part, because *that is what they were written to do*. At the same time, the university knows, in part, that it's instructions about assessment are getting across because it knows that *the correct paperwork is being used*. But it also knows that there is more to it than this. The university can trust colleges to use learning and teaching strategies *of their own design* to explicate the assessment process, but only in a secondary or supplementary role, to support the documentation and procedures that the university has established. And anyway, it would be highly impractical to monitor physically all of what goes on in the different colleges. So the university needs to do more than just provide text-based artefacts to keep the system moving. Other actors are needed as well, and these need to be people.

TRACING ASSOCIATIONS: PEOPLE AND PLACES, NOT JUST THINGS

Immutable mobiles work the way that they are supposed to because people, as well as things, are involved with them, in getting things done in certain ways, in the work of ordering assessment as a social project. People not only write and interpret them, but they accompany them, sponsor them, champion them, remind others of their importance. And this is where the issue of trust, raised above, comes to the fore. The university

cannot or will not leave the tutors in the colleges to get on with using these handbooks, or artefacts, or immutable mobiles, on their own: they need to be accompanied.

There are several ways to accomplish this. To begin with, it is necessarily to acculturate tutors in colleges: all new tutors on the course attend a "development day" at the University, run by an experienced member of academic staff who teaches on the course and has responsibility for quality assurance. There are monthly meetings, when representatives from the course delivery teams at the colleges come to the university. Invariably, these meetings cover both bureaucratic issues (such as admissions policy, which, like assessment, is ordered by the university but carried out in the colleges themselves), and academic issues (such as the introduction of e-learning, curriculum development, and occasional scholarly presentations by internal and external speakers). And the university comes to the colleges as well. Twice a year, each college will hold a course meeting, where a member of the university department will attend in a liaison tutor capacity. These meetings are minuted, and a copy of the minutes must go back to the university. Once every three years, a panel of university staff visit each college in order to revalidate formally the course provision. It perhaps goes without saying that this visit is preceded by the creation of a significant text artefact by the college in question that is submitted to the university before the visit. There are two annual conferences (also open to external delegates) and a host of other training events for non-teaching staff. In sum, there is a significant number of ways by which interested people accompany or travel alongside the artefacts of the network. Or, to put it another way, there are many different kinds of social actions by which actors, which can be people or things, across a number of sites, can coordinate activity. And many of these activities involve people, and texts, and talk around these texts. What is important, in ANT, is the fact that

BRINGING THE ASSESSMENTS TO INTERNAL MODERATION

Once students' work has been completed, a sample of this work goes to internal moderation. As already mentioned, the processes of internal moderation have to be organised across significant physical and temporal boundaries. As such, the university has created a series of written documents that carry the rules and regulations surrounding the process to the different colleges where the course is delivered. These rules govern details such as the timing of internal examination, the amount of work to be sampled and the location for the meetings. In this way, a uniformity can be applied to the process. The course leader at each college is responsible for selecting a sample of student work. As well as bringing along all assignments that are marked as having failed, course leaders select at their own discretion a representative sample of work, some excellent, some borderline. The size of the sample is set at 5%. Colleges are divided into groups (of about five or six) that come to regional meetings where work is distributed and moderated. Normally each assignment is read by one other tutor. A brief feedback sheet is completed for each moderated file. A representative from Holgate University also attends these meetings, and takes a chief moderator role, with any disputes referred to them, although the internal moderation meeting does not have the power to reverse an assessment decision. Each region holds a moderation meeting twice a year. At the end of the meeting, an internal moderation report is completed. Eventually, a single internal moderation report, effectively a compilation of the dozen or so produced during the two rounds of regional meetings, is produced at the university.

If the number of people, places and written documents for the process as a whole were ag-glomerated, the tally would be considerable: over 400 assignments, each with an internal moderation sheet attached, and a dozen regional internal moderation reports, all completed during 12 day-long meetings in six different locations and involving over 100 tutors; one overall internal moderation report, written by the course examinations tutor at the university; five or six external examiners' reports, written after a two-day external examiners' meeting at the university; one overall chief external examiner's report. This last report is the final product of the process: four or five sides of A4 paper.

But the problem of over-simplification remains. Such detailed processes speak to a discourse of accountability and transparency, but they lack the fine-grained detail that an actor-network account would provide. If the actor-network relies on the cooperation and engagement of all of the actors within the network, then an actor-network account would also insist on a scrupulous examination of how and why these actors work the way that they do, thereby restoring the richness and complexity to the story of (in this example) internal moderation, that the audit trail silences.

As already mentioned, the 5% representative sample of student work that goes to internal moderation is selected by the course leaders at the colleges. But this selection process is far from straightforward. In fact, it is a locus for considerable professional doubt and scrutiny:

Debbie (course leader, Nunthorpe College)*: ... we only take five per cent, we select [the assignments] ourselves. Now although we're encouraged to select the borderline, the middle of the road and the high flyers, you have to be quite brave to take along the borderline ones, and I, I've tried to be brave sometimes and taken [borderline] ones, and then we get into academic discussions about whether it was good enough or not. But I'm being brave because I'm opening myself up to why I passed them, when I might be having an internal debate as to whether I should have passed them* *or not, and what the cut off point is between not quite good enough, and good enough. I think we should have more debates about this, perhaps. [...]*

Jonathan: *and do you think we should take more than five per cent to the moderation event?*

Debbie: *it's the sheer practicalities of getting through the amount of work. Is it better to look at the work and take our time and do a thorough read through? I'm very slow at reading, other people are very quick. I could take a cursory look but that's not, may not be good enough. So five per cent is probably okay but what I do wonder about, and this is really contentious, is whether we should be given some names of who we should take, because it depends on how I'm feeling, as to whether I think "let me just take some standard, you know, some good work. If we've got some excellent work I'll take that along." I know no-ones going to quibble with me about the level but if there are some who are on the borderline, I may think not. "No, I won't take that piece of work."*

PAYING ATTENTION TO DETAIL: ACTOR-NETWORK THEORY AND THE ORDERING OF ASSESSMENT

Accounts of other actor-networks have taken time to expound the conceptual tools of ANT in more or less greater amounts of detail (Clarke, 2002; Edwards, 2003; Fox, 2000; Fox, 2005; Hamilton, 2001, 2009). Briefly, a network can grow like this: first, one group of actors identify a problem or activity or thing that needs to be done; a project that needs to be ordered. Crucially, this group has a monopoly on the means by which the problem can be solved, or the thing can get done: other actors have to follow their orders and employ the same means. Secondly, it is necessary to gain the commitment of these others to the course of action needed, as defined by the first group. Next, the others need to be persuaded, or induced, or

threatened into enrolling into the course of action that the initial group of actors have proposed. And so, finally, these others have been mobilised. The actors have translated the interests of the others into their own, reduced them to a representative sample so that they can communicate with them, using both voices and texts.

Therefore, this actor-network can be seen as being 'an actor-network' in several ways. Firstly, there is a social project to be ordered: the project of assessment. The desirability and importance of the project is not questioned or challenged in any sense thanks to the emergence of broadly shared practices on assessment on part-time courses for professionals which are run on an HE in FE basis (Brown, 1999a; Brown, 1999b; Taylor 1997; Young 1999). Secondly, the university manages to gain the *commitment* and then *cooperation* of other actors within the network. This is achieved through a number of means. To some extent the college-based actors are self-selecting: tutors have often chosen to work as teacher educators, or have been encouraged to do so (Noel, 2006). To some extent the historical background of the network serves to normalise the processes of commitment and cooperation: the vast majority of colleges within the network have been in the network for fifteen years, and some have been working with Holgate University for much longer. For colleges as institutions, the capital, both financial and political, generated by HE in FE provision is a powerful incentive for participation and cooperation. Moreover, the dominant discourses of quality assurance have created a culture within FE that is receptive to the audit demands of HE in FE provision (Parry and Thompson 2002; Parry et. al., 2003). Finally, the university is able to *mobilise* the actors within this network. By this I mean that tutors, students and colleges are made to do things: to explain assessment briefs; to mark assessments; to take a sample of assessments to internal moderation. Firstly, this is achieved through the mobilisation of a variety of immutable mobiles, text-based objects that carry instructions ranging from which books should be read, to how feedback should be written, to when the results of assessment need to be returned to the university. These objects also perpetuate and reinforce the practices of the network: meetings, whether for bureaucratic or for moderation purposes, are captured in text-based artefacts so that those things that happen in them, that are important for the work of the actor-network, can be perpetuated, although it is important to remember that such reifications can lead to a loss of complexity (Wenger, 1998). Secondly, *mobilisation* is achieved through people: internal moderators, liaison tutors, all the other people in the big monthly meetings who tell the college-based tutors what is coming next, or what procedures are now due, or what the new look syllabus might be like.

Ordering the social project of assessment is a technologically complex task, therefore, consisting of a chain made up of links that are both human and non-human. The actions taken by all of these different actors are many, varied and complex. They are circumscribed by the other actors within the network as a whole, some of whom are more powerful and influential than others. But all of the actors' accounts matter, and need to be listened to. Debbie's narrative highlights the complex and ambiguous decisions that surround the selection of assignments to take to moderation, a process that is far from straightforward – although audit discourses might say otherwise. What might be termed Debbie's professional ambiguity in no way militates against her broader professional expertise and ethical approach: yet the process is clearly a fraught one. Emma's narrative shows a different, but no less important, example of professional expertise at work: here, a professional judgement about the legibility, the usability, and perhaps the worth of the kind of documentation that a network of this size relies on. For Emma, the professional challenge is in interpreting this document (and others) so that her students can access them. Finally, there is Richard's narrative, embodying the perspective of the university at the

centre that has the ability, the power, to shape and influence the work that is being done throughout the network as a whole to order the process of assessment. Some of this is done by people and some is done by artefacts, predominantly literacy artefacts. Both the people and the artefacts, or to put it another way, the human actors and the non-human actors, make things happen. The things that happen, and the ambiguities that surround them, are not privileged by audit discourses. But their traces – Debbie's hard choices over moderation, Emma's profound reservations about the course documentation, Richard's ability to shape how the course is done, – are abundant, within an actor-network. And it is through writing actor-network accounts that the story can be told in full, with the detail that it both requires and deserves, in order to demonstrate how rich and how complex these processes are.

REFERENCES

Atkins, M. (1995). What should we be assessing? In Knight, P. (Ed.), *Assessing for Learning in Higher Education*. London: Kogan Page.

Avis, J. (2002). Developing Staff in Further Education: discourse, learners and practice. *Research in Post-Compulsory Education*, 7(3), 339–352. doi:10.1080/13596740200200135

Avis, J. (2005). Beyond performativity: reflections on activist professionalism and the labour process in further education. *Journal of Education Policy*, 20(2), 209–222. doi:10.1080/0268093052000341403

Barnett, R. (2003). *Beyond All Reason: living with ideology in the university*. Buckingham: Open University Press/Society for Research into Higher Education.

Barton, D., & Hamilton, M. (2005). Literacy, reification and the dynamics of social interaction. In Barton, D., & Tusting, K. (Eds.), *Beyond Communities of Practice: Language, Power and Social Context*. Cambridge, UK: Cambridge University Press. doi:10.1017/CBO9780511610554.003

Bird, J., & Crawley, G. (1994). Franchising and other further education/higher education partnerships: the student experience and policy. In Haselgrove, S. (Ed.), *The Student Experience*. Buckingham, UK: Open University Press/SRHE.

Brandt, T., & Clinton, K. (2002). Limits of the local: expanding perspectives on literacy as a social practice. *Journal of Literacy Research*, *34*(3), 337–356. doi:10.1207/s15548430jlr3403_4

Brown, S. (1999a). Assessing practice. In Brown, S., & Glasner, A. (Eds.), *Assessment Matters in Higher Education: choosing and using diverse approaches*. Buckingham, UK: Open University Press/Society for Research into Higher Education.

Brown, S. (1999b). Institutional strategies for assessment. In Brown, S., & Glasner, A. (Eds.), *Assessment Matters in Higher Education: choosing and using diverse approaches*. Buckingham: Open University Press/Society for Research into Higher Education.

Clarke, J. (2002). A new kind of symmetry: actor-network theories and the new literacy studies. *Studies in the Education of Adults*, *34*(2), 107–122.

Connolly, M., Jones, C., & Jones, N. (2007). Managing collaboration across further and higher education: a case in practice. *Journal of Further and Higher Education*, *31*(2), 159–169. doi:10.1080/03098770701267630

Crooke, C., Gross, H., & Dymott, R. (2006). Assessment relationships in higher education: the tension of process and practice. *British Educational Research Journal*, *32*(1), 95–114. doi:10.1080/01411920500402037

Ecclestone, K. (2001). 'I know a 2:1 when I see it': understanding criteria for degree classifications in franchised university programmes. *Journal of Further and Higher Education*, *25*(3), 301–313. doi:10.1080/03098770126527

Edwards, R. (2003). Ordering subjects: Actor-networks and intellectual technologies in lifelong learning. *Studies in the Education of Adults*, *35*(1), 54–67.

Fox, S. (2000). Communities of practice, Foucault and actor-network theory. *Journal of Management Studies*, *37*(6), 853–867. doi:10.1111/1467-6486.00207

Fox, S. (2005). An actor-network critique of community in higher education: implications for networked learning. *Studies in Higher Education*, *30*(1), 95–110. doi:10.1080/0307507052000307821

Gleeson, D., Davies, J., & Wheeler, E. (2005). On the making and taking of professionalism in the further education workplace. *British Journal of Sociology of Education*, *26*(4), 445–460. doi:10.1080/01425690500199818

Hamilton, M. (2001). Privileged literacies: policy, institutional process and the life of the IALS. *Language and Education, 15*(2 and 3), 178-196.

Hamilton, M. (2009). Putting words in their mouths: the alignment of identities with system goals through the use of individual learning plans. *British Educational Research Journal, 35*(2), 221–242. doi:10.1080/01411920802042739

Hilborne, J. (1996). Ensuring quality in further and higher education partnerships. In Abramson, M., Bird, J., & Stennett, A. (Eds.), *Further and Higher Education Partnerships: the Future for Collaboration*. Buckingham, UK: Open University Press/Society for Research into Higher Education.

Ivanic, R. (1998). *Writing and Identity: the discoursal construction of identity in academic writing*. Amsterdam: John Benjamins.

Katz, T. (2000). University Education for Developing Professional Practice. In Bourner, T., Katz, T., & Watson, D. (Eds.), *New Directions if Professional Higher Education*. Buckingham: Open University Press/Society for Research into Higher Education.

Klenowski, V. (2002). *Developing Portfolios for Learning and Assessment*. London: Routledge.

Latour, B. (2005). *Reassembling the Social: an introduction to Actor-Network Theory*. Oxford: Oxford University Press.

Law, J. (1994). *Organising Modernity*. Oxford, UK: Blackwell.

Law, J. (2004). *After Method: mess in social science research*. London: Routledge.

Lillis, T. (2001). *Student Writing: Access, Regulation, Desire*. London: Routledge.

Noel, P. (2006). The Secret Life of Teacher Educators: becoming a teacher educator in the learning and skills sector. *Journal of Vocational Education and Training, 58*(2), 151–170. doi:10.1080/13636820600799577

Parry, G., Davies, P., & Williams, J. (2003). *Dimensions of Difference: higher education in the learning and skills sector*. London: Learning and Skills Development Agency.

Parry, G., & Thompson, A. (2002). *Closer By Degrees: the past, present and future of higher education in further education colleges*. London: Learning and Skills Development Agency.

Price, M. (2005). Assessment standards: the role of communities of practice and the scholarship of assessment. *Assessment & Evaluation in Higher Education, 30*(3), 215–230. doi:10.1080/02602930500063793

Scollon, R. (2001). *Mediated Discourse: The Nexus of Practice*. London: Routledge.

Shain, F., & Gleeson, D. (1999). Under new management: changing conceptions of teacher professionalism and policy in the further education sector. *Journal of Education Policy, 14*(4), 445–462. doi:10.1080/026809399286288

Shore, C., & Wright, S. (1999). Audit culture and anthropology: new-liberalism in British higher education. *The Journal of the Royal Anthropological Institute, 5*(4), 557–575. doi:10.2307/2661148

Shore, C., & Wright, S. (2000). Coercive accountability – the rise of audit culture in higher education. In Strathern, M. (Ed.), *Audit Cultures: Anthropological Studies in Accountability, Ethics and the Academy*. London: Routledge.

Swales, J. (1990). *Genre Analysis: English in academic and research settings*. Cambridge, UK: Cambridge University Press.

Taylor, I. (1997). *Developing Learning in Professional Education*. Buckingham, UK: Open University Press/Society for Research into Higher Education.

Thomas, L. (2001). *Widening Participation in Post-Compulsory Education*. London: Continuum.

Tigelaar, D., Dolmans, D., Wolfhagen, I., & van der Vleuten, C. (2005). Quality issues in judging portfolios: implications for organizing teaching portfolio assessment procedures. *Studies in Higher Education, 30*(5), 595–610. doi:10.1080/03075070500249302

Tummons, J. (2008). Assessment, and the literacy practices of trainee PCET teachers. *International Journal of Educational Research, 47*(3), 184–191. doi:10.1016/j.ijer.2008.01.006

Tummons, J. (2010). *Becoming A Professional Tutor in the Lifelong Learning Sector*. Exeter, UK: Learning Matters.

Wenger, E. (1998). *Communities of Practice: learning, meaning and identity*. Cambridge, UK: Cambridge University Press.

West, J. (2006). Patrolling the borders: accreditation in further and higher education in England. *Journal of Further and Higher Education*, *30*(1), 11–26. doi:10.1080/03098770500431957

Young, G. (1999). Using portfolios for assessment in teacher preparation and health sciences. In Brown, S., & Glasner, A. (Eds.), *Assessment Matters in Higher Education: choosing and using diverse approaches*. Buckingham, UK: Open University Press/Society for Research into Higher Education.

Chapter 13
Managing Multi–Organizational Interaction Issues:
A Case Study of Information Technology Transfer in Public Sector of Malaysia

Hasmiah Kasimin
Universiti Kebangsaan, Malaysia

Huda Ibrahim
Universiti Utara, Malaysia

ABSTRACT

In Malaysia, major information technology transfers in public sector agencies are usually due to policy implementation. This policy-led technology transfer involves central government directives to the implementation agencies. The technology transfer process usually not only involves multi-organizations that consist of many public agencies and private sector organizations but also involved many phases. Each organization plays certain roles and contributes to the achievement of the technology transfer objectives. Each phase serves a different purpose and each role during each phase has different requirements. Coordinating and encouraging the multiple organization participation in each phase is complex and a challenge that may at least result in project delays or technological decision-making that based on non-technical considerations. In such a case, understanding and managing interactions between stakeholders are important in designing activities and strategies for effective technology transfer process suitable to local environment. This is especially true for technology that requires further development to adapt with local environment. This paper explores this issue in a case study of XYZ technology transfer in a Malaysian public agency. We make use an approach based on actor-network theory and the concepts of technology transfer stages. We found that ignoring issues emerged from interactions between stakeholders will not only delay the transfer process but will also render the project's original objectives as not fully achieved.

DOI: 10.4018/978-1-60960-197-3.ch013

INTRODUCTION

Malaysia is a developing country in the process of transforming her economy from a manufacturing economy to a knowledge-based economy. Malaysia believes that information technology should play the role of a catalyst to this transformation process. It is not surprising that the Malaysian government has given a serious focus on IT not only on using IT for development but also to develop the IT industry. One of the important IT related policies is the development of the Multimedia Super Corridor (MSC) launched in the Seventh Malaysia Plan (1996-2000) which cover a designated area in the state of Selangor. In order to develop the MSC, a number of MSC Flagship Applications such as Smart-School, E-Government, Telemedicine, Government Multi-purpose Card, R & D Clusters, Worldwide Manufacturing Web and Borderless Marketing were launched. The MSC development was extended into the Eight Malaysia Plan (2001-2005). And later in the Ninth Malaysia Plan (2006-2010) the coverage of the MSC area includes several other states in Malaysia as well. The implementation of this policy involves IT technology transfer from overseas suppliers to local IT industries and from local IT industries to local users which includes public sector agencies, private sector organizations and public individuals. Thus issues related to information technology transfer are important to Malaysia. They are critical to Malaysia as investments on the seven Flagship Applications are costly. At the same time, the technology progress in IT is very fast, in that any delay in the technology transfer will make the application less effective. The policy-led technology transfer process is complex as it involves many stakeholders from both public and private sector agencies. Thus information technology transfer involved in the IT policy implementation is not a matter to be taken lightly in order to achieve maximum benefit from it. This paper explores issues related to managing multi-organization interactions in a case study of XYZ technology transfer in a public sector agency of Malaysia. Analysis of the case study makes use of an approach that combined technology transfer stages and actor-network theory. We found that ignoring issues emerged from interactions between stakeholders will not only delay the transfer processes but will also render the project's original objectives as not fully achieved. The experience may be useful in the implementation of any E-Government applications as they also involve information technology transfer.

LITERATURE REVIEW, CONCEPTS AND FRAMEWORK OF THE STUDY

All technology transfer process is a complex and difficult process, especially where secondary uses of innovations are involved or it occurs across different organization boundaries (Buxton & Malcolm, 1991; Frutkin, 1975; Sung, 2009). It is not simply moving technology from one point to another but involves an iterative process with a great deal of back-and-forth exchange among individuals over an extended period of time. The technology has to be absorbed, mastered, and controlled (Montealegre, 1998). Its application requires the existence of capability to insert new ideas, new practices, and new elements into a flexible system. It also requires new intellectual skills, abstract thinking, problem-solving and inference that are very scarce in most developing countries.

According to Gibson and Smilor (1991) technology transfer requires a profoundly human endeavor. It usually requires collaborative activity between two or more individuals or functional units that are often separated by a range of structural and cultural barriers (Gibson & Harlan, 1995). According to Kahen (1997), technology transfer is multi-dimension and multi-factor. It involves economic, social, political and organizational dimensions (Buxton & Malcolm, 1991). Previous study also shows that there are many factors that affect technology transfer effectiveness such as technical, human resources and technology transfer process (Madu, 1992). Buxton and Malcolm (1991) found that, the process of transfer is complex and involves many roles and phases. Each phase serves different purpose and each role, during each phase, has requirements for a different type of information. If any role is mishandled or if any phase is inadequately carried out, it is probable that the effort will not succeed. Technology transfer also requires cooperative activities from many individuals or functional units that are structurally and culturally different (Gibson & Harlan, 1995; Sung & Gibson, 2000). According to Dudley (2006), there are two important aspects in technology transfer, (i) the science and technology about the technology transfer, and (ii) the working relationships between parties involved in the technology transfer process. Interactions that occur between many parties and between the technology and the relevant parties may affect the transfer process. Coordinating and encouraging the multiple organization participation in each phase is complex and a challenge that may at least result in project delays. In such a case, understanding and managing interactions between stakeholders are important in designing activities and strategies for effective technology transfer process suitable to local environment (Buono, 1997; Montealegre, 1999). This means that the process and interaction management between those parties depends on an organized strategy and action toward accomplishing the technology transfer objective in an integrated and effective mode. This paper gives focus on the technology transfer process and how the interactions between various stakeholders, including the technology involved, affects the process.

Technology Transfer Process

Technology transfer process refers to the implementation process of a technology that is developed in a particular context to another different context. The implementation of the technology requires adaptation of the systems as well as procedures and work flows in the new environments. Technology transfer process involves a number of activities. Technology transfer activities describe what is being done in the transfer process. These activities vary according to local environment where the transfer takes place. Previous studies show technology transfer activities may be summarized into a number of main activities such as planning (Madu, 1992), assimilation and use (Baark & Heeks, 1998), adaptation (Narasimhan, 1984; Lall, 1987; Schmitz & Hewitt, 1991; innovation (Quitas, 1994; Rogers, 1995), and diffusion (Dooley, 1990). Baark and Heeks(1998) called their model the model of donor-funded ICT transfer from industrialized to developing countries. This model conceptualized technology transfer activities as a life cycle comprising a sequence of five steps: choice technology, purchase and installation, assimilation and use, adaptation and diffusion. This view provides a useful structure for analyzing technology transfer, but in practice the process hardly follows the sequence. In general information technology transfer may be grouped into three stages: planning or pre-technology transfer (Pre-TOT), technology of transfer implementation (TOT implementation) and technology of transfer innovation and diffusion (Post-TOT). Pre-TOT includes activities related to technology transfer planning such as requirement analysis, decision to adopt new technology, investigation of the relevant technology, identifying the technology provider, identifying possible collaboration and required resources. Pre-TOT is important to ensure the whole technology transfer process is efficient and effective. Previous experiences (Madu, 1992; Capps & Fairley, 2002) show that an improper strategic planning and management is one of the significant sources of failure for many technology transfer initiatives. Without strategic planning, technology transfer will get slow and in worse case the transfer could not proceed or being abandoned at any time. TOT implementation includes activities related to installation and operation of technology such as technology delivery and installation, absorption and operation, maintenance and evaluation. TOT implementation should be carried out properly because there are a number of common problems occur such as human resource, training and lack of implementation monitoring (Chung & Chik, 1997). Post-TOT includes activities related to technology innovation and diffusion such as new technology innovation, research and development, developing sub industry and technology development center, decision to diffuse new technology and sharing and diffusing new knowledge. Post-TOT activities need to be carried out in order to encourage technology applications and development of new products according to local needs (Derakhshani, 1983).

Each level of technology transfer process involves many different entities whom interact to each other to attain their objectives respectively. Entities include individual, groups of individual and non-human elements that represent various roles, such as technology recipients, technology messenger, employee, management, trainee, trainer, customer, partner and consultant. Non-human elements include technology, machine, business report, document, business strategy, policy, plans and culture. Interactions between human and non-human elements might raise problems and conflicts which will influence the success or failure of a technology transfer. The concept of technology transfer process however does not explain how management of interactions between entities in every level should be done to determine the efficiency and effectiveness of the technology transfer. This paper therefore would use an actor network theory (ANT) to analyze processes which occur in every level of technology transfer. In terms of ANT, entities are called actors.

Actor-Network Theory

Previous studies show that in real world, technology transfer process is not a linear and systematic process (Flannery & Dietrich, 2000). Other studies (Jegathesan et al, 1997; Schnepp et al, 1990; Derakhshani, 1983) show that technology transfer process involves change in various forms such as products' function, human knowledge and skills, organizational behaviors and cultures. According to Buono (1997) technology transfer involves many agents and participants. It also requires participation from many stakeholders at various levels such as national, organization, local workers and individuals. Interactions between various stakeholders may influence activities carried out in the transfer process. In this paper we make use of the actor-network theory (ANT) to study how interactions between participants and agents of technology transfer affect the activities in the process of technology transfer. ANT is an approach that refers to how a network of actors is formed through heterogeneous of human and non-human actors with multiple roles, relations and activities in order to address a real problem defined by a focal actor. According to ANT, the implementation potential will be in the hands of those who are able to translate problems and needs to support their own enterprise (Berntsen & Seim, 2007). ANT was first proposed by Michel Callon and Bruno Latour in the early 1980s [(Callon & Latour, 1981; Callon, 1986). The theory was born out of on-going efforts within the social studies of science and technology.

ANT involves two main processes, namely *translation* and *inscription*. *Translation* is the process that creates an actor network. *Inscription* is a process of inscribing interests and/or agreement between actors. It may be in the form of a number of texts and graphical representations to protect the interests or agreement between actors. It prescribes a program of action for others, which may or may not be followed. ANT introduces a number of concepts to describe and analyze the actor-network formed such as actor, boundary objects, obligatory point of passage (OPP), irreversibility, betrayal and intermediaries such as text, technical objects, human beings and money.

OPP refers to a situation that has to occur in order for all the actors to satisfy the interests that have been attributed to them by the focal actor. OPP is defined by the focal actor through which the other actors must pass and by which the focal actor becomes indispensible (Callon, 1986).

Translation Process

It occurs when actors start to define roles, distribute and redistribute roles and power, describe a scenario, and through these, alliances of human and nonhuman actors are formed and consolidated. Translation presents an interaction between actors as they convince and negotiate with each other. It is unlike a usual interaction where two (or more) relatively stable entities are linked together in a stimulus-response relation. Translation, instead, focuses on the mutual (inter)definition of actors as they become linked together. Translation involves a process of change, which occur via four major 'moments': problematization, interessement, enrolment and mobilization.

Problematization involves an identification of actors and a determination of OPP. It involves a number of steps such as:

1. Identification of an issue or problem that initiates the stage. The issue will guide the main actor in identifying other actors to be involved in stage one.
2. Identify the multiple actors to be involved in the stage.
3. Identify the multiple interests or roles of actors in the stage. It is advisable to take into account the nature of actors' current activities and objectives before assigning roles and functions to each of them.
4. Identify an OPP.
5. Identify potential obstacles. Obstacles may be in the form of the business and technical problems, conflicts, changes that could possibly happened in each stage of IT transfer.

Ignored obstacles may affect the achievement of OPP.

In the creation of an actor-network, a number of text and graphical representations are produced to protect the interests and/or agreement of/between actors. The process of inscribing interests and/or agreement is known as inscription. The process tends to prescribe a program of action for other actors, which may or may not be followed.

Interessement moment is a group of actions in which the focal actor attempts to impose and stabilize the identity of other actors (Callon, 1986). This is to convince other actors to accept roles given by the focal actor. *Interessement mechanism* is activities to encourage cooperation between actors to face any obstacles so that an agreed OPP can be achieved.

Enrolment is a situation where actors accept interest defined for them by the focal actor. *Enrolment mechanism* is the effort to build and reinforce all actors' commitments in facing and meeting obstacles (challenges, threats or pressures in their way to achieve the OPP), which eventually helps create an actor-network. It may be in the form of strategies and intermediaries. *Strategies* are efforts such as multilateral negotiations, trial of strength and tricks to support enrolment of actors in the actor network of technology transfer.

Mobilization is the effort to ensure the network starts to operate the strategies in terms of activities to implement the proposed solution. A set of methods are required to ensure that supposed spokesmen for various collectivities are properly able to represent those collectivities and are not betrayed by the latter. Figure 1 shows the four moments in the creation of an actor-network.

Approach of the Study

This paper examines a case study of XYZ technology transfer to public sector of Malaysia. The transfer was intended to support the development of a national IT project henceforth to be referred to

Figure 1. Translation process in creating an actor network

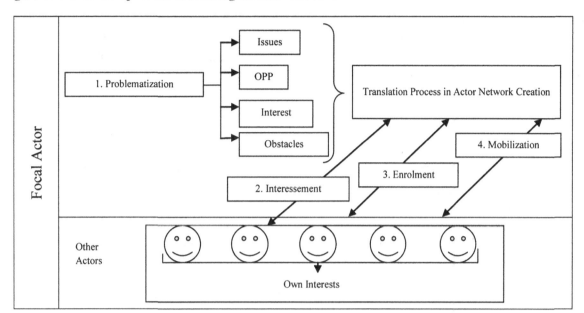

Figure 2. A framework to analyze technology of transfer

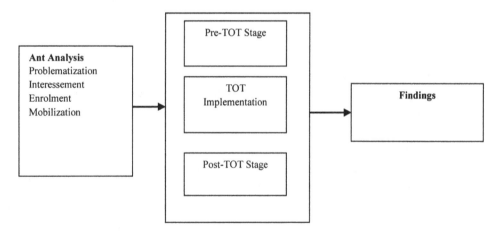

as XYZ-based System. The study was conducted one year after the commencement of the transfer. Analysis on the case was carried out using the framework as depicted in Figure 2 which utilized the stages of technology transfer process and ANT.

Previous studies show that an efficient and effective technology transfer should focus on several phases categorized as Pre-TOT, TOT Implementation and Post-TOT. Pre-TOT is necessary so that an organization can prepare and set up action plans to acquire the new technology while TOT implementation is important to be carried out efficiently and effectively. Post-TOT, on the other hand, is essential to encourage technology development and adaptation with the current situation and needs.

From ANT perspectives, each phase would involve variations in an organization, which will bring about an efficient and effective technology transfer. At Pre-TOT level, an organization changes from an unprepared to a prepared level in acquiring a new technology. At TOT implementation phase, organization moves from having no new technology to possess a new technology whilst at Post-TOT level, organization is advancing to modifying and disseminating the use of that technology. In order to realize the changes in every level, the management of technology transfer should give focus on aspects such as problematization, interessement, enrolment and mobilization.

Data for this study was gathered by carrying out personal interviews based on structured questionnaires. Respondents include 26 recipients, 7 transferors and one respondent from management. The questions in the interview were divided into five sections; (i) agency profile, (ii) the planning process and decision making before a new technology is being transferred to the agency, (iii) the implementation of the actual technology transfer, (iv) the post activities and future planning after the technology has been transferred to the agency, (v) issues, challenges and actions taken by the agency during the whole technology transfer process. To support the interviews section, the study had also relied on secondary data gathered from the agency's library, which include the agency's annual report, XYZ Technology of Transfer Plan and other related documents. Data from the interviews was recorded and analyzed based on TOT phases and from the perspectives of ANT. To support data analysis and interpretation, the study applied the concept of translation from ANT to the three phases of TOT. As shown in Figure 1, translation is applied to Phase 1 (Pre-TOT and Planning), Phase 2 (TOT Implementation), and Phase 3 (Post-TOT). Each translation on each phase of TOT involves three major moments: a) problematization, b) interessment, and c) enrolment. These three moments explain the details of human and non-human interaction in all three stages of TOT.

ANT was chosen to interpret and analyze the data in this qualitative study since its approach is intended to help understand the behavior of relevant actors in the process of TOT. ANT is the best choice since it provides a framework to help the study understand and describe actors' actions and interaction in IT transfer. The use of ANT does not only identify the success and failures factors of a particular IT project but also goes beyond it by understanding the complex interactions associated between the factors (Walsham, 1995).

CASE STUDY OF XYZ TECHNOLOGY TRANSFER IN PUBLIC SECTOR OF MALAYSIA

The case study is based on a consulting intervention with a real public agency henceforth to be referred to as Agency A. The project is one of the seven flagship applications that are deployed by the Malaysian Government to attract leading edge technology development to Malaysia. The key technologies used to deliver the project are the chips and biometrics technology. The main challenge was to devise a new system and process redesign to accommodate various security aspects and to cater the incorporation of eight applications from government agencies and private sectors into a single XYZ-based system. As there was no other similar system deployed in Malaysia or in other countries, the Malaysia government has to design and develop all the components, including the procedures and methodologies necessary to achieve the objectives of the XYZ-based system.

To realize the overall of XYZ-based system, a well-structured organization was formed to manage and coordinate the implementation of the case and XYZ technology. The organization comprised of several committees and bodies with the support of local technology consortiums that had been awarded to deploy XYZ technology. At the bottom, the planning and management of the case was led by Unit Y and Agency A. Unit Y is under Agency A, a public-sector organization providing all sorts of registration services to

Malaysian public. This organization is a non-IT organization with very minimum IT experts and experiences in IT transfer.

The deployment of XYZ technology first started with a pilot project covering the MSC-KL areas. Today, the deployment has covered the whole states in Malaysia with more applications than before. Initially, the transfer of XYZ technology in this case has brought up some complaints related to the transfer practices among transferors and recipients. Among the complaints heard are: lack of enforcement on the planning and implementation of the transfer, the requirements of XYZ technology were not well stated, the requirements of XYZ technology kept changing from time to time, some vendors were not very committed to the project, lack of sense of ownership among the agencies involved, and no incentives were given to the individuals selected for trainings and other development programs. The analysis is to diagnose and describe the good and poor technology transfer practices in the case from actor network theory perspectives.

ANALYSIS OF THE CASE STUDY

In general, the purpose of a technology transfer process is to achieve an efficient and effective technology transfer. This process involves several levels where each level relates to another and influences one another. However each TOT level has different issue and problem. In order to have a clear understanding on the problem that exists at every level, an analysis using ANT is made at every level of TOT process. Verification on the accuracy of the outcome from the analysis was made at three levels:

1. Identifying the existence of the three levels of TOT (based on the characteristics of activities). The existence was revealed by the interviews and references of documents related to the activities.

2. Existence of information in terms of ANT concepts by referring to information gathered during interview and the company's documents.

3. Confirmation with the interviewees after data analysis.

ANT Analysis in Stage One

Problematization in stage one (Pre-TOT) involves identifying actors to be involved, interests of each actors, issues to be given focus and obstacles and mechanism to face the obstacles. There are five main agencies to be involved directly with five XYZ-based applications implementation into a single system. These agencies have multiple requirements, their own specific data, and shared data for some applications. The technology involves the use of chip and biometric technology. XYZ technology provides a new solution for these purposes. The technology must be developed with specific applications and components since it needs to address the multiple requirements and functions from multiple agencies. Other actors are TOT Consortium (consists of Foreign Technology Partners and a number of local IT companies) have interests in designing and developing the applications and components of smart card technology. The technology was being transferred to Malaysia by foreign technology partners (FTPs). They have interest to widen their business opportunity through their contact with local Technology Consortiums. External advisors have interest to provide advices and assistance in the research and development of smart card technology. In response to the multiple interests, a specific OPP has been created to bring the actors together. The OPP created was a question on the capacity and responsibility to manage the implementation of XYZ technology. The issue focus in stage one is the need to implement a new technology namely XYZ technology to upgrade the Malaysian public services.

Figure 3. Interessement mechanism (activities) to overcome obstacles in stage 1

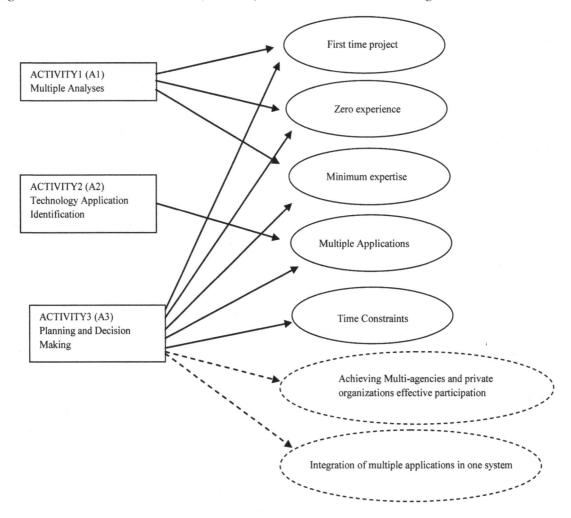

In order to achieve the OPP, a number of obstacles (Figure 3) were identified such as it being the first of such project in the country, having minimum experiences and expertise, involves multiple data and applications owned by multiple public agencies and must be completed within a specific time frame. XYZ technology was such a unique and first time project in Malaysia. It was a big challenge since it involved a development of multiple applications to meet multiple requirements from public and private agencies. Apart from that, there was insufficient information regarding the multiple requirements, resources, infrastructure, cost and benefits and social impacts of the project. In Malaysia, there were also not enough experts to support the necessary technology operation and maintenance.

In order to overcome these obstacles, two activities (Activity-1: multiple analyses and Activity-2: technology application identification) were created as the *interessement mechanisms*. To *enroll and mobilize* the two activities, a special committee was formed as the *enrolment mechanism*, known as Project Management Committee (PMC). PMC has representatives from public agencies as well as from the consortiums. The committee has acted on a collaboration strategy to facilitate the actors' negotiations and interaction in defining business requirements, technology requirements, human requirements, cost and benefit and social impact of the project. With the supports from the committee, the agencies were convinced to identify their business requirements while technology consortiums were convinced to identify the technology requirements. Together they focused on determining the design and features of the smart card technology applications. The rest of the deployment of XYZ technology was under the consortiums' responsibilities. The input and output of the actors' negotiation, persuasion, and agreement in Activity-1 and Activity-2 are represented in multiple forms of *intermediaries* including the government directives to implement the XYZ technology, project proposal, project evaluation, business requirement analysis, social-impact analysis, cost-benefit analysis and financial appraisal.

The last obstacle identified was a challenge to complete the project under the given time frame. To overcome this obstacle, other actors were engaged in other activity: planning and decision making activity (Activity-3). The planning and decision making activity created cover a lot of implementation aspects. Activity-3 was also created to overcome the rest of other obstacles: i.e. first time project, zero experiences, minimum expertise, and multiple applications. To support Activity-3, two strategies as the enrolment and mobilization mechanism: technology transfer (TOT) workgroup and training workgroup were set up. Two types of intermediaries such as the TOT Consortium Plan and TOT Programs are used to support these strategies. In order to mobilize the XYZ-based project, Unit Y in Agency A (one of the five public agencies involved in the XYZ-based project) was appointed as the lead agency of the project.

It is found that at this stage, the issue pertaining the integrated cooperation and collaboration to develop the integrated applications among all the agencies was not given enough priority and was taken for granted. Obstacles in terms of the multi-agencies participation were not identified (dotted lines in Figure 3). There were no formal mechanisms to encourage and foster knowledge and skill exchange between agencies to be set up. The issue regarding the technology innovation and diffusion was also not given due attention. Obstacles to integrate multiple applications in a single XYZ-based system were not identified (dotted lines in Figure 3). There was no plan to initiate post technology of transfer activities especially to encourage innovation and technology diffusions in the country.

ANT Analysis in Stage 2

The issue in stage two is the need for Unit Y and Agency A (as the focal actor) to lead and manage XYZ technology transfer. This issue had forced Unit Y and Agency A to recruit other actors: Technology consortiums, Public agencies, FTPs, TOT consortiums plan, TOT Program, XYZ technology, Trainees, and Trainers. It is realized that TOT Consortiums Plan and TOT Program have been produced earlier in stage-1 translation as the output intermediary. These actors have multiple interests. XYZ technology was embedded with certain capacity and limitation. It has interest to be further developed with multiple applications. The interests of the consortiums were to develop smart card applications, make money, create new business and collaboration and provide knowledge and skills development program. TOT Consortium Plan's interest was to explain and guide the implementation of XYZ technology transfer. It contains the important components of TOT Programs such as the program's objectives, requirements, content, and expectations. Finally, TOT Programs' were to produce knowledgeable and skillful people. Trainers were representatives from TOT Consortium that would install and develop the system. Trainees were staff from relevant public agencies that were supposed to acquire knowledge and skills.

To align the different interests of actors, Unit Y and Agency A have created a specific target (OPP)

Figure 4. Interresement mechanisms (activities) in stage 2

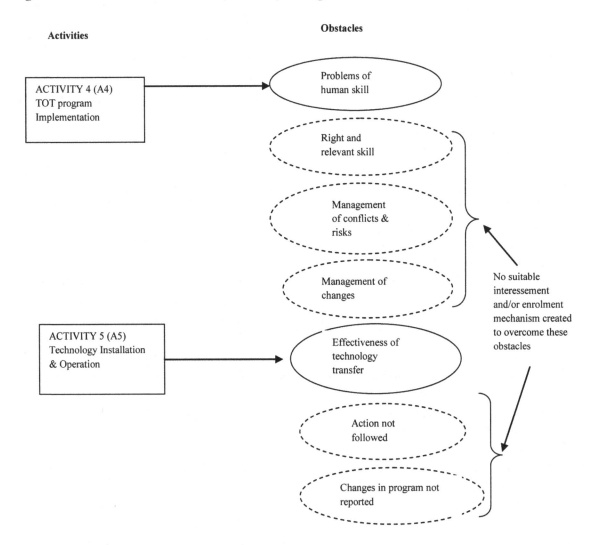

identified as a question on the ability of Unit Y to implement XYZ technology transfer effectively. Actors again have encountered obstacles. The first and second obstacles (Figure 4) identified were associated with the problems of human skills. Unit Y did not have the right and relevant skills to operate XYZ technology. To overcome the first obstacle, Unit Y must convince its employees to acquire certain knowledge and skills prior to operating the technology. This is made through the creation of TOT program implementation. To support the implementation of TOT programs, three programs strategies with five approaches

were set up to meet different levels of recipients. Each approach has a specific objective designed to develop knowledge and skills relevant to the technology functions.

The selection of trainees for TOT program was made under multiple negotiations. Unit Y had also been facing other obstacles. It did not have enough people with the required background to attend the programs. The Unit tried to overcome the obstacle by selecting any available people. Some of the employees, however, were not qualified and some were selected for the wrong program. There was a mismatch between the qualification of the trainee and the program he/she attended. As a result, the benefits of some programs were not fully achieved. The trainees who were selected without the right requirements and background did not fully benefit from the programs. There was no other supportive mechanism created to overcome this obstacle. On the other hand, TOT program was also designed to educate people from other agencies who have participated in the transfer of the smart card technology. Some of these trainees were supposed to be attached to Agency A for a specific time period with regards to the operation of the technology. But Unit Y did not have full control on the selection of the trainees and the benefits afterwards. Upon completing their tasks, the trainee went back to their agency and leave Unit Y with minimum benefits. Unit Y needs to devise additional strategies and mechanisms to mobilize TOT program effectively.

The OPP is a question on the ability of Unit Y to implement XYZ technology transfer effectively. In order to realize the OPP, a number of obstacles were identified: problems of human skills; right and relevant skills; management of conflicts, changes and risks; and an effective technology transfer program.

A number of *interresement* mechanisms were introduced to start implementation actions. They are in the form of activities: TOT program implementation (Activity-1) and technology installation and Operation (Activity-2). Enrolment mechanism to forge collaboration between actors is through TOT program. This strategy is supported by a number of intermediaries such as TOT program materials, knowledge and skills, technology components and applications and user manual.

The study found that a number of changes in the training program were not reported and the effectiveness of the TOT program was not evaluated. Activities to carry out monitoring and evaluation of TOT implementation by agencies were non existence. This has rendered it difficult for Agency A to measure the progress of the TOT implementation as a whole. The problem is also related to the absent of TOT Implementation Plan for each participating agencies. The TOT Consortium Plan is developed by the TOT Consortium in delivering the technology. TOT Implementation Plan for each participating agency should be developed to guide the mobilization of TOT implementation at each agency level as well as a basis for monitoring and evaluation of implementation progress.

ANT Analysis in Stage 3

We found that there is no technology transfer activity which reflects Post-TOT stage. This stage is important to encourage integrated participation from other participant agencies to develop their applications in XYZ-based application system. Although all participating agencies were willing to cooperate and to implement TOT Consortium Plan together, these were not enough to facilitate actual participation. Strategic alliance between participating agencies should be encouraged. When our study took place, that is one year after the project was launched, XYZ-based system is still made up of one application, specifically, just the one for identification application. Participation from other agencies needs to be supported by Post-TOT stage. An actor-network needs to be developed to encourage Post-TOT activities. Furthermore, research and development should be encouraged to work on developing other applications.

CONCLUSION

The study has identified a number of possible reasons that may help to explain the slow progress of the technology transfer. These reasons are due to the weaknesses in the translation process in stage one, stage two and the non-existence of a stage-3 translation. The weaknesses of the translation processes started with the absence of two elements of translation namely the issue and obstacle. The absence of critical issues to be considered in a translation process may result in an incomplete set-up of OPP and no related obstacles identified. As a result actors to solve the issues were not identified; obstacles occurred were ignored and finally led to poor or incomplete translation and ended-up with poor actor network of IT transfer.

In some cases such as in stage 1, the issues and actors to solve the issues were identified, relevant OPP was also created but the obstacles such as lack of effective collaboration between participating agencies that could affect OPP in stage two and three were ignored due to ignorance. As a result the OPP in stage 2 was not achieved and this ended-up with poor or incomplete translation, which eventually created a poor actor-network of IT transfer.

The importance of Stage-3 was not given due attention. As a result, issues and obstacles related to stage-3 were ignored. This will lead to failure in achieving an integrated XYZ-based application.

The study also gives a number of recommendations to improve the XYZ transfer technology. Activity 3 in stage 1 needs to be initiated again in order to produce Post-TOT Program, Organization-based TOT Implementation Plan, Knowledge Sharing and Documentation Management System Plan and Strategic Collaboration between Agencies Plan.

Stage- 2 needs to include issue on the need for monitoring and evaluating of the progress of IT transfer. A number of missing obstacles also need to be given focus. It is recommended that stage-2 is to implement monitoring systems at both the recipient agencies' and technology providers' levels. Development of well-defined change management system is also needed to be planned and implemented. Stage-2 should also implement the Organization-based TOT Implementation Plan.

Stage-3 should be included in the transfer process. Major actors such as the five public agencies, technology providers and TOT-programs' recipients should be involved. Activities related to innovation and diffusion should be developed.

A number of plans such as Knowledge sharing and Document Management System, Strategic Collaboration between Agencies and Post-TOT Plan should be implemented.

Our analysis emphasizes that effective TOT needs to carry out the three stages of technology transfer process and to manage the interrelationships between actors involved in the process. Interrelationships between actors are unique to a particular environment. They are even more important in cases where the technology transfer is involved with a multi-organization environment. They need to be taken into account in devising strategies, methods and approach to carry out activities in TOT process.

Stages in technology transfer may be generic but the actual activities in each stage may be different according to the need of the local environment. ANT provides the framework to identify what activities to be carried out in each stage. In terms of ANT, it can be regarded as interessement moment. Activities identification will take into account problems, issues and obstacles that are unique for that particular environment.

Organizational culture, norms and politics will shape the interrelationships. Events that happen due to interrelationships between actors need to be monitored and their effects need to be evaluated. This is to ensure that any negative effect will be handled accordingly. Any positive effect, conversely, should be encouraged. In this case, ANT provides a good framework to analyze interrelationships critically and in a systematic way. ANT helps to trace where the problems crops up in stages of the TOT process as it occurs, and identify who (actors) is involved in the process. This will help the management to find solutions which will be taking the local environment into account.

ANT analysis is not an easy feat to carry out; as conceptually it depends on how one views the process for unstructured analysis. It may be useful if we can structure the use of ANT in each analysis to capture the experience into a framework that is easy to understand and follow for future reference. It will help other potential users explore many other possibilities in using ANT.

REFERENCES

Baark, E., & Heeks, R. (1998). *Evaluation of Donor-Funded Information Technology Transfer Projects in China: A Lifecycle Approach, Development Informatics Working Paper Series*, paper No.1, Institute for Development Policy and Management, University of Manchester, Manchester U

Berntsen, H. O., & Seim, R. (2007). Design Research through the Lens of Sociology of Technology. Retrieved August 18, 2007, from http:www2.uiah.fi/sefun/DSIU%20Berntsen%20_%Design%20research.pdf

Buono, A. F. (1997). Technology transfer through acquisition, *Management Decision, 35/3*, MCB University Press, 194-204.

Buxton, J. N., & Malcolm, R. (1991, January). Software technology transfer. *Software Engineering Journal*.

Callon, M. (1986). Some elements of a sociology of translation: domestification of the scallops and fisherman of St Brieuc Bay. In Law, J. (Ed.), *Power, Action and Belief: a new sociology of knowledge* (pp. 196–233). London: Routledge and Keagan Paul.

Callon, M., & Latour, B. (1981). Unscrewing the big leviathan: how actors macrostructure reality and how sociologists help them to do so. In Knorr-Cetina, K. D., & Cicourel, A. V. (Eds.), *Advances in Social Theory and Methodology: Toward an Integration of Micro-and Macro-Sociologies* (pp. 277–303). Boston, MA: Routledge and Keagan Paul.

Capps, B., & Fairley, B. E. (2002). PROSM: A systematic approach to planning technology transfer campaigns. Retreieved January 3, 2003, from http://www.cse.ogi.edu/~dfairley/PRISM.pdf

Chung, W. W. C., Lee, W. B., & Chik, S. K. O. (1997). *Technology Transfer at The Hong Kong Polytechnic University*, IEEE.

Derakhshani, S. (1983). Factors Affecting Success in International Transfers of Technology- A Synthesis and a Test of a New Contingency Model. *The Developing Economies*, 21.

Dooley, K. E. (1999). Towards a holistic model for the diffusion of educational technologies: an integrative review of educational innovation studies. *Journal of Educational Technology & Society, 2*(4). Retrieved from http://ifets.ieee.org/periodical/vol_4_99/kim_dooley.html.

Dudley, J. R. (2006). Successful Technology Transfer Requires More Than Technical Know-How. *BioPharm International, 19*(10). Retrieved May 20, 2008, from http://biopharminternational.findpharma.com/biopharm/Article/Successful-Technology-Transfer-Requires-More-Than-/ArticleStandard/Article/detail/377759

Flannery, W. T., & Dietrich, G. (2000). Technology Transfer in a Complex Environment: Exploring Key Relationships. In *Proceedings of the 2000 IEEE Engineering Management Society, EMS-2000,* August 13-15, 2000 Albuquerque, New Mexico.

Frutkin, S. (1975). The Technology Transfer Process-The Case of the LNG Tanker [IEEE]. *OCEAN, V7*, 855–859.

Gibson, D. V., & Harlan, G. T. (1995). Inter-Organizational Technology Transfer: The Case of the NSF Science and Technology Centers, In *Proceedings of the 28th Annual Hawaii International Conference on System Sciences*.

Gibson, D. V., & Smilor, W. (1991). Key Variables in Technology Transfer: A field – Study Based on Empirical Analysis. *Journal of Engineering and Technology Management, 8,* 287–312. doi:10.1016/0923-4748(91)90015-J

Jegathesan, J., Gunasekaran, A., & Muthaly, S. (1997). Technological development & transfer: experiences from Malaysia. *International Journal of Technology Management, 13*(2), 196–214. doi:10.1504/IJTM.1997.001655

Kahen, G. (1997). Building a Framework for Successful Information Technology Transfer to Developing Countries: Requirements and Effective Integration to a Viable IT Transfer, *Int. Journal of Computer and Applications Technology, 9*(1), 1–8.

Lall, S. (1987). *Learning to industrialize.* Basingstoke, UK: Macmillan.

Madu, C. N. (1992). *Strategic planning of technology transfer to less developed countries.* New York: Quorum Books.

Montealegre, R. (1998). Managing information technology in modernizing "against the odds": lessons from an organization in less-developed country. *Information & Management, 34*(2), 103–116. doi:10.1016/S0378-7206(98)00051-2

Montealegre, R. (1999). A case for more case study research in the implementation of Information Technology in less-developed countries. *Information Technology for Development, 8*(4), 199–207. doi:10.1080/02681102.1999.9525310

Narasimhan, R. (1984). *Guidelines for Software Development in Developing Countries, IS.439.* Vienna: UNIDO.

Quitas, P. (1994). A product-process model of innovation in software development. *Journal of Information Technology, 9*(1), 3–17. doi:10.1057/jit.1994.2

Rogers, E. M. (1995). *Diffusion of innovations,* Fourth Edition, (1995), New York: The Free Press, A Division of Macmillan, Inc.

Schmitz, H., & Hewitt, T. R. (1991). Learning to raise infants: a case study in industrial policy. In Colclough, C., & Manor, J. (Eds.), *States or Markets?* Oxford, UK: Oxford University Press.

Schnepp, Von G., Mary Ann and Bhambri, A. (1990). United States- China Technology Transfer, Eaglewood Cliffs. NJ: Prentice-Hall, in Min Chen, *Managing International Technology Transfer,* International Thompson Business Press, 1996.

Sung, T. K. (2009). Technology transfer in the IT industry: A Korea perspective, Technological Forecasting & Social Change. *International Journal (Toronto, Ont.), 76*(5), 700–708.

Sung, T. K., & Gibson, D. V. (2000). Knowledge and Technology Transfer: Key Factors and Levels. Brazil, In *Proceeding of 4th International Conference on Technology Policy and Innovation.*

Walsham, G. (1995). Interpretive case studies in IS research: nature and method. *European Journal of Information Systems, 4*(2), 74–81. doi:10.1057/ejis.1995.9

Section 4

Chapter 14
Reassembling the Problem of the Under–Representation of Girls in IT Courses

Leonie Rowan
Griffith Institute for Educational Research, Australia

Chris Bigum
Griffith Institute for Educational Research, Australia

ABSTRACT

The percentages of girls in developing countries undertaking information technology subjects in the post-compulsory years of education has remained persistently low: often under 25%. This is despite the fact that this particular phenomenon has been the subject of sustained international enquiry for at least three decades. This article investigates data collected during an Australian Research Council Linkage Grant project (2005-2007) that aimed to identify some of the contemporary reasons for this under-representation in Australian schools. The original phases of data collection proceeded from the belief that there was a clear and agreed understanding that the low numbers of girls was a problem worthy of analysis. As the project evolved, however, significant differences between the researchers' perception of the underrepresentation and the participants' views about the same issue. In this paper we make use of actor-network theory to ask key questions about the extent to which the enrolment of girls in IT is indeed 'a problem'.

INTRODUCTION

The percentages of girls in Australian schools who elect to enrol in post compulsory information communication and computing technologies units has barely changed over the past twenty years hovering consistently around (and often below) 25% (James, et al., 2004). Analysis of this statistic

(and its persistence) has often focused on such factors as the impact this under representation has upon the total numbers of students studying information technology or related courses at university (hereafter referred to as IT); the looming personnel shortages in information technology professions (Wentling & Thomas, 2004); the implications that opting out of IT as an area of study has on girls' future career paths, including the potential to reduce their chances of employ-

DOI: 10.4018/978-1-60960-197-3.ch014

ment within lucrative and "in demand" industries, and, indeed, curtailing their ability to contribute to the construction of the kinds of technologically mediated futures that impact upon their lives into the short and long term future (Wajcman, 1991).

Despite the fact that these various versions of 'a problem with girls and IT' have received a reasonable amount of attention from researchers and industry professionals over the past twenty years, during this time there has been little impact upon the numbers of girls following the pathway to tertiary study of information technology. Indeed, the numbers of girls studying IT in schools are actually trending down (AAUW, 2000; James et al., 2004).

In response to this complex set of factors a range of researchers[1] and industry partners from NSW, South Australia and Victoria designed a mixed-method project intended to identify the processes that lead to this gender gap and possible ways in which the situation could be challenged. The project was tilted: *From High School to Higher Education: Gendered pathways in information communication and computer technology education* and ultimately received funding through the Australian Research Council (ARC) Linkage Project scheme. The project aimed to:

- identify the educational pathways and career outcomes for males and females in IT fields;
- ascertain why the proportion of girls who enter education pathways leading to IT careers is so small;
- identify strategies that might lead increased numbers of girls to qualify for, choose, and enter IT courses at the higher education level.

Over the three year period, the research team collected data from across 28 schools and more than 1400 students. As a result of the themes found within questionnaires, focus groups and interviews, the research team identified a range of factors that influenced girls' and boys' subject selections, and the reasons why they would choose or reject post-compulsory IT pathways. In response to this data the team put forward a number of recommendations discussed in detail elsewhere (see Lynch, 2007) but summarised briefly here:

- Provide more accurate and timely career advice and subject information, to counter common misconceptions This includes differentiating between the different kinds of IT career pathways
- Emphasise the relevance of senior IT subjects to university studies in software engineering and information technology.
- Use learning activities that align with work practices in IT industries and that make links with the local community. Make particular use of group based learning, project learning, and 'real world' tasks.
- Make use of new leisure and lifestyle technologies to help break down the divide between everyday technologies and IT studies.
- Recognise that many students will achieve high levels of computer literacy at home and will need a more challenging IT program if their interest in the IT field is to be sustained.
- Affirm girl's interest and competence in difficult technical tasks; affirm boys' interest and competence in communication and design activities; and, affirm the behaviours and attitudes of girls who express an interest in computing technology.
- Provide opportunities for commonly held notions about gender and IT to be aired, debated and challenged.

This list of recommendations—like many formal documents—points to some of the key issues to emerge from the project and offers important advice to practitioners, curriculum developers and, indeed, those working in teacher education.

This list, however, also partially obscures one of the most interesting points to emerge from the project. Recommendations and 'solutions' only make sense in a context where one believes there is a problem. One of the most powerful themes to emerge through the data, however, was that for many of the people at the heart of the research the low numbers of girls in IT related subjects was not, in fact, something to worry about.

Despite the fact that the researchers, the industry partners and the funding body saw the low enrolment of girls in IT units as significant a problem worthy of investing time, resources and money, teachers and students, for the most part, did not. From the very beginning, researchers found it difficult to recruit schools into the project, and spent far more time than anticipated in the recruitment phase. In reports about research projects these kinds of difficulties are often glossed over and read merely as the project background. This paper, however, seeks to position the context not as a hurdle that had to be overcome in order to get to the 'real' source of the problem. Rather, this lack of interest in girls and IT as a research problem is the explicit focus *of* the paper.

The paper has three sections. In the first we look specifically at the various moves and countermoves employed by the researchers in the Victorian arm of the project in order to recruit and maintain participants into the project. In the second we look at some of the data that emerged from the study, with particular attention to the ways in which this data helps make sense of the recruitment difficulties outlined in the previous section. We discuss the difference between the *researchers'* perception of the problem under consideration, and the *participants'* perception of the same issue. In the third we use the resources of actor network theory to re-visit the official recommendations and to highlight what an innovative approach to the girls and IT "problem" might actually look like.

Throughout the paper we will focus primarily on data collected by members of the Victorian

research team as this is the data one of the authors was responsible for collecting.[2]

"THIS WASN'T IN THE ORIGINAL PLAN BUT..." RECRUITMENT CHALLENGES

The project was conceptualised as a mixed method study (Creswell, & Plano Clark, 2007, 5): that is, one that "focuses on collecting, analyzing, and mixing both quantitative and qualitative data in a single study or series of studies (Creswell, & Plano Clark, 2007, p. 5). The original plan was for a project that would involve principals, teachers, career advisors and students (boys and girls) from schools across three Australian states: New South Wales, South Australia and Victoria. The project involved interviews with teachers and career advisors; the administration of a survey to students in years 10 and 11 and focus groups with a range of selected case study schools.

The original project design argued that we would recruit schools through written invitations. The schools to be approached would be selected after analysis of data concerning the percentages of girls enrolled in IT at the school and other factors such as the school's location, and its socio-economic environment. After they rushed responded to our invitation principals from the participating schools would be asked to nominate 2 members of the teaching staff who may be willing to share their insights and valuable local knowledge about the study of IT at the school. These nominees would be invited to participate in a 20 to 40 minute telephone, or in some cases face-to-face, interview. The interview would take the form of a semi-structured conversation consisting mainly of open-ended questions. Topics relating to the characteristics of the schools - such as population and location details – would be discussed, along with participation and performance levels of male and female students in the areas of IT. Teachers were to be asked for their opinions and beliefs about probable factors that might be influencing current student participation and performance rates in IT at their school.

The next phase of the research would see year ten students at each of the participating schools asked to complete a survey focusing on their computer usage at home and at school, their ideas for subject choices in Year 11 and 12 (the post-compulsory years), their opinions of Year eight, nine and ten computer subjects, and their beliefs about how effectively boys and girls work with computer technology studies. Students would also be asked if they were willing to be contacted again with regard to participating later in a 40-minute follow-up discussion session.

In the final data collection phase focus groups would be held with groups of six to eight including boys and girls who have a high or low interest in IT. The focus groups would explore issues around students' constructions of IT education and careers, their attitudes towards computer technology and uses at home and at school, and their plans and aspirations in terms of post-compulsory subject selection.

Our plan was to achieve maximum variation in terms of the location, socioeconomic status (SES), and IT participation rates of girls. We therefore planned to conduct focus groups in schools:

- located in areas identified by the Australian Bureau of Statistics as high and low SES areas.
- within rural/remote areas and urban/metropolitan areas
- with above and below average rates of female participation in post-compulsory information technology subjects. A year 12 participation rate above 40% was described as high, a rate between 20% and 40% was described as moderate, and a rate below 20% was considered low.

It was a good plan and seemed very logical and persuasive on paper. In reality, the Victorian mem-

bers of the project team struggled to find schools willing to participate right from the beginning. Letters disappeared into a void. Telephones rang out. Emails went ignored...or were simply not noticed. We soon abandoned attempts to 'cold call' the 'ideal' schools and started drawing on a range of networks. We approached education department employees for recommendations about interesting schools so that we were able to 'name drop' when phoning schools ("your school has been recommended to us by person x in the department of y"). We drew upon schools that we had worked with for other projects, hopeful that our existing contacts could recruit their IT department into the project. And we called upon personal friendships with teachers to see if they could connect us to the relevant people in their school.

As we continued to modify our original plan it was tempting to abandon the original goal of finding schools that met all of the criteria on our original grid (rural high socio-economic status or SES; rural Low socio-economic status (hereafter SES) + high and low percentages of girls; regional High SES+ Regional Low SES + high and low percentages of girls; metropolitan high SES + metropolitan Low SES + high and low percentages of girls). Indeed, we considered just trying to find schools in the different locations and, in some particularly bleak moments, just finding any school at all.

However, the researchers were able to resist the urge to take any school they could find, and managed to recruit 8 schools that were consistent with the original criteria. The recruitment process took more than 16 months and involved approaches to more than 30 schools, teacher and principals.

The schools (represented here by their pseudonyms) had the following characteristics:

- **Crocodile:** Rural, low SES, low diversity, mid female participation
- **Otter (H):** Rural, low SES, low diversity, mid female participation

- **Bandicoot:** Regional, high SES, low diversity, low female participation
- **Dragon:** Metro, low SES, high diversity, mid female participation
- **Angelfish:** Metro, low SES, high diversity, low female participation
- **Black Mare:** Regional, mid SES, low diversity, low female participation
- **Sheepdog:** Rural, low SES, low diversity, low female participation

Once we achieved an invitation into the schools, there were yet further hurdles to climb. Ethical clearance procedures required us to receive signed parental consent forms for all students who were asked to participate in surveys and focus groups. Like much school based research this raised serious challenges. We initially sent letters home, via the teachers, along with small postcards outlining our interests and asking students to participate. Session after session was postponed and rescheduled when our coordinating teachers/contacts advised that only a few students had returned the consent forms. Regular phone calls and emails to teachers to check on the progress of the consent form resulted in requests for more copies of the form or, better still, for a form (to cover both the surveys and the focus groups) and for more time.

The original plan had been to survey students, and then select some from the survey group to interview. As the months went on it became apparent that getting access to the students for one session was going to be hard enough, let alone trying to get them back twice. In addition to this, two separate sessions had twice the impact upon school timetables, and at the time of the research, many schools were implementing major reforms and had little 'free time'. The times that we were offered were generally at the end of terms and usually fairly short: somewhere between 40 and 60 minutes on average. The phrase "this wasn't in the original plan but…" seemed to dominate every project team meeting. Ultimately we agreed

to 'fast track' the data collection and to follow the surveys with brief focus group discussions.

We adopted a different recruitment strategy whereby we offered a free lunch (usually pizza) to students (and teachers) willing to participate. Before and during the lunches we grouped students and conducted focus groups. Many of the discussions were conducted during the lunch itself with significant impact upon the quality of audio recordings that resulted. We also commonly had two researchers interviewing groups at the same time in the same location in a desperate move to get the most out of limited time we had.

At the end of a two year period we had collected almost exactly the range of data we had aimed for. The huge amount of negotiation involved in this process, however, was far more than we originally planned. The moves and countermoves outlined here provide much more than interesting and mildly amusing background to the project. Rather, the need for this ongoing re-invention of project design provided us with the first key finding from the project. Whilst all our initial moves took for granted the fact that the underrepresentation of girls in the IT subjects of our targeted schools was an important and legitimate problem requiring close attention, most teachers and students in the schools approached, did not share our opinion. Where the researchers saw 'problem' students and teachers just saw 'life'. As the project progressed it became clear that for the majority of the participants there was nothing remarkable about the extent to which students, boys or girls, enrolled in or avoided IT. Rather, the low numbers were seen as logical, natural and easily explained by a range of commonly cited factors. We'll turn to an exploration of these factors in the second section.

"I JUST DON'T LIKE COMPUTERS"… PERSPECTIVES ON THE 'PROBLEM'

The moves and counter moves outlined above provided a clear indication that there was a significant difference between the *researchers'* perception of the problem under consideration, and the *participants'* perception of the same issue. As we will outline below, teachers, students and (by proxy, their parents) looked at the IT enrolment patterns and saw, not a narrowing of employment pathways, or missed professional opportunities, or limited financial futures, or a perpetuation of limited and limiting gender norms. Rather, the majority of the participants saw patterns that could be explained by several 'logical' and 'obvious' factors that would explain girls' (and, indeed, boys') lack of interest.

First: it was widely acknowledged that students' previous experiences with 'computers' (both in dedicated IT subjects and as part of their cross-curricular learning) up to and including year 10 often lead to particular beliefs about the likely focus of year 11 and 12 IT subjects. Students and teachers agreed that many kids came to secondary school thinking that they knew all that they needed to know about IT and made the point that they didn't want to waste any more time. One exception to this were some of the (few) students who *did* study IT because they thought it was easy and a "bludge" (Angelfish focus group 2; Blackmare focus group 2; Dragon focus group 2).

From this point of view, the problem was that students have already done enough IT in the compulsory years of schooling, and could see no compelling reason to do any more. As one boy commented: "I did a year 11 course in year 10 and we were still learning how to download programs and how to run programs. It was pretty boring" (Angelfish Focus group)

Second, IT subjects were routinely described as "boring" (a very common description): this was often linked to the fact that the content was repetitive—"It's the same old stuff over and over again" (Boy, Bandicoot focus group 2)–and seen to be irrelevant. As one boy commented: "Most of it is stuff that you're not going to learn or use"… (Dragon, focus group 2).

When asked to reflect in more detail upon the issue of relevance students continually critiqued the focus and content of the subjects:

Interviewer: So what about it makes it boring at the school?

Girl G: I don't know, all the programs. If you've learnt new things and you know. You don't need to use that many programs. You only need to know a couple and they teach you all these you [know your not going] to use.

Interviewer: Give me an example of a dodgy one?

All: MicroWorld.

Interviewer: What was that about? I don't even know what that is.

Girl G: Making chickens green.

Girl C: And you have to type these little codes in …

Girl M: And the thing I don't like about it is the fact that you have to write in all these … like from a text book, you get a text book and its got all this information and then you have to type it with your class and like I just think this is … you're typing in what's already in the text book. Just looking and you're typing it in so it's on the computer …. (Blackmare Mare, focus group 3)

This exchange captures a common theme in the data collected: students were often able to understand why they were doing particular activities, and they resented what they saw as low level and repetitive 'data entry' type tasks particularly those that asked them to work in silence and isolation.

Indeed, from the point of view of many students the 'problem' related to the low numbers of students studying IT was fundamentally connected to pedagogy. When asked to comment on what makes a good IT teacher one group of girls answered:

Girl J: Someone who's got the patience to stay there and like teach us. There's nothing worse when you don't get it and they're getting frustrated ...[inaudible]....

Girl C: Make it interesting, I reckon, what you do.

Boy A: Do different things every week. (Otter focus group 3)

A further, but less commonly cited, reason put forward to account for the low enrolment was the simple fact of competition between subjects to recruit students. Some saw that particular subjects were far more appealing particularly for those who were more 'active'. As one boy commented: "when I talked to other classes they'd rather do sport than sit in front of a computer typing code" (Bandicoot focus group 6). A group of girls also acknowledged that IT had a low profile:

Girl J: ...see I don't think IT for our unit was every really put out there as a subject ... I think our school is more orientated on trades and more science subjects I think. Like with physics, chemistry, biology, they've very sort of [sold] that.... (Angelfish focus group 2)

One group of girls who *were* interested in IT indicated that students needed to be made more aware of what exactly goes on in IT classes in order to counteract stereotypes. As Girl S from Blackmare suggested "Just like advertise the stuff more. Like what we do in the classes. Like we make websites and movies and stuff and not just typing and...I don't know, Excel work and stuff. We do kind of projects as well" (focus group 1).

From this perspective, the problem could be that, as a subject area that bids for a share of post-compulsory student enrolment, IT does not have a strong or consistent image. Nor does it appear

to have a unified group of teachers who might promote the interests of the discipline. Indeed, at each school within the project "IT Teacher" meant something quite different: some were working solely in IT subjects; most were working in a combination of IT and maths; and others were working in IT and commerce, or English or another discipline area altogether.

A different reason put forward by participants to account for the low enrolments in IT units was the belief that IT would not help them in their attempt to get into university. Rather, IT was seen as a subject field that was too easy, and which would add little to their tertiary entrance score. As one person commented:

Girl T: It's just a bludge and people are trying to get serious like VCE. Like it just doesn't help... (Blackmare focus group 2)

The problem from this perspective concerns the ways in which various subjects and areas are ranked against each other and either scaled up or down as a result of their relative difficulty during the process of calculating a tertiary entrance score.

Similarly, students wanting to enter the workforce did not see IT as an area of high employment. Whilst the industry partners and the research team was convinced that IT was an area of considerable employment growth and a field characterized by diverse career options, for teachers and *students* (and indeed their parents) IT was seen as a field that had few employment opportunities. As one girl commented:

Girl E: a lot of our parents and that say, "Oh there's no jobs out in the IT world because there was a big boom last time" and yeah that's what they tell us so we just don't need to do it.. (Crocodile focus group 1)

To summarise, then, teachers and students throughout the project consistently argued that students would be 'naturally' discouraged from studying IT as a result of the subjects' image; the kinds of curriculum and pedagogy employed; their career aspirations; and their own personal interests.

For the purposes of this paper, the key point is that this selection of data defines the IT problem in a number of different—but all compelling and logical—ways. By extension each version of the problem outlined above seems to lead to equally logical recommendations (already cited above) that might increase IT enrolments overall: these include interventions designed to improve pedagogy, raise the profile of the area and improve publicity and promotion materials; ensure greater articulation between early and later IT units; and so on.

In other words, each assemblage of the problem (and associated 'solutions') effectively position girls' decision making as something that occurs in a neutral environment characterized by 'free choice'. Indeed, when asked whether or not there was any form of social pressure on girls or boys to choose, or not choose IT as an area of study, students consistently commented that people "didn't care" what areas students studied and that an individual's choices would be respected.

It would be tempting to leave the analysis of the data at this point, and to take at face value the students' observations of the key barriers to girls' participation. However, a closer reading of the data reveals the presence of a number of contradictory perspectives. These contradictions emerge first when the 'image' of the subjects were raised, and second when the impact of gender was explicitly discussed by the research team.

As outlined above, students generally insisted that students could please themselves in terms of what they chose to study and it was widely accepted that "interest" was the bottom line. Students consistently attributed decision making to the broad phenomenon of 'interest'. Students stated that they just "don't find it interesting" (Girl T Bandicoot focus group) and that other girls would avoid IT because "they're not interested in computers (Boy D Bandicoot focus group).

A similar sentiment is expressed by a teacher at Fairy Wren (a school from the New South Wales arm of the study) who argues that:

Male Teacher: I guess it probably or maybe gets down to interests. Like we try to encourage the kids to take the courses that they're interested in. I guess, I don't know, it probably comes down to the girls probably aren't interested in it, I guess, the programming as well as computing. (Fairy Wren Interview)

Positioning girls' choices as one related to the seemingly neutral issue of interests suggests that researchers need to focus on improving those problems outlined above which might be to blame for a lack of interest.

However, there are other strands to the data which suggest that even if the subjects were made more 'fun' and 'relevant' that there might still be problems relating to the relationship between understandings about gender, and the image of IT. We turn now to data that was, from the point of view of the researchers, indicative of another set of serious problems. These problems, however, were rarely taken seriously by the students or the teachers.

There are two specific dimensions to this problem as seen by the researchers: the first concerns the image of IT; the second concerns the relationship between this image, and dominant understandings of masculinity and femininity.

In terms of the first point, students throughout the project shifted between arguing, on the one hand, that there was no longer any negative image associated with IT *per se*—it was only individuals who might have an image problem—whilst also acknowledging, on the other hand, that the image of IT subjects wasn't that positive.

For example when asked: "what about the whole computer nerd thing? Do you think that still exists anymore?" some students responded:

Boy J: You get that off TV shows and that but no not really.

Girl C: Depends on the way people have been brought up or their personalities. (Angelfish focus group 2)

One student referred to the 'nerdy' image of her cousin:

Girl E: ...antisocial I reckon. My cousin is on the computer all weekend, doesn't talk to anybody. Like 12 hours a day on the computer. (Crocodile focus group 1)

But although they attempted to argue that it was personality that determined 'nerdiness' rather than subject choice, when asked to account for girls lack of interest, many students explicitly suggested that "Girls don't want to be known as nerds or something" (Boy Otter Focus group 3) and that they "probably think it's nerdy" (Boys Bandicoot, focus group 4). Indeed, the 'nerd' word was liberally sprinkled throughout the project. Even though students were generally raising the word in order to dismiss its power, in this very act they reveal the fact that any decision to pursue IT carries with it at least the risk of being branded 'uncool'.

In stark contrast to the earlier data that suggested that is was simple things like curriculum and pedagogy or timetables which were at fault this related data defines 'the problem' quite differently, emphasizing wider cultural attitudes towards the industry itself. This leads to the second strand of subordinated explanations: students' beliefs about impact that dominant discourses about masculinity and femininity have upon subject choices.

As an opening point it is important to acknowledge that throughout the project students and teachers were generally emphatic that gender was *not* a key influence and that gender was not part of the problem. However, these denials of the impact of cultural norms associated with in-

formation technology or gender were frequently accompanied by entirely unselfconscious depictions of boys and girls as naturally different.

Girl 1: I think guys ... it's probably the way guys' brains work more than anything. Cause you know how they do physics well a larger portion, maybe that's how they ... [think] ... (Otter focus group 1)

Boy 3: While the boys are on computers, all girls want to do is just put on makeup and do dress ups and stuff. ... (Bandicoot focus group 6)

An extreme version of this biologically determinist perspective is seen in this quote where a group of boys link their interest in computers and game playing to hormones in their brains:

Boy 2: Guys have less of some hormone in their brain and got video games tend to trigger it and it basically gives people a high. It's one of the...

Boy 3: It's one of those situations you can get because guys have less of it and it's the main thing behind video game addiction cause they get addicted to the adrenalin in their brain. (Bandicoot focus group 7)

Similar sentiments were expressed by several teachers. For example, one teacher commented that "girls love things like MS Messenger, sending messages, communication" (Woman Teacher K, Sediment interview). She went onto say that in a subject focusing on Flash skills, the girls would focus on building "picture houses" whereas the boys would do "stick death".

Similarly narrow and essentialist perspectives were aired when students were asked to identify any possible ways to make IT more attractive to girls. One group of boys were particularly enlightening:

Boy 1: Paint the computers pink.

Boy 5: That's what I said.

Boy 2: I see sequins around the screen!

Boy 4: I just reckon if you made the stuff more girl like it would be more appealing to them. Instead of like doing an assignment on making Ziggy's Luge Emporium, make like a dress or just something they like. (Bandicoot focus group 6)

A more extreme version of this kind of thinking is found in a different conversation. It started with a reflection on the extent to which portraying IT career women as 'sexy' would improve girls' interest in the subject area. The boys quickly turned this into a reflection upon what would appeal to them:

Interviewer: One of the things…some group are trying to put together, to encourage girls to do IT is a calendar. Well this is one of IT women all dressed as models or in bikini's or as movie stars, that kind of thing. Do you think that would help girls?

Boy 1: Like you get a bunch of chicks in bikinis…

Boy 2: …with computers.

Boy 1: That's just what those guys in the class would go for.

Interviewer: So you think that would be more appealing for guys than the girls?

Boy 2: If it was women models, yeah.

Boy 1: A bunch of half naked girls standing near computers is just like…turn anyone on.

Boy 2: And you see a big intro saying "I want an Intel Processor". (Bandicoot focus group 6)

There are two points to be made here. On the one hand, as outlined at the start of this section, students were able to put forward a whole range of logically sounding explanations to account for girls' lack of interest in IT subjects while casually, but consistently, denying that it was anything to do with gender. On the other hand, whilst talking about issues to do with technology, computers and the study of IT, they were just as consistent in representing boys and girls as naturally different, and biologically better suited to different activities.

In the light of this set of data, the 'girls and IT' problem becomes more complex: for the researchers this data points to the ways in which girls' attitudes towards information technology must be read as shaped, not only by issues relating to curriculum or pedagogy, but also by widely circulated and powerful stories about what it means to be a girl. Data which indicates the persistence of narrow, limiting, gendernorms that continue to circulate, even less contested than they may have been ten years ago was, for the researchers, another important take on 'the problem'. For the students, however, the comments about what boys are like, or what girls are like, and how both prefer to act, were nothing more than barely remarkable portrayal of reality.

When this gender based version of the problem is set alongside other versions of the problem, the task of implementing recommendations becomes vastly more complicated. Suddenly the challenge is not simply recruiting students into IT units through more sophisticated and coordinated approaches to career planning or changes to pedagogy and curriculum that might perhaps be facilitated by professional development or alternative assessment regimes. Suddenly the challenge is recruiting students who see themselves as naturally and biologically *unsuited* to the area.

To make matters even more complex, each version of the problem appears to demand different kinds of responses. This poses significant challenges when, as researchers reporting on our findings, we are asked the inevitable "well what do we do now questions" (both conceptually and practically) to engage with these understandings of the "girls and IT problem in schools". It is this 'what happens next' question which informs the final section of the chapter.

REASSEMBLING THE PROBLEM

The discussion in the previous section indicates that there are more than one way in which 'the problem' is understood. By extension, there is more than one way in which a solution can be imagined. This raises a challenging set of questions for those wishing to improve girls' participation rates:

- How do we determine which of the competing explanations to believe? Do we accept all of them, and develop responses to all? Do we pick one above the others and focus efforts on that one?
- How can we get the people who would presumably need to be involved in any intervention to care about the problem anyway?
- Given the failure of so many previous interventions to disrupt these long standing patterns of access, is there any point in trying?

It was an attempt to respond to these questions that initially led us to turn to the resources offered by Actor-Network Theory (ANT) to discuss some of the issues that need to be reconsidered if an intervention is to be realistically considered or, indeed, considered as realistic. In this concluding section we seek, not so much to provide a definitive set of answers to these questions, but rather to explore the different kinds of recommendations that might emerge by bringing ANT resources to bear on the 'problem' of girls under enrolment in IT units.

ANT has grown from a modest set of interests largely concerned with social studies of science and technology, something of an *enfant terrible* in social theory, to a point where interest in it now spans a broad range of disciplines. ANT-informed studies tend to ask anthropological questions, such as: "what is going on here?". What distinguishes ANT-informed studies from anthropology and related social sciences is that they do away with the differences between people and things in order to "…find a way of talking about the social-and-the-technical all in one breath" (Law, 1991, 8).

Early ANT literature was characterised by studies that traced the relational shifts associated with projects, things in the making. A key consideration was the principle of generalised symmetry (Callon, 1986), in which all projects, regardless of their outcomes, were examined the same way. More specifically, in following the actors engaged in the formation of a particular socio-technical assemblage that the same status and hence mode of interrogation is afforded each actor, human or non-human.

We are also conscious of a commitment in all ANT-informed work to be holistic in approaching any complexity, and to avoid essentialist simplifications. So this broad sketching of ANT acknowledges the multiple enactments (Mol, 2001) of ANT and signals our intent to trace the study reported here in a similar manner. In other words, we draw on recent work loosely called "the performative turn" in science and technology studies[3]. This turn or move is ontological. It shifts from the view that objects are single entities with particular essential attributes to one in which an object is a texture or pattern of partially co-ordinated, partly coherent performances. Just as most sociologies accept the human as decentred and the product of multiple subjectivities, so too in this stance, are objects. That is, an object does not exist in and of itself as some kind of stand-alone entity but is performed through multiple practices.

In a now famous study, Annemarie Mol (2001) reports an ethnography of a common disease, atherosclerosis. She argues, employing a performative approach, that the disease is multiple: more than one due to the multiple performances of the disease but less than many due to the interconnectedness of the enactments. Further, there is no single thing or cause at the base of these performances. The disease *is* the various performances.

How does this help us make sense of the girls and IT Data?

Firstly, the resonances between Mol's study and the girls and IT data outlined above are strong. Clearly there is no one, single, coherent performance of either "IT in schools" or "girls and IT in schools". Rather both these phenomenon have multiple enactments that partially overlap, contradict and cohere. From teachers, and students we have heard variously that IT is too easy. IT is too hard. IT is too boring. IT is too theoretical. It is too familiarly practical. IT has no particular image. IT has a negative image. Enrolment is influenced by 'interests'. Enrolment is influenced by biology. Teachers are committed to the IT programs. Teachers are consumed by other factors. There are lots of jobs. There are no jobs. It is a crisis. It is not a crisis. It just is what it is.

Whilst the design, conduct and analysis of the study generally continued to pursue the starting premise that the low numbers of girls enrolled in IT *was* a problem, taking the ANT dictum to 'follow the actors' and to accord the same status to each actor must inevitably challenge the 'the researchers know best' stance which underpins this study and much of social science research. Every move the researchers made in the project was designed to convince students, teachers, principals and parents that opting out of IT at high school and in university was a bad thing for students generally and girls even more specifically. From this premise action seems immediately called for.

An ANT perspective on the data challenges us to pursue a different pathway. There are three points to be made about this.

First, as the ANT-informed approach suggests, girls participation in IT can be seen as an intricately inter-related set of enactments that overlap with a broad set of "realities" in schools to do with IT

generally and gender-based thinking and related practices. The approach we have taken here is to resist the urge to blame, name or simplify. Tinkering or focussing on one or a few won't solve the problem. When the enactments of the set of inter-related "realities" are taken together, it is clear that broad brush sets of recommendations, no matter how comprehensive they may appear on paper are likely to have the same limited impact of all previous reforms, and to persist, if at all, only so long as there are external resources to keep them in place locally.

Second, in order to move on from the patterns identified in this research, we need to acknowledge not just the current patterning of relationships but the previous layers of patterning that have been laid down over many years, what John Law (2004, p. 27 & ff.) calls the hinterland. He draws upon and extends the work of Latour and Woolgar in their account of science to develop this concept, describing it as (Law, 2004):

A bundle of indefinitely extending and more or less routinised and costly literary and material relations that include statements about reality and the realities themselves; a hinterland includes inscription devices and enacts a topography of reality possibilities, impossibilities, and probabilities. A concrete metaphor for absence and presence. (p. 160)

Or, perhaps, more succinctly, "if a statement is to last it needs to draw on—and perhaps contribute to—an appropriate hinterland" (Law, 2004, p. 28).

In the beginning of this project, the research enacts the participation by girls in IT in school as a serious problem, one of significance and importance to a range of stake holder groups external to schools. What became equally apparent was that locally, in the schools in which we worked, participation by girls in IT was not enacted, in the main, as a problem by the principals, teachers, students or parents. At the school level it is enacted as a more or less natural consequence of a variety of practices and competing enactments of IT. The difficulty of interesting schools in the research, and of collecting data underlines the misalignment that bedevilled the research from the beginning. Borrowing from Law (2004, p. 29), it is the character of this hinterland and its practices which determines what girls and IT *is* in schools.

Open endings, as Mol (2001, p. 184) suggests, does not imply immobilization. What this ANT-informed analysis does say is, yes, it, the low participation by girls in IT is hard, is difficult and complex, something the many previous studies about this phenomenon would confirm and which are underlined by the many recommendations of this study. Further, it is also clear that the problem of interest in this research, generated from rationalising systems of aggregated statistics has a lot of work to do in order to engage the realities of contemporary schooling for some young women.

And this is the third and final point we make and which we draw on the work of Latour (2004) to develop. The matter of fact at the core of the research reported here is the <25% of girls who elect to enrol in post compulsory IT units. In the logic of this research project, this fact, assembled at a point of calculation remote from all the sites from which data was gathered, is the framing rationale for what was proposed. In many ways, this type of research is typical of research that identifies a pattern, more often than not via statistical techniques, and then seeks an explanation as to why the pattern is not as might or should be. Latour (2003) argues that this style of research epitomizes the laboratory age of the 20th century in which there was a sharp distinction between expert, scientific analysis that took place in research centres of various kinds and the outside where "began the realm of mere experience - not experiment." But, as he goes on to argue (Latour, 2003), this separation is rapidly fading,

The sharp divide between a scientific inside, where experts are formulating theories, and a political

outside, where nonexperts are getting by with human values, is evaporating. And the more it does, the more the fate of humans is linked to that of things, the more a scientific statement ("The Earth is warming") resembles a political one ("The Earth is warming!"). The matters of fact of science become matters of concern of politics (np)

These changing circumstances are those in which this study took place. Latour's work points a way forward in terms of what he calls hybrid forums, in the case of this research we suggest a greater participation of the local sites in exploring the patterns of subject enrolments in the post-compulsory years and that, symmetrically, questions can be asked of not only the pattern but also the pattern makers, of their logics, concerns and practices.

This is unchartered territory. We are not harking back to forms of participatory research that, despite their good intentions, largely maintained the asymmetry of the researcher and the researched, the humans and the non-humans, the centre of calculation and the sources of data. Some of the current scientifically driven debates about things like global warming or genetic engineering point towards what we have in mind.

Thus, this paper is not about closing off debate about girls and IT in school but of broadening the debate. Presenting the multiple enactments of girls in IT at school as the reality that is found in schools is not a solution to the problem but a way of challenging and perhaps shifting the intellectual patterns that have thus far characterised research in this field. If we accept the ontological argument that the enrolment of girls in IT is seen as a set of overlapping, contradicting and partially cohering enactments then any reforms based upon simplification cannot succeed. Further, the simplifying move that, on average, girls ought to participate more in IT denies the nuanced and indeed, in many instances, sensitive approaches to the IT needs and interests of young women locally that is identified in this research.

Finally, this paper has brought to mind, what Bruno (Latour, 2005; 2008) has been saying about the separation of matters of fact and matters of concern in recent publications (Latour, 2004):

We explain the objects we don't approve of by treating them as fetishes; we account for behaviors we don't like by discipline whose makeup we don't examine; and we concentrate our passionate interest on only those things that are for us worthwhile matters of concern. (np)

This, indeed, may well sum up much of the experiences of this project. We started with the assumption that a certain percentage of girls in IT was a problem. All the data we collected 'explained' why this problem arose. But this same data could just as easily be read as evidence that boys AND girls were actually making extremely sensible and intelligent decisions about not studying IT for entirely 'valid' reasons. And there are as likely many other logics at play that we did not draw from our data. The key point is that despite three years that constitute—in an academic world—a project completed, we still do not fully understand the hinterland of girls in IT OR ways to challenge it or, indeed what, precisely, is most worth challenging nor what, in fact, actually *can* be challenged. And whilst this whole project was premised upon the need to mount a challenge to the percentages of girls in IT, it may well be that the project asks us to return to a related but distinct concern: the ways in which schooling systems participate in the construction, circulation and naturalization of historically marginalizing gendernorms. In this way, the recommendations of this project can never be read outside of recommendations for us to follow these actors to a space that is no longer deemed worthy of much discussion or time or space in school, university or teacher education curriculum: the issue of gender.

REFERENCES

AAUW. (2000). *Tech-savvy: educating girls in the new computer age*. Washington: AAUW Educational Foundation.

Callon, M. (1986). In Law, J. (Ed.), *Some Elements of a Sociology of Translation: Domestication of the Scallops and the Fishermen of St. Brieuc Bay* (pp. 196–233). London: Routledge & Kegan Paul.

Creswell, J., & Plano Clark, V. (2007). *Designing and conducting mixed methods research*. Thousand Oaks, CA: Sage.

James, R., Baldwin, G., Coutes, H., Krawse, K., & McInnis, C. (2004). *Analysis of equity groups in higher education 1991-2002*. Canberra: DEST.

Latour, B. (2003). The World Wide Lab. RESEARCH SPACE: Experimentation Without Representation is Tyranny. *Wired, 11*(06). Retrieved from http://www.wired.com/wired/archive/11.06/research_spc.html

Latour, B. (2004). Why has critique run out of steam? From matters of fact to matters of concern. *Critical Enquiry, 30*(2), 225-248. Retrieved from http://criticalinquiry.uchicago.edu/issues/v30/30n2.Latour.html

Latour, B. (2005). *Reassembling the Social: An Introduction to Actor-Network-Theory*. Oxford: Oxford University Press.

Latour, B. (2008). *What is the style of matters of concern? Two lectures in empirical philosophy*. Amsterdam: Van Gorcum.

Latour, B., & Woolgar, S. (1986). *Laboratory Life: The Construction of Laboratory Facts* (2nd ed.). Princeton, NJ: Princeton University Press.

Law, J. (Ed.). (1991). *A Sociology of Monsters: Essays on Power, Technology and Domination*. London: Routledge.

Law, J. (2004). *After Method: mess in social science*. London: Routledge.

Lynch, J. (Ed.). (2007). *Gender and IT: Challenges for Computing and Information Technology education in Australian secondary schools*. Melbourne: ACSA & Common Ground.

Mol, A. (2001). *The Body Multiple: Artherosclerosis in Practice*. Durham, N.Ca. and London: Duke University Press.

Wajcman, J. (1991). *Feminism Confronts Technology*. Pennsylvania: Pennsylvania State University Press.

Wentling, R. M., & Thomas, S. P. (2004). Women in information technology. *Proceedings of the Academy of Human Resource Development, Austin, 1-2,* 90-97.

ENDNOTES

[1]   Industry partners: New South Wales Department of Education and Training; Australian National Schools Network; South Australian Department of Education and Children's Services ; Office for Women, NSW Premier's Department. Academic partners: Deakin University (Catherine Harris, Julianne Lynch, Leonie Rowan); University of Western Sydney (Margaret Vickers, Toni Downes – *now CSU*, Susanne Gannon, Carol Reid, Kerry Robinson). Research Assistants: Cristyn Davies (UWS), My Trinh Ha (UWS), Clare Sidoti (UWS), Karen Tregenza (Deakin), Vianne Tourle (CSU), and Josina van den Akker (UWS); Consultant: Fred Kleydish

[2]   The views expressed in this paper are the views of the authors, and not necessarily the views of the project team.

[3]   Here the work of John Law, Annemarie Mol, Donna Haraway, Marilyn Strathern, Bruno Latour, Michel Callon, Vicky Singleton, Anni Dugdale, Ingunn Moser is useful.

Chapter 15
Using S'ANT for Facilitating Superior Understanding of Key Factors in the Design of a Chronic Disease Self–Management Model

Nilmini Wickramasinghe
RMIT University, Australia

Rajeev Bali
Coventry University, UK

Steve Goldberg
INET International, Canada

ABSTRACT

The S'ANT approach (Wickramasinghe and Bali, 2009) - namely the incorporation of Actor-network Theory and Social Network Analysis as proposed by Wickramasinghe and Bali 2009 in order to support a network centric healthcare solutions is proffered in the following as an appropriately rich lens of analysis in the context of the development of a chronic disease self-management model.

SOCIAL NETWORK ANALYSIS (SNA)

SNA is a technique that facilitates the mapping and measuring of relationships and flows between people, groups, organizations, systems as well as all information/knowledge processing organizations and thereby enhances metacognition with respect to the representation of organizational knowledge in networks (Wasserman and Faust, 1994; Niessen 2007). People and groups are represented as nodes while the relationships or flows are represented by links. Taken together, this analysis of nodes and links builds the network under consideration. The location of actors in such a network is critical to a deeper understanding of the network as a whole and the participation of individual actors. Location is measured by finding the centrality of the node.

DOI: 10.4018/978-1-60960-197-3.ch015

In terms of centrality, three considerations become important in any SNA; degree of centrality – in other words how many people connect with you, betweenness – or whether or not you are located between 2 key actors in the network and thus may play a "broker" role, and closeness – or ones position relative to others (especially key players) in the network. In addition, it is important to note if there exist boundary spanners - actors who bridge or overlap into different networks, or peripheral players. Such actors maybe perceived as unimportant but in reality they play key roles.

To illustrate the value for SNA in the context of supporting diabetes self-care let us return to figure 3. What becomes of crucial importance in supporting diabetes self-care is the distance or centrality of key actors since the key actors are the important decision makers and in such a context rapid prudent decision-making can facilitate prudent care options. Clearly then, the understanding of who/where the boundary spanners are as well as the betweenness and closeness constructs are key in designing a superior network that will enable at all times appropriate and speedy decision-making to ensue. It is also useful to note that SNA can be used in post facto analysis to facilitate necessary lessons learnt that can be applied to the future state. Thus the incorporation of SNA into the continuous design and development of the diabetes self-care model is going to facilitate the realization of a well structured network that will indeed support all the complex and dynamic operations in healthcare.

ACTOR-NETWORK THEORY

Actor-network Theory (ANT) provides a rich and dynamic lens of analysis. Essentially, it embraces the idea of an organizational identity and assumes that organizations, much like humans, possess and exhibit specific traits (Brown, 1997). Although labeled a "theory", ANT is more of a framework based upon the principle of generalized symmetry, which rules that human and non-human objects/subjects are treated with the same vocabulary. Both the human and non-human counterparts are integrated into the same conceptual framework.

ANT was developed by British sociologist, John Law and two French social sciences and technology scholars Bruno Latour and Michel Callon (Latour, 1987, 2005; Law and Hassard, 1999; Law, 1992, 1987; Callon, 1986. It is an interdisciplinary approach that tries to facilitate an understanding of the role of technology in specific settings, including how technology might facilitate, mediate or even negatively impact organizational activities and tasks performed. Hence, ANT is a material-semiotic approach for describing the ordering of scientific, technological, social, and organizational processes or events.

CONCEPTS OF ACTOR-NETWORK THEORY

Table 1 presents the key concepts of ANT and their relevance to the diabetes self-care model

THE S'ANT APPROACH TO RESEARCHING THE DIABETES SELF-CARE MODEL

The S'ANT approach is a hybrid approach that combines the respective strengths of SNA and ANT in order to facilitate the realization of superior diabetes self-care. Such an approach requires the identification and tracing of specific healthcare events and networks to "follow the actors" (Latour, 1996) and investigate all the relevant leads each new actor suggests. The first step is thus to identify these actors (or actants), remembering that an actor is someone or something that can make its presence individually felt and can make a difference to the situation under investigation. Thus, in healthcare networks the actors would include: medical practitioners, nurses, medical instruments, healthcare organizations, regulators,

Table 1. Key concepts of ANT

Concept	Relevance to Diabetes self-care
Actor/Actant: Typically actors are the participants in the network which include both the human and non-human objects and/or subjects. However, in order to avoid the strong bias towards human interpretation of Actor, the neologism ACTANT is commonly used to refer to both human and non-human actors. Examples include humans, electronic instruments, technical artifacts, or graphical representations.	In the diabetes self-care model this includes the web of healthcare players such as provides, healthcare organizations, regulators, payers, suppliers and the patient as well as the clinical and administrative technologies that support and facilitate healthcare delivery.
Heterogeneous Network: is a network of aligned interests formed by the actors. This is a network of materially heterogeneous actors that is achieved by a great deal of work that both shapes those various social and non-social elements, and "disciplines" them so that they work together, instead of "making off on their own" (Latour, 2005).	The wireless technology combined with the specific application is clearly the technology network in this context. However it is important to conceptualize the heterogeneous network not as the technology alone but as the aligning of the actors through the various interactions with the technology so that it is possible to represent all interests and thereby provide the patient with superior healthcare delivery. The key is to carefully align goals so that healthcare delivery is truly patient centric at all times.
Tokens/Quasi Objects: are essentially the success outcomes or functioning of the Actors which are passed onto the other actors within the network. As the token is increasingly transmitted or passed through the network, it becomes increasingly punctualized and also increasingly reified. When the token is decreasingly transmitted, or when an actor fails to transmit the token (e.g., the oil pump breaks), punctualization and reification are decreased as well.	In the diabetes self-care model this translates to successful healthcare delivery, such as treating a patient in a remote location by having the capability to access critical information to enable the correct decisions to be made. Conversely, and importantly, if incorrect information is passed throughout the network errors will multiply and propagate quickly hence it is a critical success factor that the integrity of the network is maintained at all times.
Punctualization: is similar to the concept of abstraction in Object Oriented Programming. A combination of actors can together be viewed as one single actor. These sub actors are hidden from the normal view. This concept is referred to as Punctualization. An incorrect or failure of passage of a token to an actor will result in the breakdown of a network. When the network breaks down, it results in breakdown of punctualization and the viewers will now be able to view the sub actors of the actor. This concept is often referred to as depunctualization.	For example, an automobile is often referred to as an unit. Only when it breaks down, is it seen as a combination of several machine parts. Or in the diabetes self-care model the uploading task of one key actor, be it a provider or a patient is in reality a consequence of the interaction and co-ordination of several sub-tasks. This only becomes visible when a breakdown at this point occurs and special attention is given to analyse why and how the problem resulted and hence all sub tasks must be examined carefully.
Obligatory Passage Point: broadly refers to a situation that has to occur in order for all the actors to satisfy the interests that have been attributed to them by the focal actor. The focal actor defines the OPP through which the other actors must pass through and by which the focal actor becomes indispensable (Callon, 1986).	In the diabetes self-care model we can illustrate this by examining the occurrence of the diabetes or secondary complications that have resulted because of the primary disease. Such incidents form the catalyst for developing shared goals and united focus of effort so necessary to effect superior healthcare delivery.
Irreversibility: Callon (1986) states that the degree of irreversibility depends on (i) the extent to which it is subsequently impossible to go back to a point where that translation was only one amongst others and (ii) the extent to which it shapes and determines subsequent translations.	Given the very complex nature of healthcare operations (von Lubitz and Wickramasinghe, 2006b-e) irreversibility is generally not likely to occur. However it is vital that chains of events are continuously analyzed in order that future events can be addressed as effectively and efficiently as possible.

patients, equipment suppliers, medical administrators, administrative computer systems, medical researchers, and so on. In a particular operation (or event) it is important to identify all relevant actors before proceeding further.

The next step is to 'interview' the actors. With human actors this is, of course, quite straightforward, but with non-humans it is necessary to find someone (or something) to speak on their behalf. For an item of medical technology this might be its designer or user, or it might just be the instruction manual. The aim of this step is to see how these actors relate to each other and the associations they create – to identify how they interact, how they negotiate, and how they form alliances and networks with each other. These 'heterogeneous networks' consists of the aligned interests held by each of the actors.

Human actors, such as medical practitioners, can 'negotiate' with non-human actors such as

X-Ray or dialysis machines by seeing what these machines can do for them, how easy they are to use, what they cost to use, and how flexible they are in performing the tasks required. If negotiations are successfully completed then an association between the medical practitioner and the machine is created and the machine is used to advantage – the network has become durable. If the negotiations are unsuccessful then the machine is either not used at all, or not used to full advantage.

Once this is developed it is then important to apply the techniques of SNA to map the flows of pertinent information and germane knowledge throughout this network and thereby not only enhancing the metacognition of the system but also the ability to rapidly extract and utilize the critical knowledge to support prudent decision making and at always a state of being prepared and ready (Wickramasinghe and von Lubitz, 2007; von Lubitz and Wickramasinghe, 2006 a;f)

The main advantage of the S'ANT approach to considering the diabetes self-care model is in being able to identify and explore the real complexity involved. Other approaches to technological innovation, Innovation Diffusion for example, put much stress on the properties of the technology or organization themselves, at the expense of looking at how these interact. Unfortunately in doing this they often tend to oversimplify very complex situations and so miss out on a real understanding. To develop a better appreciation of the vital role the S'ANT approach plays in the development of a self-care model for chronic disease it is now necessary to understand the seriousness of one of the major chronic diseases; diabetes, and the key factors in a particular self-care model.

DIABETES

Diabetes is a chronic disease that occurs when there is too much glucose in the blood because the body is not producing insulin or not using insulin properly (DA, 2007).

Diabetes management involves a combination of both medical and non-medical approaches with the overall goal for the patient to enjoy a life which is as normal as possible (AIHW, 2008; AIHW, 2007). Critical to this management regimen is the systematic monitoring of blood sugar levels. However, as there is no cure for diabetes, achieving this goal can be challenging because it requires effective lifestyle management and careful and meticulous attention and monitoring by the patient and health professionals (Britt, 2007). In particular, to be totally successful, this requires patients to be both informed and active in their treatment regimen. A solution is therefore required which provides the possibility for "anytime anywhere" monitoring of an individual's diabetes, thereby contributing to diabetes management. In response to this, this chapter suggests the application of a pervasive technology solution in the form of a wireless-enabled mobile phone to facilitate superior diabetes management.

CHRONIC DISEASE MANAGEMENT

Containment of cost whilst offering the highest quality healthcare has become a global priority for healthcare delivery. In such an environment, prevention and/or early detection becomes critical since initiatives that prevent the occurrence of a disease help to circumvent costly healthcare interventions while initiatives that detect early the occurrence of a disease usually enable better control of this disease (and thereby less costly healthcare interventions). Moreover, in both instances, quality is high since the patient is subjected to less invasive healthcare interventions and can enjoy a higher quality of life. In such an environment, the effective management of chronic disease becomes particularly important.

If detected early, chronic diseases (such as diabetes, asthma or hypertension) can be contained and sufferers can continue to lead full and high quality lives. Conversely, if these diseases are not well managed, they can develop into more complicated healthcare problems and life for such patients can become less than satisfactory. Critical to effective chronic disease management is regular monitoring leading to an informed patient who takes responsibility for managing his/her wellness.

As identified by Rachlis (2006), a chronic care model requires the interaction and co-ordination of numerous areas. In particular, it requires the interaction of four key components of the health-care system including self-management support, delivery support, decision support and clinical information systems and support from the community at large. Taken together, this provides a conducive environment to have productive interac-

tions between an informed and activated patient and a prepared and proactive healthcare team.

Diabetes is an important chronic disease increasing in prevalence throughout not only North America but also the World (figure 1). Given the treatment costs for this increasing population, coupled with the increased non-working hours due to treatment requirements, increases in the prevalence of diabetes as is projected is indeed alarming to any healthcare system.

Regular monitoring of diabetes is necessary to control this particular chronic disease to prevent it from evolving into more complicated healthcare problems. To do this efficiently and effectively, we believe that ICT (information and communication technologies) can play a critical role by

Figure 1. The global picture

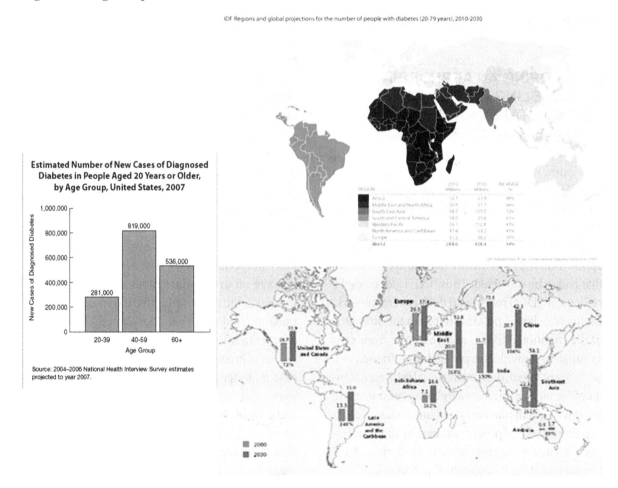

providing a means to enable superior monitoring "anywhere, anytime" thereby allowing the patient to enjoy a high quality lifestyle. However, technology initiatives in healthcare to date have had mixed results at best (Kulkarni and Nathanson, 2005; Lacroix, 1999; Frost and Sullivan, 2004; Wickramasinghe and Goldberg, 2004; Wickramasinghe and Mills, 2001; Wickramasinghe and Silvers, 2003). We believe this is connected with the failure of current IS (information systems) methodologies to correctly capture the richness and complexities of a modern healthcare environment. To address this issue (and, in so doing, provide an environment enabled by ICT that facilitates superior chronic disease management) we describe the results from a seven year longitudinal study conducted between INET and CMMT (Goldberg, 2002a-e; Wickramasinghe and Goldberg, 2004; Wickramasinghe and Goldberg, 2003; Wickramasinghe, Goldberg and Bali, 2007).

DEVELOPING AN APPROPRIATE ICT ENABLING ENVIRONMENT TO FACILITATE CHRONIC DISEASE MANAGEMENT

The journey began by realizing that the tradition SDLC (systems development life cycle) was fundamentally flawed for any healthcare initiative. This was due to several reasons including the length of time it would take to realize the final application and the structures and inflexible stages that had to be traversed. Thus, INET developed a refocused SDLC model and delivery framework. In this way it was possible to retain the strengths of the traditional SDLC and yet move from start to finish in a much compressed time frame.

Simply stated, the research goal is to use a standardized mobile Internet (wireless) environment to improve patient outcomes with immediate access to patient data and provide the best available clinical evidence at the point of care. To do this, INET International Inc's research (Goldberg, 2002a-e;

Wickramasinghe and Goldberg, 2003, 2004) starts with a 30-day e-business acceleration project in collaboration with many key actors in hospitals (such as clinicians, medical units, administration, and I.T. departments). Together they follow a rigorous procedure that refocuses the traditional 1-5 year systems development cycle into concurrent, 30-day projects to accelerate health care delivery improvements. The completion of an e-business acceleration project delivers a scope document to develop a handheld technology application (HTA) proof-of-concept specific to the unique needs of the particular environment. The proof-of-concept is a virtual lab case scenario. A virtual Lab operates within a mobile Internet (wireless) environment by working with hospitals and technology vendors. The final step is the collection of additional data with clinical HTA trials consisting of two-week hospital evaluations.

From the refocused SDLC model it was then possible to design a robust and rigorous web-based business model, the INET web-based business model (figure 2) (Wickramasinghe et al., 2005; Wickramasinghe and Misra, 2004; Goldberg, 2002a; 2002b; 2002c; 2002d; 2002e; Wickramasinghe and Goldberg, 2004). The business model then provides the necessary components to enable the delivery framework to be positioned in the best possible manner so it can indeed facilitate the key components of the chronic disease model being successfully enacted.

In order to successfully implement the business model described above it was however necessary to have an appropriate methodology. Based on this need, the AMR (adaptive mapping to realization) methodology was developed. The idea of the methodology was to apply a systematic rigorous set of predetermined protocols to each business case and then map the post-prior results back to the model. In this way it was possible to compare and contrast both *a priori* and *post priori* findings. From such a comparison, a diagnosis of the current state was made and then prescriptions were made for the next business case. Hence each pilot

Figure 2. INET-web-based-business model

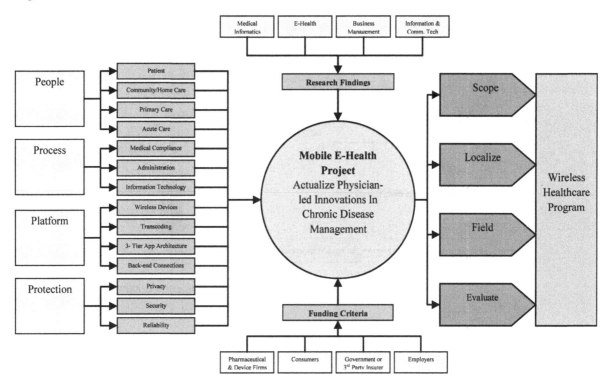

study incorporated the lessons learnt from the previous one and the model was adapted in real time.

By applying the tools and techniques of today's knowledge economy, as presented in the intelligence continuum (IC), it is possible to make the AMR methodology into a very powerful knowledge-based systems development model (figure 3). The IC was developed by Wickramasinghe and Schaffer (2006) to enable the application of the tools and technologies of the knowledge economy to be applied to healthcare processes in a systematic and rigorous fashion and thereby ensure superior healthcare delivery. The collection of key tools, techniques and processes that make up the IC include, but are not limited to data mining, business intelligence/analytics and knowledge management. Taken together, they represent a very powerful system for refining the data raw material stored in data marts and/or data warehouses, thereby maximizing the value and

utility of these data assets for any organization. In order to maximize the value of the data generated through specific healthcare processes and then use this to improve processes, the techniques and tools of data mining, business intelligence and analytics and knowledge management must be applied in a systematic manner. Once applied, the results become part of the data set that are reintroduced into the system and combined with the other inputs of people, processes, and technology to develop an improvement continuum.

Thus, the intelligence continuum includes the generation of data, the analysis of these data to provide a "diagnosis" and the reintroduction into the cycle as a "prescriptive" solution. In this way, the IC is well suited to the dynamic and complex nature of healthcare environments and ensures that the future state is always built upon the extant knowledge-base of the preceding current state. Through the incorporation of the IC with the AMR methodology we then have a

Figure 3. Knowledge-based systems development model

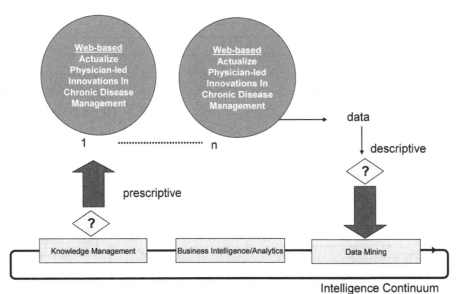

knowledge-based systems development model that can be applied to any setting not necessarily chronic disease management. The power of this model is that it brings best practices and the best available germane knowledge to each iteration and is both flexible and robust.

DISCUSSION AND CONCLUSION

In the current context healthcare delivery especially in the US is in need of fundamental re-design (Porter and Tiesberg, 2006). The focus on cost containment also necessitates a shift to prevention

Figure 4. ICT support for diabetes

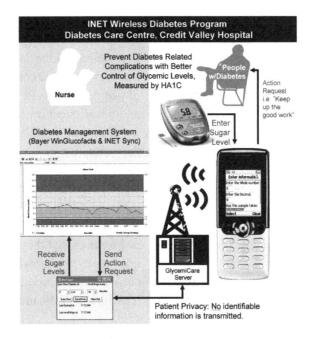

rather than cure. This is particularly important in the case of chronic diseases such as diabetes.

Diabetes is the fifth-deadliest disease in the United States. Since 1987, the death rate due to diabetes has increased by 45 percent, while the death rates due to heart disease, stroke, and cancer have declined. The total annual economic cost of diabetes in 2002 was estimated to be $132 billion. Direct medical expenditures totaled $92 billion and comprised $23.2 billion for diabetes care, $24.6 billion for chronic diabetes-related complications, and $44.1 billion for excess prevalence of general medical conditions. Indirect costs resulting from lost workdays, restricted activity days, mortality, and permanent disability due to diabetes totaled $40.8 billion. The per capita annual costs of health care for people with diabetes rose from $10,071 in 1997 to $13,243 in 2002, an increase of more than 30%. In contrast, health care costs for people without diabetes amounted to $2,560 in 2002. One out of every 10 health care dollars spent in the United States is spent on diabetes and its complications.

The preceding then has outlined an ICT enabled solution that in itself is not exorbitantly expensive in order to facilitate the superior monitoring of diabetes (figure 4). Moreover, the chapter has outlined the critical success factors and necessary steps required to traverse from idea generation to implementation of this solution. Diabetes affects all members of the community and is indeed a silent epidemic. Currently and in the near future there is no foreseeable cure available to most suffers thus management of this disease is vital. As confirmed by recent studies just a small 1% decrease in blood sugar can facilitate a significant decrease in secondary problems including kidney disease and heart problems (figure 5). This serves to underscore the importance of the proposed diabetes self-care model. However, such a model cannot move from idea to realization without a rich lens to analyse the key areas and hence we have proffered the adoption of the S'ANT approach in order to facilitate the realization of the full power of the outlined self-care model.

Figure 5. Impact of a 1% decrease on likelihood of developing secondary issues

UKPDS: decreased risk of diabetes-related complications associated with a 1% decrease in A1C

Observational analysis from UKPDS study data

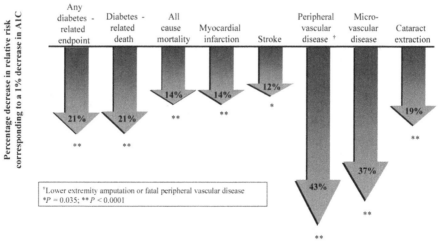

Adapted from Stratton IM, *et al.* UKPDS 35. *BMJ* 2000; 321:405 –412.

REFERENCES

AIHW. (2007). National Indicators for Monitoring Diabetes: Report of the Diabetes Indicators Review Subcommittee of the National Diabetes Data Working

AIHW. (2008). *Diabetes: Australian Facts 2008.* Canberra: Australian Institute of Health and Welfare.

Britt, H., Miller, G. C., Charles, J., Pan, Y., Valenti, L., & Henderson, J. (2007). *General Practice Activity in Australia 2005-06, Cat. no. GEP 16.* Canberra: AIHW.

DA. (2007). *Diabetes Facts.* New South Wales: Diabetes Australia Frost and Sullivan Country Industry Forecast (n.d.). *European Union Healthcare Industry.* Retrieved May 11, 2004 from http://www.news-medical.net/print_article. asp?id=1405

Goldberg, S., et al. (2002a). *Building the Evidence For A Standardized Mobile Internet* (wireless) Environment in Ontario, Canada, January Update, internal INET documentation.

Goldberg, S. et al. (2002b). *HTA Presentational Selection and Aggregation Component Summary,* internal documentation.

Goldberg, S. et al. (2002c). *Wireless POC Device Component Summary.,* internal INET documentation.

Goldberg, S. et al. (2002d). *HTA Presentation Rendering Component Summary.,* internal INET documentation.

Goldberg, S. et al. (2002e). *HTA Quality Assurance Component Summary,* internal INET documentation.

Kulkarni, R., & Nathanson, L. A. (2005). *Medical Informatics in medicine, E-Medicine.* Retrieved from http://www.emedicine.com/emerg/topic879. htm

Lacroix, A. (1999). International concerted action on collaboration in telemedicine: G8sub-project 4, Sted. Health Technol. *Inform (Silver Spring, Md.), 64,* 12–19.

Porter, M., & Tiesberg, E. (2006). *Re-defining health care delivery.* Boston: Harvard Business Press.

Rachlis, M. (2006). *Key to sustainable healthcare system.* Retrieved from http:www.improveingchroniccare.org

Wickramasinghe, N. Schaffer, J., & E. Geisler 2005 "Assessing e-health" forthcoming in Eds T. Spil and R. Schuring *E-Health Systems Diffusion and Use: The Innovation, The User and the User IT Model,* Hershey, PA: Idea Group Publishing.

Wickramasinghe, N. (2007). Fostering knowledge assets in healthcare with the KMI model. *International Journal of Management and Enterprise Development, 4*(1), 52–65. doi:10.1504/ IJMED.2007.011455

Wickramasinghe, N., & Bali, R. (2009)... *The S'ant Imperative For Realizing The Vision Of Healthcare Network Centric Operations Intl J Actor-network Theory and Technology Innovation, 1*(1), 45–59.

Wickramasinghe, N., & Goldberg, S. (2003). The Wireless Panacea for Healthcare. In *Proceedings of the 36th Hawaii International Conference on System Sciences* (HICSS-35) January 6-10, 2003, Hawaii (CD-ROM), Copyright 2002 by the Institute of Electrical & Electronic Engineers, Inc (IEEE).

Wickramasinghe, N., & Goldberg, S. (2004). How M=EC2 in Healthcare. *International Journal of Mobile Communications, 2*(2), 140–156. doi:10.1504/ IJMC.2004.004664

Wickramasinghe, N., & Goldberg, S. (2007a). Adaptive mapping to realisation methodology (AMR) to facilitate mobile initiatives in healthcare. *International Journal of Mobile Communications, 5*(3), 300–318. doi:10.1504/IJMC.2007.012396

Wickramasinghe, N., Goldberg, S., & Bali, S. (2008). Enabling superior m-health project success: a tri-country validation. *International Journal of Services and Standards*, *4*(1), 97–117. doi:10.1504/IJSS.2008.016087

Wickramasinghe, N., & Mills, G. (2001). MARS: The Electronic Medical Record System The Core of the Kaiser Galaxy. *International Journal of Healthcare Technology and Management*, *3*(5/6), 406–423. doi:10.1504/IJHTM.2001.001119

Wickramasinghe, N., & Misra, S. (2004). A Wireless Trust Model for Healthcare. *Int. J. e-Health (IJEH)*, *1*(1), 60-77

Wickramasinghe, N., & Schaffer, J. (2006). Creating Knowledge Driven Healthcare Processes With The Intelligence Continuum. [IJEH]. *International Journal of Electronic Healthcare*, *2*(2), 164–174.

Wickramasinghe, N., & Silvers, J. B. (2003). "IS/IT The Prescription To Enable Medical Group Practices To Manage Managed Care. *Health Care Management Science, 6* pp-75-86.

Chapter 16
The Impact of Network of Actors on the Information Technology

Tiko Iyamu
Tshwane University of Technology, South Africa

Arthur Tatnall
Victoria University, Australia

ABSTRACT

Organisations' reliance on Information Technology (IT) is rapidly increasing. IT strategy is developed and implemented for particular purposes by different organizations. We should therefore expect that there will be network of actors within the computing environment, and that such network of actors will be the key to understanding many otherwise unexpected situations during the development and implementation of IT strategy. This network of actors has aligned interests. Many organizations are developing and implementing their IT strategy, while little is known about the network of actors and their impacts, which this paper reveals. This paper describes how Actor-Network Theory (ANT) was employed to investigate the impact of network of actors on the development and implementation of IT strategy in an organisation. ANT was used as it can provide a useful perspective on the importance of relationships between both human and non-human actors. Another example: design and implementation of a B-B web portal, is offered for comparison.

INTRODUCTION

Technical and non-technical factors are crucial in the various phases of IT strategy development and implementation, and provide opportunities for those in positions of power in the organisation to exercise the most explicit influence. IT strategy serves as the 'road map' to guide an organisation on technology issues over a period of time. To this end, IT strategy allows all parts of the organisation to gain a shared understanding of priorities and goals for the time period as defined by the strategy.

A definition of IT strategy by itself cannot influence development of this strategy as both the development and implementation stages encompass components including Technology, People and Process. Technology is what people make of the definition – how they internalise

DOI: 10.4018/978-1-60960-197-3.ch016

it – this matters as it shapes the development and implementation processes. Salzman (1998) emphasises that the outcome of IT strategy is as a result of a continual process from development to implementation, of many actors' influence on IT strategy. In spite of the importance associated with IT, some experts such as Carr (2003) have controversially challenged its use. In his article "IT Doesn't Matter", Carr (2003, 2004) argues about whether IT actually mattered in an organisation's performance and competitiveness. The uses, techniques, power and presence of IT have increased tremendously over the years (Andreu & Ciborra, 1998), and Kling (1980) addresses how, on the one hand, computing has affected social structures while, on the other hand, the underlying social structures influence computing processes. Kling provides a very helpful scheme to examine theories accounting for people's resistance to the introduction and implementation of technologies and identified six distinct theoretical perspectives, namely: rational, structural, human relations, interactionist, organisational politics and class politics. According to Walsham & Waema (1994), both the development and implementation stages are critical in an effective IT strategy. They base their argument on the end product of development and implementation of IT strategy, which to them, determines to a certain extent what level of service the organisation offers to its clients through the application of technology services. Iyamu and Roode (2010) argues that the various interests in IT strategy are either individual or team based. Individual interests are mostly based on 'stocks of knowledge'.

Even though work has been done in the area of IT strategy both in the academic and professional domains, it is considered that many problems still exist in the development and implementation phases. Some of the works include that of Walsham and Waema (1994), Wyatt (2001), Mack (2002) and Papp & Fox (2002). Even the most ambitious business vision still needs an IT strategy to enable it (Benamati & Lederer, 1999),

and what is more important is that the connection between IT strategy and business strategy must be understood.

IT strategy is only a means to an end, and to achieve its goals and objectives, it needs to be implemented (Ward & Peppard, 2002). According to Gottschalk (1999), implementation is important for four reasons: opportunities can be lost, efforts could be duplicated resulting in technology incompatibilities and a waste of resources, the extent to which the IT strategy achieves its goals and objectives is determined by the implementation, lack of implementation leaves the organisation dissatisfied with and reluctant to continue strategy development, and lack of implementation creates problems of establishment and maintenance priorities in future IT strategy development.

RESEARCH METHODOLOGY

Qualitative, interpretive case study research methodology was employed in the study, which involved, in the main study, an insurance organisation in South Africa, and in the second study, a semi-government authority in Australia. An interpretive approach was adopted to explore the relationship between actors in the development and implementation of IT strategy in the organisation, and the analysis was done through the Translation perspective of Actor Network Theory to investigate the impact of non-technical factors on the development and implementation of IT strategy. According to Denzin & Lincoln (1994), qualitative research is multi-method in focus, involving an interpretive, naturalistic approach to its subject matter. This means that qualitative researchers study things in their natural settings, attempting to make sense of or interpret phenomena in terms of the meanings people bring to them.

In the case study, data sources included interviews and documentation. The study employed the semi-structured approach. In a semi-structured interview the interviewer has the freedom to probe the interviewee to elaborate on the original response or to follow a line of inquiry introduced by the interviewee. The semi-structured approach allows fairly informal interviews. More advantageously, it makes interviewees feel as though they are participating in a conversation or discussion rather than in a formal question and answer situation. The case studies took cognisance of the fact that an actor can be part of many networks at the same time, manifesting him/herself differently within each particular network. Also, the actors play decisive roles in the construction of the networks that they are part of.

Demographic information, such as race, gender, grade or level in the organisational structure, as well as the years of service in the organisation were criteria for nominating and identifying participating respondents. Number of years of service was used as a criterion to ensure that the respondent understood the organisational systems and could therefore provide rich data. Three years was thought to be enough for an employee to understand the organisation in terms of business activities, structures, strategies and policies and to be able to give an assessment based on opinion and perception. The data collection through interview was stopped at the point of saturation. 33 employees were interviewed: 17 were whites and the others were non-white. On the level of organisational hierarchy 14 of the interviewees were senior and 18 were junior. The computing environment of the organisation consisted of 122 whites and 30 non-whites employees.

ANT was employed for the analysis, primarily because it can explain and interpret social and technological evolution using neither technical-material nor social reductionism. Rather, it incorporates principles that integrate both humans and non-humans into the same conceptual framework (Callon, 1986). According to Tatnall & Gilding (1999), neither the social nor the technical elements in these 'heterogeneous networks' should then be given any special explanatory status. Callon (1991) defined actors as all entities that are able to connect texts, humans, money, etc., to build more or less effectively a world that is filled with other entities having their own history, identity and relations. When actors and their interactions are taken together they form a network (Callon, 1987; 1991; and Law, 1992). A network incorporates both technical and non-technical actors with linkages consisting of stabilised translations and interactions between actors.

An ANT perspective was applied in analysis of the study in order to gain an understanding of the spheres of influence that the actors have on the development and implementation of IT strategy. In terms of ANT this happens through a 'processes of translation', and in this context actors are entities that have the ability to constrain, facilitate or influence action.

The analysis of the case study from an ANT perspective draws upon the sociology of translation. The focus is on how the 'actor-network' grows, changes and stabilises during the development and implementation of IT strategy, specifically examined in the context of the organisation's computing environment. Interactions between actors are the primary building blocks of actor-networks and their many manifestations are called 'translations' (Callon 1986; Latour 1987). Between humans and objects, translation occurs during design when the object is imbued with its purpose, program or script as to how it would interact with or affect other actors (Akrich, 1992).

The concept of translation is particularly important in situations where an innovation, or an implementation, is either not adopted or carried out in full, or is adopted or used in a different way to that expected. In these cases the human actors can be seen to adapt, or translate, the innovation into a form that suits them by leaving out certain parts or aspects, or by modifying others (Tatnall, 2009). Singleton and Michael (1993:229) define translation as "... the means by which one entity gives a role to others." Latour (1986) argues that the mere 'possession' of power by an actor does not automatically confer the ability to cause

Figure 1. Four moments of translation (Callon, 1986)

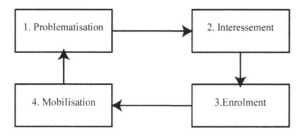

change unless other actors can be *persuaded* to perform the appropriate actions for this to occur. Latour (1986) maintains that with innovation translation, people may react to an innovation in different ways. On the one hand they may modify it or add to it, and on the other they may let it drop. He suggests that each of these actors works to shape the innovation to their own ends. The key to innovation is the creation of a powerful enough consortium of actors to carry it through, and when an innovation fails to be taken up this can be considered to reflect on the inability of those involved to construct the necessary network of alliances amongst the other actors (McMaster, Vidgen, & Wastell, 1997)

The case study was analysed on the basis of the four moments of translation outlines by (Callon, 1986): problematisation, interessement, enrolment and mobilisation, in the order as shown in Figure 1.

- **Problematisation:** is the stage where an actor defines an issue in their own terms. An actor then analyses, defines and proposes a solution for the problematised issue. The idea of problematisation is to foster relationships and to allocate and reallocate power between the actors involved. In relation to this, Callon (1986) refers to an Obligatory Passage Point (OPP) as a situation that has to occur in order for all the actors to satisfy the interests that have been attributed to them by the focal actor. The focal actor defines the OPP through which the other actors must pass and by which the focal actor becomes indispensable.

- **Interessement:** is the set of actions by which an entity attempts to impose and stabilise the identity of other actors in the same network for the cause of problematisation. As described by Callon (1986), it involves a process of convincing other actors to accept the solution proposed by the focal actor. The initiators seek to lock the other actors into the roles that are proposed for them. In other words, actors are engaged in the process of confirming the OPP. This succeeds when other actors become interested in the solution proposed. They change their affiliation to a certain group in favour of the new actor.

- **Enrolment:** involves consolidation of these alliances through bargaining and mutual concessions. As defined by the focal actor, the solution is accepted as a new concept through a process of negotiation, and a new network of interests is created or generated. Actors accept the roles defined for them when enrolling in the network (Callon, 1986). Enrolment can be seen as a successful outcome of the 'problematisation' and the 'interessement' processes.

- **Mobilisation:** of allies is a set of methods used to represent the group effectively. "Who speaks in the name of whom?" (Callon, 1986). Some actors are used as (new) initiators and become delegates or spokespersons for the focal actor. The new network starts to operate with a target-oriented approach to implement the solution proposed. This leads to strengthening and stabilisation of the network.

In a stabilised network, irreversibility is the key to consistency and success. Network building is a search for stability which is achieved when changes set in train during network construction become irreversible (Callon, 1991; Law & Callon, 1997), either because it would be too costly to reverse them or because to do so becomes unthinkable. Callon's (1991) concept of irreversibility describes how translations between actor-networks are made durable and how they can resist assaults from competing translations.

ANALYSIS THROUGH ANT

The most important actors involved in the actor-network, along with their relevant interests, are first described using the four moments of translation.

Executive Committee (Exco) was the highest decision making body in the organisation. It consisted of executive members, of which some were heads of departments. It was headed by the Chief Executive Officer (CEO) of the organisation. The HOD concerned was the head of the IT department and was responsible and accountable for the development and implementation of IT strategy including related issues such as relevant people and processes. IT Management was the highest decision making body in the computing environment of the organisation and was headed by the HOD. This body was responsible and accountable for all IT strategy-related issues in the organisation and consisted of the most senior employees in the hierarchy of the computing environment as each member was the Head of a unit. Each of the IT managers controls at least one team and is responsible for development and, largely, implementation of the components of IT strategy in the organisation. The rest of the employees in the IT department are referred to as IT Employees. Their responsibilities vary, but all were involved in the implementation of IT strategy in the organisation. Non-human actors included Technology: the different technologies were vital in enabling the business processes and activities through IT strategy and skill-set: the employees

have different technical skill sets. Also, some of the employees were more highly skilled than others.

ANT Translation: Problematisation

The organisation, through its executive committee, provided the Head of Department (HOD) in the computing environment with the business strategy. The HOD was requested to develop and implement an IT strategy to align with the business strategy, and to achieve this, a set of requirements was formulated. The requirements were then problematised by the HOD for the employees to develop and implement an IT strategy to align and support the organisation's business strategy.

The organisation's rules prohibit the organisation or any of the units from soliciting or contracting information technology services from external sources, and all IT solutions rendered to the organisation or part of the organisation were through its IT department. Also, only through the IT strategy were the business processes and activities enabled and supported. All IT solutions were defined and dictated by IT strategy in the organisation.

The HOD must approve of any and all components of the IT strategy in the organisation before it is implemented. The HOD sometimes delegated members of the IT Management team to approve IT strategy-related requests on her behalf. Subsequently IT Management (including the IT managers) dictated tasks and activities to their employees. After the development of IT strategy, the HOD IT Management and the IT managers present this to the rest of the employees at a workshop.

During this stage the HOD thus uses the main goal and objective of IT strategy, namely to align with the organisation's business strategy, to formulate a set of requirements. These requirements were problematised by the HOD, and under the leadership of the CEO the development and implementation of IT strategy was presented as a solution to the problematised issue. The processes of development and implementation of the IT strategy were defined as the Obligatory Passage Point through the assignment of individual tasks related to the development and implementation of the IT strategy to all employees, to be monitored through performance appraisal schemes.

ANT Translation: Interessement

The HOD submits the developed IT strategy to the organisation's Executive Committee for approval. Thereafter, implementation starts and the HOD and the IT Management team become the key stakeholders in the implementation of IT strategy in the organisation. However, without the active participation of the rest of the employees all efforts would be wasted.

IT Management was able to build interest among the IT managers reporting to them, the individual members of the IT Management Team. The building of interest was to take a step further through the presentation of IT strategy to employees at a workshop. The IT management team also used the opportunity to explain the services that would be made available to the organisation, and this was done by giving examples of improvements that could be made within the computing environment.

Managers were then appointed to oversee the implementation of the IT strategy within the organisation, and they helped to ensure that their individual employees committed to the implementation of the IT strategy through further team meetings and workshops. The success of these efforts was not guaranteed, however, as is evidenced during the interviews. This state of affairs was acknowledged by management but not effectively addressed beyond acknowledgement. Some employees, again, were not interested because they could not work with others. This was often due to the fact that certain employees insisted on speaking Afrikaans, which their colleagues do not understand.

The building of interest among employees was further hampered by issues of mistrust, alluded to, when it was pointed out that some employees feel that the information shared or communicated to them was either not complete or was incorrect. As a result they did not trust the IT Management team. Thus, while management made several efforts to build interest for the proposed solution to the problematised issue, the building of interest among employees could not be regarded as a success. As a result, enrolment of employees to the processes of implementation, presented as the OPP of the actor-network, was also only partially successful, with employees reluctantly accepting the tasks allocated to them and their roles in the implementation of the IT strategy.

ANT Translation: Enrolment

Workshops held to inform employees about the developed IT strategy were followed up with team meetings, which were used as vehicles to discuss the objectives of the IT strategy and to allocate tasks to individuals. Also, one-on-one meetings between employees and their various managers offered another opportunity in which IT strategy was discussed and roles and responsibilities were negotiated.

While enrolment at the highest level was not a problem, with the IT managers supporting IT Management in the development as well as in the implementation of IT strategy, the rest of the employees were divided – some supported the process and enrolled in the implementation, while others showed little support and as such enrolled only reluctantly.

IT managers used their authority to enrol employees in the implementation process allocating tasks and resources to them, coupled with the organisation's mandatory performance appraisal system. Also, some IT managers were able to use their personal relationship with employees, especially those who were of the same racial or language group to them, to enrol them in the IT strategy. Some employees, who wouldn't have enrolled otherwise, did so to please their individual IT manager. These managers were compelled to return the favour at the expense of the organisation.

Some members of the IT management team and the HOD were aware of the challenges of the enrolment of employees in the implementation of IT strategy in the organisation. Thus, as expected from a relatively unsuccessful stage of building interest for implementation among employees, enrolment was likewise only partially successful. What enrolment actually took place was more the result of employees being coerced into accepting the tasks allocated to them, because this was coupled to their performance appraisal, than that it was due to their interest having been successfully translated to coincide with the interests of the focal actors.

ANT Translation: Mobilisation

During mobilisation, some actors would be used as new initiators by becoming delegates or spokespersons for the focal actor. This leads to strengthening and stabilisation of the network. Depending on how successful mobilisation is, the actor-network would then start to operate with a target-oriented approach to implement the solution proposed.

The HOD successfully mobilised the IT Management team and IT managers and expected them to enrol their various employees in the IT strategy development and implementation processes. The IT managers were motivated by the task of mobilisation, which was linked to their performance appraisals. They responded by speaking on behalf of the HOD and the IT Management team on the aims and objectives of IT strategy in the organisation, but there was some difficulty in mobilising the newer employees, especially of the older generation and this was attributed to the tension between them. The newer employees

benefited from the South African Government's 'Affirmative Action Policy'.

Some of the employees, who attend the workshops, understood the value of IT strategy and as a result, spoke to and encourage their colleagues on the need for IT strategy in the organisation and the proposed developmental processes. They could be seen as third level spokespersons for the focal actor, and contributed a further element of mobilisation of the network. However, the mobilisation efforts of managers often broke down due to their poor understanding of the developed IT strategy.

Obviously, such situations have a severe negative influence on mobilisation. While it is recognised that managers do not wittingly set out to create further spokespersons amongst employees, their general lack of knowledge about and understanding of the developed IT strategy and the implementation implications simply means that a further cascading of mobilisation does not take place to the extent that is required for effective stabilisation of the network. Mobilisation starts off relatively successfully at a high level, but peters out through the ranks and leaves most of the employees' unconvinced and unenthusiastic contributors to the implementation of the IT strategy.

INTERPRETATION

Based on the above analysis, key non-technical factors which influence and impact the development and implementation of IT strategy were identified. A discussion of the interpretation follows.

Language Used for Communication

It was the policy of the organisation to allow both Afrikaans and English as languages of communication. Some employees, however, were not fluent in Afrikaans and found it difficult to understand and interpret IT strategy related documents written in this language, and it was difficult for them to participate in meetings where the development and implementation of IT strategy were discussed in Afrikaans. Historically, only Afrikaans speaking people were employed in the organisation, and accordingly the language of communication in processes and activities had always been Afrikaans. In the new setting of the computing environment, these employees were finding it difficult to adjust and accept the changes that were taking place in the new dispensation. Their response to these changes was to be uncooperative. Some of the managers preferred to allocate critical tasks to people they could easily communicate with, and this would often exclude those who were not fluent in Afrikaans. Also, in terms of team work, language took preference. Afrikaans speaking employees preferred to work with those who could also communicate in Afrikaans. The language policy of the organisation therefore had an adverse effect on the implementation of IT strategy: a divide of the workforce along language lines, poor communication between individuals and groups, and, in general, problems of co-operation to get the work done.

Coping with Diversity

There was rich cultural diversity in the computing environment of the organisation, but instead of celebrating their diversity, pervasive elements of conservatism counteracted the advantages that could have been gained from this. The diversity manifested itself in terms of different generations, language groups and racial groups. The response of the older generation to the changes in the environment was to be uncooperative. This did not alleviate the plight of the new intakes, who were mostly from other language and racial groups in comparison to the older generation, and who had difficulty in performing their tasks in the new cultural setting.

It was not always possible for employees from the older generation to avoid working with new employees – invariably from the younger generation, since the rules of the organisation made it possible to enforce such arrangements. This 'generation gap' co-operation was then based on a foundation of unwillingness to work together and led to the younger employees not getting enough information from their older colleagues who were more knowledgeable about the organisation. The younger generation employees were not only divided from the older generation in terms of age and language, but also in terms of race, since many of them were appointed in terms of the organisation's transformation efforts required by the 'Employment Equity Act'. There was a reluctance to co-operate, or a complete lack of co-operation from both the affirmative action employees and other employees, including managers. The organisation was clearly unable to cope with the rich diversity amongst its employees, and the diversity was used in many subtle and not-so-subtle ways to undermine work procedures and co-operative work.

Practices of Favouritism and Nepotism

IT managers had autonomous control over resources under their auspices. This rendered them vulnerable to favouritism and nepotism and created conflicts of interest. Some of the IT managers accorded preferences to employees as they wished, and some preferred to allocate critical tasks to people they could easily communicate with. There was no performance contract for employees in the computing environment of the organisation and as a result, employees did not believe that the organisation could fairly judge their performance and qualification for salary increases and promotion. Consequently, employees resorted to manoeuvring because they believed that managers had no objective way of differentiating effective people from those who were less effective, and were in fact practising nepotism and favouritism.

Pursuit and Protection of Personal and Group Interests

Feelings of insecurity resulted in some employees from the older generation acting individually in order to achieve and satisfy their own goals and objectives. They exploited the fact that certain senior managers had more respect for them because of their age, and that whatever they said would carry more weight than the words of a younger employee in achieving personal objectives. They also used their greater knowledge of the organisation and the computing environment to maintain job security and to dominate younger employees. Personal interests also mediated early decisions about IT strategy in the organisation that eventually wielded their greatest influence during the implementation stage. The absence of performance contracts led to employees resorting to manoeuvring to ensure favourable appraisals from their managers. Such practices were not restricted to individuals and various groups, divided along language, race or age lines, all pursued their group interests first and not that of the organisation in the implementation of the IT strategy.

Implementing Transformation

To balance the number of employees in the computing environment along racial lines, the organisation implemented the affirmative action policy of the Employment Equity Act, which was promulgated by the Government of South Africa. Employees at the lower levels, who mainly came from non-white (coloured, Indian and black) origins, were referred to as affirmative action candidates. This was considered to be discriminatory in the organisation. The employees concerned were also considered as not having the same organisational values or ways of operating as their white colleagues. As such, they were allocated few tasks or opportunities in the implementation of IT strategy.

Quite rightly, the affirmative action employees felt they were being discriminated against. This led to uncooperative actions and manifestations of defensive behaviour by the affirmative action employees, and antagonism between them and the rest of the employees. The affirmative action candidates claimed that because of the discrimination, information about IT strategy was not appropriately circulated or shared with them and they felt that their white colleagues had more power as a result of the resources within their reach. In response to this domination, the affirmative action candidates acted in their individual interests and only half-heartedly supported the implementation of IT strategy in the organisation.

Affirmative action, in terms of the Employment Equity Act, therefore became an obstacle within the organisation rather than a doorway to the future, and was resented by employees and managers from both sides of the 'divide'.

The five non-technical factors identified are, of course, not independent. In order to discover the relationships between the factors, they were analysed based on the discussion above. This was further illustrated in Figure 2 below and shows that the following relationships hold between the non-technical factors:

- Language used for communication ↔ Coping with diversity
- Language used for communication ↔ Practice of favouritism and nepotism
- Language used for communication ↔ Pursuit and protection of personal and group interests
- Language used for communication ↔ Implementing transformation
- Coping with diversity ↔ Practice of favouritism and nepotism
- Coping with diversity ↔ Pursuit and protection of personal and group interests
- Coping with diversity ↔ Implementing transformation
- Practice of favouritism and nepotism ↔ Pursuit and protection of personal and group interests

Figure 2. Impact of non-technical factors on IT strategy

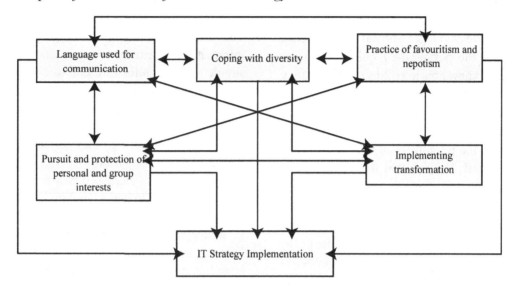

- Practice of favouritism and nepotism ↔ Implementing transformation
- Pursuit and protection of personal and group interests ↔ Implementing transformation

The five non-technical factors all have an impact on the development and implementation of IT strategy. Since implementation produces the final outcome of the strategy this was seen as even more critical, thus, Figure 2 only shows the impact on the implementation of IT strategy.

ANOTHER EXAMPLE: DEVELOPMENT OF A WEB PORTAL

Almost ten years ago in Melbourne, Australia, a not-for-profit organisation's implementation of a Business-Business (B-B) Web Portal provides another example of systems development and implementation strategies (Tatnall & Burgess, 2002). We will call this organisation Westernesse. The idea was to develop a B-B portal, complete with a payment gateway, to facilitate trading between small to medium enterprises (SME) in the local area. Westernesse knew *why* they wanted

the portal and the need it was to fulfil, but they had only a rough idea of *what* the development would involve – development of a portal of this type was very new at this time. Not having the in-house expertise themselves to develop a portal, they approached a software developer: Instaport, to build and host it for them. They also approached one of the major banks regarding the payment gateway. Westernesse thought all the rest would be easy, but in this they were much mistaken.

Identification of the actors is always the first step in an ANT study. The principal actors in this case were: Westernesse, and in particular their portals project manager and CEO; Instaport (the portal developer), and in particular their development manager and programmers; the bank, and in particular its portals manager; and portal software itself. At one level it is convenient to consider the organisations themselves: Westernesse, the portals developer and the bank, as black boxes, but at another level it is necessary to look inside to see the motives and operational style of the people involved and making the decisions within these organisations.

The first problem that arose was due to Westernesse and Instaport not fully understanding the other's interpretation of the problem: the problematisation proposed by Westernesse was not accepted by the developer who did not appreciate exactly why the portal was required. Instaport thought they knew how to build a portal, but they had not properly allowed for the needs and nature of the potential SME users, who typically had little or no knowledge or expertise with computers and little idea of the possible uses and the potential of a web portal. The problem was compounded further as it took Westernesse a while to discover that the developer had not fully understood their problematisation of the portal, and when they did, and spoke with Instaport about this, some of the development work had to be re-done. In actor-network terms, Westernesse had not succeeded in properly enrolling the developer in the early stages of the development, and wasted a lot of time in correcting this mistake.

The next problem was with the bank. Developers at the bank knew about portal payment gateways, but they had only ever implemented these for use by large enterprises, and most of their expertise went to earlier, pre-Internet, times and the use of EDI (Electronic Data Interchange). They also did not understand or accept the Westernesse problematisation of their portal, or that of Instaport, the portal developer. To make matters even more difficult it was necessary for the bank to co-operate with the portal developer, and a clash of personalities in each organisation created problems here.

Nevertheless, the portal was built and in the end it did match what Westernesse wanted as the project manager at Westernesse did finally manage an interessement to get both the portals developer and the bank on side and working for the same outcome. They were eventually enrolled. The next problem involved enrolling the SME users into productive use of the portal, but that is another story (Pliaskin & Tatnall, 2005; Tatnall, 2007; Tatnall & Pliaskin, 2007).

CONCLUSION

The strategy involved in the development of an information system in an organisation is neither simple nor straightforward and it involves many actors, as shown in this article. Often, the success of an implementation has more to do with interactions between the people involved, and between these people and the technology they are using than with the actual technology itself.

This article has discussed how and why decision makers need to understand the functions, the dynamics and the causes of what, why and how IT strategy or any of its components succeeds or fails at the micro-level, and how these issues can be addressed. For example, many of the employees in one of the case studies were either reluctant or were non-participators in the implementation of the IT strategy in the organisation, yet the organisation still had to address the causes of this phenomenon. The principal actors in the other case study at first did not except the same problematisation of the portal and only after a good deal of discussion were able to come to a common understanding of the problem.

An analysis of the interplay between both technical and non-technical factors, and a better understanding of the contribution of socio-technical elements to IT strategy is likely to result in better future implementations. The two organisational case studies discussed in this article are quite different in many ways, but show in common the need to allow for socio-technical factors in any IT development strategy. An organisation that does not do this, and does not allow for human as well as technical factors and for their interactions, is much less likely to achieve successful IT systems implementation.

REFERENCES

Akrich, M. (1992). The description of technical objects. In Bijker, W. E., & Law, J. (Eds.), *Shaping technology, building society* (pp. 205–224). Cambridge, MA: MIT Press.

Andreu, R., & Ciborra, C. (1998). *Organisational learning and core capabilities development. Information Technology and Organisational Transformation: Innovation for the 21st Century Organisation* (Galliers, D. R., & Baets, R. J. W., Eds.). New York: John Wiley & Sons Ltd.

Benamati, J., & Lederer, A. L. (1999). An empirical study of IT management and rapid IT change, In *Proceedings of the SIGCPR conference on Computer personnel research, Communication of the ACM*, pp.144-153, New Orleans; Louisiana.

Callon, M. (1986). Some elements of the sociology of translation: Domestication of the scallops and the fisherman of St Brieuc Bay. In Law, J. (Ed.), *A New Sociology of Knowledge, power, action and belief* (pp. 196–233). London: Routledge.

Callon, M. (1987). Society in the Making: The Study of Technology as a Tool for Sociological Analysis. In Bijker, W. E., Hughes, T. P., & Pinch, T. (Eds.), *The Social Construction of Technological Systems* (pp. 83–103). Cambridge, MA: MIT Press.

Callon, M. (1991). Techno-economic networks and irreversibility. In Law, J. (Ed.), *A sociology of monsters. Essays on power, technology and domination* (pp. 132–164). London: Routledge.

Carr, N. G. (2003). IT Doesn't Matter. *Harvard Business Review, 81*(5).

Carr, N. G. (2004). *Does IT Matter? Information Technology and the Corrosion of Competitive Advantage*. Boston, USA: Harvard Business School press.

Daniels, C. N. (1994). *Information Technology: The Management Challenge*. Reading, MA: Addison-Wesley publishing Ltd.

Denzin, N. K., & Lincoln, Y. S. (1994). Introduction: Entering the field of Qualitative Research. In Denzin, N. K., & Lincoln, Y. S. (Eds.), *Handbook of qualitative research* (pp. 1–17). California: Sage Publications.

Gottschalk, P. (1999). Implementation Predictors of Formal Information Technology Strategy. *Information & Management, 36*(2), 77–91. doi:10.1016/S0378-7206(99)00008-7

Iyamu, T., & Dewald, R. (2010). The use of Structuration and Actor Network Theory for analysis: A case study of a financial institution in South Africa. *International Journal of Actor-Network Theory and Technological Innovation, 2*(1), 1–26.

Kling, R. (1980). Social analysis of computing: Theoretical perspectives in recent empirical research. *ACM Computing Surveys, 1*(12), 61–110. doi:10.1145/356802.356806

Latour, B. (1986). The Powers of Association. In Law, J. (Ed.), *Power, Action and Belief. A New Sociology of Knowledge? Sociological Review monograph 32* (pp. 264–280). London: Routledge & Kegan Paul.

Latour, B. (1987). *Science in Action: How to follow Scientists and Engineers through Society*. Cambridge, MA: Harward University Press.

Law, J. (1992). Notes on the theory of the actor-network: ordering, strategy, and heterogeneity. *Systems Practice, 5*(4), 379–393. doi:10.1007/BF01059830

Mack, R. (2002). *Creating an Information Technology (IT) Strategy: An Alternative Approach, Gartner, Inc*. Retrieved June 28, 2004, from www.gartner.com.

McMaster, T., Vidgen, R. T., & Wastell, D. G. (1997, 9-12 August, 1997). Towards an Understanding of Technology in Transition. Two Conflicting Theories. Paper presented at the Information Systems Research in Scandinavia, IRIS20 Conference, Hanko, Norway.

Papp, R., & Fox, D. (2002). Information strategy development: The strategic alignment imperative, *Eighth Americas Conference on Information Systems*.

Pliaskin, A., & Tatnall, A. (2005). Developing a Portal to Build a Business Community. In Tatnall, A. (Ed.), *Web Portals: The New Gateways to Internet Information and Services* (pp. 335–348). Hershey, PA: Idea Group Publishing.

Salzman, H. (1998). *Beyond User Participation: The Politics of Software Development, Center for Industrial Competitiveness*. USA: University of Massachusetts.

Singleton, V., & Michael, M. (1993). Actor-Networks and Ambivalence: General Practitioners in the UK Cervical Screening Programme. *Social Studies of Science*, *23*(2), 227–264. doi:10.1177/030631293023002001

Tatnall, A. (2007, 4-6 June 2007). *Business Culture and the Death of a Portal. Paper presented at the 20th Bled e-Conference* - eMergence: Merging and Emerging Technologies, Processes and Institutions Bled, Slovenia.

Tatnall, A. (2009). Information Systems, Technology Adoption and Innovation Translation. *International Journal of Actor-Network Theory and Technological Innovation*, *1*(1), 59–74.

Tatnall, A., & Burgess, S. (2002, June 2002). Using Actor-Network Theory to Research the Implementation of a B-B Portal for Regional SMEs in Melbourne, Australia. Paper presented at the 15th Bled Electronic Commerce Conference - 'eReality: Constructing the eEconomy', Bled, Slovenia.

Tatnall, A., & Gilding, A. (1999). Actor-Network theory and Information Systems Research, In *Proceeding of the 10th Australian Conference on Information Systems*, (ACIS), Wellington, Victoria University of Wellington.

Tatnall, A., & Pliaskin, A. (2007). The Demise of a Business-to-Business Portal. In Radaideh, M. A., & Al-Ameed, H. (Eds.), *Architecture of Reliable Web Applications Software* (pp. 147–171). Hershey, PA: Idea Group Publishing.

Walsham, G., & Waema, T. (1994). Information Systems Strategy and Implementation: A Case Study of a Building Society. *ACM Transactions on Information Systems*, *12*(2), 159–173. doi:10.1145/196734.196744

Ward, J., & Peppard, J. (2002). *Strategic Planning for Information Systems* (3rd ed.). England, West Sussex, UK: John Wiley & Sons.

Wyatt, JC. (2001). The New NHS Information Technology Strategy: Technology will change practice, 322 (7299), 1378. *MIS Quarterly*.

Chapter 17
A Potential Application of Actor Network Theory in Organizational Studies:
The Company as an Ecosystem and its Power Relations from the ANT Perspective

Magdalena Bielenia-Grajewska
University of Gdansk, Poland

ABSTRACT

In this chapter, an attempt will be made to discuss the place of Actor Network Theory in organizational studies. To narrow the scope of the research, attention will be focused solely on companies. The concept of ANT researched within the corporate setting has been one of the author's interests for some years. Consequently, in this work the author will try to show some aspects related to Actor Network Theory in contemporary organizations. Since not every concept related to ANT within the corporate environment can be investigated in greater detail, two issues, namely ecosystem and power, have been selected to discuss the possible application of ANT in the studies on corporations.

INTRODUCTION

Modern life is complex and consists of different relations and networks determining the private and social sphere of one's existence (Castells, 2009). Thus, the issues related to organizational studies can be discussed by taking the network concept into consideration. The idea of networking did not originate in the twentieth century since *any*

sociotechnical system, ancient or modern, primitive or industrialized, stems from the efforts of system builders who attempt to create a network capable of resisting dissociation (Pfaffenberger, 2004 p. 81) and one which is flexible and adaptable (Vuokko and Karsten, 2007). Corporate networking consists of both internal and external networks which determine the organizational capability to be efficient and competitive (Boons, 2009). One of the methods of studying the grids and lattices of corporations is Actor Network Theory.

DOI: 10.4018/978-1-60960-197-3.ch017

APPLICATION OF ANT IN ORGANIZATIONAL STUDIES

There are several reasons for the possibilities of using ANT concepts in the discussion on corporations. One of them is the technological advancement of modern companies. Since the study of technology has been incorporating many ideas from the sociology of scientific knowledge and both *scientific facts and technological artifacts are to be understood as social constructs* (Woolgar, 1989 p. 311), the boundaries between social and technological entities are of secondary importance. What is more, the increasing role of technology has given rise to the appearance of technology-related theories, including ANT (Kien, 2009b) since, among others, they offer the possibilities of studying the complicated relations between technology, human beings and organizations. The author will try to discuss this aspect in greater detail when referring to the two selected notions in the coming sections.

The second reason for the popularity of networking in organizational studies is related to the recognition of postmodern theories in various scientific domains. Taking only management into account, postmodern organizations are changeable in nature since they have to respond all the time to the alternating conditions of their fluid environment (Bauman, 2003). What is more, postmodern organizations are not anchored in one place and their activities are shaped by changing media images, techno-images, finance-images and idea-images (Appadurai, 2005) or the reshaping character of the economic field (Bourdieu, 1990). Consequently, this leads to the fusion of different elements and the creation of hybrid identities (e.g. Bielenia-Grajewska, 2010). Actor Network Theory shares several features with postmodern studies (Breiger, 2003; Grant, 2005; Ward, 1996) since, among other similarities, they both question the existence of strong boundaries, stress the role of process and opt for non-hierarchical approaches. What is more, both Actor Network

Theory and postmodernism rely on a semiotic heritage in their studies. Semiotics is defined as *the study of signs and codes that make up culture and that organize everyday social existence* (Catt and Eicher-Catt, 2010 p. 18). Taking a more dynamic approach, it is the *intersubjective mediation by signs* (Gunaratne, 2009 p. 49). ANT is defined as *a semiotics of materiality* (Law in Smith and Jenks, 2006 p. 161) and shares some features with semiotics. For example, as in semiotics, actors have no fixed identity but their individual and social character is created during relations with other network constituents (Barry, 2006). Since *a sign is anything which produces meaning* (Thwaites, Davis and Mules, 2002 p. 9), both living and non-living entities, regardless of their size, can be very powerful elements, for example, in corporate communication (Pickering, 1995). Communication studied from the perspective of cognitive semiotics can be basically understood as the process of exchanging as well as interpreting signs by using other signs (Origlio, 2007; Rosengren, 2000). In the case of companies, it is possible to investigate the role of human (e.g. managers, workers, stakeholders) and non-human signs (e.g. computers, faxes, telephones, interior design) in the speed and efficiency of corporate dialogue. The other reason for looking at corporations through the sign perspective is the state of post-industrial or information goods which have limited material content but are rather perceived as signs, being the embodiment of some aesthetic values (Lash and Urry, 1994). The sign perspective makes it possible to account for the historic context in studying companies through ANT. Some claim that ANT pays attention to the social processes within and outside the network, and, consequently, *there often remains a limited exploration of both human agency and its historical construction* (Newton, 2007 p. 32). The semiotic perspective offers the possibility to consider the origin and background of studied entities since *all communications are taken through semiotic codes which have a history, by which we simply mean that they exist outside of and prior to any situated use* (Scollon and Wong Scollon, 2001 p. 272).

Moreover, ANT has much in common with post-structuralism (Crawford, 2005), especially with the ideas presented by Michel Foucault, Michel Serres and Gilles Deleuze (e.g. Barry, 2006; Clarke, 2005; Phillips, 2005). For example, Deleuze's notion of rhizome bears resemblance to networks, being a collection of connected elements which undergo constant changing (Colman, 2005). Thus, the approach taken by the author of this paper reflects the current tendency of applying different theories, including Actor Network Theory, to business areas. Actor Network Theory is adapted for general discussions on management and organization studies (e.g. Alcadipani and Hassard, 2010; Lee and Hassard, 1999) as well as being used in more specific domains of managerial interests. For example, public relations (Verhooven, 2009), corporate communication (Luoma-aho and Paloviita, 2010), intercultural communication (Bielenia-Grajewska, 2009), stakeholder behavior (Pouloudi, Gandecha, Atkinson and Papazafeiropoulou, 2004), strategies (Gao, 2005), customer-relationship management (Monteiro, 2001), budgeting system (Ezzamel, 1994), teleworking (Jackson and Van der Wielen, 1998), portals in business (Tatnall and Davey, 2005), electronic markets (Baygeldi and Smithson, 2004) and auditing (Spira, 2002) are studied through the ANT perspective. One of the reasons for the popularity of ANT in organizational studies, regardless of the investigated domain, is the fact that it is suited to explore the complexities of organizations (Law, 2001) since it offers important methodological tools for the examination of substantial enterprises with a long history and available data (Spira, 2002). What is more, modern companies are rather judged by taking into account their profit and abilities than their physical dimensions. Since what really counts are the actors and their networks, not the space as such (Pedersen, 2009), a smaller ecosystem can be more effective and more innovative than its larger competitor (Andersson, Curley and Formica, 2010).

Other aspects of the potential application of ANT in organizational studies will be discussed in the following sections by narrowing the scope of interest to companies as such.

ACTOR NETWORK THEORY IN STUDYING CORPORATIONS

Taking into account the multinational and multicultural character of modern companies, ANT can be very useful in discussing how global techniques and standards are translated for the local needs (Pinch, 2003). Thus, in the case of corporations, ANT can be used for discussing how different strategies are localized to meet the expectations of specific consumers. One of the ways of discussing localization is through the actor perspective.

According to ANT, actors are divided into language-bearing and non-language-bearing entities (Rowan and Bigum, 1991). The important characteristic is that living and non-living elements of a network are equally important for networking (e.g. Bauchspies, Croissant and Restivo, 2006; Burton and Hamilton, 2005; Del Casino, 2009; Schäfer, 2010). Thus, *Actor Network Theory rejects the solace of humanism, 'man's mastery of technology'* (Munro, 2005 p. 125) and, consequently, it can be said that it in a way *would breathe life into commodities and their supporting cast allowing them in principle to throw off their chains* (Wilkinson, 2006 p. 14). Although human and non-human elements progress together in networks (Pickering, 1995), non-human actors contribute to the network in a different way since, for example, they cannot speak (Jaeger, 2005). Non-human elements are rather perceived as fixed and stable, and, consequently, the possibility of rearranging and reconfiguring them within the networks makes them mobile, fluid and adaptable at the same time (Thompson, 2003). Not only the entity is changed by the network, but at the same time the network is changed by the entity since any introduction of a new element in the network does not go unnoticed since it transforms or at least changes the network (Geels, 2005). But some also say that since the position of non-humans is considerably stronger in Actor Network Theory in comparison with other theories, human beings in ANT are rather treated as cogs in machines, *much like a Kodak camera since they can be assumed to act in a certain way given a certain actor network configuration* (Newton, 2007 p. 32). However, it is rather connected with shifting *attention away from humans and the social to collectives and complex ecologies* (Murdoch, 2005 p. 292) than with depriving human beings of their outstanding characteristics.

What is more, actor networks are *assemblages of socio-material entities* (Mitev, 2009 p. 13) or, in other words, *a heterogeneous amalgamation of textual, conceptual, social and technical actors* (Crawford, 2005 p. 1). Thus, ANT takes into account that there are no strict boundaries between the natural and the social world (Murdoch, 2005; Porsander, 2002; Thrift, 2000). Thus, the elements constituting the corporate world, regardless of their origin, can be studied by applying the same methodology. It gives the possibility of concentrating rather on the flows and processes than on single entities as such which, consequently, leads to a more concise and dynamic picture of corporations. It also draws the attention to the immense role of technological devices in the creation of a company's position on the market as well as the interaction between nature, technology and human beings and their potential implications for innovativeness and competitiveness.

To digress, it should be stated that the lack of strong demarcation between living and non-living entities is not exclusive for ANT. In synechism, as in ANT, both living and non-living entities are treated with equal respect (e.g. Philström, 2007). The same notion can be observed in the systems approach, in which it is stressed that a system is combined of living and non-living entities (e.g.

Trivedi, 2002) which evolve together. As far as systematic theories are concerned, the General Systems Theory stresses interconnectedness (Avis, 2009) and the role of holons (systems being a part of other systems) in the environment (Beerel, 2009). Some characteristics related to both systems and networks will be further elaborated in the coming section on ecosystems.

ECOSYSTEMS AND CORPORATIONS

The term ecosystem comes from the studies on natural systems and it is generally defined as *a bordered part of nature, where a large number of elements (e.g. plants, animals) are under consideration* (Popp and Meyer, 2010 p. 120). What is more, *an ecosystem is all the living organisms that interact together in a place, combined with all the nonliving characteristics of that place* (Marchetti and Moyle, 2010 p. 92). It should be noted that the idea of ecosystem in management studies results from the complex nature of modern companies and their environment. In the age of globalization, companies do not operate autonomously but they belong to the ecosystem which is characterized by sharing technological advancement (Iansiti and Levien, 2004) and offering symbiotic cooperation between different organizations and other elements (Andrew and Sirkin, 2006). The ecosystem constitutes of individual and collective actors who are perceived through their relationships with other actor network members (Doolin and McLeod, 2005). The business ecosystem is not limited to one company or one domain but it consists of different industries (Aurik, Jonk and Willen 2003; Iansiti and Levien, 2004), comprising different companies which aim to benefit from shared resources and flows (Abe, Dempsey and Bassett, 1998), but at the same time *whose choices and actions are interdependent* (Boudreau and Hagia, 2010 p. 168). This approach especially holds true in the case of modern global companies since *metanationals build an ecosystem* to identify and access this dispersed knowledge ahead of competition (Williamson, 2007 p. 83). Their ecosystem entails different networks. For example, the business ecosystem may consist of companies which perform outsourcing for the given company or which provide financing, technology, regulatory agencies and media outlets (Davenport, Leibold and Voelpel, 2006). Taking the managerial networks as an example, they make use of their internal expertise as well as external resources, such as the legal system (Grint, 2005). What is more, the surrounding space is also important in studying ecosystems. The environment of any business ecosystem consists of political, cultural, social and legal spheres. This ecosystem is *a system formed by the interaction of a community of organizations and their environment* (Daft, 2009 p. 176) and it is determined by external environment, internal structure, leadership and internal management systems (Rainey, 2009). The relation between the business ecosystem and its environment is mutual since *this environment has an impact on the business ecosystem, but the business ecosystem may also have an impact on the environment* (Allen and Andriani, 2007 p. 26).

Thus, the word ecosystem seems to be more appropriate for the discussion on enterprises than the more anachronic term industry (Nankervis, 2005) in order to encompass the environment related to modern companies. Since the topic of this investigation is ANT, it is important to discuss the distinction between the two, often used interchangeably, terms: (eco)system and network. As Ho (in Gilbert 2007 p. 81) states, *system usually means a linkage of differing members and channels (passages), such as cars on highways, or blood in veins; whereas network, as used in actor network theory, implies a virtual relation of the co-constitution between the actor and the linkages. The network only exists when the actor is in transit through it; the actor only exists as a point particle of the network.* However, there are several similarities between these two concepts. In ecosystems, as in networks, the boundaries are not

static and clear (Iansiti and Levien, 2004; Popp and Meyer, 2010; Saunier and Meganck, 2009) but they are chosen according to the conditions demanded (Leibold, Probst and Gibbert, 2005). In both networks and systems, living and non-living entities are equally important (Pfaffenberger, 2004) and their existence is related to the performance of other entities (Corallo, 2007). Companies may compete with each other since they want to achieve a better position in the ecosystem (Leibold, Probst and Gibbert, 2005), but at the same time they are all interested in the outstanding condition of their industry, or, in the systemic terminology, in the mutual ecosystem (Iansiti and Levien, 2004). What is more, both network and system are related to innovation since companies cooperate to launch new products or services or meet customers' needs (Freeman and Liedtka, 2005) and change their capabilities to adapt to changing market demands (Gibbert, 2010). These are some of the reasons why the contemporary economy has been named the business ecosystem or the networked economy (Aurik, Jonk and Willen, 2003).

POWER IN CORPORATIONS

As has already been mentioned in the introductory part of this article, modern organizations are characterized by changeability and fluidity. Thus, ANT, which turns out to be very useful in discussing concepts undergoing changes and being characterized by unclear boundaries (Usher and Edwards, 2007), can be applied with success in organizational studies. Taking into account the discussed features of modern times, the environment and the company itself, ANT stresses the necessity to create and recreate (Grint and Woolgar, 1997), or in other words, define and redefine the network (Callon, 1989; Clegg, Courpasson and Phillips, 2006). What is more, ANT also reflects the current role of change in organizational studies since it stresses the flows between the links (Thrift, 2000) rather than concentrating on the nodes themselves and highlights that stability *is always provisional and precarious because the aim of the fact is that it may be undone by antagonistic actors* (Pfaffenberger, 2004 p. 72). As far as ANT theory is concerned, it is also stressed that the aim of those constituting an actor network is to achieve their mutual goal (Abrahall, Cecez-Kecmanovic and Kautz, 2007). The same applies to organizations and their purpose to gain profit, competitive position or recognition on the market. The other important aspect of modern companies is the role of innovation and knowledge exchange. Network structure, being informal and interactive, constitutes an innovation-friendly corporate environment (Corallo, 2007; Sundbo, 2003). Having other methods of achieving cohesion than the hierarchy itself (Josserand, 2004), network serves as a perfect place for creating and implementing innovations. Consequently, power can be exercised in other ways than by relying exclusively on the corporate social stratum. However, it should be stated that networks are not places completely devoid of any hierarchical relations, of any stronger and weaker ties. Rather, these relations are continually undergoing constant reorganization (Thompson, 2003 p. 77), being the *result of negotiation, trade-off and compromises between actors* (Rowan and Bigum, 1991 p. 180) since they are *the uncertain consequences of the ordering of heterogeneous materials* (Law 2001 p. 864) *with the need to make actions (scientific or otherwise) durable through space and time* (Murdoch, 2006 p. 78). The focus on power in ANT is not on *the power differentials and imbalances in such networks* (Erickson, 2005 p. 85), but on *the organizing powers of combinations* (Munro, 2005 p. 125). Power is studied on the social rather than on the individual level since power is treated as the network property (Rowan and Bigum, 1991) and it is evaluated by taking into account the participants in the studied network (Crawford, 2005; Kien, 2009b), of both human and non-human type since, as has already been stated, they both possess power (Rose and Truex III, 2000). It is also

connected with the intensity of power which is related directly to convergence. High convergence leads to stable networks, and, consequently, to powerful networks. These networks can even be perceived as black boxes (Baygeldi and Smithson, 2004). Since *a black box is any actant so firmly established that we are able to take its interior for granted* (Harman, 2009 p. 33), the power is also treated as a collective feature in the corporate setting. Black box results from one type of translation, being the *process of network stabilization* (Löwer, 2006 p. 27), namely the simplifying of constituting entities (Crawford, 2005), comprising various actors with diversified interests (Monteiro, 2001). In the case of any corporate setting, it can be performed by unifying norms of communication, sharing common values and acting according to the demanded corporate standards. Network has little influence on loosely connected actors (Jaeger, 2005), thus the network, in this case the company, will want to encompass members on a fixed basis and become a powerful black box on the market.

Taking into account the fluid size of networks, the micro network can become as powerful as the macro one since it may be more adaptable to appearing circumstances (Wilkinson, 2006). What is more, according to ANT, *in the last instance, there is no difference in kind, no great divide, between the powerful and the wretched* (Law, 2001 p. 864). Thus, even those less powerful are of importance in corporate networks.

CONCLUSION

The aim of this short chapter was to draw the attention to the potential possibilities of discussing organizational issues through the prism of ANT concepts. The author has decided to concentrate on the issue of ecosystem and power to show the suggested application of Actor Network Theory in the studies on companies. The aim was to show that ANT offers an interesting perspective to study the role of non-living and living entities in creating and maintaining the market position of modern companies. Due to the limitations imposed on the paper, the author has only managed to highlight some concepts taken from Actor Network Theory and their possible contribution to organizational studies. Thus, the author hopes that this discussion on ANT in management can be enriched in the future, e.g. with the cross-cultural perspective in comparative company studies.

REFERENCES

Abe, J. M., Dempsey, P. A., & Bassett, D. A. (1998). *Business ecology: giving your organization the natural edge*. Woburn, MA: Butterworth-Heinemann.

Abrahall, R., Cecez-Kecmanovic, D., & Kautz, K. (2007). Understanding strategic ISD Project in practice- An ANT account of success and failure. In G. Magyar, G. Knapp, W. Wojtkowski, W.G. Wojtkowski & J. Zupančič (Eds.), *Advances in information systems development: new methods and practice for the networked society*. New York, Dordrecht, Heidelberg, London: Springer Science + Business Media, LCC, 23-36.

Alcadipani, R., & Hassard, J. (2010). Actor-Network Theory, organizations and critique: towards a politics of organizing. *Organization*, *17*(4), 419–435. doi:10.1177/1350508410364441

Allen, P. E., & Andriani, P. (2007). Diversity, interconnectivity and sustainability. In J. Bogg, & R. Geyer (Eds.), *Complexity, science and society*. Abingdon: Radcliffe Publishing Ltd, 1-32.

Andersson, T., Curley, M. G., & Formica, P. (2010). *Knowledge-Driven Entrepreneurship: The Key to Social and Economic Transformation*. New York, Dordrecht, Heidelberg, London: Springer Science + Business Media.

Andrew, J. P., & Sirkin, H. L. (2006). *Payback: reaping the rewards of innovation*. Boston, MA: Harvard Business School Press.

Appadurai, A. (2005). *Nowoczesność bez granic. Kulturowe wymiary globalizacji*. Cracow: Universitas.

Aurik, J. C., Jonk, G. J., & Willen, R. E. (2003). *Rebuilding the corporate genome: unlocking the real value of your business*. Hoboken, NJ: John Wiley & Sons.

Avis, P. (2009). General Systems Theory. In Avis, P. (Ed.), *Psychological Perspectives* (pp. 113–128). Cape Town: Pearson Education South Africa.

Barry, A. (2006). Actor-Network-Theory. In A. Harrington, B.L. Marshall & H.P. Müller (Eds.), *Encyclopedia of social theory*. Abingdon: Routledge, 4-5.

Bauchspies, W. K., Croissant, J., & Restivo, S. (2006). *Science, technology, and society: a sociological approach*. Oxford, Malden, Victoria: Blackwell Publishing.

Bauman, Z. (2003). *Liquid Modernity*. Cambridge: Polity Press.

Baygeldi, M., & Smithson, S. (2004). Ability of the Actor Network Theory (ANT) to Model and Interpret an Electronic Market. In Gupta, J. N. D., & Sharma, S. K. (Eds.), *Creating knowledge based organizations* (pp. 109–126). London: Idea Group Publishing.

Beerel, A. (2009). *Leadership as change management*. New Delhi: Sage Publications India Pvt Ltd.

Bielenia-Grajewska, M. (2009). Actor-Network Theory in Intercultural Communication: Translation through the Prism of Innovation, Technology, Networks and Semiotics. *International Journal of Actor-Network Theory and Technological Innovation*, *1/4*, 53–69.

Bielenia-Grajewska, M. (2010). The Linguistic Dimension of Expatriatism- Hybrid Environment, Hybrid Linguistic Identity. *European Journal of Cross-Cultural Competence and Management, 1/2,* 212–231. doi:10.1504/EJCCM.2010.031998

Boons, F. (2009). Ecology in the social sciences: an overview. In Boons, F., & Howard-Grenville, J. A. (Eds.), *The social embeddedness of industrial ecology* (pp. 28–46). Cheltenham: Edward Elgar Publishing Limited.

Boudreau, K. J., & Hagia, A. (2010). Platform rules: multi-sided platforms as regulators. In Gawer, A. (Ed.), *Platforms, Markets and Innovation* (pp. 163–191). Cheltenham: Edward Elgar Publishing Limited.

Bourdieu, P. (1990). *In Other Words: Essays Towards a Reflexive Sociology.* Stanford: Stanford University Press.

Breiger, R. L. (2003). Emergent Themes in Social Network Analysis: Results, Challenges, Opportunities. In Breiger, R., Carley, K., & Pattison, P. (Eds.), *Dynamic Social Network Modeling and Analysis: workshop summary and papers* (pp. 19–38). Washington: The National Academic Press.

Burton, D., & Hamilton, M. (2005). Literacy, reification and the dynamics of social interaction. In Burton, D., & Tusting, K. (Eds.), *Beyond Communities of Practice: Language, Power and Social Context* (pp. 14–35). New York: Cambridge University Press. doi:10.1017/CBO9780511610554.003

Callon, M. (1989). Society in the Making: The Study of Technology as a Tool for Sociological Analysis. In Bijker, W. E., Hughes, T. P., & Pinch, T. (Eds.), *The Social construction of technological systems: new directions in the sociology and history of technology* (pp. 83–106). Boston, MA: MIT Press.

Castells, M. (2009). *Communication power.* Oxford: Oxford University Press.

Catt, I. E., & Eicher-Catt, D. (2010). Communicology: a Reflexive Human Science. In Eicher-Catt, D., & Catt, I. E. (Eds.), *Communicology: The New Science of Embodied Discourse* (pp. 15–32). Cranbury, NJ: Associated University Presses.

Clarke, A. (2005). *Situational analysis: grounded theory after the postmodern turn.* Thousand Oaks, CA: Sage Publications Inc.

Clegg, S., Courpasson, D., & Phillips, N. (2006). *Power and organizations.* London: Sage Publications Ltd.

Colman, F. J. (2005). Rhizome. In Parr, A. (Ed.), *The Deleuze dictionary* (pp. 231–233). Edinburgh: Edinburgh University Press.

Corallo, A. (2007). The business ecosystem as a multiple dynamic network. In Corallo, A., Passiante, G., & Prencipe, A. (Eds.), *The digital business ecosystem* (pp. 11–32). Cheltenham: Edward Elgar Publishing Limited.

Crawford, C. S. (2005). Actor Network Theory. In Ritzer, G. (Ed.), *Encyclopedia of Social Theory* (pp. 1–3). Thousand Oaks, CA: Sage Publications, Inc.

Daft, R. (2009). *Organization Theory and Design.* Mason, OH: South-Western Cengage Learning.

Davenport, T.H., Leibold, M., & Voelpel, S. (2006). *Strategic management in the innovation economy: strategy approaches and tools for dynamic innovation capabilities.* Erlangen: Publicis Corporate Publishing and Wiley-VCH Verlag.

Del Casino, V. J. (2009). *Social Geography.* Chichester: John Wiley & Sons Ltd.

Doolin, B., & McLeod, L. (2005). Towards critical interpretivism in IS research. In Howcroft, D., & Trauth, E. M. (Eds.), *Handbook of critical information systems research: theory and application* (pp. 244–271). Cheltenham: Edward Edgar Publishing Limited.

Erickson, M. (2005). *Science, culture and society: understanding science in the twenty-first century.* Cambridge: Polity Press.

Ezzamel, M. (1994). Organizational change and accounting: understanding the budgeting system in its organizational context. *Organization Studies, 15*(2), 213–240. doi:10.1177/017084069401500203

Freeman, E., & Liedtka, J. (2005). Stakeholder Capitalism and the Value Chain. In Bettley, A., Mayle, D., & Tantoush, T. (Eds.), *Operations management: a strategic approach* (pp. 35–47). London: Sage Publications, Ltd.

Gao, P. (2005). Using actor-network theory to analyse strategy formulation. *Information Systems Journal, 15*(3), 255–275. doi:10.1111/j.1365-2575.2005.00197.x

Geels, F. W. (2005). *Technological transitions and system innovations: a co-evolutionary and socio-technical analysis.* Cheltenham: Edward Edgar Publishing.

Gibbert, M. (2010). *Strategy Making in a Crisis: From Analysis to Imagination.* Cheltenham: Edward Elgar Publishing Limited.

Gilbert, K. W. (2007). Slowness: notes towards a economy of différencial rates of being. In P. Ticineto Clough & J. Halley (Eds.), *The affective turn: theorizing the social.* Duke University Press, 77-105.

Grant, I. H. (2005). Postmodernism and science and technology. In S. Sim (Ed.), *The Routledge companion to postmodernism.* Abingdon: Routledge, 58-70.

Graves, M. (2008). *Mind, brain and the elusive soul: human systems of cognitive science and religion.* Aldershot: Ashgate Publishing.

Grint, K. (2005). *The sociology of work: introduction.* Cambridge: Polity Press.

Grint, K., & Woolgar, S. (1997). *The machine at work: technology, work, and organization.* Oxford: Blackwell Publishers Ltd.

Gunaratne, S. A. (2009). Asian Communication Theory. In Littlejohn, S. W., & Fos, K. A. (Eds.), *Encyclopedia of Communication Theory* (pp. 46–52). Thousand Oaks, CA: Sage Publications Inc.

Harman, G. (2009). *Prince of networks: Bruno Latour and metaphysics.* Melbourne: Re. Press.

Iansiti, M., & Levien, R. (2004). *The keystone advantage: what the new dynamics of business ecosystems mean.* Boston, MA: Harvard Business School Publishing Corporation.

Jackson, P. J., & Van der Wielen, J. (1998). *Teleworking: international perspectives: from telecommuting to the virtual organisation.* London: Routledge.

Jaeger, B. (2005). Digital Visions- the role of politicians in transition. In Bekkers, V., & Homburg, V. (Eds.), *The information ecology of e-government: e-government as institutional and technological innovation in public administration* (pp. 107–126). Amsterdam: IOS Press.

Josserand, E. (2004). *The network organization: the experience of leading French multinationals.* Cheltenham: Edward Edgar Publishing Limited.

Kien, G. (2009a). Actor-Network Theory: Translation as Material Culture. In Vannini, P. (Ed.), *Material culture and technology in everyday life: ethnographic approaches* (pp. 27–44). New York: Peter Lang Publishing.

Kien, G. (2009b). *Global Technography: ethnography in the age of mobility.* New York: Peter Lang Publishing.

Lash, S., & Urry, J. (1994). *Economies of sign and space.* London: Sage.

Law, J. (2001). Notes on the theory of the actor-network: ordering, strategy and heterogeneity. In Warwick Organizational Behaviour Staff (Eds.), *Organizational Studies. Critical Objectives on Business and Management. Vol II: Objectivity and Its Other*. London, New York: Routledge, 853-868.

Lee, N., & Hassard, J. (1999). Organization unbound: actor network theory, research strategy and institutional flexibility. *Organization, 6*(3), 391–404. doi:10.1177/135050849963002

Leibold, M., Probst, G., & Gibbert, M. (2005). *Strategic management in the knowledge economy: new approaches and business applications*. Erlangen: Publicis Corporate Publishing and Wiley-VCH Verlag.

Löwer, U. M. (2006). *Interorganisational standards: managing web services specifications for flexible supply chains*. Heidelberg: Physica Verlag.

Luoma-aho, V., & Paloviita, A. (2010). Actor-networking stakeholder theory for today's corporate communications. *Corporate Communication: An International Journal, 15*(1), 49–67. doi:10.1108/13563281011016831

Marchetti, M. P., & Moyle, P. B. (2010). *Protecting Life on Earth: An Introduction to the Science of Conservation*. Berkeley and Los Angeles, CA: University of California Press.

Mitev, N. (2009). In and out of actor-network theory: a necessary but insufficient journey. *Information Technology & People, 22*, 1, 9–25. doi:10.1108/09593840910937463

Monteiro, E. (2001). Actor-Network Theory and Information Infrastructure. In Ciborra, C. U., Braa, K., & Cordella, A. (Eds.), *From control to drift: the dynamics of corporate information infastructures* (pp. 71–86). New York: Oxford University Press.

Munro, R. (2005). Actor Network Theory. In Clegg, S., & Haugaard, M. (Eds.), *The SAGE Handbook of Power* (pp. 125–139). Thousand Oaks, CA: Sage Publications Inc.

Murdoch, J. (2005). Ecologising sociology. Actor-Network Theory, co-construction and the problem of human exemptionalism. In D. Inglis, J. Bone & R. Wilkie (Eds.), *Nature: From nature to natures: contestation and reconstruction*. Abingdon: Routledge, 282-305.

Murdoch, J. (2006). *Post-structuralist geography: a guide to relational space*. London: Sage Publications, Ltd.

Nankervis, A. R. (2005). *Managing services*. New York: Cambridge University Press. doi:10.1017/CBO9780511481260

Newton, T. (2007). *Nature and sociology. Abingdon*. Routledge.

Origlio, B. (2007). Antropological Semiotics: A Methodological and Conceptual Approach to Intercultural Communication Studies in Organizations. In Ch. M. Schmidt and D. Neuendorff (Eds.), *Sprache, Kultur und Zielgruppen: Bedingungsgrößen für die Kommunikationsgestaltung in der Wirtschaft*. Wiesbaden, DUV, 9-26.

Pedersen, M. A. (2009). At Home Away from Homes: Navigating the Taiga in Northern Mongolia. In Kirby, P. W. (Ed.), *Boundless worlds: an anthropological approach to movement* (pp. 135–152). New York, NY: Berghahn Books.

Pfaffenberger, B. (2004). The social anthropology of technology. In Buchli, V. (Ed.), *Material culture: critical concepts in the social sciences* (pp. 61–89). London: Routledge.

Phillips, M. (2005). Philosophical Arguments in Human Geography. In Phillips, M. (Ed.), *Contested worlds: an introduction to human geography* (pp. 13–86). Aldershot: Ashgate Publishing Limited.

Philström, S. (2007). Synechism. In Lachs, J., & Talisse, R. (Eds.), *American philosophy: an encyclopedia* (pp. 774–746). New York: Routledge.

Pickering, A. (1995). *The mangle of practice: time, agency, and science.* Chicago, London: University of Chicago Press.

Pinch, P. (2003). Making the wrecker seem not all malevolent: re-regulating the UK's china clay mining industry. In S. Buckingham (Ed.), *Local environmental sustainability.* Abingdon: Woodhead Publishing Limited, 46-73.

Popp, K., & Meyer, R. (2010). *Profit from Software Ecosystems: Business Models, Ecosystems and Partnerships in the Software Industry.* Norderstedt: Books on demand GmbH.

Porsander, L. (2002). Things that Matter: A Computerized System as a Part of an Emerging Action Net. In Hedberg, B., Baumard, P., & Yakhlef, A. (Eds.), *Managing imaginary organizations: a new perspective on business* (pp. 117–136). Oxford: Elsevier Science Ltd.

Pouloudi, A. Gandecha, R. Atkinson, C., & Papazafeiropoulou, A. (2004). How Stakeholder Analysis can be Mobilized with Actor-Network Theory to Identify Actors. In B.M. Kaplan, D.P. Truex III, D. Wastell, A.T. Wood-Harper & J.I. De Gross (Eds.), *Information systems research: relevant theory and informed practice.* Norwell, MA: Kluwer Academic Publishers, 705-712.

Radder, H. (1996). *In and about the world: philosophical studies of science and technology.* Albany, NY: State University of New York Press.

Rainey, H. G. (2009). *Communication power.* San Francisco: Jossey-Bass.

Rose, J., & Truex, D., III. (2000). Machine Agency as Perceived Autonomy: An Action Perspective. In R. Baskerville, J. Stage & J.I. DeGross, J.I. (Eds.), *Organizational and social perspectives on information technology: IFIP TC8 WG8.2 International Working Conference on the Social and Organizational Perspective on Research and Practice in Information Technology, June 9-11, 2000, Aalborg, Denmark.* Norwell, MA: Kluwer Academic Publishers, Norwell, 371- 390.

Rosengren, K. E. (2000). *Communication: An Introduction.* London: SAGE.

Rowan, L., & Bigum, Ch. (1991). Actor Network Theory and the Study of Online Learning. New Perspectives on Quality. In Potelli, A. (Ed.), *The death of Luigi Trastulli, and other stories: form and meaning in oral history* (pp. 179–188). Norwell, MA: Kluwer Academic Publishers.

Saunier, R. E., & Meganck, R. A. (2009). *Dictionary and Introduction to Global Environmental Governance.* London: Earth Scan.

Schäfer, J. (2010). Reassembling the literary. In Schäfer, J., & Gendolla, P. (Eds.), *Beyond the Screen: Transformations of Literary Structures, Interfaces and Genre* (pp. 25–71). Bielefeld: Transcript Verlag.

Scollon, R., & Wong Scollon, S. (2001). *Intercultural communication: a discourse approach.* Oxford: Blackwell Publishing.

Smith, J. A., & Jenks, Ch. (2006). *Qualitative Complexity: Ecology, Cognitive Processes and the Re-emergence of Structures in Post-humanist Social Theory.* Abingdon. Routledge.

Somerville, I. (1999). Agency versus identity: actor-network theory meets public relations. *Corporate Communications-. International Journal (Toronto, Ont.), 4,* 1, 6–13.

Spira, L. F. (2002). *The audit committee: performing corporate governance.* Norwell, MA: Kluwer Academic Publishers.

Sundbo, J. (2003). Innovation and Strategic Reflexivity: An Evolutionary Approach Applied to Services. In Shavinina, L. (Ed.), *The international handbook on innovation* (pp. 97–114). Oxford: Elsevier. doi:10.1016/B978-008044198-6/50008-5

Tatnall, A., & Davey, B. (2005). An Actor Network Approach to Informing Clients through portals. In Cohen, E. B. (Ed.), *Issues in informing science and information technology* (pp. 771–780). Santa Rosa, CA: Informing Science Press.

Thompson, G. (2003). *Between hierarchies and markets: the logic and limits of network forms of organization.* New York: Oxford University Press.

Thrift, N. (2000). Actor-Network-Theory. In Johnston, R. J. (Ed.), *The dictionary of human geography* (pp. 4–6). Malden: Blackwell Publishing Ltd.

Thwaites, T., Davis, L., & Mules, W. (2002). *Introducing Cultural and Media Studies A Semiotic Approach.* Basingstoke: Palgrave Macmillan.

Trivedi, M. L. (2002). *Managerial Economics. Theory and application.* New Delhi: Tata McGraw Hill.

Usher, R., & Edwards, R. (2007). *Lifelong learning: signs, discourses, practices.* Dordrecht: Springer.

Verhooven, P. (2009). On Latour: Actor-Network-Theory (ANT) and Public Relations. In Ihlen, O., van Ruler, B., & Fredriksson, M. (Eds.), *Public relations and social theory: key figures and concepts* (pp. 166–186). New York: Routledge.

Vuokko, R., & Karsten, H. (2007). Working with technology in complex networks of interaction. In McMaster, T., Wastell, D., Ferneley, E., & DeGross, J. I. (Eds.), *Organizational dynamics of technology-based innovation: diversifying the research agenda* (pp. 331–344). New York: Springer. doi:10.1007/978-0-387-72804-9_22

Ward, S. C. (1996). *Reconfiguring truth: postmodernism, science studies, and the search for a new model of knowledge.* Lanham, MA: Rowman and Littlefield Publishers, INC.

Wilkinson, J. (2006). Network theories and political economy: from attrition to convergence? In Marsden, T., & Murdoch, J. (Eds.), *Between the local and the global: confronting complexity in the contemporary agri-food sector* (pp. 11–38). Oxford: JAI Press.

Williamson, P. J. (2007). From a national to a metanational ecosystem: harnessing the value of global knowledge diversity. In A. Corallo, G. Passiante, G., & A. Prencipe (Eds.), *The digital business ecosystem.* Cheltenham: Edward Elgar Publishing Limited, 82-102.

Woolgar, S. (1989). Reconstructing Man and Machine. A note on Sociological Critiques of Cognitivism. In Bijker, W. E., Hughes, T. P., & Pinch, T. (Eds.), *The Social construction of technological systems: new directions in the sociology and history of technology* (pp. 311–328). Boston, MA: MIT Press.

Compilation of References

Aanestad, M., & Hanseth, O. (2000, 10-12 June). *Implementing Open Network Technologies in Complex Work Practices: A case from telemedicine.* Paper presented at the IFIP 8.2, Aalborg, Denmark.

AAUW. (2000). *Tech-savvy: educating girls in the new computer age.* Washington: AAUW Educational Foundation.

Abe, J. M., Dempsey, P. A., & Bassett, D. A. (1998). *Business ecology: giving your organization the natural edge.* Woburn, MA: Butterworth- Heinemann.

Abel-Smith, B. (1989). Health economies in developing countries. *The Journal of Tropical Medicine and Hygiene*, *92*, 229–241.

Abrahall, R., Cecez-Kecmanovic, D., & Kautz, K. (2007). Understanding Strategic ISD Project in Practice – An ANT Account of Success and Failure. In G. Magyar, G. Knapp, W. Wojtkowski, W. G. Wojtkowski & J. Zupančič (Eds.), *Advances in Information Systems Development*, *1*, 23-33. Springer US.

Abrea de Paula, R. (2004). The construction of usefulness: How uses and context create meaning with a social networking system. [http://www.ics.uci.edu/~depaula/publications/dissertation-depaula-2004.pdf]

Adelakun, O., & Jenne, M. E. (2002) Stakeholder Process Approach to Information Systems Evaluation. *Eighth Americas Conference on Information Systems.*

AIHW. (2007). National Indicators for Monitoring Diabetes: Report of the Diabetes Indicators Review Subcommittee of the National Diabetes Data Working

AIHW. (2008). *Diabetes: Australian Facts 2008.* Canberra: Australian Institute of Health and Welfare.

Ajzen, I. (1991). The Theory of Planned Behavior. *Organizational Behavior and Human Decision Processes*, *50*(2), 179–211. doi:10.1016/0749-5978(91)90020-T

Ajzen, I., & Fishbein, M. (1980). *Understanding Attitudes and Predicting Social Behavior. London.* Englewood Cliffs: Prentice-Hall.

Ajzen, I., & Madden, T. (1986). Prediction of Goal-Directed Behavior: Attitudes, Intentions, and Perceived Behavioral Control. *Journal of Experimental Social Psychology*, *22*, 453–474. doi:10.1016/0022-1031(86)90045-4

Ajzen, I. (1985). From intentions to actions: a theory of planned behaviour [Electronic Version]. *Action Control: From Cognition to Behavior*, 11-39. Retrieved February 2, 2004, from http://search.epnet.com/login.aspx?direct=true&db=aph&authdb=epref&an=ACFCB.AJZEN.SPRINGER.AIHE.AA

Akrich, M., & Latour, B. (1997). A summary of a convenient vocabulary for the semiotics of human and non-human assemblies. In Bijker, W. E., & Law, J. (Eds.), *Shaping technology/building society: Studies in sociotechnical change* (pp. 259–264). Cambridge, MA: MIT Press.

Akrich, M. (1992). The description of technical objects. In Bijker, W. E., & Law, J. (Eds.), *Shaping technology, building society* (pp. 205–224). Cambridge, MA: MIT Press.

Alawneh, A., & Hattab, E. (2009). E-Banking Diffusion in the Jordanian Banking Services Sector: An Empirical Analysis of Key Factors. *International Journal of Actor-Network Theory and Technological Innovation*, *1*(2), 50–65.

Alawneh, A., & Hattab, E. (2008). E-Business Value Creation in Jordanian Banking Services Industry: An Empirical Analysis of Key Factors. In *Proceedings of the International Arab Conference on e-Technology* (IACeT'2008). Arab Open University, Amman-Jordan. October 15-16, 2008.

Alawneh, A., & Hattab, E. (2009). An Empirical Study of the Sources Affecting E-Business Value Creation in Jordanian Banking Services Sector. *The International Arab Journal of e-Technology (IAJeT)., 1*(2).

Alberts, D. S., Garstka, J. J., & Stein, F. P. (2000*). Network Centric Wardare: Developing and Leveraging Information Superiority, CCRP Publication Series* (Dept. of Defense), Washington, DC, pp 1-284. Retrieved from http://www.dodccrp.org/publications/pdf/Alberts_NCW.pdf

Alcadipani, R., & Hassard, J. (2010). Actor-Network Theory, organizations and critique: towards a politics of organizing. *Organization, 17*(4), 419–435. doi:10.1177/1350508410364441

Alexander, M. (2000, 23 April 2000). Be Online or Be Left Behind - the Older Crowd Head for Cyberspace. *Boston Globe*.

Al-Gahtani, S. S. (2003). Computer technology adoption in saudi arabia: Correlates of perceived innovation attributes. *Information Technology for Development, 10*(1), 57–69. doi:10.1002/itdj.1590100106

Al-Hajri, S., & Tatnall, A. (2007, 4-6 June 2007). *Internet Technology in Omani Banks – a Case of Adoption at a Slower Rate.* Paper presented at the 20th Bled e-Conference - eMergence: Merging and Emerging Technologies, Processes and Institutions Bled, Slovenia.

Allen, P. E., & Andriani, P. (2007). Diversity, interconnectivity and sustainability. In J. Bogg, & R. Geyer (Eds.), *Complexity, science and society*. Abingdon: Radcliffe Publishing Ltd, 1-32.

AlMarzouq, M., Zheng, L., Rong, G., & Grover, V. (2005). Open Source: Concepts, Benefits, and Challenges. *Communications of the AIS, 16*, 756–784.

Al-Yaseen, H., Eldabi, T., & Paul, R. J. (2004) A Quantitative Assessment of Operational Use Evaluation of Information Technology: Benefits and Barriers. *Proceedings of the Tenth Americas Conference on Information Systems.* New York, New York, USA.

American University. (2008). *Visualizing data.* Retrieved 16 Sept 2008, from http://www.j-learning.org/present_it/page/visualizing_data

Anderson, J. C., & Gerbing, D. W. (1988). Structural Equation Modelling in practice: a review and recommended two-step approach. *Psychological Bulletin, 103*(3), 411–423. doi:10.1037/0033-2909.103.3.411

Andersson, T., Curley, M. G., & Formica, P. (2010). *Knowledge-Driven Entrepreneurship: The Key to Social and Economic Transformation.* New York, Dordrecht, Heidelberg, London: Springer Science + Business Media.

Andreu, R., & Ciborra, C. (1998). *Organisational learning and core capabilities development. Information Technology and Organisational Transformation: Innovation for the 21st Century Organisation* (Galliers, D. R., & Baets, R. J. W., Eds.). New York: John Wiley & Sons Ltd.

Andrew, J. P., & Sirkin, H. L. (2006). *Payback: reaping the rewards of innovation.* Boston, MA: Harvard Business School Press.

Appadurai, A. (2005). *Nowoczesność bez granic. Kulturowe wymiary globalizacji.* Cracow: Universitas.

Atkins, M. (1995). What should we be assessing? In Knight, P. (Ed.), *Assessing for Learning in Higher Education.* London: Kogan Page.

Atkinson, C. J. (2000). The 'Soft Information Systems and Technologies Methodology' (SISTeM): An actor network contingency approach to integrated development. *European Journal of Information Systems, 9*, 104–123.

Aurik, J. C., Jonk, G. J., & Willen, R. E. (2003). *Rebuilding the corporate genome: unlocking the real value of your business.* Hoboken, NJ: John Wiley & Sons.

Avis, J. (2002). Developing Staff in Further Education: discourse, learners and practice. *Research in Post-Compulsory Education, 7*(3), 339–352. doi:10.1080/13596740200200135

Avis, J. (2005). Beyond performativity: reflections on activist professionalism and the labour process in further education. *Journal of Education Policy, 20*(2), 209–222. doi:10.1080/0268093052000341403

Avis, P. (2009). General Systems Theory. In Avis, P. (Ed.), *Psychological Perspectives* (pp. 113–128). Cape Town: Pearson Education South Africa.

Baark, E., & Heeks, R. (1998). *Evaluation of Donor-Funded Information Technology Transfer Projects in China: A Lifecycle Approach, Development Informatics Working Paper Series*, paper No. 1, Institute for Development Policy and Management, University of Manchester, Manchester U

Babcock, C. (2007). What Will Drive Open Source? *InformationWeek, Mar 19, 2007,* 36-44.

Back, J., & Oppenheim, C. (2001). *A model of cognitive load for IR: implications for user relevance feedback interaction, Information Res. 2*. Retrieved from http://InformationR.net/ir/6-2/ws2.html

Bandura, A. (1986). *Social Foundations of Thought and Action: a Social Cognitive Theory*. Englewood Cliffs, NJ: Prentice-Hall.

Banjeri, D. (2004). The people and health service development in India: a brief overview. *International Journal of Health Services, 34*, 123–142. doi:10.2190/9N5U-4NFK-FQDH-J46W

Barad, K. (2003). Posthumanist Performativity: Toward an Understanding of How Matter Comes to Matter. *Signs: Journal of Women in Culture and Society, 28*, 801–831. doi:10.1086/345321

Bardini, T. (1994). A Translation Analysis of the Green Revolution in Bali,'. *Science, Technology & Human Values, 19*(2), 152–168. doi:10.1177/016224399401900202

Barile, S. & Polese, F. (2010). Smart service systems and viable service systems

Barile, S., Spohrer, J. & Polese, F. (2010). System thinking for service research advances Volume 2 • Number 1/2 • Spring/Summer 2010, *Service Science* 2(1/2) © 2010 SSG

Barnett, T. P. M. (2004). *The Pentagon's New Map* (pp. 1–435). New York: G.P. Putnam & Sons.

Barnett, R. (2003). *Beyond All Reason: living with ideology in the university*. Buckingham: Open University Press/Society for Research into Higher Education.

Barry, A. (2006). Actor-Network-Theory. In A. Harrington, B.L. Marshall & H.P. Müller (Eds.), *Encyclopedia of social theory*. Abingdon: Routledge, 4-5.

Barton, D., & Hamilton, M. (2005). Literacy, reification and the dynamics of social interaction. In Barton, D., & Tusting, K. (Eds.), *Beyond Communities of Practice: Language, Power and Social Context*. Cambridge, UK: Cambridge University Press. doi:10.1017/CBO9780511610554.003

Barua, A. (2001). P., Konana, A. B., & Whinston, F. (2001). Driving e-business excellence. *MIT Sloan Management Rev., 34*(1), 36–44.

Basel Committee Report on Banking Supervision. (1998). Bank of International Settlements. In *Molina and Ben-Jadeed 2004*. Basel: Risk Management for Electronic Banking and Electronic Money Activities.

Bauchspies, W. K., Croissant, J., & Restivo, S. (2006). *Science, technology, and society: a sociological approach*. Oxford, Malden, Victoria: Blackwell Publishing.

Bauman, Z. (2003). *Liquid Modernity*. Cambridge: Polity Press.

Baygeldi, M., & Smithson, S. (2004). Ability of the Actor Network Theory (ANT) to Model and Interpret an Electronic Market. In Gupta, J. N. D., & Sharma, S. K. (Eds.), *Creating knowledge based organizations* (pp. 109–126). London: Idea Group Publishing.

Beerel, A. (2009). *Leadership as change management*. New Delhi: Sage Publications India Pvt Ltd.

Belk, R. W., & Tumbat, G. (2005). The cult of Macintosh. *Consumption Markets and Culture, 8*(3), 205–217. doi:10.1080/10253860500160403

Benamati, J., & Lederer, A. L. (1999). An empirical study of IT management and rapid IT change, In *Proceedings of the SIGCPR conference on Computer personnel research, Communication of the ACM*, pp.144-153, New Orleans; Louisiana.

Berghout, E., Nijland, M., & Grant, K. (2005). Seven Ways to get Your Favoured IT Project Accepted – Politics in IT Evaluation. *Electronic Journal of Information Systems Evaluation, 8*, 31–40.

Berntsen, H. O., & Seim, R. (2007). Design Research through the Lens of Sociology of Technology. Retrieved August 18, 2007, from http:www2.uiah.fi/sefun/DSIU%20Berntsen%20_%Design%20research.pdf

Bielenia-Grajewska, M. (2009). Actor-Network Theory in Intercultural Communication: Translation through the Prism of Innovation, Technology, Networks and Semiotics. *International Journal of Actor-Network Theory and Technological Innovation, 1/4*, 53–69.

Bielenia-Grajewska, M. (2010). The Linguistic Dimension of Expatriatism- Hybrid Environment, Hybrid Linguistic Identity. *European Journal of Cross-Cultural Competence and Management, 1/2*, 212–231. doi:10.1504/EJCCM.2010.031998

Bijker, W. E., Hughes, T. P., & Pinch, T. J. (1987). *The social construction of technological systems: New directions in the sociology and history of technology*. Cambridge, Mass.: MIT Press.

Bijker, W. E., & Law, J. (1992). *Shaping technology/building society: Studies in sociotechnical change*. Cambridge, MA: MIT Press.

Bijker, W. E. (1993). Do Not Despair: There is life after constructivism. *Science, Technology & Human Values, 18*(1), 113–138. doi:10.1177/016224399301800107

Bijker, W. E. (1995). *Of Bicycle, Bakelite and Bulbs: Towards a theory of sociotechnical change*. Cambridge, MA: MIT Press.

Bingley, S., & Burgess, S. (2009). A framework for the adoption of the Internet in local sporting bodies: A local sporting association example. In Pope, N., Kuhn, K. L., & Forster, J. J. H. (Eds.), *Digital sport for performance enhancement and competitive evolution: Intelligent gaming technologies* (pp. 212–227). Hershey, PA: IGI Global.

Bird, J., & Crawley, G. (1994). Franchising and other further education/higher education partnerships: the student experience and policy. In Haselgrove, S. (Ed.), *The Student Experience*. Buckingham, UK: Open University Press/SRHE.

Bloomfield, B. P., Coombs, R., Knights, D., & Littler, D. (Eds.). (1997). *Information Technology and Organizations: Strategies, Networks, and Integration*. Oxford, UK: Oxford University Press.

Bloomfield, B. P., & Vurdubakis, T. (1997). Paper Traces: inscribing organizations and information technology. In Bloomfield, B. P., Coombs, R., Knights, D., & Littler, D. (Eds.), *Information Technology and Organizations: Strategies, Networks, and Integration* (pp. 85–111). Oxford, UK: Oxford University Press.

Bodner, G. M., & McMillen, T. L. B. (1986). Cognitive restructuring as an early stage in problem solving. *Journal of Research in Science Teaching, 23*, 727–737. doi:10.1002/tea.3660230807

Bonaccorsi, A., & Rossi, C. (2003). Why Open Source software can succeed. *Research Policy, 32*(7), 1243–1258. doi:10.1016/S0048-7333(03)00051-9

Boons, F. (2009). Ecology in the social sciences: an overview. In Boons, F., & Howard-Grenville, J. A. (Eds.), *The social embeddedness of industrial ecology* (pp. 28–46). Cheltenham: Edward Elgar Publishing Limited.

Bosler, N. (2001, 22 May 2001). *Communication, E-Commerce and Older People*. Paper presented at the E-Commerce, Electronic Banking and Older People, Melbourne.

Bottomley, J. E. J., Chehab, M. C., Gleixner, T., Hellwig, C., Jones, D., Kroah-Hartman, G., et al. (2006). *The Dangers and Problems with GPLv3*. Retrieved January 9, 2008, from http://lwn.net/Articles/200422/

Boudourides, M. A. (2001). The Politics of Technological Innovations: Network Approaches,' presented in International Summer Academy on Technological Studies.

Boudourides, M. A. (2002). *Governance in Science and Technology*, contributed paper at the EASST 2002 Conference.

Boudreau, K. J., & Hagia, A. (2010). Platform rules: multi-sided platforms as regulators. In Gawer, A. (Ed.), *Platforms, Markets and Innovation* (pp. 163–191). Cheltenham: Edward Elgar Publishing Limited.

Bourdieu, P. (1990). *In Other Words: Essays Towards a Reflexive Sociology*. Stanford: Stanford University Press.

Boyd, J. R. COL USAF, (1987). Patterns of Conflict. (Unpubl Briefing). Retrieved from http://www.d-n-i.net

Boyle, A., Macleod, M., Slevin, A., Sobecka, N., & Burton, P. (1993). The use of information technology in the voluntary sector. *International Journal of Information Management*, *13*(2), 94–112. doi:10.1016/0268-4012(93)90076-G

Brailer, D. J., & Terasawa, A. B. (2003). *Use and Adoption of Computer-Based Patient Records* (pp. 1–42). California HealthCare Foundation.

Brandt, T., & Clinton, K. (2002). Limits of the local: expanding perspectives on literacy as a social practice. *Journal of Literacy Research*, *34*(3), 337–356. doi:10.1207/s15548430jlr3403_4

Breiger, R. L. (2003). Emergent Themes in Social Network Analysis: Results, Challenges, Opportunities. In Breiger, R., Carley, K., & Pattison, P. (Eds.), *Dynamic Social Network Modeling and Analysis: workshop summary and papers* (pp. 19–38). Washington: The National Academic Press.

Britt, H., Miller, G. C., Charles, J., Pan, Y., Valenti, L., & Henderson, J. (2007). *General Practice Activity in Australia 2005-06, Cat. no. GEP 16*. Canberra: AIHW.

Brynjolfsson, E. (1993). The productivity paradox of information technology. *Communications of the ACM*, *36*, 66–77. doi:10.1145/163298.163309

Buono, A. F. (1997). Technology transfer through acquisition, *Management Decision, 35/3*, MCB University Press, 194-204.

Burgess, S., & Trethowan, P. (2002, April). *GPs and their Web sites in Australia: Doctors as Small Businesses*. Paper presented at the IS OneWorld, Las Vegas.

Burton, D., & Hamilton, M. (2005). Literacy, reification and the dynamics of social interaction. In Burton, D., & Tusting, K. (Eds.), *Beyond Communities of Practice: Language, Power and Social Context* (pp. 14–35). New York: Cambridge University Press. doi:10.1017/CBO9780511610554.003

Buse, K. (1999). Keeping a tight grip on the reins: donor control over aid coordination and management in Bangladesh. *Health Policy and Planning*, *14*, 219–228. doi:10.1093/heapol/14.3.219

Buxton, J. N., & Malcolm, R. (1991, January). Software technology transfer. *Software Engineering Journal*.

Buzzacchi, L. M., Colombo, G., & Mariotti, S. (1995). Technological regimes and innovation in services: the case of the Italian banking industry. *Research Policy*, *24*, 151–168. doi:10.1016/0048-7333(93)00756-J

Byrne, B. M. (2001). *Structural Equation Modelling with AMOS: Basic Concepts, Applications, and Programming*. Mahwah, NJ: Lawrence Erlbaum Associates, Inc.

Byrne, B. M. (2006). *Structural Equation Modelling with EQS: Basic concepts, applications, and programming* (2 ed.). Mahwah, NJ: Lawrence Erlbaum Associates, Inc.

Cadili, S., & Whitley, E. A. (2005). *On the Interpretive Flexibility of Hosted ERP Systems* (Working Paper Series No. 131). London: Department of Information Systems, The London School of Economics and Political Science.

Callon, M., Courtial, J. P., Turner, W. A., & Bauin, S. (1983). From Translations to Problematic Networks: An Introduction to Co-Word Analysis. *Social Sciences Information. Information Sur les Sciences Sociales*, *22*(2), 191–235. doi:10.1177/053901883022002003

Callon, M. (1986). *Some elements of a sociology of translation: domestication of the scallops and the fisherman of St. Brieuc Bay,' in J. Law, Power, action and belief: a new sociology of knowledge?* London: Routledge.

Callon, M., & Law, J. (1982). On Interests and their Transformation: Enrolment and Counter-Enrolment. *Social Studies of Science*, *12*, 615–625. doi:10.1177/030631282012004006

Callon, M. (1987). Society in the Making: the study of technology as a tool for sociological analysis. In Bijker, W. E., Hughes, T. P., & Pinch, T. (Eds.), *The Social Construction of Technological Systems* (pp. 83–103). Cambridge, MA: MIT Press.

Callon, M., & Latour, B. (1981). Unscrewing the big leviathan: How actors manufacture reality and how sociologists help them to do so. In Knorr-Cetina, K. D., & Cicourel, A. V. (Eds.), *Advances in social theory and methodology: Toward an integration of micro- and macro-sociologies* (pp. 277–303). Boston, MA: Routledge & Kegan-Paul.

Callon, M. (1991). Techno-economic networks and irreversibility. In Law, J. (Ed.), *A sociology of monsters: Essays on power, technology and domination* (pp. 132–161). London: Routledge.

Callon, M. (1986). Some Elements of a Sociology of Translation: Domestication of the Scallops and the Fishermen of St Brieuc Bay. In Law, J. (Ed.), *Power, Action & Belief. A New Sociology of Knowledge?* (pp. 196–229). London: Routledge & Kegan Paul.

Callon, M., & Law, J. (2003). *On Qualculation, Agency and Otherness*. published by the Centre for Science Studies, Lancaster University, Lancaster LA1 4YN, UK. Retrieved August 8, 2007 from http://www.comp.lancs.ac.uk/sociology/papers/Callon-Law-Qualculation-Agency-Otherness.pdf

Capps, B., & Fairley, B. E. (2002). PROSM: A systematic approach to planning technology transfer campaigns. Retreived January 3, 2003, from http://www.cse.ogi.edu/~dfairley/PRISM.pdf

Carr, N. G. (2003). IT Doesn't Matter. *Harvard Business Review*, *81*(5).

Carr, N. G. (2004). *Does IT Matter? Information Technology and the Corrosion of Competitive Advantage*. Boston, USA: Harvard Business School press.

Castells, M. (2009). *Communication power*. Oxford: Oxford University Press.

Catt, I. E., & Eicher-Catt, D. (2010). Communicology: a Reflexive Human Science. In Eicher-Catt, D., & Catt, I. E. (Eds.), *Communicology: The New Science of Embodied Discourse* (pp. 15–32). Cranbury, NJ: Associated University Presses.

Cavusgil, S. T., Calantone, R. J., & Zhao, Y. (2003). Tacit knowledge transfer and firm innovation capability. *Journal of Business and Industrial Marketing*, *18*(1), 6–21. doi:10.1108/08858620310458615

Cebrowski, A. K., & Garstka, J. J. (1998). Network-centric warfare: its origin and future. *US Nav. Inst. Proc.*, *1*, 28–35.

Cetina, K. K. (1993). Strong Construtivism- From a sociologist's Point of View. *Social Studies of Science*, *23*(3), 555–563. doi:10.1177/0306312793023003005

Chandrasekaran, D., & Tellis, G. J. (2008). The global takeoff of new products: culture, wealth, or vanishing differences. *Marketing Science*, *27*(5), 844–860. doi:10.1287/mksc.1070.0329

Charity Commission for England and Wales. (2002). *Giving confidence in charities: Annual* Report 2001–2002. London.

Chatterjee, D., Grewal, R., & Sambamurthy, V. (2002). Shaping up for e-commerce: Institutional enablers of the organizational assimilation of Web technologies. *Management Information Systems Quarterly*, *26*(2), 65–89. doi:10.2307/4132321

Chau, P. Y. K., & Hu, P. J. (2002). Examining a model of information technology acceptance by individual professionals: An exploratory study. *Journal of Management Information Systems*, *18*(4), 191–229.

Chau, P. Y. K., & Tam, K. Y. (1997). Factors affecting the adoption of open systems: An exploratory study. *Management Information Systems Quarterly*, *21*(1), 1–21. doi:10.2307/249740

Chun, I. C. J. (2003). Tasks and theories in the marketing strategy of innovative new product. *Korean Journal of Marketing*, *5*(1), 1–16.

Chung, W. W. C., Lee, W. B., & Chik, S. K. O. (1997). *Technology Transfer at The Hong Kong Polytechnic University*, IEEE.

Ciborra, C. (1996). *Groupware and teamwork*. Chichester: Wiley.

Claessens, J., Dem, V., Decock, D., Preneel, B., & Vandewalle, J. (2002). On the security of today's online electronic banking systems. *Computers & Security, 21*(3), 257–269. doi:10.1016/S0167-4048(02)00312-7

Clarke, J. (2002). A new kind of symmetry: actor-network theories and the new literacy studies. *Studies in the Education of Adults, 34*(2), 107–122.

Clarke, A. (2005). *Situational analysis: grounded theory after the postmodern turn*. Thousand Oaks, CA: Sage Publications Inc.

Clegg, S., Courpasson, D., & Phillips, N. (2006). *Power and organizations*. London: Sage Publications Ltd.

Cohen, M. A., Eliashberg, J., & Ho, T. (1996). New product development: The performance and time-to-market trade-offs. *Management Science, 42*(2), 173–186. doi:10.1287/mnsc.42.2.173

Collins, C., & Green, A. (1994). Decentralization and primary health care: some negative implications in developing countries. *International Journal of Health Services, 24*, 459–475.

Collins, H. M., & Yearley, S. (1992). Epistemological Chicken. In Pickering, A. (Ed.), *Science as Practice and Culture* (pp. 301–326). Chicago: The Universty of Chicago Press.

Collins, H. M. & Yearley, S. (1992) Journey into Space. *Science as Practice and Culture*, 369–89.

Colman, F. J. (2005). Rhizome. In Parr, A. (Ed.), *The Deleuze dictionary* (pp. 231–233). Edinburgh: Edinburgh University Press.

Commission of Higher Education. (2007). Commission of Higher Education. Retrieved January 15, 2007, from http://www.mua.go.th/default1.php

Compeau, D. R., & Higgins, C. A. (1991). *A Social Cognitive Theory Perspective on Individual Reactions to Computing Technology*. Paper presented at the Proceedings of the 12th International Conference on Information Systems, New York.

Computer Desktop Encyclopedia. (2008). *ZDNet definition for: Visualization*. Retrieved 17 Sept 2008, from http://dictionary.zdnet.com/definition/Visualization.html

Connolly, M., Jones, C., & Jones, N. (2007). Managing collaboration across further and higher education: a case in practice. *Journal of Further and Higher Education, 31*(2), 159–169. doi:10.1080/03098770701267630

Cooper, R. B., & Zmud, R. W. (1990). Information technology implementation research: A technological diffusion approach. *Management Science, 36*(2), 123–139. doi:10.1287/mnsc.36.2.123

Corallo, A. (2007). The business ecosystem as a multiple dynamic network. In Corallo, A., Passiante, G., & Prencipe, A. (Eds.), *The digital business ecosystem* (pp. 11–32). Cheltenham: Edward Elgar Publishing Limited.

Cornford, T., Ciborra, C., & Shaikh, M. (2005). Do penguins eat scallops? *European Journal of Information Systems, 14*(5), 518–521. doi:10.1057/palgrave.ejis.3000583

Council on the Ageing. (2000). Older People and the Internet Focus Group: Unpublished.

Crawford, C. S. (2005). Actor Network Theory. In Ritzer, G. (Ed.), *Encyclopedia of Social Theory* (pp. 1–3). Thousand Oaks, CA: Sage Publications, Inc.

Creswell, J., & Plano Clark, V. (2007). *Designing and conducting mixed methods research*. Thousand Oaks, CA: Sage.

Crooke, C., Gross, H., & Dymott, R. (2006). Assessment relationships in higher education: the tension of process and practice. *British Educational Research Journal, 32*(1), 95–114. doi:10.1080/01411920500402037

D'Aveni, R. A. (1994). *Hypercompetition: Managing the dynamics of strategic maneuvering*. New York: Free Press.

DA. (2007). *Diabetes Facts*. New South Wales: Diabetes Australia Frost and Sullivan Country Industry Forecast (n.d.). *European Union Healthcare Industry*. Retrieved May 11, 2004 from http://www.news-medical.net/print_article.asp?id=1405

Daft, R. (2009). *Organization Theory and Design*. Mason, OH: South-Western Cengage Learning.

Damanpour, F. (1996). Organizational complexity and innovation: Developing and testing multiple contingency models. *Management Science, 42*(5), 693–716. doi:10.1287/mnsc.42.5.693

Daniels, C. N. (1994). *Information Technology: The Management Challenge*. Reading, MA: Addison-Wesley publishing Ltd.

Davenport, T.H., Leibold, M., & Voelpel, S. (2006). *Strategic management in the innovation economy: strategy approaches and tools for dynamic innovation capabilities*. Erlangen: Publicis Corporate Publishing and Wiley-VCH Verlag.

Davis, F. D. (1986). *A Technology Acceptance Model for Empirically Testing New End-User Information Systems: Theory and Results*. Boston: MIT.

Davis, F. D. (1989). Perceived usefulness, perceived ease of use and user acceptance of information technology. *Management Information Systems Quarterly, 13*(3), 319–340. doi:10.2307/249008

Davis, F. D., Bagozzi, R., & Warshaw, P. (1989). User Acceptance of Computer Technology: A Comparison of Two Theoretical Models. *Management Science, 35*(8), 982–1003. doi:10.1287/mnsc.35.8.982

Dawson, R., & Horenkamp, M. (2007). *Service delivery innovation: creating client value and enhancing profitability*. SAP Ag.

de Bruijn, H., van der Voort, H., Dicke, W., de Jong, M., & Veeneman, W. (2004). *Creating System Innovation: How Large Scale Transitions Emerge*. London, UK: A. A Balkema Publishers.

de Laat, P. B. (2005). Copyright or copyleft? An analysis of property regimes for software development. *Research Policy, 34*(10), 1511–1532. doi:10.1016/j.respol.2005.07.003

Deering, P. (2008). *The Adoption of Information and Communication Technologies in Rural General Practice: A Socio Technical Analysis*. Melbourne: Victoria University.

Del Casino, V. J. (2009). *Social Geography*. Chichester: John Wiley & Sons Ltd.

Dempsey, B. J., Weiss, D., Jones, P., & Greenberg, J. (2002). Who is an Open Source Software Developer? *Communications of the ACM, 45*(2), 67. doi:10.1145/503124.503125

Denzin, N. K., & Lincoln, Y. S. (1994). Introduction: Entering the field of Qualitative Research. In Denzin, N. K., & Lincoln, Y. S. (Eds.), *Handbook of qualitative research* (pp. 1–17). California: Sage Publications.

Departemen ESDM. (2007). *Pokok-pokok Materi Untuk Dilaporkan pada Rakortas Energi Alternatif*.Presented in Jakarta, May 23.

Derakhshani, S. (1983). Factors Affecting Success in International Transfers of Technology- A Synthesis and a Test of a New Contingency Model. *The Developing Economies, 21*.

Dewan, R., Freimer, M., & Seidmann, A. (2000). Organizing Distribution Channels for Information Goods on the Internet. *Management Science, 46*(4), 483–496. doi:10.1287/mnsc.46.4.483.12053

Dikbas, T. E., Kocak, U. Y., & Ilgaz, H. (2008). Teachers' adoption of laptops in the stages of innovation decision process. *Proceedings of World Conference on Educational Multimedia, Hypermedia and Telecommunications 2008*, Vienna, Austria. 3147-3152.

Dooley, K. E. (1999). Towards a holistic model for the diffusion of educational technologies: an integrative review of educational innovation studies. *Journal of Educational Technology & Society, 2*(4). Retrieved from http://ifets.ieee.org/periodical/vol_4_99/kim_dooley.html.

Doolin, B., & McLeod, L. (2005). Towards critical interpretivism in IS research. In Howcroft, D., & Trauth, E. M. (Eds.), *Handbook of critical information systems research: theory and application* (pp. 244–271). Cheltenham: Edward Edgar Publishing Limited.

Doolin, B. & Lowe A (2002) "To reveal is to critique: actor–network theory and critical information systems research", Journal of Information Technology, Vol.17, No.2, June 2002, pp. 69-78(10)

du Plessis, M. (2007). The role of knowledge management in innovation. *Journal of Knowledge Management, 11*(4), 20–29. doi:10.1108/13673270710762684

Dudley, J. R. (2006). Successful Technology Transfer Requires More Than Technical Know-How. *BioPharm International, 19*(10). Retrieved May 20, 2008, from http://biopharminternational.findpharma.com/biopharm/Article/Successful-Technology-Transfer-Requires-More-Than-/ArticleStandard/Article/detail/377759

Ecclestone, K. (2001). 'I know a 2:1 when I see it': understanding criteria for degree classifications in franchised university programmes. *Journal of Further and Higher Education, 25*(3), 301–313. doi:10.1080/03098770126527

Edge, D. (1995). The Social Shaping of Technology. In Heap, N., Thomas, R., Einon, G., Mason, R., & Mackay, H. (Eds.), *Information Technology and Society: A reader*. The Open University.

Edwards, R. (2003). Ordering subjects: Actor-networks and intellectual technologies in lifelong learning. *Studies in the Education of Adults, 35*(1), 54–67.

Erickson, M. (2005). *Science, culture and society: understanding science in the twenty-first century*. Cambridge: Polity Press.

Etzkowitz, H. (2000). The Triple Helix of University-Industry-Government: Dynamics of Innovation Spaces and Implications for Policy and Evaluation," *Proceedings from the 2000 US-EU Workshop on Learning from Science and Technology Policy Evaluation*, Bad Herrenalb, Germany.

Everitt, P., & Tatnall, A. (2003). *Investigating the Adoption and Use of Information Technology by General Practitioners in Rural Australia and Why This is Less Than it Might Be*. Paper presented at the ACIS 2003, Perth.

Ezzamel, M. (1994). Organizational change and accounting: understanding the budgeting system in its organizational context. *Organization Studies, 15*(2), 213–240. doi:10.1177/017084069401500203

Farbey, B., Land, F., & Targett, D. (1994). Matching an IT project with an appropriate method of evaluation: a research note on 'Evaluating investments in IT'. *Journal of Information Technology, 9*, 239–243. doi:10.1057/jit.1994.23

Fichman, R. G. (2000). *The diffusion and assimilation of information technology innovations. R. Zmud, ed. framing the Domains of IT Management: projecting the future through the past*. Cincinnati, OH: Pinnaflex publishing.

Fishbein, M., & Ajzen, I. (1975). *Belief, Attitude, Intention, and Behavior: An Introduction to Theory and Research*. Reading, MA: Addison-Wesley.

Fisher, E., Mahajan, R. L., & Mitcham, C. (2006). Midstream Modulation of Technology: Governance From Within,'. *Science, Technology & Society, 26*(6), 485–496. doi:10.1177/0270467606295402

Fitzgerald, B. (2006). The Transformation of Open Source Software. *Management Information Systems Quarterly, 30*(3), 587–598.

Flannery, W. T., & Dietrich, G. (2000). Technology Transfer in a Complex Environment: Exploring Key Relationships. In *Proceedings of the 2000 IEEE Engineering Management Society, EMS-2000*, August 13-15, 2000 Albuquerque, New Mexico.

Fogelgren-Pedersen, A. (2005). The mobile internet: The pioneering users' adoption decisions. *Proceedings of the 38th Hawaii International Conference on Systems Sciences*, Hawaii.

Fontana, J. (2008). *Torvalds Breaks Down Linux*. Retrieved January 11, 2008, from http://www.networkworld.com/news/2008/011008-torvalds-linux.html

Fosfuri, A., Giarratana, M. S., & Luzzi, A. (2008). The Penguin Has Entered the Building: The Commercialization of Open Source Software Products. *Organization Science, 19*(2), 292–305. doi:10.1287/orsc.1070.0321

Fox, S. (2000). Communities of practice, Foucault and actor-network theory. *Journal of Management Studies, 37*(6), 853–867. doi:10.1111/1467-6486.00207

Fox, S. (2005). An actor-network critique of community in higher education: implications for networked learning. *Studies in Higher Education, 30*(1), 95–110. doi:10.1080/0307507052000307821

Franck, E., & Jungwirth, C. (2003). Reconciling Rent-Seekers and Donators–The Governance Structure of Open Source. *Journal of Management and Governance, 7*(4), 401–421. doi:10.1023/A:1026261005092

Free Software Foundation. (2008). *Free Software and the GNU Operating System.* Retrieved December 17, 2008, from http://www.fsf.org/about

Free Software Foundation, & Software Freedom Law Center. (2006). *GPLv3 Process Definition.* freshmeat. net. (2008). *Statistics and Top 20: License breakdown.* Retrieved December 11, 2008, from http://freshmeat. net/stats/#license

Freeman, E., & Liedtka, J. (2005). Stakeholder Capitalism and the Value Chain. In Bettley, A., Mayle, D., & Tantoush, T. (Eds.), *Operations management: a strategic approach* (pp. 35–47). London: Sage Publications, Ltd.

Friendly, M. (2006). A brief history of data visualization. In C. Chen, W. Hardie & A. Unwin (Eds.), *Handbook of Data visualization,* Springer-Verlag, 15-54

Frutkin, S. (1975). The Technology Transfer Process-The Case of the LNG Tanker [IEEE]. *OCEAN, V7,* 855–859.

Gao, P. (2005). Using actor-network theory to analyse strategy formulation. [Blackwell Publishing]. *Information Systems Journal, 15*(3), 255–275. .doi:10.1111/j.1365-2575.2005.00197.x

Garstka, J. J. (2000). Network Centric Warfare: an overview of emerging theory. *Phalanx, 4,* 28–33.

Geels, F. W. (2005). *Technological transitions and system innovations: a co-evolutionary and socio-technical analysis.* Cheltenham: Edward Edgar Publishing.

Gefen, D., & Straub, D. W. (1997). Gender differences in the perception and use of e-mail: An extension to the Technology Acceptance [Electronic Version]. *MIS Quarterly,* 21, 389. Retrieved 7 September 2004 from http://search. epnet.com/login.aspx?direct=true&db=aph&an=36297

Gibbert, M. (2010). *Strategy Making in a Crisis: From Analysis to Imagination.* Cheltenham: Edward Elgar Publishing Limited.

Gibson, D. V., & Smilor, W. (1991). Key Variables in Technology Transfer: A field – Study Based on Empirical Analysis. *Journal of Engineering and Technology Management, 8,* 287–312. doi:10.1016/0923-4748(91)90015-J

Gibson, D. V., & Harlan, G. T. (1995). Inter-Organizational Technology Transfer: The Case of the NSF Science and Technology Centers, In *Proceedings of the 28th Annual Hawaii International Conference on System Sciences.*

Gilbert, K. W. (2007). Slowness: notes towards a economy of différencial rates of being. In P. Ticineto Clough & J. Halley (Eds.), *The affective turn: theorizing the social.* Duke University Press, 77-105.

Gleeson, D., Davies, J., & Wheeler, E. (2005). On the making and taking of professionalism in the further education workplace. *British Journal of Sociology of Education, 26*(4), 445–460. doi:10.1080/01425690500199818

Goldenberg, J., Libai, B., & Muller, E. (2002). Riding the saddle: How cross-market communications can create a major slump in sales. *Journal of Marketing, 66,* 1–16. doi:10.1509/jmkg.66.2.1.18472

Golder, P., & Tellis, G. (2004). Growing, growing, gone: cascades, diffusion, and turning points in the product life cycle. *Marketing Science, 23,* 207–218. doi:10.1287/mksc.1040.0057

Gottschalk, P. (1999). Implementation Predictors of Formal Information Technology Strategy. *Information & Management, 36*(2), 77–91. doi:10.1016/S0378-7206(99)00008-7

GPSRG. (1998). *Changing the Future Through Partnerships.* Canberra: Commonwealth Department of Health and Family Services, General Practice Strategy Review Group.

Grant, I. H. (2005). Postmodernism and science and technology. In S. Sim (Ed.), *The Routledge companion to postmodernism.* Abingdon: Routledge, 58-70.

Graves, M. (2008). *Mind, brain and the elusive soul: human systems of cognitive science and religion.* Aldershot: Ashgate Publishing.

Grint, K. (2005). *The sociology of work: introduction.* Cambridge: Polity Press.

Grint, K., & Woolgar, S. (1997). *The machine at work: technology, work, and organization*. Oxford: Blackwell Publishers Ltd.

Grönroos, C. 2006. What can a service logic offer marketing theory? in R.F. Lusch and S.L. Vargo, (Eds.), *The service–dominant logic of marketing dialog, debate, and directions*. 320–333. Armonk: M.E. Sharpe

Gross, J. (1998, 1998). Wielding Mouse and Modem, Elderly Remain in the Loop. *The New York Times*.

Grover, V. (1993). An empirically derived model for the adoption of customer-based inter organizational systems. *Decision Sciences*, *24*(3), 603–640. doi:10.1111/j.1540-5915.1993.tb01295.x

Gunaratne, S. A. (2009). Asian Communication Theory. In Littlejohn, S. W., & Fos, K. A. (Eds.), *Encyclopedia of Communication Theory* (pp. 46–52). Thousand Oaks, CA: Sage Publications Inc.

Hair, J., Black, W., Babin, B., Anderson, R., & Tatham, R. (2006). *Multivariate data analysis* (6th ed.). Upper Saddle River, NJ: Pearson Education, Inc.

Hall, M., & Banting, K. (2002). *The nonprofit sector in Canada: An introduction*. Working Paper, School of Policy Studies, Queen's University.

Hamilton, M. (2009). Putting words in their mouths: the alignment of identities with system goals through the use of individual learning plans. *British Educational Research Journal*, *35*(2), 221–242. doi:10.1080/01411920802042739

Hamilton, M. (2001). Privileged literacies: policy, institutional process and the life of the IALS. *Language and Education, 15*(2 and 3), 178-196.

Hanneman, R. (2002). Introduction to social network methods. Retrieved from www.faculty.ucr.edu/hanneman/

Hanseth, O., & Monteiro, E. (1997). Inscribing Behaviour in Information Infrastructure Standards. *Accounting. Management and Information Technology, 7*(4), 183–211. doi:10.1016/S0959-8022(97)00008-8

Hanseth, O., Monteiro, E., & Hatling, M. (1996). Developing Information Infrastructure: The Tension between Standardization and Flexibility. *Science, Technology & Human Values*, *21*(4), 407–426. doi:10.1177/016224399602100402

Hanseth, O., & Braa, K. (1998, 13-16 December). *Technology as Traitor: emergent SAP infrastructure in a global organization*. Paper presented at the Nineteenth International Conference on Information Systems (ICIS), Helsinki, Finland.

Harman, G. (2009). *Prince of networks: Bruno Latour and metaphysics*. Melbourne: Re. Press.

Hart, P. J., & Saunders, C. S. (1998). Emerging electronic partnerships: Antecedents and dimensions of EDI use from the supplier's perspective. *Journal of Management Information Systems*, *14*(4), 87–111.

Hayduk, L. A. (1987). *Structural equation modelling with LISREL: Essentials and advances*. Baltimore, MD: The Johns Hopkins University Press.

Heilbroner, R. L. (1967). Do Machines Make History? *Technology and Culture*, (July): 335–345. doi:10.2307/3101719

Hess, C. M., & Kemerer, C. F. (1994). Computerized loan origination systems: An industry case study of electronic markets hypothesis. *Management Information Systems Quarterly*, *18*(3), 251–275. doi:10.2307/249618

Hilborne, J. (1996). Ensuring quality in further and higher education partnerships. In Abramson, M., Bird, J., & Stennett, A. (Eds.), *Further and Higher Education Partnerships: the Future for Collaboration*. Buckingham, UK: Open University Press/Society for Research into Higher Education.

Hironaka, W. (1992, March). We must tackle population problems. *Integration (Tokyo, Japan)*, *31*(27).

Hirschheim, R. & Smithson, S. (1988) A critical analysis of IS evaluation. *Information Systems Assessment: Issues and Challenges*, 17-37.

Howard, L. M. (1991). Public and private donor financing for health in developing countires. *Infectious Disease Clinics of North America*, *5*, 221–234.

Hughes, T. P. (1983). *Networks of Power: Electrification in Western Society, 1880-1930*. Baltimore: Johns Hopkins University Press.

Hughes, T. P. (1986). The Seamless Web: Technology, Science, Etcetera, Etcetera. *Social Studies of Science, 16*(2), 281–292. doi:10.1177/0306312786016002004

Hughes, T. P. (1987). The Evolution of Large Technological Systems. In Bijker, W. E., Hughes, T. P., & Pinch, T. J. (Eds.), *The Social Construction of Technological Systems: New direction in the sociology and history of technology*. Cambridge, MA: MIT Press.

Hughes, T. P. (1999). Edison and electric light. In Mackenzie, D., & Wajcman, J. (Eds.), *The Social Shaping of Technology* - (2nd ed.). Buckingham, Philadelphia: Open University Press.

Hughes, T. P. (1994). Technological Momentum. In Smith, M. R., & Marx, L. (Eds.), *Does Technology Drive History? The dilemma of technological determinism*. Cambridge, MA: MIT Press.

Hyperdictionary. (2006). *Internet: Definition*. Retrieved July 5, 2006, from http://www.hyperdictionary.com/dictionary/Internet

Iansiti, M., & Levien, R. (2004). *The keystone advantage: what the new dynamics of business ecosystems mean*. Boston, MA: Harvard Business School Publishing Corporation.

IDRC/UNCTAD. (1997). *An Assault of Poverty: Basic Human Needs, Science and Technology*. Retrieved March, 6, 2008 from http://www.idrc.ca/en/ev-9364-201-1-DO_TOPIC.html.

IfM & IBM. (2008). *Succeeding through service innovation: a service perspective for education, research, business and government*. Cambridge, UK: University of Cambridge Institute of Manufacturing. ISBM.

Igbaria, M., Zinatelli, N., Cragg, P., & Cavaye, A. L. M. (1997). Personal computing acceptance factors in small firms: A structural equation model. *Management Information Systems Quarterly, 21*(3), 279–305. doi:10.2307/249498

Industry Canada. (2008). *Technology roadmaps: Geomatics technology roadmap — appendix D: Glossary*. Retrieved 17 Sept 2008, from http://www.ic.gc.ca/epic/site/trm-crt.nsf/en/rm00196e.html

Internet Usage and population in Oceania. (2006). *Internet Usage and population in Oceania*. Retrieved July 7, 2006, from http://www.internetworldstats.com/stats6.htm

Internet Usage for Asia. (2006). *Internet Usage for Asia*. Retrieved July 7, 2006, from http://www.internetworldstats.com/stats3.htm#asia

Internet Usage Statistics for the Americas. (2006). *Internet Usage Statistics for the Americas*. Retrieved 7 July 7, 2006, from http://www.internetworldstats.com/stats2.htm#north

Internet Usage Statistics-The Big Picture. (2006). Retrieved July 7, 2006, from http://www.internetworldstats.com/stats.htm

Internet World Stats. (2006). *Internet Usage in Asia*. Retrieved 9 January, 2007, from http://www.internetworldstats.com/stats3.htm#asia

Introna, L. D. & Whittaker, L. (2002) The Phenomenology of Information Systems Evaluation: Overcoming the Subject/Object Dualism. *Global and Organizational Discourse about Information Technology*, 155-175.

Islam, T., & Meade, N. (1997). The diffusion of successive generations of a technology: A more general model. *Technological Forecasting and Social Change, 56*(1), 49–60. doi:10.1016/S0040-1625(97)00030-9

Ivanic, R. (1998). *Writing and Identity: the discoursal construction of identity in academic writing*. Amsterdam: John Benjamins.

Iyamu, T., & Dewald, R. (2010). The use of Structuration and Actor Network Theory for analysis: A case study of a financial institution in South Africa. *International Journal of Actor-Network Theory and Technological Innovation, 2*(1), 1–26.

Jackson, P. J., & Van der Wielen, J. (1998). *Teleworking: international perspectives: from telecommuting to the virtual organisation*. London: Routledge.

Jaeger, B. (2005). Digital Visions- the role of politicians in transition. In Bekkers, V., & Homburg, V. (Eds.), *The information ecology of e-government: e-government as institutional and technological innovation in public administration* (pp. 107–126). Amsterdam: IOS Press.

James, R., Baldwin, G., Coutes, H., Krawse, K., & McInnis, C. (2004). *Analysis of equity groups in higher education 1991-2002*. Canberra: DEST.

Jayasuriya, R. (1997). Evaluating health information systems: an assessment of frameworks. *Australian Health Review*, *20*, 68–85. doi:10.1071/AH970068a

Jegathesan, J., Gunasekaran, A., & Muthaly, S. (1997). Technological development & transfer: experiences from Malaysia. *International Journal of Technology Management*, *13*(2), 196–214. doi:10.1504/IJTM.1997.001655

Jones, S., & Hughes, J. (2001). Understanding IS evaluation as a complex social process: a case study of a UK local authority. *European Journal of Information Systems*, *10*, 189–203. doi:10.1057/palgrave.ejis.3000405

Jones, M., & Samalionis, F. (2008). From small ideas to radical service innovation, *Design Management* [http://www.ideo.com/images/uploads/thinking/publications/pdfs/08191JON20.pdf]. *RE:view*, *19*(1).

Jöreskog, K. G. (1993). Testing structural equation models. In *B.M. Byrne (2006), Structural Equation Modelling with EQS: basic concepts, applications, and programming* (2nd ed.). Mahwah, NJ: Lawrence Erlbaum Associates, Inc.

Josserand, E. (2004). *The network organization: the experience of leading French multinationals*. Cheltenham: Edward Edgar Publishing Limited.

Kahen, G. (1997). Building a Framework for Successful Information Technology Transfer to Developing Countries: Requirements and Effective Integration to a Viable IT Transfer, *Int. Journal of Computer and Applications Technology*, *9*(1), 1–8.

Kandampully, J. (2002). Innovation as the core competency of a service organisation: the role of technology, knowledge and networks. *European Journal of Innovation Management*, *5*(1), 18–26. doi:10.1108/14601060210415144

Kappelman, L. A. (1995). Measuring user involvement: A diffusion of innovation perspective. *ACM SIGMIS Database*, *26*(2-3), 65–86. doi:10.1145/217278.217286

Karahanna, E., Straub, D. W., & Chervany, N. L. (1999). Information technology adoption across time: a cross-sectional comparison of pre-adoption and post-adoption beliefs [Electronic Version]. *MIS Quarterly*, *23*, 183-213. Retrieved August 31, 2004 from http://search.epnet.com/login.aspx?direct=true&db=aph&authdb=epref&an=MQ.BC.AHC.KARAHANNA.ITAATC

Katz, M., & Shapiro, C. (1994). Systems competition and network effects. *The Journal of Economic Perspectives*, *8*(2), 93–115.

Katz, T. (2000). University Education for Developing Professional Practice. In Bourner, T., Katz, T., & Watson, D. (Eds.), *New Directions if Professional Higher Education*. Buckingham: Open University Press/Society for Research into Higher Education.

Katzan, H. (2008). Foundations of service science concepts and facilities. *Journal Of Service Science*, *1*(1), 1–22.

Kendall, J., Tung, L., Chua, K. H., Ng, C. H. D., & Tan, S. M. (2001). Receptivity of Singapore's SMEs to electronic commerce adoption. *The Journal of Strategic Information Systems*, *10*(3), 223–242. doi:10.1016/S0963-8687(01)00048-8

Kerner, S. M. (2008). *Torvalds Still Keen On GPLv2: The Linux creator explains why he's sticking with the older version of the General Public License*. Retrieved January 11, 2008, from http://www.internetnews.com/dev-news/article.php/3720371

Klenowski, V. (2002). *Developing Portfolios for Learning and Assessment*. London: Routledge.

Kline, R. B. (1998). *Principles and practice of Structural Equation Modelling*. New York: Guilford Press.

Kling, R. (1980). Social analysis of computing: Theoretical perspectives in recent empirical research. *ACM Computing Surveys*, *1*(12), 61–110. doi:10.1145/356802.356806

Klischewski, R. (2000). *Systems Development as Networking*. Paper presented at the Americas Conference on Information Systems (AMCIS), Long Beach, CA.

Kolodinsky, J. M., & Hilgert, M. A. (2004). the adoption of electronic banking technologies by US consumers. *International Journal of Bank Marketing, 22*(4), 238–259. doi:10.1108/02652320410542536

Kripanont, N. (2007). *Examining a Technology Acceptance Model of Internet Usage by Academics within Thai Business Schools.* Melbourne: Victoria University.

Kuan, K. K. Y., & Chau, P. Y. K. (2001). A perception-based model for EDI adoption in small business using a technology-organization-environment framework. *Information & Management, 38*(8), 507–512. doi:10.1016/S0378-7206(01)00073-8

Kulkarni, R., & Nathanson, L. A. (2005). *Medical Informatics in medicine, E-Medicine.* Retrieved from http://www.emedicine.com/emerg/topic879.htm

Lacovou, C. L., Benbasat, I., & Dexter, A. S. (1995). Electronic data interchange and small organizations: Adoption and impact of technology. *Management Information Systems Quarterly, 19*(4), 465–485. doi:10.2307/249629

Lacroix, A. (1999). International concerted action on collaboration in telemedicine: G8 sub-project 4, Sted. Health Technol. *Inform (Silver Spring, Md.), 64*, 12–19.

Lall, S. (1987). *Learning to industrialize.* Basingstoke, UK: Macmillan.

Lambert, D., & Slater, S. F. (1999). Perspective: first, fast, and on time: the path to success. or is it? *Journal of Product Innovation Management, 16*(5), 427–438. doi:10.1016/S0737-6782(99)00017-X

Lanzara, G. F., & Morner, M. (2005). Artifacts Rule! How Organizing Happens in Open Source Software Projects. In Czarniawska, B., & Hernes, T. (Eds.), *Actor-Network Theory and Organizing* (pp. 197–206). Malmo, Sweden: Liber & Copenhagen Business School Press.

Lash, S., & Urry, J. (1994). *Economies of sign and space.* London: Sage.

Latour, B. (2005). *Reassembling the Social: An Introduction to Actor-Network-Theory.* USA: Oxford University Press.

Latour, B., & Woolgar, S. (1979). *Laboratory life.* Beverly Hills, CA: Sage.

Latour, B. (1993). *We have never been modern.* Hemel Hempstead Harvester, Wheatsheaf.

Latour, B. (2005). *Reassembling the social: An introduction to actor-network-theory.* Oxford: Oxford University Press.

Latour, B. (1987). *Science in Action: How to Follow Scientists and Engineers Through Society.* Milton Keynes, UK: Open University Press.

Latour, B. (2001). *Technology is Society Made Durable," A Sociology of Monsters: Essays on Power, Technology and Domination.* London: Routledge.

Latour, B. (1994). Pragmatogonies. *The American Behavioral Scientist, 37*(6), 791–808. doi:10.1177/0002764294037006006

Latour, B. (1999). *Pandora's Hope: Essays on the reality of science studies.* Cambridge, MA: Harvard University Press.

Latour, B. (2008). *What is the style of matters of concern? Two lectures in empirical philosophy.* Amsterdam: Van Gorcum.

Latour, B., & Woolgar, S. (1986). *Laboratory Life: The Construction of Laboratory Facts* (2nd ed.). Princeton, NJ: Princeton University Press.

Latour, B. (1986). The power of association. In Law, J. (Ed.), *Power, action and belief: a new sociology of knowledge?* (pp. 196–223). London: Routledge & Kegan-Paul.

Latour, B. (1991). Technology is Society Made Durable. In Law, J. (Ed.), *Sociology of Monsters: essays on power, technology and domination* (pp. 103–131). London: Routledge.

Latour, B. (1986). The Powers of Association. In Law, J. (Ed.), *Power, Action and Belief. A New Sociology of Knowledge? Sociological Review monograph 32* (pp. 264–280). London: Routledge & Kegan Paul.

Latour, B. (1996). *Aramis or the Love of Technology.* Cambridge, Ma: Harvard University Press.

Latour, B. (1999) On recalling ANT. *Actor-network Theory and After*, 15–25.

Latour, B. (2003). The World Wide Lab. RESEARCH SPACE: Experimentation Without Representation is Tyranny. *Wired, 11*(06). Retrieved from http://www.wired.com/wired/archive/11.06/research_spc.html

Latour, B. (2004). Why has critique run out of steam? From matters of fact to matters of concern. *Critical Enquiry, 30*(2), 225-248. Retrieved from http://criticalinquiry.uchicago.edu/issues/v30/30n2.Latour.html

Law, J. (2002). *Aircraft Stories: Decentering the Object in Technoscience*. Duke University Press.

Law, J. (2004). *After Method: Mess in Social Science Research*. Routledge.

Law, J. (1992). Notes on the theory of actor-network: ordering, strategy and heterogeneity. *Systems Practice, 5*(4), 379–393. doi:10.1007/BF01059830

Law, J., & Hassard, E. (Eds.). (1999). *Actor Network Theory and After. Oxford and Keele*. UK: Blackwell and the Sociological Review.

Law, J., & Callon, M. (1988). Engineering and Sociology in a Military Aircraft Project: A Network Analysis of Technological Change. *Social Problems, 35*(3), 284–297. doi:10.1525/sp.1988.35.3.03a00060

Law, J., & Callon, M. (1988). Engineering and Sociology in a Military Aircraft Project: A network analysis of technological change. *Social Problems, 35*(3), 284–297. doi:10.1525/sp.1988.35.3.03a00060

Law, J. (1992). *Notes on the Theory of Actor Network: Ordering, Strategy and Heterogeneity*. Center for Sciences Studies.

Law, J. (1994). *Organising Modernity*. Oxford, UK: Blackwell.

Law, J. (2004). *After Method: mess in social science research*. London: Routledge.

Law, J. (Ed.). (1991). *A Sociology of Monsters: Essays on Power, Technology and Domination*. London: Routledge.

Law, J. (2004). *After Method: mess in social science*. London: Routledge.

Law, J. (1992). Notes on the theory of the actor-network: ordering, strategy, and heterogeneity. *Systems Practice, 5*(4), 379–393. doi:10.1007/BF01059830

Law, J. (1987). Technology and Heterogeneous Engineering: The case of the Portuguese Expansion. In Bijker, W. E., Hughes, T. P., & Pinch, T. (Eds.), *The Social Construction of Technological Systems: New directions in the sociology and history of technology* (pp. 111–134). Cambridge, MA: MIT Press.

Law, J. (1986). The Heterogeneity of Texts. In Callon, M., Law, J., & Rip, A. (Eds.), *Mapping the dynamics of science and technology* (pp. 67–83). UK: Macmillan Press.

Law, J. (1986). On the Methods of Long-Distance Control: vessels, navigation and the Portuguese route to india. In J. Law (Ed.), *Power, Action and Belief: a new sociology of knowledge* (pp. 234-263): Routledge & Kegan Paul plc.

Law, J. (1992). Notes on the Theory of the Actor Network: Ordering, Strategy, and Heterogeneity.", http://www.lancs.ac.uk/fss/sociology/papers/law-notes-on-ant.pdf

Law, J. (1999) After ANT: complexity, naming and topology. *Actor-network Theory and After*, 1–14.

Law, J. (2001). Notes on the theory of the actor-network: ordering, strategy and heterogeneity. In Warwick Organizational Behaviour Staff (Eds.), *Organizational Studies. Critical Objectives on Business and Management. Vol II: Objectivity and Its Other*. London, New York: Routledge, 853-868.

Law, J. (2003). Notes on the Theory of the Actor Network: Ordering, Strategy and Heterogeneity,' published by Centre for Science Studies, Lancaster University. Retrived March 20, 2008 from http://www.comp.lancs.ac.uk/sociology/papers/Law-Notes-On-ANT.pdf

Law, J. (2007). *Actor Network Theory and Material Semiotics*,' 25 April version. Available online at http://www.heterogeneities.net/publications/Law-ANTandMaterialSemiotics.pdf

Lederer, A. L., Maupin, D. J., Sena, M. P., & Zhuang, Y. (1998). The role of ease of use, usefulness and attitude in the prediction of world wide web usage. In *Proceedings of the 1998 Association for computing machinery special interest group on computer personnel research conference*, 195-204.

Lee, N., & Brown, S. (1994). Otherness and the Actor Network. *The American Behavioral Scientist, 37*(6), 772–790. doi:10.1177/0002764294037006005

Lee, N., & Hassard, J. (1999). Organization unbound: actor network theory, research strategy and institutional flexibility. *Organization, 6*(3), 391–404. doi:10.1177/135050849963002

Lefley, F., & Sarkis, J. (2005). Applying the FAP Model to the Evaluation of Strategic Information Technology Projects. *International Journal of Enterprise Information Systems, 1*, 69–90.

Leibold, M., Probst, G., & Gibbert, M. (2005). *Strategic management in the knowledge economy: new approaches and business applications*. Erlangen: Publicis Corporate Publishing and Wiley-VCH Verlag.

Leidner, D. E., & Jarvenpaa, S. L. (1995). The use of information technology to enhance management school education: a theoretical view. *Management Information Systems Quarterly, 19*(3), 265–292. doi:10.2307/249596

Lepa, J., & Tatnall, A. (2006). Using Actor-Network Theory to Understanding Virtual Community Networks of Older People Using the Internet. *Journal of Business Systems. Governance and Ethics, 1*(4), 1–14.

Li, Y., & Lindner, J. R. (2007). Faculty adoption behaviour about web-based distance education: A case study from china agricultural university. *British Journal of Educational Technology, 38*(1), 83–94. doi:10.1111/j.1467-8535.2006.00594.x

Liebowitz, J. (2005). Linking social network analysis with the analytic hierarchy process for knowledge mapping in organizations. *Journal of Knowledge Management, 9*(1), 76–86. doi:10.1108/13673270510582974

Lilley, S. (1998). Regarding Screens for Surveillance of The System. *Accounting. Management and Information Technology, 8*, 63–105. doi:10.1016/S0959-8022(97)00012-X

Lillis, T. (2001). *Student Writing: Access, Regulation, Desire*. London: Routledge.

Linux Online, I. (1994-2008). *The Linux Home Page at Linux Online*, 2008, from http://www.linux.org/

Lopez, D. A., & Manson, D. P. (1997). *A study of individual computer self-efficacy and perceived usefulness of the empowered desktop information system* [Electronic Version], 83–92. Retrieved December 5, 2005 from www.csupomona.edu/~jis/1997/Lopez.pdf.

Löwer, U. M. (2006). *Interorganisational standards: managing web services specifications for flexible supply chains*. Heidelberg: Physica Verlag.

Luna-Reyes, L. F., Zhang, J., Gil-García, J. R., & Cresswell, A. M. (2005). Information systems development as emergent socio-technical change: a practice approach. *European Journal of Information Systems, 14*, 93–10. doi:10.1057/palgrave.ejis.3000524

Luoma-aho, V., & Paloviita, A. (2010). Actor-networking stakeholder theory for today's corporate communications. *Corporate Communication: An International Journal, 15*(1), 49–67. doi:10.1108/13563281011016831

Lynch, J. (Ed.). (2007). *Gender and IT: Challenges for Computing and Information Technology education in Australian secondary schools*. Melbourne: ACSA & Common Ground.

Machiavelli, N. (1515). *The Prince* (1995th ed.). (Bull, G., Trans.). London: Penguin Classics.

Mack, R. (2002). *Creating an Information Technology (IT) Strategy: An Alternative Approach, Gartner, Inc.* Retrieved June 28, 2004, from www.gartner.com.

Mackay, H., & Gillespie, G. (1992). Extending the Social Shaping of Technology Approach: Ideology and Appropriation. *Social Studies of Science, 22*(4), 685–716. doi:10.1177/030631292022004006

MacKay, N., Parent, M., & Gemino, A. (2004). A model of electronic commerce adoption by small voluntary organizations. *European Journal of Information Systems*, *13*(2), 147–159. doi:10.1057/palgrave.ejis.3000491

Mackay, H. (1995). Theorising the IT/ Society Relationship. In Heap, N., Thomas, R., Einon, G., Mason, R., & Mackay, H. (Eds.), *Information Technology and Society: A reader*. The Open University.

Mackenzie, D., & Wajcman, J. (Eds.). (1999). *The Social Shaping of Technology - second edition* (The second edition ed.). Bukingham and Philadelphia: Open University Press.

MacMillan, I., McCaffrey, M. L., & Van Wijk, G. (1985). Competitor's responses to easily imitated new products: Exploring commercial banking product introductions. *Strategic Management Journal*, *6*, 75–86. doi:10.1002/smj.4250060106

Madon, S. (1999). International NGOs: Networking, information flows and learning. *The Journal of Strategic Information Systems*, *8*(3), 251–261. doi:10.1016/S0963-8687(99)00029-3

Madu, C. N. (1992). *Strategic planning of technology transfer to less developed countries*. New York: Quorum Books.

Maglio, P. P., Srinivasan, S., Kreulea, J. T., & Spohrer, J. (2006, July). Service, systems, service scientists. *MMME and Innovation, CACM*, *49*(7), 81–85.

Maguire, C., Kazlauskas, E. J., & Weir, A. D. (1994). *Information Services for Innovative Organizations*. Sandiego, CA: Academic Press.

Mahajan, V., Muller, E., & Srivastava, R. (1990). Determination of adopter categories by using innovation diffusion models. *JMR, Journal of Marketing Research*, *27*(2), 37–50. doi:10.2307/3172549

Manurung, R. (2007). "Valorisation of *Jatropha* curcas using the Bio-refinery Concept," Presented in United Nations Expert Group Meeting on Bio fuel Meeting, New York, 29-30 March.

Marchetti, M. P., & Moyle, P. B. (2010). *Protecting Life on Earth: An Introduction to the Science of Conservation*. Berkeley and Los Angeles, CA: University of California Press.

Markoff, J., & Schenker, J. L. (2003). Europe exceeds US in refining grid computing, *The New York Times, November 10*

Markus, M. L. (2007). The governance of free/open source software projects: monolithic, multidimensional, or configurational? *Journal of Management and Governance*, *11*(2), 151–163. doi:10.1007/s10997-007-9021-x

Martens, C. (2007). *GPLv3 third draft: Linus likes it, ACT hates it*. Retrieved January 11, 2008, from http://www.computerworld.com/action/article.do?command=viewArticleBasic&articleId=9014878

Marx, L., & Smith, M. R. (1994). Introduction. In Marx, L., & Smith, M. R. (Eds.), *Does Technology Drive History? The dilemma of technological determinism*. Cambridge, MA: MIT Press.

McGrath, K. (2001, June 27-29). *The Golden Circle: A case study of organizational change at the London Ambulance Service (Case Study)*. Paper presented at the The 9 th European Conference on Information Systems, Bled, Slovenia.

McMaster, T., Vidgen, R. T., & Wastell, D. G. (1997). Towards an understanding of technology in transition: Two conflicting theories. *Information System Research in Scandinavia*, IRIS20 Conference, University of Oslo, Hanko, Norway.

Metcalfe, J. (2005). Ed Mansfield and the diffusion of innovation: an evolutionary connection. *The Journal of Technology Transfer*, *30*(1/2), 171–181.

Mick, D., & Fournier, S. (1998). Paradoxes of technology:consumer cognizance, emotions,and coping strategies. *The Journal of Consumer Research*, *25*, 123–143. doi:10.1086/209531

Misa, T. J. (1994). Retrieving Sociotechnical Change from Technological Determinism. In Smith, M. R., & Marx, L. (Eds.), *Does Technology Drive History? The dilemma of technological deteminism*. Cambridge: The MIT Press.

Mitev, N. (2009). In and out of actor-network theory: a necessary but insufficient journey. *Information Technology & People, 22,* 1, 9–25. doi:10.1108/09593840910937463

Mol, A. (2002). *The Body Multiple: Ontology in Medical Practice.* Duke University Press.

Mol, A. (2001). *The Body Multiple: Artherosclerosis in Practice.* Durham, N.Ca. and London: Duke University Press.

Möller, K., Rajala, R., & Westerlund, M. (2007). Service myopia? A new recipe for client-provider value creation, *The Berkeley-Tekes Service Innovation Conference in Berkeley, California* April 27-28, 2007.

Montealegre, R. (1998). Managing information technology in modernizing "against the odds": lessons from an organization in less-developed country. *Information & Management, 34*(2), 103–116. doi:10.1016/S0378-7206(98)00051-2

Montealegre, R. (1999). A case for more case study research in the implementation of Information Technology in less-developed countries. *Information Technology for Development, 8*(4), 199–207. doi:10.1080/02681102.1999.9525310

Monteiro, E. (2001). Actor-Network Theory and Information Infrastructure. In Ciborra, C. U., Braa, K., & Cordella, A. (Eds.), *From control to drift: the dynamics of corporate information infastructures* (pp. 71–86). New York: Oxford University Press.

Monteiro, E., & Hanseth, O. (1996). Social shaping of information structure: on being specific about technology. In Orikowski, W. J., Walsham, G., Jones, M. R., & DeGross, J. I. (Eds.), *Information technology and changes in organisational work* (pp. 325–343). London, UK: Chapman & Hall.

Moore, G. A. (1991). *Crossing the Chasm.* New York: Harper Business.

Moore, G. A. (1995). *Inside the Tornado: Marketing Strategy from Sillicon Valley's Cutting Edge.* New York: Harper Collins.

Morgon, G. (1995). ITEM: A strategic approach to information systems in voluntary organisations. *The Journal of Strategic Information Systems, 4*(3), 225–237. doi:10.1016/0963-8687(95)96803-G

Mulligan, P., & Gordon, S. R. (2002). The impact of information technology on customer and supplier relationships in the financial services. *International Journal of Service Industry Management, 13*(1), 29–46. doi:10.1108/09564230210421146

Munro, R. (2005). Actor Network Theory. In Clegg, S., & Haugaard, M. (Eds.), *The SAGE Handbook of Power* (pp. 125–139). Thousand Oaks, CA: Sage Publications Inc.

Murdoch, J. (1997). Towards a geography of heterogeneous associations. *Progress in Geography, 21,* 321–337. doi:10.1191/030913297668007261

Murdoch, J. (2006). *Post-structuralist geography: a guide to relational space.* London: Sage Publications, Ltd.

Murdoch, J. (2005). Ecologising sociology. Actor-Network Theory, co-construction and the problem of human exemptionalism. In D. Inglis, J. Bone & R. Wilkie (Eds.), *Nature: From nature to natures: contestation and reconstruction.* Abingdon: Routledge, 282-305.

Murphy, K. E., & Simon, S. J. (2001) Using Cost Benefit Analysis for Enterprise Resource Planning Project Evaluation: A Case for Including Intangibles. *Proceedings of the 34th Annual Hawaii International Conference on System Sciences, 2001.* Hawaii

Myers, M. (1999). Qualitative techniques for data collection, Qualitative Research in Information Systems. *IS World Net.* http://www2.auckland.ac.nz/msis/isworld/#Qualitativetechniques

Nankervis, A. R. (2005). *Managing services.* New York: Cambridge University Press. doi:10.1017/CBO9780511481260

Narasimhan, R. (1984). *Guidelines for Software Development in Developing Countries, IS.439.* Vienna: UNIDO.

NECTEC. (2007). *Internet Users in Thailand.* Retrieved January 12, 2007, from http://iir.ngi.nectec.or.th/internet/user-growth.html

Nelson, R. R. (Ed.). (1993). *National Innovation Systems: A Comparative Analysis*. New York: Oxford University Press.

Newby, G. B. (2001). Cognitive space and information space. *J. Am.Soc. Info. Sci. Technol., 12*, 1026–1048. doi:10.1002/asi.1172

News, B. B. C. (2010) University system needs radical change; http://news.bbc.co.uk/1/hi/education/ [Accessed 15 June 2010]

Newton, T. (2007). *Nature and sociology. Abingdon*. Routledge.

Nijland, M. H. J. (2004). *Understanding the Use of IT Evaluation Methods in Organisations*. University of London.

Nissen, M. (2007). Keynote paper: Enhancing Organisational metacognition – flow visualization to make the knowledge network explicit. *Intl J Networking and Virtual Organisations, 4*(4), 331–350. doi:10.1504/IJNVO.2007.015728

Noel, P. (2006). The Secret Life of Teacher Educators: becoming a teacher educator in the learning and skills sector. *Journal of Vocational Education and Training, 58*(2), 151–170. doi:10.1080/13636820600799577

Noertjayo, J. A. (2005). *Dari Ladang sampai Kabinet: Menggugat Nasib Petani*. Jakarta: Kompas.

Norton, J., & Bass, F. (1992). Evolution of technological generations: The law of capture. *Sloan Management Review, 33*(2), 66–77.

O'Mahony, S. (2003). Guarding the commons: how community managed software projects protect their work. *Research Policy, 32*(7), 1179–1198. doi:10.1016/S0048-7333(03)00048-9

Office of the Education Council. (2004). *Education in Thailand*. Retrieved January 29, 2005, from http://www.edthai.com/pulication/edu2004/content.

Olazabal, N. G. (2002). Banking: The IT paradox. *The McKinsey Quarterly, 1*, 47–51.

Oliver, C. (1991). Strategic responses to institutional processes. *Academy of Management Review, 16*, 145–179. doi:10.2307/258610

Olutimayin, J. (2002). Communication in health care delivery in developing countries: which way out? *Pacific Health Dialog, 9*, 237–241.

Onen, C. L. (2004). Medicine in resource-poor settings: time for a paradigm shift? *Clinical Medicine (London, England), 4*, 355–360.

Open Source Development Network. (2006). *Software Map*. Retrieved December 17, 2008, from http://www.dwheeler.com/frozen/sourceforge-stats-20031110.html

Open Source Initiative. (2005). *The Open Source Definition*. Retrieved December 10, 2008, from http://www.opensource.org/docs/osd

Origlio, B. (2007). Antropological Semiotics: A Methodological and Conceptual Approach to Intercultural Communication Studies in Organizations. In Ch. M. Schmidt and D. Neuendorff (Eds.), *Sprache, Kultur und Zielgruppen: Bedingungsgrößen für die Kommunikationsgestaltung in der Wirtschaft*. Wiesbaden, DUV, 9-26.

Orlikowski, W. J. (2007). Sociomaterial Practices: Exploring Technology at Work. *Organization Studies, 28*, 1435. doi:10.1177/0170840607081138

Orlikowski, W. J., & Scott, S. V. (2008) *The Entangling of Technology and Work in Organizations*, Working Paper Series. Department of Management, Information Systems and Innovation Group. London School of Economics and Political Science.

Oxford (1973). *The Shorter Oxford English Dictionary* (3rd edition (reprinted with corrections and revisions) ed.). Oxford: Clarendon Press.

Papp, R., & Fox, D. (2002). Information strategy development: The strategic alignment imperative, *Eighth Americas Conference on Information Systems*.

Park, S., & Yoon, S.-H. (2005). Separating early-adopters from the majority: the case of broadband internet access in korea. *Technological Forecasting and Social Change, 72*, 301–325. doi:10.1016/j.techfore.2004.08.013

Parry, G., Davies, P., & Williams, J. (2003). *Dimensions of Difference: higher education in the learning and skills sector*. London: Learning and Skills Development Agency.

Parry, G., & Thompson, A. (2002). *Closer By Degrees: the past, present and future of higher education in further education colleges*. London: Learning and Skills Development Agency.

Pedersen, M. A. (2009). At Home Away from Homes: Navigating the Taiga in Northern Mongolia. In Kirby, P. W. (Ed.), *Boundless worlds: an anthropological approach to movement* (pp. 135–152). New York, NY: Berghahn Books.

Perdue, P. C. (1994). Technological Determinism in Agrarian Societies. In Smith, M. R., & Marx, L. (Eds.), *Does Technology Drive History? The dilemma of technological determinism*. Cambridge, MA: MIT Press.

Perry, J. (2000). Retirees stay wired to kids - and to one another. *U.S. News & World Report*, ¾¾¾, 22.

Peters, T. (1994). *Crazy time call for crazy organisations. Tom Peters' Seminar* (p. 10). London: Macmillan.

Pfaffenberger, B. (1992). Technological Dramas. *Science, Technology & Human Values*, *17*(3), 282–312. doi:10.1177/016224399201700302

Pfaffenberger, B. (2004). The social anthropology of technology. In Buchli, V. (Ed.), *Material culture: critical concepts in the social sciences* (pp. 61–89). London: Routledge.

Phillips, M. (2005). Philosophical Arguments in Human Geography. In Phillips, M. (Ed.), *Contested worlds: an introduction to human geography* (pp. 13–86). Aldershot: Ashgate Publishing Limited.

Philström, S. (2007). Synechism. In Lachs, J., & Talisse, R. (Eds.), *American philosophy: an encyclopedia* (pp. 774–746). New York: Routledge.

Pickering, A. (1995). *The mangle of practice: time, agency, and science*. Chicago, London: University of Chicago Press.

Pinch, T. J., & Bijker, W. E. (1987). The Social Construction of Facts and Artifacts: Or How the Sociology of Science and the Sociology of Technology Might Benefit Each Other. In Bijker, W. E., Hughes, T. P., & Pinch, T. J. (Eds.), *The Social Construction of Technological Systems: New Directions in the Sociology and History of Technology*. The MIT Press.

Pinch, P. (2003). Making the wrecker seem not all malevolent: re-regulating the UK's china clay mining industry. In S. Buckingham (Ed.), *Local environmental sustainability*. Abingdon: Woodhead Publishing Limited, 46-73.

Pliaskin, A., & Tatnall, A. (2005). Developing a Portal to Build a Business Community. In Tatnall, A. (Ed.), *Web Portals: The New Gateways to Internet Information and Services* (pp. 335–348). Hershey, PA: Idea Group Publishing.

Polese, F. (2010). The influence of networking culture and social relationships on value creation. [forthcoming].

Popp, K., & Meyer, R. (2010). *Profit from Software Ecosystems: Business Models, Ecosystems and Partnerships in the Software Industry*. Norderstedt: Books on demand GmbH.

Porsander, L. (2002). Things that Matter: A Computerized System as a Part of an Emerging Action Net. In Hedberg, B., Baumard, P., & Yakhlef, A. (Eds.), *Managing imaginary organizations: a new perspective on business* (pp. 117–136). Oxford: Elsevier Science Ltd.

Porter, M., & Tiesberg, E. (2006). *Re-defining health care delivery*. Boston: Harvard Business Press.

Pouloudi, A. Gandecha, R. Atkinson, C., & Papazafeiropoulou, A. (2004). How Stakeholder Analysis can be Mobilized with Actor-Network Theory to Identify Actors. In B.M. Kaplan, D.P. Truex III, D. Wastell, A.T. Wood-Harper & J.I. De Gross (Eds.), *Information systems research: relevant theory and informed practice*. Norwell, MA: Kluwer Academic Publishers, 705-712.

Powell, P. (1992). Information Technology Evaluation: Is It Different? *The Journal of the Operational Research Society*, *43*, 29–42.

Prakoso, T. dan Tatang H. Soerawidjaja (2007). "Perkembangan Teknologi Penyediaan Energi Alternatif(Bio fuel)," Presented on Aternative Energy for Human Welfare Seminar in Aula Barat ITB, Bandung, September 5.

Price, M. (2005). Assessment standards: the role of communities of practice and the scholarship of assessment. *Assessment & Evaluation in Higher Education, 30*(3), 215–230. doi:10.1080/02602930500063793

Prihandana, R. (2007). *Meraup Untung dari Jarak Pagar (Cet.2).* Jakarta: AgroMedia Pustaka.

Prout, A. (1996). Actor-network theory, technology and medical sociology: an illustrative analysis of the metered dose inhaler. *Sociology of Health & Illness, 18*(2), 198–219. doi:10.1111/1467-9566.ep10934726

Quitas, P. (1994). A product-process model of innovation in software development. *Journal of Information Technology, 9*(1), 3–17. doi:10.1057/jit.1994.2

Rachlis, M. (2006). *Key to sustainable healthcare system.* Retrieved from http:www.improveingchroniccare.org

Radder, H. (1996). *In and about the world: philosophical studies of science and technology.* Albany, NY: State University of New York Press.

Rainey, H. G. (2009). *Communication power.* San Francisco: Jossey-Bass.

Ram, S., & Sheth, J. (1989). Consumer resistance to innovations: The marketing problem and its solutions. *Journal of Consumer Marketing, 6*(2), 5–14. doi:10.1108/EUM0000000002542

Ramamurthy, K., Premkumar, G., & Crum, M. R. (1999). Organizational and inter organizational determinants of EDI diffusion and organizational performance: A causal model. *Journal of Organizational Computing and Electronic Commerce, 9*(4), 253–285. doi:10.1207/S153277440904_2

Ramayah, T., & Aafaqi, B. (2004). Role of self-efficacy in e-library usage among students of a public university in Malaysia [Electronic Version]. *Malaysian Journal of Library and Information Science, 19,* 39-57. Retrieved December 8, 2006 from http://majlis.fsktm.um.edu.my/document.aspx?FileName=276.pdf.

Rappert, B. (2001). The Distribution and Resolution of the Ambiguities of Technology, or Why Bobby Can't Spray. *Social Studies of Science, 31*(4), 557–591. doi:10.1177/030631201031004004

Rayna, T., & Striukova, L. (2008). (forthcoming). The curse of the first-mover: When incremental innovation leads to radical change. *International Journal of Collaborative Enterprise.*

Remenyi, D., & Sherwood-Smith, M. (1999). Maximise information systems value by continuous participative evaluation. *Journal of Enterprise Information Management, 12,* 14–31.

Rip, A., Thomas, J., Misa, D., & Schot, J. (1995). *Managing Technology in Society: The approach of Constructive Technology Assessment.* London: Pinter Publishers.

Roberts, L. W., & Clifton, R. A. (1992). Measuring the cognitive domain of the quality of student life: an instrument for faculties of education. *Canadian Journal of Education, 2,* 176–191. doi:10.2307/1495319

Rogers, E. (2003). *Diffusion of innovations* (5th ed.). New York: Free Press.

Rogers, E. M. (2002). Diffusion of preventive innovations. *Addictive Behaviors, 27*(6), 989–993. doi:10.1016/S0306-4603(02)00300-3

Rogers, M. (1998). The definition and measurement of Innovation Melbourne Institute Working papers No. 10/98, ISSN 1328-4991 or ISBN 07325 0973 4, [Http://www.ecom.unimelb.edu.au/iaesrwww/home.html]

Rose, J., & Truex, D., III. (2000). Machine Agency as Perceived Autonomy: An Action Perspective. In R. Baskerville, J. Stage & J.I. DeGross, J.I. (Eds.), *Organizational and social perspectives on information technology: IFIP TC8 WG8.2 International Working Conference on the Social and Organizational Perspective on Research and Practice in Information Technology, June 9-11, 2000, Aalborg, Denmark.* Norwell, MA: Kluwer Academic Publishers, Norwell, 371- 390.

Rosen, P. (1993). The Social Construction of Mountain Bikes: Technology and Postmodernity in the Cycle Industry. *Social Studies of Science*, *23*(3), 479–513. doi:10.1177/0306312793023003003

Rosen, L. (2005). *Open source licensing: software freedom and intellectual property law*. Upper Saddle River, NJ: Prentice Hall PTR.

Rosengren, K. E. (2000). *Communication: An Introduction*. London: SAGE.

Rowan, L., & Bigum, Ch. (1991). Actor Network Theory and the Study of Online Learning. New Perspectives on Quality. In Potelli, A. (Ed.), *The death of Luigi Trastulli, and other stories: form and meaning in oral history* (pp. 179–188). Norwell, MA: Kluwer Academic Publishers.

Ryan, S. D., Harrison, D. A., & Schkade, L. L. (2002). Information-Technology Investment Decisions: When Do Costs and Benefits in the Social Subsystem Matter? *Journal of Management Information Systems*, *19*, 85–127.

Salzman, H. (1998). *Beyond User Participation: The Politics of Software Development, Center for Industrial Competitiveness*. USA: University of Massachusetts.

Sanderson, S., & Uzumeri, M. (1995). Managing product families: The case of the sony walkman. *Research Policy*, *24*(5), 761–782. doi:10.1016/0048-7333(94)00797-B

Sarker, S., Sarker, S., & Sidorova, A. (2006). Understanding Business Process Change Failure: An Actor-Network Perspective. *Journal of Management Information Systems*, *21*(1), 51–86. doi:10.2753/MIS0742-1222230102

Sato, S., Hawkins, J., & Berentsen, A. (2001). *E-finance: Recent developments and policy implications. In Tracking a Transformation: E-Commerce and the Terms of Competition in Industries*. Washington, DC: Brookings Institution Press, pp.64-91.

Sauer, C., & Cuthbertson, C. (2003). *The state of IT project management in the UK. Templeton College*. Oxford University.

Saunier, R. E., & Meganck, R. A. (2009). *Dictionary and Introduction to Global Environmental Governance*. London: Earth Scan.

Schäfer, J. (2010). Reassembling the literary. In Schäfer, J., & Gendolla, P. (Eds.), *Beyond the Screen: Transformations of Literary Structures, Interfaces and Genre* (pp. 25–71). Bielefeld: Transcript Verlag.

Schatzki, T. R. (2002). *The Site of the Social: A Philosophical Account of the Constitution of Social Life and Change*. Pennsylvania State University Press.

Schmitz, H., & Hewitt, T. R. (1991). Learning to raise infants: a case study in industrial policy. In Colclough, C., & Manor, J. (Eds.), *States or Markets?* Oxford, UK: Oxford University Press.

Schnaars, S. P. (1994). *Managing Imitation Strategies: How Late Entrants Seize Marketing from Pioneers*. New York: The Free Press.

Schneider, H., & Gilson, L. (1999). Small fish in a big pond? External aid and the health sector in South Africa. *Health Policy and Planning*, *14*, 264–272. doi:10.1093/heapol/14.3.264

Schnepp, Von G., Mary Ann and Bhambri, A. (1990). United States- China Technology Transfer, Eaglewood Cliffs. NJ: Prentice-Hall, in Min Chen, *Managing International Technology Transfer*, International Thompson Business Press, 1996.

Schot, J. W. (1992). Constructive Technology Assessment and Technology Dynamics: The Case of Clean Technologies. *Science Technology Human Values, Sage Publications*, *17*(1), 36–56. doi:10.1177/016224399201700103

Schumacker, R. E., & Lomax, R. G. (1996). *A beginner's guide to Structural Equation Modelling*. Mahwah, NJ: Lawerence Erbaum.

Scollon, R. (2001). *Mediated Discourse: The Nexus of Practice*. London: Routledge.

Scollon, R., & Wong Scollon, S. (2001). *Intercultural communication: a discourse approach*. Oxford: Blackwell Publishing.

Scranton, P. (1994). Determinism and Indeterminacy in the History of Technology. In Smith, M. R., & Marx, L. (Eds.), *Does Technology Drive History? The dilemma of Technological determinism*. Cambridge, MA: The MIT Press.

SEAMEO RIHED. (2007). Higher Education System of Thailand. Retrieved January 15, 2007, from http://www.rihed.seameo.org/hesystem/thailandHEIs.htm

Sekaran, U. (2003). *Research methods for business: a skill-building approach* (4 th ed.). New York: John Wiley and Sons, Inc.

Serafeimidis, V. (2000). Information systems evaluation in practice: a case study of organizational change. *Journal of Information Technology*, *15*, 93–105. doi:10.1080/026839600344294

Shaikh, M., & Cornford, T. (2003). *Version Management Tools: CVS to BK in the Linux Kernel.* Paper presented at the Taking Stock of the Bazaar, 3rd Workshop on Open Source Software Engineering, Portland, OR.

Shaikh, M., & Cornford, T. (2005). *Learning/organizing in Linux: a study of the 'spaces in between'.* Paper presented at the Open Source Application Spaces: Fifth Workshop on Open Source Software Engineering, St. Louis, MO.

Shain, F., & Gleeson, D. (1999). Under new management: changing conceptions of teacher professionalism and policy in the further education sector. *Journal of Education Policy*, *14*(4), 445–462. doi:10.1080/026809399286288

Shankland, S. (2007). *Open-source Solaris makes GPL 3 more attractive: Linus Torvalds.* Retrieved January 11, 2008, from http://www.zdnet.com.au/news/software/soa/Open-source-Solaris-makes-GPL-3-more-attractive-Linus-Torvalds/0,130061733,339278528,00.htm

Sharif, N. (2006). Emergence and Development of the National Innovation System Concept. *Research Policy*, *35*, 745–766. doi:10.1016/j.respol.2006.04.001

Sharma, S. (1996). *Applied Multivariate Techniques.* New York: John Wiley and Sons, Inc.

Sheehan, J. (2006). Understanding service sector innovation. *Communications of the ACM*, *49*(9), 43–47.

Sheppard, B. H., Hartwick, J., & Warshaw, P. R. (1988). The Theory of Reasoned Action: a meta-analysis of past research with recommendations for modifications and future research [Electronic Version] [from http://search.epnet.com/login.aspx?direct=true&db=aph&authdb=epref&an=JCR.AE.CBE.SHEPPARD.TRAMAP]. *The Journal of Consumer Research*, *15*, 325–343. Retrieved March 4, 2004. doi:10.1086/209170

Shore, C., & Wright, S. (1999). Audit culture and anthropology: new-liberalism in British higher education. *The Journal of the Royal Anthropological Institute*, *5*(4), 557–575. doi:10.2307/2661148

Shore, C., & Wright, S. (2000). Coercive accountability – the rise of audit culture in higher education. In Strathern, M. (Ed.), *Audit Cultures: Anthropological Studies in Accountability, Ethics and the Academy.* London: Routledge.

Shy, O. (1996). Technology revolutions in the presence of network externalities. *International Journal of Industrial Organization*, *14*(6), 785–800. doi:10.1016/0167-7187(96)01011-9

Sims, C. (2007). Defining services for designers: Services as systems of social and technical relations, *UCB iSchool Report* 2007-002, February 2007. http://repositories.cdlib.org/cgi/viewcontent.cgi?article=1001&context=ischool

Singh, P. J., & Smith, A. J. R. (2001). *TQM and Innovation: An empirical examination of their relationship.* Paper presented at the 5th International and 8th National Research Conference on Quality and Innovation Management. from http://www.eacc.unimelb.edu.au/pubs/proceedings6.pdf#search=%22TQM%20and%20Innovation%3A%20An%20Empirical%20Examination%22.

Singleton, V., & Michael, M. (1993). Actor-Networks and Ambivalence: General Practitioners in the UK Cervical Screening Programme. *Social Studies of Science*, *23*(2), 227–264. doi:10.1177/030631293023002001

Smarr, L. (1999). Grids in context. In Foster, I., & Kesselman, C. (Eds.), *The Grid: Blueprint for a New Computing Infrastructure.* San Francisco: Morgan Kaufman Publishers.

Smith, J. A., & Jenks, Ch. (2006). *Qualitative Complexity: Ecology, Cognitive Processes and the Re-emergence of Structures in Post-humanist Social Theory. Abingdon.* Routledge.

Smith, B. (2008). A Quick Guide to GPLv3.

Soerawidjaja, T. H. (2007). "Bahan-bahan Bakar Hayati." Presented on Development of Industrial Estate Seminar, Jakarta, 24 February.

Solow, R. M. (1987) We'd Better Watch Out. *New York Times Book Review,* 12, 07-87.

Somerville, I. (1999). Agency versus identity: actor-network theory meets public relations. *Corporate Communications-. International Journal (Toronto, Ont.), 4,* 1, 6–13.

Spiegel, M. R., & Stephens, L. J. (2008). *Statistics* (4th ed.). USA: McGraw Hill.

Spira, L. F. (2002). *The audit committee: performing corporate governance.* Norwell, MA: Kluwer Academic Publishers.

Spohrer, J., Maglio, P., Bailey, J., & Gruhl, D. (2007). Steps towards a science of service systems. *IEE Computer, 40*(Issue 1), 71–77.

Spohrer, J., Vargo, S. L., Caswell, N. S., & Maglio, P. P. (2008) The service system is the basic abstraction of service science. *Hawaii International Conference on System Sciences,* Proceedings of the 41st Annual.

Spohrer, J, Golinelli, G, M. Piciocchi, P & Bassano, C. (2010). An integrated SS-VSA analysis of changing job roles *Service Science* 2(1/2), pp. 1- 20, © 2010 SSG.

Stallman, R. (2002). *Free Software, Free Society: Selected Essays of Richard M. Stallman.* Boston, MA: Gnu Press.

Stallman, R. (2007). *Why Upgrade to GPL Version 3.* Retrieved December 11, 2008, from http://gplv3.fsf.org/rms-why.html

Stein, P. 1998, Observations on the emergence of network centric warfare, http://www.dodccrp.org/research/ncw/stein/_observations/steincw.htm

Stewart, K. J., & Gosain, S. (2006). The Impact of Ideology on Effectiveness in Open Source Software Development Teams. *Management Information Systems Quarterly, 30*(2), 291–314.

Straub, D., Hoffman, D., Weber, B., & Steinfield, C. (2002). Toward new metrics for Net-enhanced organizations. *Information Systems Research, 13*(3), 227–238. doi:10.1287/isre.13.3.227.80

Stremersch, S., & Tellis, G. (2004). Understanding and managing international growth of new products. *International Journal of Research in Marketing, 21*(4), 421–438. doi:10.1016/j.ijresmar.2004.07.001

Strum, S., & Latour, B. (1987). The Meaning of the Social: From Baboons to Humans. *Information Sur Les Science Socials. Social Sciences Information. Information Sur les Sciences Sociales, 26,* 783–802. doi:10.1177/053901887026004004

Strum, S., & Latour, B. (1999). Redefining the Social Link: From baboons to humans. In Mackenzie, D., & Wajcman, J. (Eds.), *The Social Shaping of Technology.* Buckingham, Philadelphia: Open University Press.

Students of the World. (2006). *Thailand.* Retrieved January 13, 2007, from http://www.studentsoftheworld.info/country_information.php?Pays=THA

Sturken, M., & Thomas, D. (2004). Introduction: Technological visions and the rhetoric of the new. In Sturken, M., & Thomas, D. (Eds.), *Technological Visions: The hopes and fears that shape new technologies.* Philadelphia: Temple University Press.

Suchman, L. A. (2007) Human-Machine Reconfigurations: Plans and situated actions.

Sundbo, J. (2003). Innovation and Strategic Reflexivity: An Evolutionary Approach Applied to Services. In Shavinina, L. (Ed.), *The international handbook on innovation* (pp. 97–114). Oxford: Elsevier. doi:10.1016/B978-008044198-6/50008-5

Sung, T. K. (2009). Technology transfer in the IT industry: A Korea perspective, Technological Forecasting & Social Change. *International Journal (Toronto, Ont.), 76*(5), 700–708.

Sung, T. K., & Gibson, D. V. (2000). Knowledge and Technology Transfer: Key Factors and Levels. Brazil, In *Proceeding of 4th International Conference on Technology Policy and Innovation*.

Sun-Tzu on the Art of War. (1910). *Project Guthenberg*. Retrieved from http://www.kimsoft.com.polwar.htm

Suraya, R. (2005). Internet diffusion and e-business opportunities amongst Malaysian travel agencies.In *Proceedings of the Hawaii International Conference on Business*, Honolulu.

Swain, H. (2008). UK universities face 'radical' changes, Monday February 11, 2008, [Education Guardian. co.uk, http://education.guardian.co.uk/administration/ story/0,,2255736,00.html]

Swales, J. (1990). *Genre Analysis: English in academic and research settings*. Cambridge, UK: Cambridge University Press.

Swanson, E. B. (1994). Information systems innovation among organizations. *Management Science, 40*(9), 1069–1092. doi:10.1287/mnsc.40.9.1069

Szajna, B. (1994). Software evaluation and choice: predictive validation of the technology acceptance instrument [Electronic Version]. *MIS Quarterly, 17*, 319-324 from http://search.epnet.com/login.aspx?direct=true&db=ap h&authdb=epref&an=MS.DB.HE.SZAJNA.EERTAM

Szmtkowski, D. (2005). Innovation definition comparative assessment (EU), DRAFT developed under GNU, free Documentation Licence, Brussels.

Tatnall, A. (2000). *Innovation and Change in the Information Systems Curriculum of an Australian University: a Socio-Technical Perspective*. Central Queensland University, Rockhampton.

Tatnall, A. (2005). Technological Change in Small Organisations: An Innovation Translation Perspective. *International Journal of Knowledge. Culture and Change Management, 4*(1), 755–761.

Tatnall, A., & Lepa, J. (2003). The Internet, E-Commerce and Older People: an Actor-Network Approach to Researching Reasons for Adoption and Use. *Logistics Information Management, 16*(1), 56–63. doi:10.1108/09576050310453741

Tatnall, A. (2009). Information Systems, Technology Adoption and Innovation Translation. *International Journal of Actor-Network Theory and Technological Innovation, 1*(1), 59–74.

Tatnall, A. (2002). Modelling Technological Change in Small Business: Two Approaches to Theorising Innovation. In Burgess, S. (Ed.), *Managing Information Technology in Small Business: Challenges and Solutions* (pp. 83–97). Hershey, PA: Idea Group Publishing.

Tatnall, A., & Davey, B. (2005). An Actor Network Approach to Informing Clients through portals. In Cohen, E. B. (Ed.), *Issues in informing science and information technology* (pp. 771–780). Santa Rosa, CA: Informing Science Press.

Tatnall, A., Everitt, P., Wenn, A., Burgess, S., Sellitto, C., & Darbyshire, P. (2004). A Study of the Adoption of Information and Communications Technologies by Rural General Practitioners in Australia. In Hunter, M. G., & Dhanda, K. K. (Eds.), *Information Systems: Exploring Applications in Business and Government* (pp. 232–253). Washington, DC: The Information Institute.

Tatnall, A., & Pliaskin, A. (2007). The Demise of a Business-to-Business Portal. In Radaideh, M. A., & Al-Ameed, H. (Eds.), *Architecture of Reliable Web Applications Software* (pp. 147–171). Hershey, PA: Idea Group Publishing.

Tatnall, A., & Burgess, S. (2004). Using Actor-Network Theory to Identify Factors Affecting the Adoption of E-Commerce in SMEs. In Singh, M., & Waddell, D. (Eds.), *E-Business: Innovation and Change Management* (pp. 152–169). Hershey, PA: IRM Press.

Tatnall, A. (2001, 20-23 May 2001). *Adoption of Information Technology by Small Business - Two Different Approaches to Modelling Innovation*. Paper presented at the Managing Information Technology in a Global Economy - (IRMA'2001), Toronto, Canada.

Tatnall, A. (2007, 4-6 June 2007). *Business Culture and the Death of a Portal. Paper presented at the 20th Bled e-Conference* - eMergence: Merging and Emerging Technologies, Processes and Institutions Bled, Slovenia.

Tatnall, A., & Burgess, S. (2002). Using Actor-Network Theory to research the implementation of B-B portal for regional SMEs in Melbourne, Australia. *15ᵗʰ Bled Electronic Commerce Conference & Reality: Constructing the e-economy, Bled*, Slovenia, June 17-19, 2002.

Tatnall, A., & Burgess, S. (2002, June 2002). *Using Actor-Network Theory to Research the Implementation of a B-B Portal for Regional SMEs in Melbourne, Australia.* Paper presented at the 15ᵗʰ Bled Electronic Commerce Conference - 'eReality: Constructing the eEconomy', Bled, Slovenia.

Tatnall, A., & Dai, W. (2007, 18-20 August 2007). *Adoption of Collaborative Real-Time Information Services: a Study in Technological Innovation.* Paper presented at the 13th Cross-Strait Academic Conference on Development and Strategies of Information Management Beijing Jiaotong University, Beijing, China.

Tatnall, A., & Davey, B. (2003). Modelling the Adoption of Web-Based Mobile Learning - an Innovation Translation Approach. In W. Zhou, P. Nicholson, B. Corbitt & J. Fong (Eds.), *Advances in Web-Based Learning* (Vol. LNCS 2783, pp. 433-441). Berlin: Springer Verlag.

Tatnall, A., & Davey, B. (2007, 19-23 May 2007). *Researching the Portal.* Paper presented at the IRMA: Managing Worldwide Operations and Communications with Information Technology, Vancouver.

Tatnall, A., & Gilding, A. (1999). *Actor-Network Theory and Information Systems Research.* Paper presented at the 10th Australasian Conference on Information Systems (ACIS), Wellington.

Tatnall, A., & Pliaskin, A. (2005, September 2005). *Technological Innovation and the Non-Adoption of a B-B Portal.* Paper presented at the Second International Conference on Innovations in Information technology, Dubai, UAE.

Taylor, S., & Todd, P. (1995). Understanding Information Technology Usage: A Test of Competing Models. *Information Systems Research, 6*(2), 144–176. doi:10.1287/isre.6.2.144

Taylor, I. (1997). *Developing Learning in Professional Education.* Buckingham, UK: Open University Press/ Society for Research into Higher Education.

Taylor, S., & Todd, P. A. (1995a). Assessing it usage: the role of prior experience [Electronic Version]. *MIS Quarterly, 19*, 561-570. Retrieved August 30, 2004 from http://search.epnet.com/login.aspx?direct=true&db=aph &authdb=epref&an=MQ.AI.EFA.TAYLOR.AIURPE

Thomas, L. (2001). *Widening Participation in Post-Compulsory Education.* London: Continuum.

Thompson, R. L., Higgins, C. A., & Howell, J. M. (1991). Personal computing: toward a conceptual model of utilization [Electronic Version] [from http://search.epnet.com/login.aspx?direct=true&db=aph&authdb=epref&an =MQ.AE.ABD.THOMPSON.PCTCMU]. *Management Information Systems Quarterly, 15*, 124–143. Retrieved September 1, 2004. doi:10.2307/249443

Thompson, G. (2003). *Between hierarchies and markets: the logic and limits of network forms of organization.* New York: Oxford University Press.

Thong, J. Y. L. (1999). An integrated model of information systems adoption in small business. *Journal of Management Information Systems, 15*(4), 187–214.

Thrift, N. (2000). Actor-Network-Theory. In Johnston, R. J. (Ed.), *The dictionary of human geography* (pp. 4–6). Malden: Blackwell Publishing Ltd.

Thwaites, T., Davis, L., & Mules, W. (2002). *Introducing Cultural and Media Studies A Semiotic Approach.* Basingstoke: Palgrave Macmillan.

Tiemann, M. (2008). *History of the OSI (Open Source Initiative).* Retrieved December 10, 2008, from http:// www.opensource.org/history

Tigelaar, D., Dolmans, D., Wolfhagen, I., & van der Vleuten, C. (2005). Quality issues in judging portfolios: implications for organizing teaching portfolio assessment procedures. *Studies in Higher Education, 30*(5), 595–610. doi:10.1080/03075070500249302

Tim Nasional Pengembangan, B. B. N. (2007). *Bahan Bakar Nabati: Bahan Bakar alternatif dari tumbuhan sebagai pengganti minyak bumi and gas*. Jakarta: Penebar Swadaya.

Tjahjono, S. I. (1996). Perspektif Revolusi, Pembangunan, dan Transformasi Masyarakat. In *Pembaruan dan Pemberdayaan* (pp. 106–143). Jakarta: Ikatan Alumni IA ITB.

Tornatzky, L. G., & Klein, K. J. (1982). Innovation characteristics and innovation adoption-implementation: A meta-analysis of findings. *IEEE Transactions on Engineering Management, 29*(1), 28–45.

Tornatzky, L. G., & Fleischer, M. (1990). *The Processes of Technological Innovation*. Lexington, MA: Lexington Books.

Tornatzky, L., & Klein, K. (1982). Innovation characteristics and innovation adoption-implementation: a meta-analysis of findings. *IEEE Transactions on Engineering Management, 29*(1), 28–45.

Torvalds, L., & Diamond, D. (2001). *Just for fun: the story of an accidental revolutionary*. New York, NY: HarperBusiness.

Torvalds, L. (1992). *RELEASE NOTES FOR LINUX v0.12*. Retrieved January 9, 2008, from http://www.kernel.org/pub/linux/kernel/Historic/old-versions/RELNOTES-0.12

Torvalds, L. (2007). *LKML.ORG - the Linux Kernel Mailing List Archive*, from http://lkml.org/2007/6/14/306

Trivedi, M. L. (2002). *Managerial Economics. Theory and application*. New Delhi: Tata McGraw Hill.

Tummons, J. (2008). Assessment, and the literacy practices of trainee PCET teachers. *International Journal of Educational Research, 47*(3), 184–191. doi:10.1016/j.ijer.2008.01.006

Tummons, J. (2010). *Becoming A Professional Tutor in the Lifelong Learning Sector*. Exeter, UK: Learning Matters.

Tuomi, I. (2001). Internet, Innovation, and Open Source: Actors in the Network. *First Monday, 6*(1).

Turban, E., King, D., Warkentin, M., & Chung, H. M. (2003). *Electronic Commerce 2003: A managerial perspective*. Prentice Hall. In Achour and Bensedrine, 2005.

Usher, R., & Edwards, R. (2007). *Lifelong learning: signs, discourses, practices*. Dordrecht: Springer.

Valdes, I., Kibbe, D., Tolleson, G., Kunik, M., & Petersen, L. A. (2003). Metcalfe's law predicts reduced power of Electronic Medical record software. *AMIA ... Annual Symposium Proceedings / AMIA Symposium. AMIA Symposium, 2003*, 1038.

Valente, T. (1996). Social network thresholds in the diffusion of innovations. *Social Networks, 18*, 69–89. doi:10.1016/0378-8733(95)00256-1

Venkatesh, V., & Davis, F. (2000). A Theoretical Extension of the Technology Acceptance Model: Four Longitudinal Field Studies. *Management Science, 46*(2), 186–204. doi:10.1287/mnsc.46.2.186.11926

Venkatesh, V., Morris, M. G., Davis, G. B., & Davis, F. D. (2003). User Acceptance of Information Technology: Toward a Unified View. *Management Information Systems Quarterly, 27*(3), 425–478.

Venkatesh, V., & Davis, F. D. (2000). A theoretical extension of the Technology Acceptance Model: four longitudinal field studies [Electronic Version]. *Management Science, 46*, 186-204. Retrieved August 4, 2004, from http://search.epnet.com/login.aspx?direct=true&db=bth&an=2958359

Verhooven, P. (2009). On Latour: Actor-Network-Theory (ANT) and Public Relations. In Ihlen, O., van Ruler, B., & Fredriksson, M. (Eds.), *Public relations and social theory: key figures and concepts* (pp. 166–186). New York: Routledge.

Vidgen, R., & McMaster, T. (1996). Black Boxes, Non-Human Stakeholders and the Translation of IT Through Mediation. In Orlikowski, W. J., Walsham, G., Jones, M. R., & De Gross, J. I. (Eds.), *Information Technology and Change in Organizational Work* (pp. 250–271). London: Chapman and Hall.

von Hippel, E., & von Krogh, G. (2003). Open source software and the 'private-collective' innovation model: issues for organization science. *Organization Science, 14*(2), 209–223. doi:10.1287/orsc.14.2.209.14992 von Lubitz, D., & Wickramasinghe, N. (2005). Network-centric Healthcare and Bioinformatics. *Intl. J. Expert Systems with Applications.*, *30*, 11–23.

von Lubitz, D., Wickramasinghe, N., & Yanovsky, G. (2006). Networkcentric Healthcare Operations: The Telecommuniucations Structure. *Int. J. Networking and Virtual Organizations*, *3*(1), 60–85. doi:10.1504/IJNVO.2006.008785

Von Lubitz, D., et al. (2004). Medical Readiness in the Context of Operations Other Than War: Development of First Responder Readiness Using OODA–Loop Thinking and Advanced Distributed Interactive Simulation Technology. In *Proceedings EMISPHERE 2004 Symposium*, Istanbul, Turkey September 2004. For on-line version at the Defence and National Intelligence Network. Retrieved from http://www.d-n-i.net/fcs/pdf/von_lubitz_1rp_ooda.pdf

Vuokko, R., & Karsten, H. (2007). Working with technology in complex networks of interaction. In McMaster, T., Wastell, D., Ferneley, E., & DeGross, J. I. (Eds.), *Organizational dynamics of technology-based innovation: diversifying the research agenda* (pp. 331–344). New York: Springer. doi:10.1007/978-0-387-72804-9_22

Wajcman, J. (1991). *Feminism Confronts Technology*. Pennsylvania: Pennsylvania State University Press.

Walsham, G. (1993). *Interpreting Information Systems in Organizations*. New York, NY, USA: John Wiley & Sons, Inc.

Walsham, G., & Sahay, S. (1999). GIS for district-level administration in India: problems and opportunities. *Management Information Systems Quarterly*, *23*, 39–66. doi:10.2307/249409

Walsham, G. (1995). Interpretive case studies in IS research: nature and method. *European Journal of Information Systems*, *4*(2), 74–81. doi:10.1057/ejis.1995.9

Walsham, G., & Waema, T. (1994). Information Systems Strategy and Implementation: A Case Study of a Building Society. *ACM Transactions on Information Systems*, *12*(2), 159–173. doi:10.1145/196734.196744

Walsham, G. (1997). Network Theory and the IS researcher: Current status and future prospect. In Lee, A. S., Liebenau, J., & DeGross, J. I. (Eds.), *Information Systems and Qualitative Research* (pp. 466–480). London, UK: Chapman & Hall.

Ward, J., & Peppard, J. (2002). *Strategic Planning for Information Systems* (3rd ed.). England, West Sussex, UK: John Wiley & Sons.

Ward, S. C. (1996). *Reconfiguring truth: postmodernism, science studies, and the search for a new model of knowledge*. Lanham, MA: Rowman and Littlefield Publishers, INC.

Wasserman, S., & Faust, K. (1994). *Social Network Analysis*. Cambridge, UK: Cambridge University Press.

Weiss, A. (2001). The politics of free (software). *netWorker*, *5*(3), 26–31. doi:10.1145/383719.383727

Wellman, B., & Gulia, M. (1999). Virtual communities as communities: Net surfers don't ride alone. In Smith, M. A., & Kollock, P. (Eds.), *Communities in cyberspace* (pp. 167–194). New York: Routledge.

Wenger, E. (1998). *Communities of Practice: learning, meaning and identity*. Cambridge, UK: Cambridge University Press.

Wentling, R. M., & Thomas, S. P. (2004). Women in information technology. *Proceedings of the Academy of Human Resource Development, Austin, 1-2*, 90-97.

West, J. (2006). Patrolling the borders: accreditation in further and higher education in England. *Journal of Further and Higher Education*, *30*(1), 11–26. doi:10.1080/03098770500431957

Wetherell, J. L., Reynolds, C. A., Gatz, M., & Pedersen, N. L. (2002). Anxiety, cognitive performance, and cognitive decline in normal aging. *J. Gerontol (B). Psych. Sci. and Soc. Sci.*, *57*, 246–255.

Wickramasinghe, N., & von Lubitz, D. (2007). *Knowledge-Based Enterprise: Theories and Fundamentals*. Hershey, PA: IGI Global.

Wickramasinghe, N. (2007). Fostering knowledge assets in healthcare with the KMI model. *International Journal of Management and Enterprise Development, 4*(1), 52–65. doi:10.1504/IJMED.2007.011455

Wickramasinghe, N., & Bali, R. (2009)... *The S'ant Imperative For Realizing The Vision Of Healthcare Network Centric Operations Intl J Actor-network Theory and Technology Innovation, 1*(1), 45–59.

Wickramasinghe, N., & Goldberg, S. (2004). How M=EC2 in Healthcare. *International Journal of Mobile Communications, 2*(2), 140–156. doi:10.1504/IJMC.2004.004664

Wickramasinghe, N., Goldberg, S., & Bali, S. (2008). Enabling superior m-health project success: a tri-country validation. *International Journal of Services and Standards, 4*(1), 97–117. doi:10.1504/IJSS.2008.016087

Wickramasinghe, N., & Mills, G. (2001). MARS: The Electronic Medical Record System The Core of the Kaiser Galaxy. *International Journal of Healthcare Technology and Management, 3*(5/6), 406–423. doi:10.1504/IJHTM.2001.001119

Wickramasinghe, N., & Schaffer, J. (2006). Creating Knowledge Driven Healthcare Processes With The Intelligence Continuum. [IJEH]. *International Journal of Electronic Healthcare, 2*(2), 164–174.

Wickramasinghe, N., & Goldberg, S. (2003). The Wireless Panacea for Healthcare. In *Proceedings of the 36th Hawaii International Conference on System Sciences* (HICSS-35) January 6-10, 2003, Hawaii (CD-ROM), Copyright 2002 by the Institute of Electrical & Electronic Engineers, Inc (IEEE).

Wickramasinghe, N., & Misra, S. (2004). A Wireless Trust Model for Healthcare. *Int. J. e-Health (IJEH), 1*(1), 60-77

Wickramasinghe, N., & Silvers, J. B. (2003). "IS/IT The Prescription To Enable Medical Group Practices To Manage Managed Care. *Health Care Management Science, 6* pp-75-86.

Wie, T. K. (2004). *Pembangunan, Kebebasan, dan "Mukjizat Orde Baru.* Jakarta: Kompas.

Wiji, A. (2007). "Potensi Biogas Sebagai Sumber Energi Alternatif," Presented on Aternative Energy for Human Welfare Seminar in Aula Barat ITB, Bandung, September 5.

Wilkinson, J. (2006). Network theories and political economy: from attrition to convergence? In Marsden, T., & Murdoch, J. (Eds.), *Between the local and the global: confronting complexity in the contemporary agri-food sector* (pp. 11–38). Oxford: JAI Press.

Williams, M. D., & Williams, J. (2004) A Framework Facilitating Ex-Ante Evaluation of Information Systems. *Proceedings of the Tenth Americas Conference on Information Systems.* New York, New York.

Williamson, P. J. (2007). From a national to a metanational ecosystem: harnessing the value of global knowledge diversity. In A. Corallo, G. Passiante, G., & A. Prencipe (Eds.), *The digital business ecosystem.* Cheltenham: Edward Elgar Publishing Limited, 82-102.

Wilson, M., & Howcroft, D. (2000) Power, politics and persuasion: a social shaping perspective on IS evaluation. *23rd IRIS Conference,* 725-39.

Winklhofer, H. (2002). *A Case for Soft Systems Methodology Information Analysis and Information Systems Evaluation during Organizational Change.* Gdarisk, Poland: ECIS.

Winner, L. (1986). *The Whale and The Reactor.* Chicago, London: The University of Chicago Press.

Winner, L. (1999). Do Artifacts Have Politics? In *Daedalus, 109*(1) Winter 1980. Reprinted in *The Social Shaping of Technology*, edited by Donald A. MacKenzie and Judy Wajcman (London: Open University Press, 1985; second edition 1999).

Woolgar, S. (1989). Reconstructing Man and Machine. A note on Sociological Critiques of Cognitivism. In Bijker, W. E., Hughes, T. P., & Pinch, T. (Eds.), *The Social construction of technological systems: new directions in the sociology and history of technology* (pp. 311–328). Boston, MA: MIT Press.

Wreden, N. (1997). Business boosting technologies. *Beyond Computing, 6*(9), 26-32.

Wyatt, JC. (2001). The New NHS Information Technology Strategy: Technology will change practice, 322 (7299), 1378. *MIS Quarterly*.

Young, G. (1999). Using portfolios for assessment in teacher preparation and health sciences. In Brown, S., & Glasner, A. (Eds.), *Assessment Matters in Higher Education: choosing and using diverse approaches*. Buckingham, UK: Open University Press/Society for Research into Higher Education.

Yusgiantoro, P. (2007). *Kebijakan Pemerintah Dalam Penyediaan Energi Alternatif di Indonesia*. Presented on Alternative Energy for Human Welfare Seminar, Aula Barat ITB, 5 September.

Zeithaml, V. A., Bitner, M. J., & Gremler, D. D. (2006). *Services Marketing: Integrating Customer Focus Across the Firm*. New York: McGraw-Hill Irwin.

Zemlin, J. (2008). *Linus Torvalds - Part I: Open Voices: The Linux Foundation Podcast*. Retrieved January 11, 2008, from http://linux-foundation.org/weblogs/open-voices/linus-torvalds-part-i/

Zhu, K., Kraemer, K., Xu, S., & Dedrick, J. (2004). Information Technology Payoff in E-Business Environments: An International perspective on Value Creation of E-Business in the Financial Services Industry. *Journal of Management Information Systems*, *21*(1), 17–54.

Zhu, K., & Kraemer, K. L. (2002). E-commerce metrics for Net-enhanced organizations: Assessing the value of e-commerce to firm performance in the manufacturing sector. *Information Systems Research*, *13*(3), 275–295. doi:10.1287/isre.13.3.275.82

Zhu, K., & Kraemer, K. L. (2005). Post-Adoption variations in usage and value of E-Business by organizations: cross-country evidence from the retail industry. *Information Systems Research*, *16*(1), 61–84. doi:10.1287/isre.1050.0045

Zhu, K., Kraemer, K. L., & Xu, S. (2003). E-business adoption by European firms: A cross-country assessment of the facilitators and inhibitors. *European Journal of Information Systems*, *12*(4), 251–268. doi:10.1057/palgrave.ejis.3000475

About the Contributors

Arthur Tatnall is an Associate Professor in the Graduate School of Business at Victoria University in Melbourne, Australia. He has Bachelor's degrees in Science and Education, a Master of Arts and a postgraduate diploma in Computer Science. In his PhD he used actor-network theory to investigate adoption of Visual Basic in the curriculum of an Australian university. Arthur's research interests include technological innovation, history of technology, project management, information systems curriculum, information technology in educational management and electronic business. Much of his research is based on the use of actor-network theory. Arthur is a Fellow of the Australian Computer Society and active in the International Federation for Information Processing (IFIP) as Chair of IFIP WG9.7 – *History of Computing*, Vice Chair of IFIP WG3.4 – *ICT in Professional and Vocational Education* and a member of IFIP WG3.7 – *Information Technology in Educational Management.* He has published widely in journals, books, book chapters and conference proceedings and recently edited the *Encyclopaedia of Portal Technology and Applications,* and *Web Technologies: Concepts, Methodologies, Tools, and Applications* for IGI Global. Arthur is also Editor-in-Chief of the *International Journal of Actor-Network Theory and Technological Innovation*, Editor-in-Chief of the *Journal of Education and Information Technologies* and Editor of the *Journal of Business Systems, Governance and Ethics.*

* * *

Hasan Al-Refai is an assistant professor and a head of Computer Information Systems department at Philadelphia University, Jordan. He got his PhD from National University of Malaysia, 2005. He joined Philadelphia in the fall (first) semester 2006 after one year experience as assistant professor at Yarmouk University, Jordan. His research interests include Cryptography, Mobile Cryptographic protocols, E-Commerce Security, Formal Methods, Multimedia, Mobile & Distributed Computing. He has written a number of journal articles and conference papers. He is a member of IJOPCM Editorial Board, International Journal of Open Problems in Computer Science, Program Committee of the Third International Symposium on Innovation in Information & Communication Technology - ISIICT 2009 (From 15 - 17 December, 2009) Jordan. Reviewer at Third International Symposium on Innovation in Information & Communication Technology - ISIICT 2009 (From 15 - 17 December, 2009), Member of the steering committee of the fourth International Symposium on Innovation in Information & Communication Technology - ISIICT 2011 November, 2011.

Ali Alawneh is an assistant professor and a head of Management Information Systems department at Philadelphia University, Jordan. He got his PhD from Arab Academy for Banking and Financial Sciences, 2008. His PhD involved a study in e-business in which he investigated e business value creation at Jordanian Banking Sector through developing a model named e TOEECLN. His research interests include technology diffusion, e-business models and management, e-commerce, e-banking, information systems development, e-learning and knowledge management. Dr. Alawneh has 15 publications in Scientific Conferences and Journals in the area of Information Technology, e-business, e-banking and Knowledge Management. He is a member of the technical committee of The International Arab Journal of e Technology (IAJET), Excellent constructive reviewer- International Business Information Management Conference (12 IBIMA) - Malaysia. Member of technical committee (Reviewer)- ISIICT 2009 Third International Symposium on Innovation in Information & Communication Technology 15-17 December, 2009, Philadelphia University, Amman, Jordan http://www.philadelphia.edu.jo/isiict2009. Excellent constructive reviewer- International Business Information Management Conference (13 IBIMA) - Morocco. Member of Organizing committee in ISIICT 2009 Third International Symposium on Innovation in Information & Communication Technology 15 - 17 December, 2009, Philadelphia University, Amman, Jordan http://www.philadelphia.edu.jo/isiict2009. Member of the steering committee of the fourth International Symposium on Innovation in Information & Communication Technology – ISIICT 2011 November, 2011.

Khaldoun Mohammad Batiha is an associate professor and a Dean of Information Technology Faculty at Philadelphia University, Jordan. His research interests include Computer Networks and Artificial Intelligence. He has written a number of journal articles and conference papers. He has participated in authoring two books are Computer Skills and Analysis and Design Algorithms.

Magdalena Bielenia-Grajewska is an Assistant Professor at the University of Gdansk (Institute of English, Department of Translation Studies and Intercultural Communication). She is a linguist (MA in English Studies, University of Gdansk) and an economist (MA in Economics, Gdansk University of Technology). Her PhD thesis was of an interdisciplinary character, being devoted to intercultural communication, translation and investment banking. She is a member of the Editorial Board of International Journal of Actor-Network Theory and Technological Innovation (IJANTII) and serves as an ad hoc reviewer in some international journals. Her scientific interests include organizational discourse, intercultural communication, sociolinguistics, ANT and symbolism in management studies. She can be reached at: magda.bielenia@gmail.com

Rajeev K. Bali is a Reader in Healthcare Knowledge Management at Coventry University. His main research interests lie in clinical and healthcare knowledge management (from both technical and organisational perspectives). He founded and leads the Knowledge Management for Healthcare (KARMAH) research subgroup (working under BIOCORE). He is well published in peer-reviewed journals and conferences and has been invited internationally to deliver presentations and speeches. He serves on various editorial boards and conference committees and is the Associate Editor for the International Journal of Networking and Virtual Organisations as well as the International Journal of Biomedical Engineering and Technology.

Chris Bigum is an adjunct Professor at the Griffith Institute for Educational Research and lives an unretired academic life on the Gold Coast where he can access swimming pools and surf beaches all year round. His research interests are well mapped in the chapter and relate not only to actor-network theory and information technology, but also the possibilities and imperatives for doing school differently. The freedom he now enjoys has allowed a significant expansion of his collection of interesting thinkers and memes.

Scott Bingley completed an honours degree in Information Systems in 2005. After this he became a Software Test Analyst before being awarded an Australian Postgraduate Scholarship to commence his PhD, using an Innovation Diffusion Approach to examine the adoption of Internet applications in local sporting bodies. As part of his degree, Scott has undertaken study as part of a university exchange program at Slippery Rock University in the USA. Scott's research interests include the use of information systems in community based organisation, an area where he has been involved with a number of research projects.

Stephen Burgess has research and teaching interests that include the use of ICTs in small businesses (particularly in the tourism field), the strategic use of ICTs, and B2C electronic commerce. He has received a number of competitive research grants in these areas. He has completed several studies related to website features in small businesses and how well websites function over time, including his PhD from Monash University, Australia (completed in 2002). He has authored/ edited three books and special editions of journals in topics related to the use of ICTs in small business and been track chair at the international ISOneWorld, IRMA, Conf-IRM and ACIS conferences in related areas. More recently, Stephen has extended his research interests to include the use of websites by community based organisations. He has published in journals such as the Journal of Information Science, Information Systems Frontiers, the International Journal of Tourism Research and the Journal of Hospitality, Marketing and Management.

Dubravka Cecez-Kecmanovic is a professor and the head of School of Information Systems, Technology and Management at the Australian School of Business, University of New South Wales (UNSW), Sydney, Australia. Her research has spanned a wide domain from technological design and applications of formal logics in information systems, to studies of social systems of information and government information systems, to ethnographies of electronically mediated work and communication, to exploring social theoretic foundations of IS. She has published in IS journals such as Journal of Information Systems, Information Technology and People, Decision Support Systems, Journal of Information Technology, Journal of Knowledge Management Theory and Practice, etc. Her current teaching includes research methodologies in IS. Her recent research interests include IS—organization coemergence, the sensemaking approach to organizations and information systems, and the sociotechnical, ANT view of IS entanglement in organizations.

Amany Elbanna is a lecturer in Information Systems at the Business School at Loughborough University. She holds MSc and Ph.D in Information Systems from the London School of Economics and Political Science. She also holds an MBA and professional diploma in marketing. Her research interests are in the area of business and software innovation, IS implementation and project management including large packaged software such as ERP and CRM and Agile/lean software development. Amany can be contacted at: a.elbanna@lboro.ac.uk

Yuti Ariani Fatimah, M. Eng is a research assistant in School of Architecture, Planning and Policy Development at Institute of Technology Bandung, Indonesia. Her master thesis used concepts from actor-network theory to study bio-fuel innovation within the Indonesia's context. Her research interests in science and technology studies (STS) focuses on theoretical and practical aspects of actor-network theory, bio-energy governance, and open source software movement. She has published a number of popular writings on technology and democracy. In December 2009, she started her PhD degree at University of Twente on sociotechnical regime with rural areas in Indonesia as focus.

Janet Francis gained her Masters degree in Computer Science in 1986. After a brief teaching career she went on to work in the computing industry for fourteen years. After working in software development for four years and as a trainer in database software, she moved into technical services management and worked for a number of organisations over a period of ten years. During this time she held responsibility for service development and the establishment of metrics associated with technical service delivery. Mrs Francis has been lecturing in the field of Information Systems at Staffordshire University since 1999. Additionally, she is heavily involved in the specification and management of work-based learning awards with particular interests in student retention and the mentoring role. The establishment and development of academic partnerships is a key aspect of her work. Mrs Francis is currently working towards a PhD in the area of Service Science looking particularly at service innovation through partnership and measurement of the value of HE service to stakeholders.

Steve Goldberg, In 1998 INET International Inc. was founded by Steve Goldberg. As INET's President he leads the firm in data collection for international research studies, wireless healthcare programs and INET Mini-conferences. Mr. Goldberg started his 24-year information technology career at Systemhouse Ltd. At Crowntek, he developed a $30 million IT services business. During his tenure at Cybermation, he transformed the organization from mainframe to client/server solution delivery. Prior to INET, at Compugen he successfully built and managed teams to deliver enterprise e-business solutions. Mr. Goldberg has a B.A. (Economics & Computer Science) from the University of Western Ontario. He is on the Editorial Board of the International Journal of Networking and Virtual Organizations, and has many papers accepted under peer review at international conferences and published in international journals.

Huda Ibrahim is currently working as a lecturer at Universiti Utara Malaysia (UUM), Malaysia since 1995. She has PhD in System Science and Management (2006) from Universiti Kebangsaan Malaysia, Master of Computer System and Computer Management (1995) from Creighton University, Omaha, Nebraska, USA, and BA in Mathematics (1988) from University of Arkansas at Little Rock, Arkansas, USA. Her teaching areas are IT Project Management, Seminar in Information Management, System Analysis and Design, Information System Development, and Mathematics. At the postgraduate programme, she is also a supervisor to Master by Research student and PhD students. Currently she is the Coordinator of Internationalization and Quality of Applied Science, UUM College of Arts and Sciences, UUM, responsible for coordinating the quality of programs under Applied Science Division. Her research interests are in the related areas of Information Technology Transfer, ICT Adoption, Rural Communities Development, and Service-Oriented Architecture. At the moment, she is currently involved in two long-term research projects funded by the Malaysia Ministry of Higher Education, one university research project, one consultancy project under Asian Development Bank and ITU-UUM,

Malaysia, and another consultancy project under UUM and Koperasi Pekan Rabu, Kedah. She is also actively involved in writing articles for journals, conferences proceedings, as well as courses' modules.

Tiko Iyamu is presently head of Architecture and Governance at MWEB (a telecommunication company) and Extraordinaire Senior Lecturer at the Department of Computer Science, University of the Western Cape, both of South Africa. He was Chief Architect at the City of Cape Town, South Africa. Research interests include Mobile Computing, Enterprise Architecture and Information Technology Strategy. His theoretical interests are Actor Network Theory (ANT) and Structuration Theory (ST). Dr. Iyamu is author of numerous peer-reviewed journal and conference proceeding articles. The most recent articles include The Impact of non-Technical Factors on Information Technology Strategy and E-business; Strategic Approach used for the Implementation of Enterprise Architecture; and The Impact of Network of People in the Computing Environment. Dr. Iyamu is affiliated to professional organisations such as South African Institute for Computer Scientists and Information Technologists. His achieved has also been recognised by "International Who is Who" Historical Society, USA.

Hasmiah Kasimin is currently working as a lecturer at Univesiti Kebangsaan Malaysia (UKM), Malaysia since 1978. She has PhD in Management Information Systems (1987), Master in Systems Analysis and Design (1978) from London School of Economics and Political Science, University of London, London, UK, respectively and Bachelor of Economics (Statistics) (Hons) (1977) from University of Malaya, Kuala Lumpur, Malaysia. Her teaching areas are Information Systems, and Mathematics. At the postgraduate programme, she is also supervises Master and PhD students. Her research interests are in the related areas of Information Technology Transfer, E-Government, ICT and Biotechnology industry. At the moment, she is currently involved in a number of research projects funded by Fundamental Research Grant Scheme. She is also actively involved in writing articles for journals, and conference proceedings.

Napaporn Kripanont is an academic from the Department of Accounting, Kasetsart University, Thailand. She has a BA (Accounting) from Chulalongkorn University in Thailand, an MS (Accounting) from Thammasat University in Thailand, an M.C.I.S. (Information Systems) from Cleveland State University in the U.S.A, and a PhD from Victoria University in Melbourne, Australia. Her PhD topic was: *Examining a Technology Acceptance Model of Internet Usage by Academics within Thai Business Schools.*

Samuel Landau holds a PhD in Artificial Intelligence from University of Paris 6. He was formerly a software project manager at Archos and then Chief Technical Officer of Comwax SAS. At the same time, he founded the company aevobots. Beforehand, he held several Postdoctoral fellowships in renowned universities and research institutes, such as Université Pierre et Marie Curie, University of Luxembourg and INRIA, where he worked on evolutionary robotics, software frameworks and machine learning. He is now working on business development at Gostai.

Lars Linden is a doctoral candidate at the University of Central Florida. He holds an MBA from the University of Tampa. His previous experience includes a Web development and book publishing. He has presented papers at Southern AIS, AMCIS and HICSS. His current research interests include knowledge management systems and free/open source software.

Fouad Nagm has several years of commercial experience in various analytical and project capacities at Ernst & Young, BT Financial Group, and National Australia Bank. Fouad also has taught a number of undergraduate and postgraduate university subjects including—research methods, business and computer information systems, IS management, organizational finance, IS project management, as well as knowledge management and e-business applications & technologies. Fouad's expertise and research interest lie predominately in IS project assessment, business/IS strategy, as well as project portfolio management. He is a Fellow at FinSia and holds the following qualifications, BCom-IS (UWS), MPM (USYD), MAppFin (FinSia), and a PhD (UNSW).

Thierry Rayna is a Senior Lecturer (ass. prof.) at London Metropolitan Business School. Beforehand, he worked at École Polytechnique (Paris), University of Cambridge and Imperial College London. He holds a PhD in Economics and his research investigates the economic consequences of the digital nature of goods such as films, music, software and information. Dr Rayna's research has been used in numerous governmental reports (European Commission, U.S. Federal Trade Commission, French Ministry of Culture) and he has served as an advisor for major companies of the media, telecommunication and cultural industries.

Leonie Rowan is a Senior Lecturer in the School of Education and Professional Studies at Griffith University. Her research interests relate to the broad fields of equity and social justice and she is particularly interested in the concept of relationship centred schooling as a framework for disrupting traditional patterns of success and failure in diverse educational and cultural sites. With an interest in the theoretical resources provided by feminist post-structuralism and actor-network theory, Dr Rowan has published in areas such as early childhood education, new literacies/new technologies, and values education, and is currently working on projects focused on home/school partnerships. Her most passionate belief is that schools CAN make a difference to the lives of diverse kids, provided we are all willing to look at the relationships we build, in our day to day activities, with kids, parents and caregivers.

Carol Stoak Saunders is professor of MIS at the University of Central Florida. She served as General Conference Chair of ICIS'99 and Telecommuting '96. She was the chair of the Executive Committee of ICIS in 2000 and inducted as an AIS Fellow in 2003. She was editor-in-chief of MIS Quarterly from 2005-2007. Her current research interests include the organizational impacts of information technology, virtual teams, time, and interorganizational linkages. Her research is published in MIS Quarterly, Information Systems Research, Journal of MIS, Journal of AIS, Communications of the ACM, Academy of Management Journal, Academy of Management Review, and Organization Science. She and Keri Pearlson coauthored Managing and Using Information Systems: A Strategic Approach, 3rd edition.

Ludmila Striukova is a Lecturer at University College London. She holds a PhD in Management from the University of London. Her previous experience involves working as a Market Analyst for a statistical agency and as a Research Fellow at King's College, University of London. Her research interests include innovation and entrepreneurship. As a part of her research activities Ludmila worked with a large number of FTSE 100 companies, as well as numerous start-ups.

Jonathan Tummons is senior lecturer in education at Teesside University UK, winner of the Times Higher Education University of the Year award in 2009. He is course leader for the BA in Education Studies. He is in the final stages of completing PhD research, funded by the Economic and Social Research Council (ESRC), which draws on social practice theories to explore the assessment of trainee teachers, with a focus on learning, teaching and assessment practices within the teacher training curriculum for the post compulsory sector. He has particular interests in the learning and assessment experiences of part-time and non-traditional undergraduates. He is also interested in research relating to a number of particular conceptual approaches to teaching and learning: communities of practice; actor-network theory and the new literacy studies. Jonathan is a member of the international editorial review board for the International Journal of Actor-Network Theory and Technological Innovation. He has authored or co-authored five textbooks for education and teacher-training students, had contributed invited chapters to two others, and has published several articles in peer-reviewed journals relating to his research.

Lorna Uden is a Professor in the Faculty of Computing, Engineering and Technology at Staffordshire University in the UK. She has published over 120 papers in conferences, journals, chapters of books and workshops. Her research interests include Learning Technology, Web Engineering and Technology, Human Computer Interaction, Groupware, Activity Theory, E-business, Knowledge management, E-government, Semantic web, Web services , Service Science and Problem-Based Learning (PBL). She co-authored the book, 'Technology and Problem - Based Learning', published by IGI publishers. Professor Uden is program committee member for many international conferences and workshops. She is on the editorial board of several international journals including Journal of Internet Technology, International Journal of Web Based Communities, International Journal of Web Information Systems, Business Process Management Journal and International Journal of Mobile Learning and Organisation. She is founder and editor of the International Journal of Web Engineering and Technology (IJWET) and the International Journal of Learning Technology (IJLT), published by Inderscience, UK. Professor Uden is also visiting professor to universities in Australia, China, Finland, Italy, Malaysia, Slovenia, Spain, South Africa and Taiwan. She has been keynote speaker at several international conferences. On the international front, she collaborates widely with colleagues worldwide. She was conference chair for the KMO2008 in Finland, KMO2009 in Taiwan and KMO2010 in Hungary.

Nilmini Wickramasinghe received her PhD from Case Western Reserve University, USA. She researches and teaches within the information systems domain with particular focus on the applications of these areas to healthcare. Her research work focuses primarily on developing suitable models, strategies and techniques grounded in various management disciplines to facilitate more effective design, development and implementation of IS/IT solutions to effect superior, patient centric healthcare delivery. She has collaborated with leading scholars at various premier healthcare organizations throughout US and Europe. She is well published with more than 200 referred scholarly articles, several books, numerous book chapters, an encyclopedia and a well established funded research track record. As of December 13th 2009 Nilmini Wickramasinghe took up the position of Professor of Information Management and Library Science at RMIT University's School of Business IT & Logistics, Australia.

Sonny Yuliar is an Assistant Professor in the School of Architecture, Planning and Policy Development at Institute of Technology Bandung, Indonesia. While his PhD in systems engineering was conducted from a technology-content perspective, his current research interests in science and technology studies (STS) look at intertwining content/context of technological changes. His research interests include technology governance in public sectors, the role of universities in innovation and development, and diffusion of information technology in society. He is a member of the Indonesia's National Research Council. He has written a book on technology governance in Bahasa Indonesia and published a number of journal articles and conference papers.

Index

A

actants 25, 136, 224. *See also* actors

actor-network 25, 27, 29, 38, 39, 58, 69, 135, 143, 149, 150, 178, 181, 186, 187, 188, 189, 192, 193, 195, 196, 203, 204, 208, 236, 238, 239, 240, 244, 245, 255, 256, 257

actor-networks, core 10

actor-network theory (ANT) 1, 2, 3, 4, 6, 7, 9, 15, 16, 17, 18, 20, 22, 25, 26, 27, 29, 36, 37, 38, 39, 41, 42, 44, 46, 47, 48, 50, 55, 58, 59, 60, 68, 69, 78, 130, 131, 132, 133, 134, 135, 136, 137, 138, 139, 143, 146, 147, 148, 149, 150, 153, 158, 181, 182, 185, 187, 192, 193, 195, 197, 198, 199, 201, 203, 204, 205, 210, 223, 224, 225, 226, 231, 234, 235, 236, 238, 239, 240, 243, 245, 247, 248, 249, 250, 251, 252, 253, 254, 256, 257, 258

actors 1, 3, 4, 6, 7, 8, 9, 10, 11, 13, 14, 15, 16, 20, 22, 23, 25, 26, 27, 28, 29, 30, 31, 32, 33, 36, 37, 38, 41, 44, 45, 46, 47, 192, 193, 195, 196, 197, 199, 201, 203, 204, 224, 225

adaptive mapping to realization (AMR) methodology 228, 229, 232

Afrikaans language 239, 240, 241

ALFA Bank 7, 8

ALFA group management 10

ALFA Invest 7, 8, 9, 12, 14, 15, 16, 17

alternative model (AM) 103

AMOS computer package 97, 103, 106, 108

ANT literature 218

Apple 162, 163, 168, 170, 171, 172, 173, 174, 175, 177

Aramis project 6

Archos 162, 163, 168, 170, 171, 172, 173, 174, 175

argument mosaic 146, 157

assessment 178, 179, 180, 181, 182, 183, 184, 185, 186, 187, 188, 189, 190, 191

assessment systems 181

attitude 54

attitude toward behaviour (ATB) 96

Australia 208, 209, 210, 234, 235, 243, 246

Australian Research Council (ARC) 209

automatic bill payment (ABP) 115

automatic teller machine (ATM) 115, 118

B

Bantuan Langsung Tunai (BLT) compensation program 70

behavioural beliefs 54, 55, 58

behavioural intention 54, 55, 58

bio-fuel 68, 69, 70, 71, 72, 73, 74, 75, 76, 77, 79

bio-fuel development trajectory 68, 69, 76

bio-fuel innovation 68, 75

bio-fuel innovation, diffusion of 68, 69, 77

bio-fuel translations 68, 69, 71, 74, 75, 76, 77

black boxes 252

black-boxing 27

blood sugar levels 226

borderless marketing 193

boundary objects 195

C

Callon, Michel 46, 47, 49, 224, 225

chronic diseases 226, 231

communication channels 55